EDUCATING SHAKESPEARE
What he knew and how and where he learned it

❦

Stephanie Hopkins Hughes

Till his whole library shall have been discovered; till the plots of all his dramas shall have been traced to their sources; till every allusion shall be pointed out and every obscurity elucidated; somewhat will still remain to be done.
Sir Edmond Malone, 1778

© 2022 by Stephanie Hopkins Hughes

All rights reserved. No part of this publication may be reproduced, stored in a retrieval system, or transmitted, in any form or by any means, electronic, mechanical, photocopying, recording, or otherwise, without the prior written permission of Stephanie Hopkins Hughes.

First edition, April 2022.

Published by Veritas Publications, LLC.

ISBN 978-1-7335894-5-1

Cover illustration "Library Adventure" by N.C. Wyeth, cover of *The Ladies Home Journal*, March, 1922, by permission Etsy, 2021.

Dedicated to those who continue to seek and publish the truth about Shakespeare.

Educating Shakespeare

"You are quoting Shakespeare"

If you cannot understand my argument, and declare "It's Greek to me", you are quoting Shakespeare; if you claim to be more sinned against than sinning, you are quoting Shakespeare; if you recall your salad days, you are quoting Shakespeare; if you act more in sorrow than in anger; if your wish is father to the thought; if your lost property has vanished into thin air, you are quoting Shakespeare. If you have ever refused to budge an inch or suffered from green-eyed jealousy, if you have played fast and loose, if you have been tongue-tied, a tower of strength, hoodwinked or in a pickle, if you have knitted your brows, made a virtue of necessity, insisted on fair play, slept not one wink, stood on ceremony, danced attendance (on your lord and master), laughed yourself into stitches, had short shrift, cold comfort or too much of a good thing, if you have seen better days or lived in a fool's paradise—why, be that as it may, the more fool you, for it is a foregone conclusion that you are (as good luck would have it) quoting Shakespeare. If you think it is early days and clear out bag and baggage; if you think it is high time and that that is the long and short of it, if you believe that the game is up and that truth will out even if it involves your own flesh and blood, if you lie low till the crack of doom because you suspect foul play, if you have your teeth set on edge (at one fell swoop) without rhyme or reason, then—to give the devil his due—if the truth were known (for surely you have a tongue in your head) you are quoting Shakespeare. Even if you bid me good riddance and send me packing, if you wish I was dead as a door-nail, if you think I am an eyesore, a laughing stock, the devil incarnate, a stony hearted villain, bloody-minded or a blinking idiot, then—by Jove! O Lord! Tut tut! For goodness' sake! What the dickens! But me no buts! It is all one to me, for *you are quoting Shakespeare!*

Bernard Levin, *Enthusiasms* (1983)

GVLIELMO SHAKSPEARE
ANNO POST MORTEM CXXIV
AMOR PVBLICVS POSVIT

WILLIAM SHAKESPEARE 1564~1616
BURIED AT STRATFORD-ON-AVON

A Fine Mystery

Shakespeare had been around for some 300 years before the public at large became aware that there was a problem with his identity. It took that long because it was not until then that the Oxbridge (Oxford plus Cambridge) University education allowed most educated readers enough insight into the nature and immensity of his education to see that the Stratford Shakespeare was just as fictional as his plays. With Latin still the universal language of authority—plus a considerable segment of that community versed in either classical or New Testament Greek—England's intelligentsia was ripe for the shock that hit them in 1857 when Delia Bacon published the notion that the name *Shakespeare* was a front for a handful of educated courtiers.

Delia's book was only one of a series of rude awakenings that were causing this community's worldview to expand in disturbing—if exciting—new directions. In 1847, Karl Marx had upended both classical economics and the New Testament with his *Communist Manifesto*. Eight years later he struck again with *Das Kapital*. Four years after that Darwin would do the same to human evolution and the Old Testament with his *Origin of Species*.

Like these, Delia's theory has given rise to centuries of debate —but while laughed to scorn at first—she got powerful support when Queen Victoria's Lord Chancellor revealed the vast extent of the Bard's knowledge of the Law. Spurred by longtime Bardolator the Duke of Devonshire—Lord Chancellor John Campbell proclaimed Shakespeare's "minute and undeviating accuracy" in the Law, "a subject where no layman . . . has ever yet succeeded in keeping himself from tripping." This was followed by hosts of specialists intent on revealing the Bard's expertise in fields as disparate as medical science and Greek mythology.

In obvious opposition to Ben Jonson's dismissive phrase in the First Folio—"*though thou hadst* small Latin and less Greek"—it was becoming clear that Shakespeare simply could not have written as he did without a deep and intimate knowledge of the language of the Roman historians and poets, and—even more astonishing—the ancient Greek dramatists. Yet, for some reason, the universities, who've since grasped Marx and Darwin to their bosoms "with hoops of steel"—have left Shakespeare, arguably the greatest of all—to drift in a murky semi-historical void somewhere between St. Paul and Santa Claus. All but a handful of the literary giants who would build on the foundations he laid have failed him—as did Charles Dickens who is reported to have said "The life of Shakespeare is a fine mystery. . . . I tremble every day lest something should turn up." Although Dickens is no longer trembling—something has turned up.

Contents

A Fine Mystery — i

Note to the Reader — v

Chapter I *Why Shakespeare Matters* — 1

Chapter II *What Shakespeare Knew* — 45

Chapter III *Shakespeare in His Own Time* — 121

Chapter IV *Shakespeare in Our Time* — 259

Appendix A Source of the Name Shakespeare — 313

Appendix B Shakespeare's Hand — 318

Appendix C Shakespeare's Coat of Arms — 322

Appendix D The Stratford Bust — 330

Appendix E Henslowe's Spelling — 343

Works Cited — 349

Index — 357

Acknowledgements and About the Author — 363

Educating Shakespeare

Note to the Reader

Educating Shakespeare is about the great author's education, but it is about ours as well, for while he's been entertaining us for centuries with his jokes, his comic characters, his subtle twists of plot, he's also been educating us in history, science, and politics.

For ease of understanding, all but a few quotations from early works are converted here to modern spelling and punctuation. Here and there a quoted word or phrase has been italicized without notice for purposes of editorial emphasis. Because commonly accepted facts are now available online, citations are provided only for those points that address areas of controversy, or those that may be useful to readers on their own paths of discovery.

To avoid the inevitable confusion caused by using the same name for both, here the name *William Shakespeare*—as it appeared on published plays in the late sixteenth century—refers to the man who *made it famous*—while the man who was born with it is referred to here as *William of Stratford*.

While the term C*atholic* is capitalized as has been traditional for centuries—the term *protestant* is not, since it does not refer to a religion but to *a political movement* created to *protest* Catholicism, while Protestant denominations from the same Christian mythos as Catholicism are capitalized. As for "the Academy"—a term borrowed from Plato—here it refers to the universities of the world that collectively set commonly accepted standards for what is true.

I must ask the forgiveness of my friends in the Academy for using the term *academic* for those who steadfastly continue to follow the artificial paper trail created by the Lord Chamberlain's Men in the 1590s to protect the identity of their playwright. No one could be more aware than myself of our debt to the many thousands of learned individuals in the colleges and universities around the world who have provided the basic facts with which this book is constructed—including those pieces of the puzzle that E.K. Chambers labelled "the Shakespeare problem." In seeking as nonpejorative a term as possible, here we'll call these honest if limited folks *academics*—hoping that it will be understood, as when we say about an opinion or a statement that it's *academic*, meaning that it's the standard and currently accepted view—not that it's necessarily the truth. As R.G. Collingwood once commented in regard to a different issue—

> All that the historian means when he describes certain . . . facts as his data, is that for the purposes of a particular piece of work there are certain historical problems relevant to that work which for the present he proposes to treat as settled; though, if they are settled, it is only because historical thinking has settled them in the past, and they remain settled only until he or some one else decides to reopen them.

Since it's our purpose to revisit a number of these problems, we need a word for those who—to maintain their status within the university system—continue to keep their eyes and ears tightly shut to the truth.

CHAPTER I

~ Why Shakespeare Matters ~

A near-perfect copy of Shakespeare's *First Folio*, which is regarded as the most important book in English literature, set a British record at auction yesterday when it sold for £2.8 million. The 17th century volume was the most valuable book ever sold at Sotheby's in London. The auction house said the buyer . . . had paid the highest price ever recorded for the volume at a British auction house.

The Sunday Telegraph, July 14, 2006

Today, and for at least the previous two centuries, everybody who speaks English knows the name *Shakespeare*, but how many know why? Most know that he wrote plays—many know the names of two or three—*Romeo and Juliet, Hamlet, Macbeth*. Some have a deeper knowledge of a particular play having performed it when they were in school. But why are these plays so important, their plots and characters referred to as frequently by journalists and essayists as current heads of state or those from the Bible? For most of us his 400-year-old language is difficult to read. Many find it hard to follow even in the theater. Yet every year scores of books roll off the press about him or his works—year after year, decade after decade, century after century—hundreds of thousands of books, and no sign that it will ever let up. What is it about these plays and their author that has made them so important?

The same could be said for his language. In just this one lifetime English has become the most important language in the world. While third among native born speakers, it's now the second language of every culture of any size or importance, yet until the latter half of the sixteenth century it could hardly be considered a written language at all—there being as yet no established orthography. Apart from a handful of poets who saw promise in it before Shakespeare expanded it—it was spoken by no one but the inhabitants of England itself—a tiny fraction of the world's population. It was an embarrassment to English diplomats, who used Latin, French, Italian, even German, when dealing with foreign dignitaries.

In fact, before Shakespeare, English was less a language than a collection of dialects, each made up of whatever combination of Anglo Saxon, French, Norse, Gaelic, Breton, Scots, or Welsh had taken root where the speaker was born and raised—dialects reflected in the wildly impressionistic spelling of letters and manuscripts—barely intelligible to anyone from outside their own shire.

For centuries following the 1066 invasion of the French from Normandy, English lords and ladies had been conversing with each other in French, using English only when speaking with innkeepers and stable boys. Throughout the sixteenth century, while Latin remained the language of schools and diplomats, Law French was still the language of English lawyers. As for literature, while Spain and Italy had traditions that went back to the Greeks and Romans, by 1550, English literature, rooted in a version of Anglo Saxon known as Old English—consisted of little more than Chaucer, Lydgate, Mallory and a handful of poets whose names are known today only to specialists. According to C.S. Lewis, until the late 16th century the best British literature was in Scots dialect.

Separated from the Continent by twenty miles of turbulent water—troubled by internal wars—the English were much slower to awaken to the glories of the European Renaissance than the Italians, French or Spanish. The great cultural revolution that was bringing such accomplishments to the continent did not reach the English until late in the sixteenth century—when it was almost ended before it began by the political movement known as The Reformation. It wasn't until the end of that century that—led by Shakespeare—the English began to expand their artistic limits—and when they did, it was almost totally through poetry and song. For portraiture, sculpture, and architecture—they looked to the continental nations.

Although "Great Britain" has gone the way of all empires—its

Chapter I Why Shakespeare Matters

culture, spread to every corner of the earth—is more influential today than ever. And although the English language may have been spread beyond its native borders by the forces of war, colonization, and trade—were it not for its power and flexibility it would not have taken root as it has, nor gone on to become the *lingua franca* of our time—the primary language of trade and diplomacy throughout the modern world. So it matters that those who speak it know how and where this language got its start. "Know thyself" said Socrates"—"I think, therefore I am," said Descartes. More often than not—when the world thinks today—it thinks in English.

How did this happen?

Many cultural streams have converged over time to create today's English—but there was one point in the late sixteenth century when a confluence of local dialects, of Anglo Saxon, Latin, French and Italian, of courtly discourse and Cockney slang, of classical Greek, and—some think, even of Hebrew—mingled in the mind and pen of one singularly gifted individual. By weaving and blending the sounds and rhythms from all these sources—with an English shorn of its antiquated awkwardness and ambiguities—he created a bigger, better, more powerful language—one that was good for thinking and for expressing ideas—that provided a rich palate of choices with the potential for many shades of meaning—that offered more than one word for things so that thoughts could be crafted into something beautiful and graceful to the ear as well as clear and precise to the mind. And he did this by putting them into the mouths of actors—for reading books was still beyond many in his public audience.

Out of his thoughts, his literary tastes, his personal loves and hates and his need to express himself, he created—then published for the first time—thousands of words still common in everyday use. More than words alone, he either created or captured from French, Italian, Latin or ancient Greek, hundreds of phrases and turns of speech that we still read, hear, and use every day. Thus is preserved in our minds and the minds of all who read English—truths and bits of wisdom—from ancient sources—from the hearth and the pub, language as he heard it spoken, or as *he wished to hear it spoken.*

Educating Shakespeare

Not unlike the spread of English in our time to parts of America that before the invention of the radio could be understood only by those who shared their regional dialects—the actors took his language to all of England—where—like the seeds in the Bible story, some fell on fertile ground, and from thence to America, Australia, India, Africa, the Caribbean, and—eventually—the far reaches of the entire world.

It may be that not all the words for which he's listed as "first use" by the OED (Oxford English Dictionary) are purely his doing—the first author of a substantial English dictionary was, after all, Samuel Johnson, one of his greatest admirers. Yet those he didn't create himself from Latin, French, Italian or Greek were *chosen* by him—whether from the common speech of the time or from some friend, teacher, washerwoman or "Autolycus"—thereby, like bees in amber—preserving them for all time. His vocabulary ranges anywhere from 15,000 to 30,000 words, depending on which authority you read. If the lower figure it's still almost twice the size of Milton's[1] (Masson 151).

According to the Oxford English Dictionary, he gave us such commonplace words as *bare-faced, baseless, countless, courtship, critic, denote, disgraceful, dishearten, distrustful, dwindle, eventful, exposure, lonely, fitful, fretful, gloomy, hurry, impartial, misplaced, monumental, recall, suspicious, inauspicious*—among thousands of others. Had his works been lost—had he never written—would these words have come some other way? Would we have words just as good as these? Or would we simply do without them?

One way to gauge his importance might be to examine *The Oxford Dictionary of Quotations* (1953), which devotes six pages each to writers Sir Walter Scott, Charles Dickens, and Alexander Pope. Shelley gets seven, Byron gets eight, Wordsworth and Samuel Johnson each get ten. Milton rates thirteen, as does Tennyson. The Book of Common Prayer gets fourteen, while the King James Bible ranks a high of twenty-seven pages. How many pages are devoted to Shakespeare?—sixty-six—almost triple the Bible! The other great

---

[1] Argument has been made that the actual numbers may be closer, but because Milton—like all who came later—had the advantage of having read Shakespeare, the comparison should be to writers like Lydgate and poets like Wyatt or Surrey, who came before him.

Chapter I Why Shakespeare Matters

collection of English quotations, *Bartlett's* (1882, 1980) gives the Bible forty-seven pages, while Shakespeare gets sixty-six!

When we consider that the Bible was the work of hundreds of individuals over many hundreds of years, and that—all versions taken together, it is by far—for western readers at least—the best-selling book of all time—that should tell us something about *Shakespeare's* actual accomplishment. In the Table of Contents of *Bartlett's Familiar Quotations*—which lists quotes from close to 3,000 sources—only two are broken down into sub listings—the King James Bible by its books—and Shakespeare by his plays.

Clearly Shakespeare was a genius. But what exactly does that mean? Most of us would agree that there is a qualitative as well as quantitative difference between a genius and those who are simply very good at what they do. While Philip of Macedon was a great military strategist—his son was a genius. While Jean Racine was a brilliant dramatist—his friend Molière was a genius. If Robert Hooke was a great physicist—his rival, Sir Isaac Newton, was a genius.

As a writer, Shakespeare must have grown immensely over a fairly short period of time—something we see if we compare a masterpiece like *Hamlet* or *King Lear* to early works like *Pericles* or *Titus Andronicus*. Yet even *Titus* was an immense improvement over the period just preceding his—which C. S. Lewis has so aptly termed "the drab era." To understand this we have only to compare anything he wrote, early or late, to the poetry of Thomas Churchyard (active 1555-1575) or that of George Whetstone (active 1574-1587)—to plays like *Gorboduc* (1561) or *Tancred and Gismund* (1568)—or prose works like Thomas Hoby's translation of *The Courtier* (1561). Try reading any of these out loud! The difference is not just a matter of style. A gulf in wit, richness, vocabulary and ease of expression separates Shakespeare—even early Shakespeare—from everything that came before him. Yet this is not the primary reason for his fame.

The plays *are* the thing

However important the mighty language he left a world of English speakers—Shakespeare's greatest gift are his *stories*. That this is true is evident from how his plays have reached beyond English to be performed in just about every other language in the world. More than entertainment—deeper than poems, tracts, news reports, etcetera—*story* is a dynamic that ignores differences of culture, that moves to the heart of what we all hold in common.

As psychologist Bruno Bettelheim and poet Robert Bly assure us—and the ancient author of *The Arabian Nights* confirms—human psychology is best revealed, explained—even healed—through storytelling. It's *story* that reflects us to ourselves, that helps us see ourselves as humans, as members of a particular community, as a sex, as youths or elders, as professionals, thinkers, lovers. It's what Shakespearean Lily B. Campbell wisely perceived as using *the particular* as a path to *the universal*.

Out of the dead clay of history—Shakespeare brought to life for every Londoner with a penny to spare—the great Romans, Caesar, Brutus, Coriolanus—the foreigners, Shylock, Cleopatra, Othello—the British monarchs both good and bad, strong and weak—Richard II, Richard III, Henry V, Macbeth. He brought to life the great flawed heroes—Prince Hal, Mark Antony, the Bastard Falconbridge, and the greatest, most vital fictional being of all time—Hamlet the Dane.

He's been dead for 400 years but he's still with us. Hardly a day passes without a mention of his name or a phrase from one of his works in a newspaper headline, a television interview, an old movie, a novel, a magazine article—of no other writer can this be said. When we marry we walk down the aisle to music written by Mendelssohn for the wedding that ends *A Midsummer Night's Dream*. From Romeo to Lear, Silence to Falstaff, Ophelia to Cleopatra—for every role—villain to victim, hero to madman, fool to lover—each speaks, most cogently and poetically, pitifully and hilariously, of humanity in general—and ourselves and our neighbors in particular.

In the dark days of the early 1940s, when the English authorities were striving to rally frightened hearts battered by the Nazi blitz—precious time and money went into creating Laurence Olivier's version of *Henry V*. This lavish and artful production—one of the first in Britain to be filmed in color—taught its viewers the desperately needed lesson that *this wasn't the first time* that the English had faced a deadly threat from the continent and that having prevailed before, could prevail again. Who could resist the surge of energy as the King,

Chapter I Why Shakespeare Matters

portrayed by the great Olivier, rises and shouts to the frightened movie goers—"I see you stand like greyhounds in the slips, straining upon the start. *The game's afoot! Follow your spirit and cry* 'God for Harry, England, and Saint George!'"[2]

But were these stories really "his"? Didn't he find them in the works of other writers? Yes and no. He took them from every possible source, but never without fitting them to his purpose. This was nothing new—from the time of the bards and shamans, storytellers have been handing them down from one generation to the next—conforming them to their own time, place, and audience. What may be peculiar to Shakespeare is the way he combines elements from two or three (or four or five) different sources—sometimes even from two or more different genres—all grist for his theatrical mill.

He found them in ancient Greek and Latin texts—from timeless folktales told by the kitchen hearth to current events gripping the public at the time—and from the affairs and scandals of Court gossip. These he retold through characters that return to life every time a company of actors steps out onto a stage—whether in London's Covent Garden or a high school in Shawnee, Kansas—leaving his mark again and again on every facet of our lives. To Harold Bloom, Yale professor, literary critic, he's "a mortal god"—Hamlet, his mental offspring—"the secular Christ"—

> To catalogue Shakespeare's largest gifts is almost an absurdity: where begin, where end? He wrote the best poetry and the best prose in English, or perhaps in any Western language. . . . [H]e thought more comprehensively and originally than any other writer. It is startling that a third achievement should overgo these, yet I join Johnsonian tradition in arguing, nearly four centuries after Shakespeare, that he went beyond all precedents (even Chaucer) to know all he knew.

How strange, that after 350 years there should still be no definitive answer to either question. We know more about the education of Alexander the Great, who lived a thousand years earlier in another

---

[2] Shot in 1943, it was released as the Allies began the invasion of Normandy.

part of the world, than we know today about the man who created the language we speak and the stories we live by. Who was he—and how did he come to know all that he knew?

Halfway through the nineteenth century the question finally reached a public level with Delia Bacon's *The Philosophy of the Plays of Shakespeare Unfolded.* Attributing his works to a group of courtiers from the Elizabethan and Jacobean eras—their names soon shot to the forefront as candidates for his "crown of bays." As evidence grew of the incredible extent and nature of his education, the total lack of any evidence that William of Stratford could write so much as his own name added force to the push to discover the truth about his identity.

~ Why not William? ~

So how much do we know about William of Stratford? The short answer is, not much—but a great deal more than we know about most men of his class at that time due to the intensity with which he and his family have been scrutinized for the past three centuries.

It seems that William's father—one John Shakspere—was a man of ambition. A farm boy from the English Midlands, he did what he could to improve his status within that limited sphere by marrying the daughter of a distant relative of a local gentry family. Moving to a nearby market town, he set himself up as a leathercrafter. First described as "a glover"—later as "a considerable dealer in wool"—that he also dealt in other aspects of the trade in sheep (hides, meat, bones) is suggested by the evidence that he did business over the years with his neighbor—the tanner Henry Field. Their town, Stratford-on-Avon (perhaps to distinguish it from Stratford-at-Bowe, a suburb of London)—was three days ride by horseback from the center of all business in London, and one or two days from Oxford—the closest intellectual center.

Stratford was a busy market town of some 1200 souls—and while wool was central to its economy, the people of Stratford profited more from the ale they made to sell to those who came to sell

Chapter I Why Shakespeare Matters

William Shakspere of Stratford on Avon, c.1596[3]

their sheep on market day—or to buy them for their wool, their meat, even their bones—for nothing about the animal went to waste.

Rising over the years from Constable to Burgess to Alderman to Bailiff—the equivalent of Mayor—John Shakspere appears to have been seen by his community as a man of value. Sam Schoenbaum, William's 20th-century biographer, gives impressive detail on the offices and honors held by Shakspere Sr. during his years as Bailiff (34). In those days, in a country town like Stratford, such a man—even a man who could neither read nor write—could do very well for himself within walking distance of the house on Henley Street where

---

[3] Most often used as Shakespeare's portrait—known as "The Chandos" because it was owned early on by the Duke of Chandos—it makes most sense as one of the things William purchased around the time he acquired his father's Coat of Arms and the Bust of his father on the wall of Trinity Church.

he and his wife raised eight children—William their oldest boy.

But sometime in or around 1576—right about when their son turned twelve, misfortune struck the family—exactly what or why has never been determined (Schoenbaum 36-40).[4] John Shakspere lost his office and began selling off portions of the land he had accumulated[5]––making it most unlikely for a family where no one could write, that the oldest son be spared to immerse himself in literary classics. At eighteen he impregnated, then married, a woman several years older than himself—adding two more to the family table—then, two years later, another two (twins).

Over the years the Shakspere family continued to survive on their share of the local trade in wool and other sheep products—dodging creditors and in some disrepute until 1596 when William, now in his thirties, came into the modest fortune that returned them to a level of respect. This influx of treasure allowed him to pay off his father's debts, purchase a big house as an investment property, and acquire the Coat of Arms his father had tried and failed to get back in the 1570s (see Appendix B). It got his father restored to the borough council, and—when the old man died in 1601—made it all right to put his monument on a wall in the local church.

Enter *Venus and Adonis*

Following his marriage in 1582, William disappears from the record until 1593 when—without any prior indications of writing ability—a narrative poem is published in which his unusual name is included in such a way that suggests that he was its author—a poem of such sterling quality that by 1640 it had gone into 15 editions.

For those who cling to the idea that the name *Shakespeare* is all that's needed to believe that an insignificant son of a Stratford dealer

---

[4] It's conjectured that his troubles were religious, but since there's little to support that, and since by then he had ceased to be described as a glover, he may have lost the ability to make gloves from the fine silky layer of a sheepskin known as chamois. Cutting leather requires very sharp blades, chamois the most difficult of all to cut. He may simply have cut his hand too badly to make gloves.

[5] By November 1578 he had sold all his land including his wife's inheritance (Schoenbaum 37).

Chapter I Why Shakespeare Matters

in sheep products was the creator of the literary revolution inspired by this poem—the decade from the record of Will's marriage to the publication of *Venus and Adonis* is often referred to as "the lost years." But whatever William was actually doing had nothing to do with getting educated, writing plays and poems, or becoming acquainted with the young Earl of Southampton—to whom *Venus and Adonis* was dedicated.[6] Had there been any such connection, after 200 years of research, we would surely know it by now—or at least as much as we know about other poets of his time. This was not the Dark Ages. People wrote letters. Institutions kept records.

Shakespeare's name in the theatrical record

The first time the name William Shakespeare appears in any sort of theatrical record was in 1595 when it was included—along with the names of two actors from the recently formed Lord Chamberlain's Men—on a standard request to the Queen's Exchequer for payment for plays performed at Court over the winter holidays of 1594-95.

Several things about that warrant—dated March 15, 1595—are unusual.[7] A company's payee was usually its lead actor or manager, and while it happens sometimes that more than one name will appear on such a warrant—three was unique. The other two names were familiar to the world of the London theater. Writ first and largest—*Will Kempe* was London's favorite comedian, having worked for years first with Leicester's Men, then with the Queen's Men. The second name, *Richard Burbage*, was the son of the owner and manager of the great public Theatre in Shoreditch who most likely had been performing on his father's stage since he could walk.

For 400 years—no amount of finagling by the Academy has ever come up with a scenario that sensibly connects these literary bolts from the blue with what is known about the son of a dealer in wool products—a man who apparently wrote no letters to anyone,

---

[6] Dedications were normally placed ahead of the title—in *Venus and Adonis* it appears—strangely worded—on the *reverse* of the title page.

[7] Among these is the fact that Heneage, who had been the Queen's personal financial administrator since 1570, was a dying man. Having made out his will in July, he died in October, leaving his office and his records in disarray (Akrigg 50).

who left no record of any sort of education, and whose parents and offspring signed legal documents with a mark (see *Appendix B*).

William as actor

Though universally portrayed as an actor by academics—the sole evidence that William ever performed anything, anywhere, comes from Ben Jonson. In a list of names of the actors who performed in his plays up to 1616, he included "William Shake-Speare"—the strange spelling suggesting a pun-name. In any case, Ben Jonson is worthless as any sort of third party evidence for William as an actor since it was he who in 1623—in his role as editor of the First Folio, cast in stone William's name as author of the Shakespeare canon.

William as sharer

Acting companies were made up of three kinds of actor. The basic company consisted of at least six proven professionals (up to twelve in a big company) who provided the looks and talents required to perform leading roles—*hired extras* whose numbers and functions varied from play to play—and one or two young apprentices who performed as needed. Lead actors—some recorded as having to pay £200[8] to join one of these companies—were the only members guaranteed a share of the profits. With no record of any previous acting experience—it's unlikely that William could possibly have been a genuine "sharer."

William as company playwright

While it's unlikely that William's status as a sharer was due to his abilities as an actor, his supposed role as playwright is even less likely, since only actors, *lead* actors, had the right to a share of the profits. Shakespeare scholar Gerald Bentley claims that he could find

---

[8] Since £200 in 1600 would apparently be somewhere around £30,000 today, it's dubious that there were many actors who actually paid to join a company. Most likely the sum was used to keep the unworthy at bay. A much more realistic requirement was that he could provide a trunkful of his own costumes.

Chapter I Why Shakespeare Matters

no instance where a company's playwright was ever accorded that status (28-9).[9] Where we have records, they confirm that in most cases (Marlowe's company the exception)—playwrights were treated like hired extras—paid only for what they produced.

While Philip Henslowe— owner/manager of the Rose Theater on Bankside—made up for the loss of his playwright Marlowe by keeping several writers on retainers—this was in expectation of works in progress or promised. Unless he was a lead actor or manager, an actor got no share of the profits. Ergo to wit—William was not a manager! Thus to be seen by as a legitimate sharer the Company *had* to present him as an actor because there was simply no other role that would justify their claim that he was getting a share of the profits.

As time went by, and the original members of the Company began feeling their age—William's name, missing from every theatrical record from then on (until the First Folio in 1623)—turns up in the wills of two of the original sharers—Thomas Pope in 1603, and Augustine Phillips two years later. Each has bequeathed William £5 for memorial rings. Similarly—in William's own will—composed in 1616 by an anonymous scribe shortly before his death—a similar sum was set for memorial rings for Hemmings, Condell, and Burbage.[10]

That this bequest was squeezed between two lines in the already completed will (Honigmann 127-137) suggests that it was a later addition,[11] possibly by Hemmings. Evidence like this of William's supposed active role in the Company are all things that the Lord

---

[9] Except for Thomas Heywood, playwright for Worcester's Men—but Heywood was also an actor, and eventually a manager.

[10] When Joseph Greene, vicar of the Stratford Church and headmaster of its school, found William's will in 1747, he wrote—"The legacies and bequests therein are undoubtedly as he intended, but the manner of introducing them appears to me so dull and irregular, so absolutely devoid of the least particle of that spirit which animated our great poet, that it must lessen his character as a writer to imagine the least sentence of it his production."

[11] According to Honigmann, who had seen the letter—"Had it occurred to Shakespeare before the draft was completed that he ought to remember his friends and his wife, he could have added more clauses at a later point in the will—instead these were *inserted awkwardly, and none too legibly— between lines that were already written*" (130).

Educating Shakespeare

Chamberlain's Men's new manager could easily have created to support his presence as an actor during the period that the world was beginning to wonder who was writing these popular plays.

As for William's supposed shares in the Globe and Blackfriars theaters—as later claimed by the Burbages in legal depositions—that these were ordinary shares in the sense that they could be sold, transferred, or left to his heirs is exceedingly dubious, since, in lawsuits over the ownership of what by the seventeenth century had become extremely valuable properties—there are *no mentions* of such shares nor is there any mention in William's will of shares in the great Blackfriar's Theater or the Globe—as seen in the wills of genuine sharers. It's been assumed that he *must have* sold these shares at some point—but no evidence of such sales has ever been recovered.

The only possible explanation is that—no matter where the Company—more particularly their manager John Hemmings—chose to establish a record meant to portray William as a member of the Lord Chamberlain's Men—the amounts and regularity with which he was paid were not recorded.

Was William ever in London?

The Academy simply takes for granted that—as the Company's great playwright, William *must have* lived in London—but other than a trace of one or two visits of indeterminate length—there's no evidence that he was in London for anything more than the time it took in 1596 to purchase a Coat of Arms for his father—or again for a period of indeterminate length following Shakspere Sr.'s death in 1601—to arrange for the creation of a monument honoring the old man to be placed on the wall of the Trinity Church in Stratford.

According to Schoenbaum, remaining records report that sometime between 1595 and 1598 a "William Shackspere" had failed to pay tax on property worth £5 in two London neighborhoods (161-62)—but he also reports—as a "curious fact"—that "his name cannot be traced" in any list of the residents of that district in Southwark in 1597, or 1598—or in fact at any time.

A deposition from a legal case that shows him residing with a family of theatrical costumers at some point between 1602 and 1606

Chapter I Why Shakespeare Matters

is real enough—but it proves nothing beyond the fact that he spent some time in London—not how much or doing what.[12] That the costumers lived on Silver Street—just around the corner from where both Hemmings and his assistant Henry Condell were living at that time—suggests that just as it was Hemmings's job as the Company's business manager to deal with people like the costumers—it would also have been his task to find a place for their playwright's stand-in to stay where himself or Henry Condell could keep an eye on him.

William's apparent investment in the Blackfriar's Gatehouse in 1613—sometimes offered by academics as evidence of a career as a London businessman—seems to have been a one time deal organized by Hemmings—if marginally for William's benefit—seems to have no connection to the King's Men *per se*. Involving a consortium of "trustees"—as Schoenbaum tells it (223-24)—it sounds far too complicated to be seen as a simple investment. Nor can it be seen as evidence for William's residence in London—since from the start the property in question was rented to a Londoner. Created in 1613—three years before William's death—the trustees were to take over the disbursement of rental fees to William's "survivors"—which suggests that Hemmings regarded this otherwise peculiar deal as a means of providing the aging stand-in with a guarantee that his widow would continue to receive a stipend after his death—and thus could be trusted to remain silent about the source of their income.

Was William ever at Court?

Generations of academics have assumed—based on the knowledge of Court life displayed in the plays, plus the mentions of Southampton as having paid for the publication of *Venus and Adonis* and *Lucrece*—that William "must have been" a regular member of Elizabeth's Court. If true, some bit of evidence would surely have turned up over

---

[12] One is tempted to recall how Jonson described the character Sogliardo in his play for the Lord Chamberlain's Men, *Every Man Out of his Humor*—produced at the Curtain Theater in 1598—as "an essential clown . . . so enamoured of the name of a gentleman that he will have it, though he buys it. He comes up every term to learn to take tobacco and see new motions [puppet shows]. He is in his kingdom when in company where he may well be laughed at."

Educating Shakespeare

the 200 years that scholars have been seeking proof of the sort left by actors like Richard Tarleton and Richard Burbage—or for writers like George Gascoigne, Ben Jonson and Samuel Daniel—yet no evidence of any such appearance at Court—nor of any ongoing relationship with a courtier has ever turned up. Anecdotes that suggest a relationship with the proprietress of an Oxford wineshop and her son report that on occasion William would stop overnight in Oxford on his way to and from London (Aubrey 90)—though not whether going or coming, how often, or at what intervals.

In fact, if we ignore academic conjecture and go strictly by the record—it seems that no one in Stratford had any idea of the nature of William's business in London—or if they did, never discussed it with outsiders. Nor did any of the prolific letter writers of that time like Roland White or John Chamberlain—whose letters have been plumbed by scholars for mentions of persons and incidents during the period when the Shakespeare name was first surging to prominence, ever mention *William Shakspere* (Jiménez). Although Chamberlain never showed much interest in the Theater—surely the author of so many popular plays would have rated a passing mention in a letter.

Even the defenders of the Stratford myth can't find anything to suggest that William was anywhere but in Stratford from 1611 on—when the King's Men—having finally acquired the right to use the theater that had been closed to them for fifteen years—first began their rise to commercial success (Irwin Smith 247).

Thus—according to the Academy—just when the arc of his name recognition is beginning to peak—their version of this theatrical wizard has him returning to Stratford where he immerses himself in local land deals and legal actions intended to recover a few pounds. To imagine that a real playwright—particularly one on Shakespeare's level—would depart the field just as he and his actors were hitting the big time, poses no problem for the academic who may have made Shakespeare his life work—but whose own connection to the Theater amounts to seeing a play every now and then—for if they knew anything at all about the Theatre and the lives of those that become

Chapter I Why Shakespeare Matters

its stars and its creators—they certainly don't show it.[13]

His "Stratford moniment"

Even as the plays bearing his name were supposedly making him famous, when William of Stratford died in 1616, not a soul in London —or anywhere else—mentioned his passing in a letter or published comment. His death must have been acknowledged in some way in Stratford, but if so, not in any way that reached the record. Francis Beaumont—the far less important playwright who died the same year was buried with considerable fanfare in Westminster Abbey—while Richard Burbage's death three years later set all of London grieving. Yet William's death and his burial in the floor of the local Stratford church seems to have created no response at all—either from those readers who treasured *Venus and Adonis*—or from the audiences who thronged the theaters where his name was becoming famous and his actors wealthy.

Where one would think there would be some evidence of pride in the success of their home town boy—it seems that despite the thirty years of publishing works that name him as author—not a soul in Stratford was aware of his reputation.[14] This may be hard for us to grasp today—but back then it took three days to get from Stratford to London on horseback—not including the almost traditional stopover in Oxford at the halfway point—over roads that were uncertain at best—with no theaters anywhere but *in* London, no newspapers to spread the word, and a general population that, outside of London, Oxford, or Cambridge—could not have read a newspaper even if there had been one to read.

---

[13] The experts appointed by eight universities to oversee the most recent official edition of the plays, the so called NOS (New Oxford Shakespeare), published in 2016, include seven professors of Literature and one professor of Theater. All seven of the first are men—the token Theater professor is also the token female.

[14] As detailed by historian Ramon Jiménez in *The Oxfordian* (2003)— "Shakespeare in Stratford and London: Ten Eyewitnesses Who Saw Nothing."

Dr. Hall's Diary

Dr. John Hall, the Stratford physician who would marry William's daughter Susannah, kept a diary and notebooks in which he noted details about the residents in and around Stratford that he treated over the years. In it he describes with pride his meeting with playwright and renowned London impresario Michael Drayton—yet the poet that the world regards as the greatest of all time—his wife's father—is mentioned briefly by Hall—but only as his *father-in-law!*[15]

It's clear, or certainly should be, that when it comes to solid connections to the world of the Theater, the London Stage, or the periodical press—every mention of William as the author of those plays attributed to him came in some way *from the acting company that were using it to get their best plays into print*—during what has been (until recently) an unexplained flurry of publishing activity in the early to mid-1590s. Anything else can be attributed to the urge to fill a vacuum with a conundrum, a joke, or a fairy tale.

The only possible conclusion to all of this must be that the identity of the amazing individual who actually provided the Lord Chamberlain's/King's Men with the plays that were bringing them such success—was a *trade secret*—one they were driven to protect when finally, after years of uncertainty about how to deal with the issue, they put the name of the son of a provincial dealer in sheep products on those plays that they had to get published just then —most likely to stop other companies from performing them.

When we consider the many clues that point to the real playwright as a member of the Royal Court, the most reasonable explanation for the mystery surrounding his identity has to be that, were it to be revealed, it would cause problems—not just for the author, but for some other members of the Court community as well. Considering history's long accepted identification of Polonius as a satirical version of Queen Elizabeth's Lord Treasurer, William Cecil Lord Burghley—it shouldn't be too hard to see where such an inquiry might lead. Still—when it became necessary to find a name with

---

[15] If the version of the name *Shakespeare* that was put on the plays was not pronounced in Stratford as it was pronounced in London—it may not have occurred to Hall that the playwright and his father-in-law had similar names.

Chapter I Why Shakespeare Matters

which to publish the plays—what was so compelling about William's name that would cause both the author of *Venus and Adonis* and the Lord Chamberlain's Men to prefer it over anything else?

Willy (will he) "Shake a spear"?

Although clearly the real name of a real individual—there is no doubt that the name as it was spelled on the plays is what certain readers of that time would call a *conundrum*. According to the OED, the third usage of the word (labelled "obsolete") means "a pun or wordplay depending on similarity of sound in words of different meaning" — giving as an example, "pair of dice"[16] for *paradise*.

Certainly the name *William Shakespeare* is a *conundrum* in this sense. In simpler terms—it's a pun that describes what he does—he *shakes* a *spear*. "*Will I am Shake-spear*" is one way of reading it—"*I will shake a spear*" is another. That philologists—apparently deaf to poetry—continue to *ignore the fact that the name is a pun* is nothing short of malfeasance! Shakespeare was a poet! One of the greatest who ever lived! *Of course it matters!*

For 16th-century citizens, the word *spear* had connotations that it no longer has for us today—some based on its shape, some on its use. In shape a spear resembles the object with which satires were written—*the pen* that's been called mightier than *the sword*. As a weapon of combat, a spear thrust at an enemy may wound him physically just as a satires may wound someone's reputation. While a satire is a verbal thrust, a spear suggests virility since its shape and use may suggest the male appendage that when erect is capable of thrust. In addition—the word *spear* is Green Room slang[17] for a *walk-on*, a stage hand or dresser, who—when the play calls for a mob or an army—throws on a cloak, grabs a prop spear, walks onstage, waves it shouting, walks off—and returns to his backstage task with props

---

[16] First meaning, first use—Thomas Nashe, 1595; second meaning, first use:—Ben Jonson, 1605.

[17] In the Theater the Green Room is the "dressing room" where actors wait to go onstage, thus Green Room slang refers to terms peculiar to theatrical insiders.

Educating Shakespeare

or lighting.[18] In Green Room slang—handed down through the ages —a *spear* is an *extra*—someone with a task backstage who can, as T.S. Eliot would put it—"swell a scene or two"—but is not regarded, or rewarded—as one whose task is to perform a role—i.e., an *actor*.

Shakespeare and his printer

How did the Company find William? Surely it was the true author or his representative who—when stuck for a name to put on *Venus and Adonis*—was provided with one by his printer—young Richard Field, a native of Stratford-on-Avon. Richard Field's father Henry Field was a tanner. Henry Field got the hides he turned into leather[19] from William's father, that "dealer in sheep products"—leather he then sold to printers who sold leatherbound books to the wealthier readers. That Henry Field's son Richard would have been very well acquainted with John Shakspere's son William is one of the few things in this account of which we can be a hundred percent certain.

Equally certain is the fact that one of the printers that tanner Henry Field did business with in London was a Thomas Vautrollier, a French Huguenot whose monopoly on printing works in Latin and other foreign languages had been granted him by Lord Burghley, eager to provide work for skilled protestants fleeing discrimination. That Burghley had granted Vautrollier a monopoly on works in Latin guaranteed him a substantial living with the Inns of Court lawyers— as did those educated London merchants who could afford to have their books bound in leather.

By 1579, having come to know and trust Vautrollier—when it came time for Henry Field to apprentice his son to a profitable trade he apprenticed him to Vautrollier—whose print shop was located in the Blackfriars district. By 1593, when the author of *Venus and Adonis* came to Vautrollier's shop to get his book published— Richard Field had become its owner—either as a bequest from Vautrollier, who recently died—or because the old man had left it to

---

[18] For more about the punning nature of the name *Shakespeare* and its relevance to the authorship question see Appendix A—"The name."

[19] David Kathman: "Shakespeare and Richard Field."

Chapter I Why Shakespeare Matters

A printshop from Shakespeare's time.

his daughter Jacqueline—by then an accomplished shop manager herself—whom Field had either already married, or would soon.

Thus it happened that when the author of *Venus and Adonis*—or his representative—came to Field's print shop in Blackfriars in late 1592 or early 1593 to see about getting *Venus and Adonis* published—when Field realized that a cover name was needed—he naturally thought of his neighbor William Shakspere—down on his luck and burdened with a growing family. Thus William, eager to help his father, whose struggle with adversity he had watched for years—was more than willing to make an extremely profitable deal with the actors in exchange for something as simple as the use of his name.

Two years later—when the newly formed Lord Chamberlain's Men felt forced to publish their plays—their manager, the nimble John Hemmings—aware of how the author of *Venus and Adonis* had solved a similar problem—could easily have located William through Field's printshop in Blackfriars. And since Hemmings himself haled from Droitwich—another day's ride on the road leading north from London to Stratford—it was easy to locate William—who it seems was willing to trade the use of his name for the sort of benefits Hemmings had been authorized to offer.

With illiterate country folk like William of Stratford, leery of anything that required a signature—this connection to a friend of his childhood was probably enough to seal the deal with nothing more than a handshake. William would visit London (occasionally)—where Hemmings doubtless made certain that he was accompanied whenever and wherever he went.

Hemmings would continue to handle William's finances until the cares of age prompted him to pass them on to another Court insider—Thomas Russell, husband by then to Hemmings' friend Anne St. Leger (pron. *Sellinger*), widow of Thomas Digges and mother of Leonard Digges Jr., whose poems are among the handful that introduce the 1623 collection of Shakespeare's works known to Shakespeare scholars as the First Folio. By 1600, she and Russell were living in Alderminster—four miles from Stratford.

What must have been something of an issue for the author and his actors was whether or not their stand-in could keep his mouth shut about his role with the Company. It turned out that silence was William's real talent—as suggested by a 17th-century anecdote from John Aubrey, who had it from William Beeston—whose father, the theatrical entrepreneur Christopher Beeston—had launched his own acting career years earlier with the Lord Chamberlain's Men.

According to Aubrey—William "was not a company keeper" —that he "wouldn't be debauched, and if invited to, wrote he was in pain."[20] This suggests that efforts were made to pry the truth from William with spirits—that he may have been asked to demonstrate his ability to write by urging him to write a little something—which it seems he dealt with by pretending that he'd hurt his hand.

Of course no one was fooled by any of this—but that didn't matter so long as his silence continued to protect the actors and their author. What's most likely is that William himself preferred that it not be known by his neighbors in Stratford exactly what it was that he was doing in London, playacting having a low reputation amongst persons of his native class.

"Fancy's child"

The fact that the man with the necessary name was the illiterate son of an illiterate dealer in sheep products is obviously the reason that Ben Jonson—when faced in 1623 with the problem of introducing the author in the First Folio—had to do what he could to nip in the bud any curiosity over the learning that would be so evident to the

---

[20] Chambers *Facts* 1.90.

educated who would be the ones actually purchasing and reading the book. He attempted to do this by flatly stating in advance that the author was ignorant of the Classics, should they be led at some point to locate William himself. Thus was established the author as a miraculous provincial whose achievements were solely due to his unfathomable and miraculous genius.

This fantasy would continue until the general level of education in England rose to a level where enough readers had enough education to see that somehow William had acquired an amazing education—or else he was *not* the author of the Shakespeare canon.

One of the transcending realities that the Academy continues to refuse to face is the obvious fact that William was *not* educated—for had he been he would not have had so much trouble signing his name to the six legal documents which are all the evidence that remains of centuries of digging through old papers in search of something written in his hand (Appendix B). In addition—for someone on William's socio-economic level—there would have to be evidence of patronage by someone of wealth and learning. Or there would have to be some evidence of his presence at Oxford or Cambridge. Or his name would have to have appeared in the books of a college Buttery, where accounts remained of the snacks charged to the less well-to-do students.[21] Or there would be evidence of years spent in the household of a great lord or merchant who maintained a tutor for his sons and a handful of other deserving boys—relatives and neighbors.

Evidence of no evidence

A number of men from humble backgrounds similar to William's who rose to importance back then had been afforded opportunity in just these ways—but for William—centuries of investigation have turned up nothing in either category. Had he been given the education the works published under his name demand—the diligent efforts of thousands of Shakespeare scholars would have discovered evidence of it long ago. Instead, all we have from the Academy is its unceasing

---

[21] Which is how later researchers were able to track Christopher Marlowe at his university, Corpus Christi College Cambridge.

Educating Shakespeare

refusal even to acknowledge his education as an issue.

One of the more influential of the academic efforts to provide Shakespeare with an education has been the monumental two volume tome, *Shakspere's Small Latine and Lesse Greeke*, by Chicago University English professor T.W. Baldwin—published in 1944. Well grounded in the literatures of ancient Greece and Rome—Baldwin was aware of those instances in the plays that reveal Shakespeare's knowledge of certain classical sources that were not translated into English until after William was dead. Since Baldwin was also aware that 400 years of research had located no evidence of a university education—for him the only possible solution was that —despite the unfortunate lack of evidence—the Stratford grammar school must have provided instruction in Greek.

Baldwin makes it clear right off that he is not about to disturb the sacred ethos—

> Whatever critics do, I hope they will not use the term "erudite" either of Shakspere's (sic) work or of mine upon it; neither is anything of the kind. Both merely use the humdrum, everyday routines of the most commonplace grammar school of Shakspere's day. . . . 16th-century schoolmasters had a mountain of erudition, but of it Shakspere and the author claim only a mouse apiece. (vi)

If not of erudition—Baldwin's book is certainly a mountain of something. This accumulation of data on the spread of the Erasmus curriculum tracks—statistic by statistic, author by author, school by school—the rapidly growing system of English grammar schools throughout the sixteenth and seventeenth centuries. As such it's been immensely valuable for historians of education. But what it fails to do—because it couldn't—is prove that William had actually *attended* the Stratford grammar school. Had we some solid justification for assuming that he did—had there been any evidence of something more than just a version of his name published on a dozen title pages in the late 1590s—we might be justified in assuming that the author had learned both Greek and Latin at the Stratford grammar school.

Unfortunately for Baldwin and those who continue to rely on him as evidence that William knew Latin because Latin was taught at

Chapter I Why Shakespeare Matters

the Stratford school—all the evidence has been on the other side. That no letters from William in any language have ever surfaced—that apart from the pesky scribbles on a handful of legal documents—no certain holograph of his handwriting has ever turned up, either on a playscript or on anything else. So there is still nothing that might suggest that he was anything but an illiterate provincial tradesman.

Says Baldwin—"Whether or not Shakespeare ever spent a single day in petty or grammar school, nonetheless petty and grammar school were a powerful shaping influence upon him, as they were, and were planned to be, upon the whole society of that day" (vii). Thus Baldwin emits the usual squid-like cloud of ink we get from academics in place of any real evidence—for how can grammar school influence someone who cannot spell his own name?

During the 1570s—when William was in his learning years—the Stratford school would have been responding in its own way and in its own time to the wave of excitement over Learning that was driving the English to educate as many boys as possible—a period sociologist Lawrence Stone claims was "the most active school expansion" in English history (*Crisis* 309).

While Stratford school attendance records, if kept, have not survived—there's actually enough information about its teachers during the period when William was of an age to attend that suggests that these men, all graduates of Cambridge, would certainly have been equipped to teach the curriculum that Baldwin describes. And just as certainly there would have been boys in Stratford whose parents put their sons in the local grammar school because they wanted them prepared for the University. But that is not the point—the point is first—whether William's parents were of that sort, and second—whether William was of that sort himself.[22] Baldwin didn't answer either question because, without evidence, he simply couldn't.

"Small Latin and less Greek"

So obvious would the quality of Shakespeare's education have been

---

[22] According to Joan Simon, historian of Early Modern education, "grammar school was . . . far out of reach of the . . . poor husbandman who fell into the category of those needing the child's help to support the family" (370).

Educating Shakespeare

to the educated readers of later centuries that the authorship question might never have arisen had not Ben Jonson—in his dedicatory Ode to the First Folio—tossed off the comment—seemingly in passing, that his great precursor had only "small Latin and less Greek." This means nothing to us now—for how many among Shakespeare's worldwide audience today are fluent in Latin or know so much as a smidgeon of classical Greek? But to Jonson and his 17th-century readers—and to those who know what little there is to know about William's life—it had to mean that Shakespeare had—if not *no* education, then very little—for in those days even a grammar school education would have rendered him competent in basic Latin—and certainly capable of writing letters in English—while ancient Greek was hardly of use to anyone but a few scholars and poets.

Latin—originally spread throughout Europe by Caesar and the Romans who followed in his wake—was still the universal language of international communications, diplomacy and literature. Uniting officialdom and all men of learning throughout the West—it was Latin—not English—that was taught at the grammar schools that were being so enthusiastically planted all over England. Nor was there any reason for a youth to attend one of these schools unless he was preparing for the seven years at a university that it took to get the Masters degree that qualified him to advertise himself as a physician, lawyer, or clergyman—all of which required fluent Latin.[23]

So the monumental effort by T.W. Baldwin to prove that the Stratford grammar school offered enough Latin that it got William started on a lifetime of self education falls apart with the realization that had he learned what Baldwin claims he must have—due to the immense popularity of Shakespeare's plays—400 years of digging would have turned up letters from him or to him from admirers who treasured them. It would have turned up the kind of business letters that all educated men and women wrote and received back then.

Fellow poets would have mentioned him in their dedications and eulogies. Gossipy letter writers Roland White and John

---

[23] Those who studied at a university purely for the sake of acquiring knowledge often left no sign of their studies. Only medical doctors, clergymen, and lawyers required a Master's degree, which took seven years, the Bachelor's degree, acquired after the first three years, merely the first step in the process.

Chapter I Why Shakespeare Matters

Chamberlain would have mentioned him in letters to friends and business associates. Yet despite centuries of research—no evidence has ever been uncovered that William Shakspere of Stratford-on-Avon—or any member of his family—ever spent any time in a grammar school, at a university, or in an educated household—no evidence that he was prepared to write anything more than a shakily scrawled *Shakspr* on a handful of legal documents—or that any member of his family could as much.

Perhaps a better question might be—why should Ben Jonson think it mattered? In an Ode intended to praise Shakespeare—why bother to discredit his learning? Could it be that already readers were raising questions about his identity based on the evidence of his knowledge of the very classics that Jonson took such pains to deny? Was it because the actors were already being asked too often —and increasingly by too many—who was writing these plays?

According to Jonson—while Shakespeare could barely read all that "insolent" Greece or "haughty" Rome sent forth"—somehow he had managed to surpass them. This could be taken to mean that however minimal his knowledge of Latin and Greek, it was sufficient for his purpose. Instead—for the next two centuries—Shakespeare was seen by both scholars and publishers as unable to read *anything* but English—which, in effect, meant he could read nothing—there being as yet little published in English other than almanacs, sermons, and joke books.

Ten years later—Jonson's "small Latin" was reinforced by the Second Folio (1633)—in which the great John Milton describes Shakespeare as "Fancy's child, warbling native woodnotes wild." After another ten years, Leonard Digges Jr. pursued the party line in the 1640 edition of Shakespeare's poetry—"Next Nature only help'd him, for look through this whole book, thou shalt find he doth not borrow one phrase from Greeks, nor Latins imitate, nor once from vulgar languages translate"—*vulgar* meaning Italian, Spanish or French. Edition after edition, poet after poet—all were strangely obsessed with his ignorance. As one such remark would have it— made by John Dryden as if in passing—"Shakespeare, who—*taught by none*, did first impart, to Fletcher wit, to labouring Jonson Art."

How did they get from *small* to *none*? How did it happen that

Educating Shakespeare

for a good 300 years the only thing that anyone knew for certain about Shakespeare—beyond the fact that he came from a place named Stratford—was that he was un*educated*. Long before the pie face with the bald head, page boy haircut and Van Dyke beard—Shakespeare's first brand—the one that the literary establishment not only failed to question but actively fostered—was his stupendous lack of learning.

As academician John Velz puts it in his 1968 bibliographical compendium of references to Shakespeare's Classical sources—"By 1660 the notion of an untutored Shakespeare was a commonplace beginning to freeze into a tradition." According to Velz—between 1660 and 1679—John Dryden, the 17th-century Lion of English literature—alludes to Shakespeare's ignorance of antiquity "no fewer than five times." Knowing nothing about him, it seems to have been the only thing they could find to say about him. Throughout the centuries this has remained the common view—spawned by Ben Jonson in 1623, and handed on in turn by every succeeding figurehead of the English Literary establishment from Milton to Dryden to Pope and through Dr. Johnson to the English Departments of today.

What could have caused this bizarre distortion of what should have been obvious to educated readers from the start, particularly those of the eighteenth century—by which time the ancient classics had crystallized into the intellectual backbone of the standard upper-class English education, with its heavy accent on the literatures of ancient Rome and Athens.

Nicholas Rowe, editor of the first edition of Shakespeare's plays to be produced after the anti-theatrical years under Cromwell—in his 1709 "Account of the Life"—based (so he claimed) on research by London's leading actor at that time, Thomas Betterton. According to Rowe, Betterton (in his youth the favorite of Charles II) had made the three-day trip to Stratford on purpose to question those who might still remember their famous neighbor. This it appears was minimal—for all that Rowe could offer was—"His father, who was a considerable dealer in wool, had so large a family, that he could do no more for him than raise him to his own trade."

Chapter I Why Shakespeare Matters

> He had bred him, 'tis true, for some time at a free school,[24] where 'tis probable he acquired that little Latin he was master of, but the narrowness of his circumstances, and the want of his assistance at home, forced his father to withdraw him ... and unhappily prevented his further proficiency in that language. It is without controversy that *he had no knowledge of the writings of the ancient poets.*

Apparently the aging Betterton had returned from Stratford with little more than a handful of questionable anecdotes—that is, if he actually took the arduous three day trip, for he was ill by then, dying the following year. Did no one in Stratford remember anything about William Shakespeare?—"Shakspere"? "Shakyspeyr"?[25] "Shaxberd"? Why was there no information from William's remaining family members? What about Joan Hart, his younger sister, who had married the local hatter and lived until 1646? Her descendants were still in possession of the Henley Street house well into the eighteenth century (Phillipps 403).

Aubrey's anecdotes, based on Anthony á Wood's testimony, add little—though it certainly is fascinating to learn from Wood that there was a butcher's apprentice in Stratford who was just as witty as William—but who (alas!) died young! As reported by editor Samuel Monk in his introduction to the 1948 reprint of Rowe's biography —"Antiquarian research has added a vast amount of detail about the world in which Shakespeare lived, and has raised and answered questions that never occurred to Rowe, but it has recovered little more of the man himself"—a complaint equally true of more recent efforts by academics James Shapiro and Stephen Greenblatt.

In the 1679 prologue to an "amended" version of *Troilus and Cressida*, Betterton speaks as the voice of Shakespeare's ghost— "Untaught, unpractis'd, in a barbarous age, *I found not, but created first the stage.*" In 1725, after describing Shakespeare's abilities—

---

[24] The Stratford school was *free* only in that all children were allowed to attend— it did not mean that it was without cost. Parents had to pay an assortment of fees, for the masters, their ushers, winter fuel—not to mention the pens and paper books so the boys could learn to write (Simon 370 fn3).

[25] Two of the 83 spellings found in the records (Chambers *Problems* 371).

Alexander Pope ends with, "this is perfectly amazing from a man of no education or experience in those great and public scenes of life which are usually the subject of his thoughts."

～ The first Shakespeareans ～

The earliest Shakespeare scholars dealt only with the works. In 1773, George Steevens (1736-1800) produced the first variorum (scholarly) edition of the plays based on his collection of octavo editions in 10 volumes—followed in 1793 by a second in 15 volumes. As for the author—all he could add was the oft-repeated squib—

> All that is known with any degree of certainty concerning Shakespeare is that he was born at Stratford-upon-Avon, married and had children there, went to London where he commenced acting and wrote poems and plays, returned to Stratford, made his will, died, and was buried.

Steevens's efforts overlapped with the works of Malone (1741-1812)—the first modern Shakespeare scholar. Sir Edmond Malone's donation to the Bodleian Library of his collection of documents and notes would form the basis for all subsequent efforts to unlock the mysteries of the Bard's origins and sources. As for the biography—beyond quoting Steevens (above) and repeating several versions of the "Davenant scandal," he had little to add.

Shakespeare's first real biographer was the Victorian James Orchard Halliwell-Phillipps (1820-1889)—an antiquarian who, with classic 19th-century thoroughness—collected and published many thousands of documents relevant to what's termed Early Modern Literature. Altogether, his gleanings —including a collection of nursery rhymes—fill over 60 volumes. It may have been in response to the increasing interest in Shakespeare's identity raised by Delia Bacon and the Lord Chancellor that in 1870 Phillipps began to concentrate on the biography that would engage him from then on.

In his *Outlines of the Life*, first published in 1881, Phillipps avoided the problems involved with creating a narrative by choosing instead to provide the documentation on which future narratives would be based. This includes hundreds of verbatim documents

Chapter I Why Shakespeare Matters

relating to William of Stratford, his family, his neighbors, plus any and all records he could find of their births, deaths, wills, marriages and court cases—which he reproduced in the original Latin, along with numerous facsimiles of originals arranged in chronological order. His work provided the foundation for 20th-century literary historians E.K. Chambers, W. W. Greg, and Samuel Schoenbaum.

Beginning with estate records from Stratford and London—most of them in Latin—Phillipps provides the single extant letter written *to* William, three letters by Stratford neighbors in which he's mentioned, material on William's Stratford home "New Place" with illustrations, the Snitterfield estates, the Hathaway families, a short list of the various spellings of William's unusual surname, facsimiles of his attempts at a signature, a list of all the John Shaksperes in Warwickshire, and so forth. All are of great use in every area of Shakespeare Studies—every area, that is, but one—a solid *third party connection* to the London Stage—"third party" meaning one that *cannot be traced* in any way to the Lord Chamberlain's Men. Were he actually ever in London for more than a brief visit, William would have left his name in places in the record that *cannot be connected* to the actors or their patrons.

Nothing bemuses the scholar in search of a fact that will substantively connect Shakspere of Stratford with the actual creation of the dramas that bear his name than the sheer volume of material provided by Phillipps—for nowhere in this mountain of data is there a single document that shows that William could write anything beyond six barely legible scribbles on legal forms—that he had ever appeared at Court, or been introduced, as Jonson put it, to "Eliza and our James" who were both "so taken" with the plays that bore his name. In all of this mountain of data there was nothing to connect him to the world of the London Stage beyond the use of a particular version of his name by the Lord Chamberlain's Men, their publishers, printers, and patrons.

His name is found only on the title pages of plays, or on legal documents where it accompanies one or more members of the acting company that made it famous in 17th-century London. In a time of avid letter writing, when letters from people of importance were treasured, this gargantuan anomaly demands an explanation from the

Academy that purports to hold the truth about this greatest of all authors—one they have yet to provide.

Actually, there is one thing—however embarrassing to his 19th-century idolators—that suggests the means by which both William of Stratford and his brand as a man of little or no education were established and maintained over the four decades from the publication of the First Folio in 1623—to the reopening of the theaters after the decades of Civil War—and the brave new world that would follow.

⁓ The Davenant scandal ⁓

Shortly after the publication of the First Folio in 1623, a newcomer began writing plays for the King's Men. This was young William Davenant—or D'Avenant, as he preferred—a man of amazing energy and fortitude. Having risen from middle-class mediocrity to a place of leadership—first as confidante to the royal family during the twenty years of civil war when all the theaters were closed—then, following the return of Charles II—to theatrical prominence with the rebirth of the London Stage. Arriving in London during or after 1622 from Oxford, his hometown, young Davenant began by taking rooms at the Middle Temple where he was befriended by poets and Court insiders. Men like John Suckling and James Shirley, patrons like Endymion Porter, Edward Hyde, future Earl of Clarendon, and Henry Jermyn, future Earl of St. Albans—rakish young intellectuals with money to spend in the wine shops and theaters shouldering the Inns of Court in the West End, befriended William Davenant.

But this William was no playboy—he had a goal—he dreamed of writing plays for Shakespeare's company. His first effort, a travesty based on *Othello*, was rejected—but by 1627 the Company began producing his stuff. Though far from brilliant, Davenant was fortunate in having arrived on the scene just when the King's Men were losing their grip on their all-important Court audience. With both of their major playwrights gone[26]—what was Shakespeare's

---

[26] Nathan Field died in 1620—John Fletcher in 1625. With the accession of Charles I in 1625—his Queen's preference for Inigo Jones's masques left the aging Ben Jonson out in the cold.

Chapter I Why Shakespeare Matters

Company was now in competition with Queen Henrietta's Men, patronized by Her Majesty, the educated daughter of the King of France. Producing fewer plays—from fifteen sharers in 1625 the number had dropped by 1635 to nine—and with the linchpins of company management gone—Hemmings in 1630 and the last of the Burbages, Cuthbert, in 1638—management of the Court Stage had transferred to Inigo Jones, whose elaborately costumed masques were what the Court preferred. Shakespeare had become "old hat."

Despite the management skills that biographer Mary Edmond attributes to Davenant's apprenticeship under Jones—had it not been for his efforts in behalf of the royal family it's unlikely that he would be remembered today—for, as she complains, history has been unkind to Sir William. Compared unfavorably with Shakespeare, Jonson and Webster from before him—Dryden, Etheredge and Congreve after—it has failed to acknowledge his real achievements.

During the dark days of the Puritan Interregnum—the twenty years of the English Civil War when the great public stages were torn down and actors forced to seek other means of survival—Davenant found ways to keep putting on shows. When the royal troops were desperate for weapons and transportation—it was Davenant who found them horses. When the royal family and its retinue of impoverished supporters were living a marginal existence in Paris—it was Davenant who travelled through Europe raising funds to keep them in bread and butter. With plays outlawed—he managed to produce the first proto-opera in English history. Imprisoned twice by Cromwell's puritans—he used his time in jail to write an epic poem.

No one fought harder over the twenty years of Civil War for the return of the monarchy and the rights of the English to make merry in public than William Davenant. For this he was rewarded with a knighthood by Charles I, and—following the death of Ben Jonson, Jonson's office of Court poet.[27] With the return of the monarchy, he was rewarded by Charles II—that patron of beautiful actresses—with one of two royal licenses meant to reestablish the London Stage.

Only then—and with but eight years left of his long active life

---

[27] While later Jonson and Dryden would reap a steady stipend from the honor—Davenant had to be satisfied with just the prestige.

—was Sir William free to demonstrate to the fullest extent his considerable talent for management. Having the foresight to put his trust in young Tom Betterton—who soon became the most renowned actor of the age and Sir William's steadfast partner in managing their company, the Duke's Men—Davenant rose to become the leading theatrical entrepreneur of his day. Literary mavens make fun of his bowdlerization of Shakespeare, forgetting that it was only in this way that Shakespeare managed to survive the forty years of civil war and the very uncivil period that followed, until—with the dawn of the eighteenth century—his glories could be rediscovered by a fresh new generation of critics and poets.

Shakespeare's son

Thus, as the central figures of the Shakespeare era died off, Sir William became the only remaining member of the theatrical community that had known the London Stage when it was still performing Shakespeare as originally written. By the 1660s, he was also the only one left who had any memory at all of William of Stratford. Passionate about Shakespeare's works—some he had memorized—he used them either as inspiration for his own attempts, or as artefacts to cut and rearrange for the amalgamations he produced for the Court.

But whatever his literary weaknesses—Davenant had a unique claim on the Bard that no one else could match—namely that he himself was Shakespeare's son. Surrounded for most of his career by men with greater claims to talent, social standing or education—Davenant was proud to be known as the great playwright's natural son, conceived during one of his stopovers in Oxford on his way to or from London, when it seems his choice of a place to relax was the tavern owned by Davenant's parents. Davenant's mother, attractive and friendly, had been friendly with William, who took advantage of the relaxed atmosphere where she held sway—or so the story goes.

And so the story went for centuries—having originated in Oxford, where diarist Anthony á Wood—whose life overlapped with Davenant's—heard it repeated as gospel by his older contemporary John Aubrey, both of them Oxonians—and both personally

Chapter I Why Shakespeare Matters

acquainted with Davenant's parents and their wine shop. Wood passed on the story in his *Athenae Oxoniensis*—from whence it travelled from one commentator to another—twenty in all from 1629 through 1778—as recorded by Phillipps—who honored it with a separate section of its own—"The Davenant Scandal" (43-6). Far from any shame, it seems that Davenant himself was its major promoter. Phillipps repeats—from Aubrey's *Lives of Eminent Persons,* a manuscript in the Bodleian Library completed in 1680—

> Now Sir Wm. would sometimes, when he was pleasant over a glass of wine with his most intimate friends, e.g., Samuel Butler, author of *Hudibras*, etc., say that it seemed to him that he wrote with the very spirit that Shakespeare [did], and was contented enough to be thought his son.

Pope's comment was reported by Spence in 1750—the "notion of Sir William Davenant being more than a poetical child of Shakespeare was common in town, and Sir William himself seemed fond of having it taken for truth." In his edition of Shakespeare, Malone could note that Davenant's connection to Shakespeare was "always a constant tradition in Oxford" (44-5). John Dryden—who was very fond of Davenant, praising him and crediting him with his own introduction to Shakespeare—"whom first he taught me to admire"—held to the story of Davenant's origins as he had had it from Sir William.

Whether the story of his conception is true or not matters less than the fact that Davenant himself believed it—or chose to believe it—and that he was responsible for the fact that an entire literary community, including the great Dryden—chose to believe it. And while today's literary historians—if they mention it at all, tend to relegate it to the level of an anecdote, an amusing if somewhat embarrassing footnote to the life of the great Shakespeare[28]—what they fail to realize is how central it is to the first and longest lasting image of the Bard—that is, a genius whose gifts could only have come from Nature since he so obviously lacked a formal education.

---

[28] Mary Edmond, Davenant's 20th-century biographer, mentions these claims only in passing and only as a rumor with no foundation. Ignoring the testimonies of Aubrey, Wood and Dryden—she refers to William of Stratford only as Davenant's "godfather."

Educating Shakespeare

It seems certain that, as a boy, William Davenant became acquainted in some way with the man he'd been told was his godfather. Whenever it was that his mother confessed the thrilling secret of his paternity, it may have explained the differences between himself and his siblings—for while William was drawn to pursue a career in the theater, his brothers all followed their father through the Merchant Taylor's Academy into more pedestrian livings. Although history, or rumor, were pleased to ascribe Davenant's poetic and theatrical talents to William of Stratford—the true source was probably his mother, Jennet Sheppard, renowned for her wit and beauty, who shared with her husband[29] a great love of the London Stage—as reported by Aubrey—who knew them both.

Davenant could not have spent much time with his godfather, whose trips, according to the stories, took place no more than once every year or two—and whose later years were spent in Stratford, where he died when his little namesake was ten years old. By then the name *Shakespeare*—broadcast by title pages and playbills—was so famous that what to a more easily scandalized period would be considered shameful was generally seen as something William could take pride in—that inspired him to commit his plays to memory.

Did Davenant himself ever doubt the official version of the Shakespeare authorship? Why would he? For old-timers like Ben Jonson, John Hemmings, or Cuthbert Burbage—the only members of the Company left from its early days—it would have been counter productive to disillusion one whose passionate belief in his father's authorship made him so useful in maintaining the rather ambiguous authority of the First Folio.

Thus it was through William Davenant—self proclaimed son of Shakespeare—that the certainty of William of Stratford's authorship was embraced by the community most responsible for broadcasting it—and thus it may also have been through Davenant that Shakespeare's memory was humanized for his uneducated public by the fact that he seems to have lacked an education.

For what, after all, did William Jr. actually know about his

---

[29] According to Wood—Davenant Sr. attended the Merchant Taylor's Grammar School under Richard Mulcaster during the period when the students were often performing at Court (Edmond 10, 14).

Chapter I Why Shakespeare Matters

reputed father? While in reality they could have had very little actual contact, he would have needed some special knowledge to establish the intimacy of their relationship. If at some point he became aware that—according to residents of the university town—the great playwright seemed strangely ignorant of the Greek dramatists—this bit of inside information may have helped support his claim.

In fact, a university education was the only thing that William Davenant had that report had denied his famous father—for he himself had learned to read and write at the local grammar school and had even spent a few semesters at the university that dominated his home town. This may also help to explain why writers like Milton and Dryden were content to believe in the uneducated Shakespeare. It cast him as a thing apart—unlike themselves, a prodigy of Nature. As Rowe's editor Samuel Holt Monk put it in 1948—

> Dryden did not heed Jonson's caveat that, despite his lack of learning, Shakespeare did have art. He was too obsessed with the idea that Shakespeare, ignorant of . . . the ancients, was infected with the faults of his age . . . . When Dryden died in 1700, the age of Jonson had passed and the age of Shakespeare was about to begin.

Most relevant perhaps is the fact that Davenant left his theatrical legacy to his competent widow and their stable of sons, several of whom followed in his footsteps as successful theater entrepreneurs and managers—all instrumental in keeping alive the Shakespeare of their father and Milton as "Fancy's Child." In his famous *Worthies of England* (1662), Thomas Fuller—a relative of Davenant, records only Shakespeare's birth town and that he was "never any scholar."

Davenant to Dryden to Rowe

If anyone knew the whole truth about the authorship it would have to be John Hemmings, whose association with the Lord Chamberlain's Men began (officially) in 1594 when the Company was first formed by Lord Chamberlain Henry Hunsdon. Trained for a business career as an apprentice to a member of the Grocer's Guild—Hemmings left the acting to other members of the Company—taking on what by then

Educating Shakespeare

had become the full time duties of the Company's business manager. Steering it through the deaths of patrons and the adversity of London officials—he and his old friend Henry Condell —if the value of their shares through James's reign is to be believed—helped it to become one of the most successful commercial ventures of that era.

By 1630, when Hemmings died, William of Stratford and all who might have known him—either in Stratford or London—were dead—while of the original Company, only Ben Jonson remained, poor and ill and largely ignored by the Caroline Court until he too died on the eve of the government takeover by Oliver Cromwell.

Cromwell's Stalinist concept of public order would make illegal all theatrical efforts for twenty long years. The only men to survive the Puritan Interregnum were too young before it to know more than what their elders had told them. Thus the poet-playwright Nicholas Rowe—the first to attempt a biography of Shakespeare—had no one who could provide him with direct knowledge of the elusive playwright. The closest he could get was to the aging actor, Tom Betterton—

> I must own a particular obligation to [Betterton] for the most considerable part of the passages relating to his life which I have here transmitted . . . his veneration for the memory of Shakespeare having engag'd him to make a journey into Warwickshire on purpose to gather up what remains he could of a name for which he had so great a value. (Phillipps 76)

Since Rowe had little more to offer than what had been reported by Aubrey and Wood—this four-day round trip seems unlikely. By the time Betterton got around to it, he was almost seventy. Seriously ailing with gout and related infirmities—he barely made it through another year, dying in 1710. Most likely he simply repeated what he'd heard over the years from Davenant—who by 1709 had been dead for forty years—while Dryden had been gone for almost a decade.

John Dryden was only thirty-six in 1668 when—following the death of Davenant, Charles II bestowed on him the by then official title of "Poet Laurette." The ruling voice in the literary world of London for four decades—Dryden, "by his own acknowledgement, had derived his enthusiasm for Shakespeare from Davenant." Thus

Chapter I Why Shakespeare Matters

from Davenant to Dryden to Rowe to the Augustans, all that was known about Shakespeare was that he was "taught by none."

Adding to the myth of the uneducated Shakespeare is the gaping gulf that for centuries separated his arena, the London Stage, from the intellectual centers of Oxford and Cambridge—for neither university showed any interest at all in Shakespeare during the author's lifetime or for the next 200 years. Claims on 16th- and 17th-century quarto title pages that his plays were performed at a university refer to civic halls in the university town—not to anything within its walls, where —as Oxford graduate and English professor Frederick Boas makes clear in his *Shakespeare and the Universities* (1923)—the actors were anything but welcome. "For generations the predominant attitude of the university authorities towards Shakespeare was one of hostility or contempt" (Velz 1). Having disdained "vulgar" (English) drama for centuries—when the Oxbridge community finally began to take notice of the Bard—their interest was solely in the texts of his plays —as has been the case ever since.

Thus the original view—that the public theaters were no more worthy of notice than the pubs and bordellos that surrounded them in the free-wheeling London "liberties"—meant that their greatest playwright, however popular, continued for centuries to be regarded by the universities as little more than the best of a bad lot. Bemused by the bowdlerized versions of the plays as produced by Davenant[30] —versions that continued to be produced for English and Americans until the late nineteenth century—audiences saw no irony in Shakespeare's déclassé reputation. So when Romantic era poets like Keats and Coleridge, or actors like Edmund Kean and John Philip Kemble began using Shakespeare's original texts—rather than bothering to revise their opinions—the homophobic Victorians, horrified by the masculine pronoun that threatened to besmirch the purity of his *Sonnets*—turned with relief to the "prudent" Warwickshire actor— about whom they knew nothing bad because they knew nothing at all. Whatever his other problems—William of Stratford's biography made it easy for academics to ignore Shakespeare's apparent passion

---

[30] Thomas Bowdler was an early 19th-century doctor who, together with his sister, created *The Family Shakespeare*—a version of the plays they advertised as "appropriate for women and children."

for a youth of his own sex—leaving it to his popularizers to provide readers with descriptions of Stratford-on-Avon in the Spring.

Nevertheless—despite the consensus of officialdom—there could be heard, right from the start, here and there—however ignored by the mainstream of popular enthusiasts—little questioning peeps. By 1680, playwright Nahum Tate—who provided 17th-century London with a happy ending to *King Lear*—would admit—"I confess I could never yet get a true account of his learning, and am apt to think it more than common report allows him."—By the middle of the eighteenth century—passages suggesting his knowledge of both Greek and Latin were finding their way into print.

Then in 1767 all questioning came to an abrupt halt with the *Essay on the Learning of Shakespeare* by the uber-academic Richard Farmer, Vice-Chancellor of Cambridge University and pillar of the Tory Party. Farmer argued so convincingly against Shakespeare's learning that the heretics fell silent for another century.

The Birthplace Trust

Meanwhile the nation's burgeoning Bardolatry was heading in a direction unconcerned with his education or the lack thereof. Two years after Farmer's book came the Shakespeare Jubilee—a gala produced both in Stratford and London by actor/impresario David Garrick in his campaign to awaken the nation to the importance of the man he believed should be enshrined as England's National Poet.

As Garrick force fed the Stratford biography into the minds of the public—poets like Keats and Byron signed the visitors' register at the house on Henley Street. Then in 1847—purchased by a new group of enthusiasts who would make it headquarters for their *Shakespeare Birthplace Trust*—Charles Dickens pitched in to help raise funds for Stratford-on-Avon as England's Shakespeare Mecca.

Although Shakespeare's increasing popularity throughout the eighteenth century did little to arouse interest in his education, as the universities and grammar schools began creating thinkers versed in classical languages and literatures—questions arose regarding Jonson's disclaimer. In 1857, the publication of Delia Bacon's theory of group authorship sparked so much enthusiasm for Francis Bacon

Chapter I Why Shakespeare Matters

that a Society formed in 1885 to promote him as the true author. Other candidates soon followed—among them Christopher Marlowe, the Earl of Derby, and almost anyone whose name could be connected in some way to Elizabethan literature or the London Stage.

Meanwhile the public—ignorant of Latin, Greek, and sixteenth century history—were roused in defense of the dear old Birthplace. Politicians—aware as always of what is most likely to put butter on their bread—have been inclined to back them—or at least, to avoid offending them. Still it's the popular prejudice against the aristocracy that tars as snobbishness any effort to locate the author where his plays show that he so clearly belongs—at the royal Court.

"Facts and problems"

In 1923, Sir Edmund Kerchever Chambers provided what would become the cornerstone of Shakespeare studies with his massive four-volume history of *The Elizabethan Stage.* Seven years later, in a two-volume follow-up, *Shakespeare: Facts and Problems*—he dealt more directly with the kind of questions he was forced to ignore while creating its predecessor. Since it took only twenty-seven pages to cover what was known of William's life, Chambers needs must acknowledge—"As in so many other historical investigations, after all the careful scrutiny of clues and all the patient balancing of possibilities, the last word for a self-respecting scholarship can only be that of *nescience*"—a synonym for *ignorance.*

While subsequent chapters deal with what's known of the Stage from 1592 on—the acting companies and the publishing history of the plays—Chambers gave two categories chapters of their own. In "Problems of Authenticity"—i.e., *"What did Shakespeare actually write?"*—he filled 40 pages, almost double those about William's life. As for the 30 pages devoted to "Problems of Chronology"— i.e., *"When did he write them?"*—these quickly devolved into a hodgepodge of *maybe-this-maybe-that.*

Certainly this book is a must for anyone researching a particular work of the period. The bulk of Volume I is devoted to the works, some of it material not found anywhere else—but it does not attempt to resolve any of the issues it mentions—nor does it address the outstanding fact that *all of these problems* arise from a single source —*the Stratford* biography. For Chambers, Stratford remains sacred, beyond doubt or question. In Volume II he mostly repeats the same facts, dates, records, references to William and other members of his family and the acting community previously culled by Malone and Phillipps from letters, records, and other published materials. And although he adds his measure of scorn for those who seem to rely too heavily on conjecture—he simply can't resist the urge to contribute a little "imaginative reconstruction" of his own.

"Foolish questions"

The son of Victorian clergy, a graduate of Corpus Christi Oxford, a career bureaucrat in the Department of Education—Chambers (1866-1954) was, basically, a Church of England Tory—a Victorian either unwilling or unable to see past the Stratfordian anomalies to anything too radically inconsistent with what he'd been taught in school or at the family dinner table. Of a methodical nature, his way of dealing with incompatibles was primarily—and perhaps sensibly—to allow them to coexist.

When it came to Shakespeare's lack of an education, he did what he could to minimize its importance—as in his Introduction to *The Elizabethan Stage*—"The attempt . . . of Professor Churton Collins to establish a familiarity with the Greek tragedians rests largely upon analogies of thought and expression which may have had a natural origin out of analogous situations." By "analogous situations" did he mean that the resurrection of Hermione in *Winter's Tale* that so closely resembles the resurrection of Euripides's *Alcestis* came to Shakespeare from some situation in his own life? Of all such evidence of Shakespeare's learning Chambers says—

> One may reasonably assume that at all times Shakespeare read whatever books, original or translated, came his way. It has been asked where he found them in the absence of public libraries. Did he borrow them from the Earl of Southampton, or from Jonson or from Camden, or did he merely turn over their leaves on the stationers' stalls? These are foolish questions to which I propose no answers. (1.22-3)

Chapter I Why Shakespeare Matters

Although Chambers added little to the dating scheme proposed by Greg—who followed Malone—it acquired his name because his massively detailed *Elizabethan Stage* has since become so influential. But because he (and Greg) were forced to accept the Stratford biography and its dates—they were forced to create a dating scheme that sees the author, not yet thirty—having arrived in London sometime in the early 1590s—creating dramatic works at the level of an experienced and highly innovative dramatist with nothing in his resumé of any sort of theatrical experience. As for his published works, the dedication to the first (1593) edition of *Venus and Adonis* —strangely placed on the second printed page under the dedication to Southampton (not on the title page where tradition should have put it)—a minor point, but curious—particularly when added to so much else that's unusual.

With a clergyman father and an Anglican theologian mother—Chambers could not have been more of an establishment thinker. Steeped in the 19th-century view of history—Chambers does not go deeply enough into Renaissance history to show how disturbingly out of sync with the history of Shakespeare's time are the dates forced on him by the Stratford bio. Certain questions seem never to have bothered him—such as why the great language artist would continue to use outdated terms when his contemporaries were using modern Jacobean language—which he explains as "experimenting with an archaic form for comic effect." Or why the most innovative writer that ever lived wouldn't look farther afield for plots and styles than contemporary writers so inferior to himself?

Why no letters? Why no portrait? Why no mention by any contemporary writer until Ben Jonson's Ode? Why no encomia at his death? Such questions are anything but foolish. An honest scholar, Chambers was willing to admit that there were serious problems with the scenario he inherited—but it was simply not within his capacity to find or even to seek a solution. Chambers's massive four volume effort reveals even more starkly the contrast between the life of William of Stratford—the spotty history of the London Stage—and the total lack of anything but the name *William Shakespeare*—to connect them.

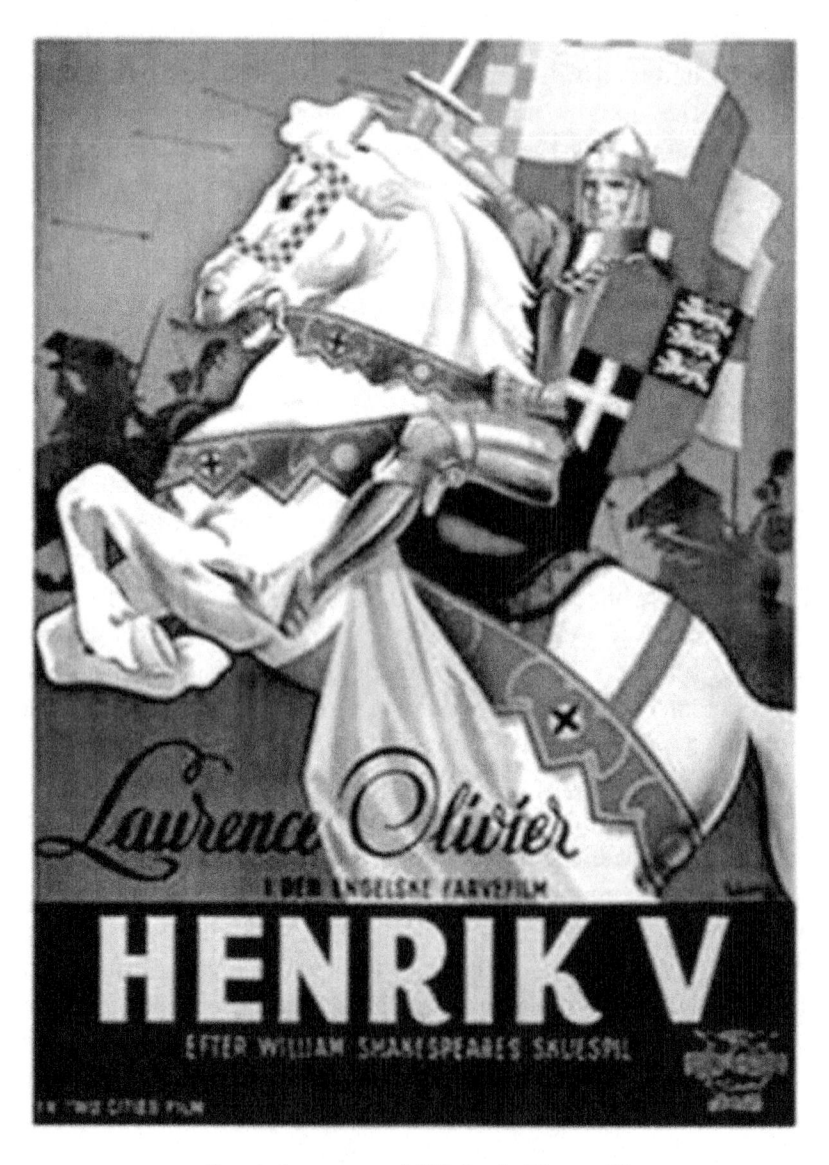

Danish poster of Olivier's Henry V

CHAPTER II

—∞— What Shakespeare Knew —∞—

What finally caused the identity issue to reach beyond insiders to the public at large was the dawning realization of the incredible[31] nature of Shakespeare's education. While lawyers had probably been discussing his knowledge of the Law among themselves for years, possibly centuries—it seems to have been Delia Bacon's *Philosophy of the Plays of Shakspeare Unfolded* that finally sent the Duke of Devonshire's librarian to England's top legal authority—Queen Victoria's Lord Chancellor, John Campbell—for his opinion.

After giving it some consideration, Campbell's response made it clear that—in his opinion—Shakespeare knew the Laws of England as well or better than most practising lawyers at that time—or any time. Said Campbell—*Sonnet 46* is "so intensely legal in its language and imagery that, without a considerable knowledge of English forensic procedure it cannot be fully understood." Examining the legal terms and issues in scenes from several of the plays—the trial scene in *Merchant of Venice*, the trials of Hermione in *Winter's Tale*, the arraignment of Goneril and Regan in *King Lear*, Campbell—clearly without the slightest notion of what a career in the Theater would have required—concluded that Shakespeare "must have been" a working lawyer who "enjoyed writing plays in his free time."

When time passed—and it became obvious that there wasn't any evidence that William of Stratford could possibly have been a practising lawyer—questioners turned to Francis Bacon. Not only was Bacon famous for his writing style, he was also considered the greatest legal mind of his time. Although his biography raised—and continues to raise—questions about his role in "the Shakespeare

---

[31] While the word *incredible*—synonymous with *unbelievable*—is mostly used for emphasis—it happens to be the correct adjective to describe the nature and extent of Shakespeare's education—which must have seemed, as it began to be revealed—simply *too vast to be believed.*

problem"—once it became clear that he simply could not have been both Shakespeare and the creator of the modern scientific method—for which, among others things, he's been lauded ever since—other candidates began popping up—so many that by the turn of the twentieth century—when the Academy grudgingly got around to adding English Literature to their curricula—the question of Shakespeare's identity had become something of a joke.

～ Shakespeare and the Law ～

Why it was the legal community that was the first to openly question Shakespeare's education is easy to understand. First, their opinions carry weight—not only because of their credentials, but because of certain traits possessed by all good lawyers. Trained in Logic and the arts of persuasion, they're also experienced in weighing evidence. They have respect for the record and for precedents handed down through time by past decisions. More even than historians—who tend to see past events in the light of their own prejudices—judges are sworn to keep an open mind. Most telling perhaps, lawyers will be aware of the human tendency to lie or obfuscate even the most innocent of truths if it will profit them or keep them out of trouble.

Versed in an ancient and specialized terminology, a lawyer will be alerted to the presence of a fellow lawyer by his correct use of Latin terms specific to the Law. They know what it takes to use such terms with accuracy—and, not least, the time, effort and money it has taken to learn how to use them—no less then than now. So it's not surprising that—as time passed—it was a group of 19th-century lawyers who took up the question of his knowledge of the Law.

This interest on the part of English lawyers can perhaps be seen as returning the favor, for so much of Shakespeare's humor is designed for their amusement—teasing them with puns and engaging their minds and expertise with imaginary trials like those in *Merchant of Venice* and *Measure for Measure*. The long and—to most laymen —boring first scene of *Henry V,* in which he argues the case for a woman's right to rule—a scene written—not for the groundlings— none of whom would have understood it any better than we do today —but for "the Gentlemen of the Inns of Court"—the lawyers and civil servants whose offices in Westminster surrounded the royal seat of government at Whitehall—who were all deeply engaged at that time with that very question.

Authorship scholar Mark Alexander has tracked this discussion from its beginning in 1778 with the first variorum edition of Shakespeare's plays—published by George Steevens, graduate of Eton, King's College Cambridge, and resident at London's Inner Temple—a task in which Steevens was supported by the highly respected Samuel Johnson. The Steevens-Johnson edition was surpassed a decade later by the first real Shakespeare scholar, Sir Edmond Malone—another lawyer, son of a judge, and friend and critic of both Steevens and Johnson. In 1881 came the popular *Annals of the Stage* by journalist John Payne Collier, in which—quoting Lord Chancellor John Campbell—he noted Shakespeare's "minute and undeviating accuracy" in matters of the Law.

Contrariwise—just as it was Bacon's status as Lord Chancellor under King James that cast him as William's first challenger—it was largely 19th-century homophobia that cast Maryland lawyer William Devecmon as Bacon's opponent[32]—and by extension—every other possible replacement for the unremarkable William of Stratford. Eventually—first Devecmon, then the pertinacious J.M. Robertson were trumped by lawyer and parliamentarian Sir Granville George Greenwood.[33] Liberal MP from Peterborough, advocate for Animal Rights and Independence for India—Greenwood may have been the most eloquent[34]—but other lawyers too turned to "radical solutions" for "the Shakespeare problem" because they understood that it was simply not possible that—back in the sixteenth century—someone with such a biography could have acquired Shakespeare's knowledge of the Law without having left some evidence of it.

---

[32] Francis Bacon was gay. Nineteenth-century England was torn by a devastating epidemic of homophobia which not only destroyed the reputations and lives of hundreds of good and great living men—among them Lord Byron and Oscar Wilde—it reached back in history to defile, where it could, the great men of yore.

33 Though Greenwood never named his choice of candidate—his books and articles attracted other notables, among them Mark Twain and Sigmund Freud.

34 Greenwood's *The Shakespeare Problem Restated* (1908) is available online via books.google.com.

The Law is itself a form of history—containing as it does the record of judgments and misdeeds of a nation—with precedence—the history of a particular issue—a factor in almost every trial. A nation's laws are the history of its social progress—its papers, parchment rolls then, preserved records of trials and decisions going back centuries. Unlike old play manuscripts and cheaply printed quartos—16th-century legal documents would never have been used as toilet paper or to stopper mustard pots. Preserved for reference—they've been lost only to disasters—earthquake, fire or flood. And what makes a particular document legal? Signatures! Had William of Stratford ever worked as a law clerk—as some have suggested—there would have been documents still in existence that contained his signature. In over 200 years of intense research—no such evidence has ever been found. In fact, the six signatures he scrawled on the three legal documents he left in the record in Stratford are the most convincing evidence of all that he could not possibly have been the author of anything. (See Appendix B—"Shakespeare's Hand")

The Merchant of Equity

One play in particular has advanced the argument beyond demur. In his 1935 article *Law vs. Equity in The Merchant of Venice*, law student Mark Edwin Andrews holds that in 1597, Shakespeare's play was presented as something of a legal brief in the long ongoing argument over which court had primacy—that of Queen's Bench, the court of Common Pleas—or Chancery, the court of Equity.

Competition between the two courts first arose centuries earlier with the establishment under Edward III of the court of Chancery, administered by the Lord Chancellor as a means of recourse for persons who felt their human rights had been violated by decisions based on English Common Law—which was solely concerned with property rights. As these two courts grew in power, they continued to vie for preeminence until Elizabeth's time when each found a champion—Attorney General Sir Edward Coke (pron. Cook) for Common Law—Sir Thomas Egerton, Master of the Rolls, for Chancery. By 1597, these two had been playing musical chairs for high legal office for some time before the arrival of young Francis

Chapter II What Shakespeare Knew

Bacon—eager to embark on the path he felt born to follow.

As MP for Melcomb Regis—Bacon aligned with Egerton, who—having just been named Lord Keeper, had therefore become the Parliamentary liaison between Lords and Commons. According to Andrews—evidence from that session shows Egerton determined to promote Bacon's program for streamlining legal procedures—over the centuries having become a maze of complications, contradictions, legal fictions and work arounds. Much later, under King James, Coke, now Chief Justice of the Queen's Bench, lost out to Egerton, now Chancellor Ellesmere, and Bacon, now Attorney General, when the latter two persuaded King James to give priority to Equity—which it has retained ever since.

The Duke of Venice

Andrews suggests that it was for the 1597 session of Parliament that Shakespeare produced *The Merchant of Venice*[35]—largely to take advantage of the confluence of lawyers and national leaders that took place only every three or four years under Queen Elizabeth.

Thus in Act IV—during the trial that will determine Antonio's fate—although Portia begins by following the rules of Common Law, which would have justified Shylock's right to a pound of Antonio's flesh—she then, in the famous switcheroo, invokes Equity. Because Common Law would cause Antonio harm—death to be precise—Shylock will lose because it's clear that his purpose all along has been purely to revenge himself on Antonio. What, after all, would anyone do with a pound of human flesh? That the flesh in question is located next to Antonio's heart is a lovely metaphor for the need for *humane* laws—laws that see the right to life as more important—or, at least just *as* important—as the right to property.

Andrews holds that by the seventeenth century Shakespeare's play had become an instrument in the argument for Equity—revealed in language used by the Attorney General and the Lord Chancellor, as in the statement attributed to Ellesmere—

He would advise the judges to maintain the power and

---

[35] The Riverside Shakespeare supports this date, though for other reasons.

prerogative of the King, and in cases in which there is no authority and precedent, to leave it to the King to order it according to his wisdom and the good of his subjects, for otherwise the King would be no more than *the Duke of Venice*.

—this reference can only have been to the play—in which the Doge is referred to as "the Duke of Venice" several times in the speeches of both Ellesmere and Bacon, references that could only have come from the play—and because its stand on Equity—as spoken by Portia (in disguise) in her "quality of mercy" speech in Act IV—was seen by the lawyers in Parliament as something of a legal brief in favor of Equity. In the greater portion of his book, Andrews lists upwards of 90 terms used by Shakespeare in the trial scene in *Merchant*— showing with quotes culled from respected sources like Holdsworth and Selden, where he found the same terminology—evidence that the author's knowledge of the issues and legal terms was totally accurate as the Law was understood at that time.

Where did Shakespeare get such precise knowledge of English Law? Not from any known source. Bullough provides the consensus on his sources for other parts of the play—Fiorentino's *Il Pecorone*, Masuccio's *Il Novelino*, Gower's *Confessio Amantis*, the *Gesta Romanorum*, Silvayn's *The Orator*, and Munday's *Zelauto*. Of these —"none of the recognized sources of the bond plot in the *Merchant of Venice* contains the strict adherence to legal forms and procedure, . . . none has the reference to contemporary legal problems and existing statutes, and . . . none makes use of the equitable devices found in the trial scene" (1.xiii).

To this day the legal community remains more engaged with the Shakespeare authorship question than any but authorship scholars and their academic opponents. In 1987 a moot court was held in Washington D.C. during which arguments against William as author were presented to three justices of the US Supreme Court. Reflecting the general attitude of their time—they agreed that there was no reason to change the story they'd grown up with. Since then however —two of the three, plus at least two later Supreme Court justices— have publicly accepted the questioners' view. In June 2004, the University of Tennessee College of Law, having hosted a symposium on "Who Wrote Shakespeare," with equal time given to traditional and authorship scholars—published the resulting standoff in a 454 page issue of the *Tennessee Law Review*.

In 1994, lawyer Daniel Kornstein ends his book *Kill All the Lawyers* with this comment on Shakespeare and the Law—

> In some ways he had a prophetic vision of the Law more real than Blackstone, more permanent than Coke, more incisive than Marshall, more comprehensive than Holmes. At long last we can acknowledge Shakespeare as one of our greatest lawgivers. (245)

Four and a half centuries later, the question remains—how, when, and where did Shakespeare acquire this incredible legal education?

—✥— Medicine and Pharmacology —✥—

Shakespeare's expert use of medical terms is another area where experts have recognized the extent of his knowledge. A considerable library has accumulated on the subject—from 1860 with Dr. J.C. Bucknill's *The Medical Knowledge of Shakespeare,* to 2011 with Sujata Iyengar's dictionary, *Shakespeare's Medical Language*.

Since issues of disease and health loomed large for everyone in the sixteenth century, references to standard treatments—bloodletting, leeches, purges, urinalysis—are common in letters and tracts. But Shakespeare goes beyond what a layman would have known. With his use of terms like *cicatrix, impostume, cataplasm, hysteria, hectic, prescription,* and *infusion*—there's also evidence that long before 1628—when William Harvey published his historic thesis on the circulation of the blood—Shakespeare was already aware that blood is circulated by and through the heart. His knowledge of the coagulation of blood—how it separates into two streams, bright and dark, and into clots and serum—is revealed in *The Rape of Lucrece* (Bucknill 283, Davis 51-53). The plot of *All's Well* turns on the need to heal the King's fistula.[36]

While childbirth and the process of dying were familiar to all

---

[36] Usually located within the body, a fistula can also appear externally as a wound that refuses to heal.

back when people were born and died in their own homes—Shakespeare's knowledge goes well beyond mere observance. In *Love's Labour's Lost,* the pedant Holofernes refers to the function of the *pia mater* in his brain—something that, according to history, would not be discovered until the nineteenth century (Davis 50-1). Similar references occur in *Troilus and Cressida* and *Twelfth Night.* Doctors feature in several of the plays—in *Merry Wives* he makes fun of Dr. Caius (pron. *Keys*) in much the same way that he makes fun of Falstaff—both satires on persons known to his Court audience.

As with the Law—Shakespeare demonstrates his knowledge of Medicine as much through imagery and metaphor as through direct reference. Hamlet's muttered remark—"Something is rotten in the State of Denmark"—initiates the themes of corruption and disease that run throughout the play. In *Troilus and Cressida, Richard III, Coriolanus, Lear* and *Timon*—the Court is befouled both physically and spiritually. Shakespeare uses terms like *infect* and *infection*—not only for disease—but also for strong emotions like love, fear, joy, delight and melancholy—what the Schmidt *Shakespeare Lexicon* describes as—"to affect in any manner, but always contrary to wishes" (1.584).

Evil as a disease

Shakespeare sees evil as a sort of moral epidemic that affects an entire community, making it almost impossible for any one member, however innocent, to remain unsullied. As Hamlet rants at poor Ophelia—"Be thou as chaste as ice, as pure as snow, thou shalt not 'scape calumny!" Shakespeare sees literature as a means of healing, as Jaques—who seems to be a writer—states in *As You Like It*—that if "invested in motley"—that is, if allowed to create stories that move hearts—he will "purge the foul body of the infected world."[37]

In the only obvious reference to Shakespeare in a contemporary work that invokes a like image—the *Return to Parnassus*—"Kempe states that [Jonson] brought up Horace giving the poets a pill, but our

---

[37] "Motley" refers to the colors worn by the Court Jester, whose job at a medieval Court was to help the King relax by making him laugh.

fellow Shakespeare hath given him a purge that made him bewray his credit."[38] However obscure the source—one thing is clear in this riposte—satire is seen as a healthy purgative.

Love and malaria

Shakespeare's characters often suffer from *agues*, or *the Ague* (pron. ay-gyew). Modern historians interpret this as another term for *fever*—but this is much too vague since it's clear that *the Ague* involved chills as well as fever, and with aching bones—as its name, similar to the word *ache*, suggests. In fact, *Ague* was the English word for *malaria*—rife at the time in the wetlands surrounding areas of the Thames and its tributaries where the villainous anopheles mosquito bred in profusion in steamy summer weather (Reiter 2006).[39]

Rather oddly, Shakespeare was fond of using the symptoms of malaria to describe how it feels to fall in love with someone one he (or she) *should not love*—someone already married or pledged to a friend or relative—or someone "out of their sphere"—someone too high or low in their social spectrum. First they *freeze* with fear, then they *fry* with desire, then freeze and fry again—in a cycle analogous to the repeated attacks of chills and fever experienced by one who suffers from malaria.

Some commentators conclude that Shakespeare's references to "the Pox" (syphilis) suggest personal experience—but there's a big difference between his references to malaria and those to syphilis. While connecting malaria's chills and fevers with the passions of love suggests personal experience—the Pox, most obvious in *Timon of Athens*[40]—shows only the disgust and horror of someone who *fears* it—a reaction common to all sexually active individuals over the

---

[38] From the anonymous *Return to Parnassus #2*—performed somewhere at or near Cambridge University over the winter holiday of 1601-02.

[39] In the 16th century it was believed that malaria was caused by *bad air* ("mal aria"). Like the humming of mosquitoes—the odor of a fetid swamp was a sign that the Ague was present—but that it was caused by a mosquito would not be known for another 200 years (Reiter).

[40] Syphilis is also described, or hinted at, in *Troilus and Cressida, Measure for Measure,* and *A Midsummer Night's Dream* (Showerman *Medical* 4-5).

Educating Shakespeare

centuries before Fleming discovered penicillin in 1928. While the chills and fever of malaria came and went—once syphilis came it never went—its bacterium digging deep within the victim's organs to resurface again and again, in a devastating cycle of destruction.[41]

Arguments have arisen, of course, over where Shakespeare acquired his amazing knowledge of methods, drugs and cures, all closely held secrets of a profession that required its practitioners to be officially licensed. Licensed physicians had the legal power to have anyone who attempted to practice medicine without a license arrested, prosecuted and imprisoned. But what Shakespeare does provide are clues that much of what he knew came from what at that time was still a revolutionary new branch of medicine.

Shakespeare and Pharmacology

Shakespeare's amazing knowledge of horticulture reveals how much he knew about what today we term *pharmacology*—the medical use of plant based drugs—as in *A Midsummer Night's Dreame*" when Puck uses juice from "the little western flower" to confuse the lovers —or *Othello,* who's accused by Desdemona's father of using drugs to seduce her. Plots of *Romeo and Juliet, Pericles* and *Much Ado* turn on the use of a drug that simulates death. As noted in an online article by Adam Tait—"Aconite and mandrake: crypto-pharmalogical botanicals in Shakespeare"—

> Shakespeare's work is rife with botanical references of both mythical, foreign, and regional origin, ranging from the anemone that sprouts from Adonis's blood in *Venus and Adonis*—to the crown imperial that Perdita in *The Winter's Tale* includes in her list of native and foreign flowers and which was first introduced to Europe in 1580 from the Middle East—to the humble rock samphire that sprawls on the cliffs of the English coast that Edgar calls upon in *King*

---

[41] Compare Shakespeare's vitality and bonhomie to Baudelaire, who died of syphilis and who called his poems *Fleurs du Mal*—"Flowers of Evil." Consider Ibsen who—though he was not infected himself—portrayed the suffering it caused in *Ghosts* and *A Doll's House.*

Chapter II What Shakespeare Knew

> *Lear*. It is his inclusion of crypto-pharmacological botanicals, however, that is especially intriguing. . . . substances that oscillate between medicine and myth, those forbidden botanicals like wolfsbane that skirt the dangerous edge between Thessalian witchcraft and aconite poisoning.

When most doctors were still relying on the authority of first century Galen and his philosophy of the four humours—Shakespeare's use of distilling as a metaphor suggests that much of his medical knowledge came from *Paracelsus*—the Swiss physician known as the "father of pharmacology"—whose plant based methods were opposed to the purges and bloodletting prescribed by Galen.

Knowledge of distilling had come to Paracelsus (Theophrastus Von Hohenheim) during travels through the Middle East that brought him into contact with Arabic medicine. The Arabs were pioneers in the art of distilling—a spinoff of their mastery of glass making. With glass vessels (alembics) capable of withstanding high temperatures, they could bring a liquid to just under a boil—siphoning off the mist as it arose, capturing it in a clean vessel to cool into a potent essence. This not only allowed them to make medicines from plant teas—but also turn flower juices into perfumes and wines into brandy.

Probably because Paracelsus's work wasn't available in his own lifetime in any language but German—it wasn't until well after his death (1541), that pharmacological medicine found its way to England. The first known distillery in London didn't go into business until the mid-1570s. Not only were the specially designed and manufactured glass retorts, furnaces and other tools expensive and hard to come by, the process—which created foul smells and the occasional explosion—required a special lab, which had to be located at some distance from where people ate and slept—plus assistants trained in its operation—something that few could afford. These constituted the first evidence of what in time would become the pharmaceutical industry—today's Big Pharma.

This aspect of Shakespeare's medical knowledge has been missed by commentators largely because so many of its terms are ordinary words like *still* or *dew*. One term that stands out is *limbec* or *limbek,* English for *alembic*—the Arabic term for the glass vessels required—specialized, expensive, and not something for which the ordinary householder would have an ordinary use.

Distilling as a metaphor isn't as prevalent in Shakespeare as some scientific terms—but where it appears it's significant, as in Hamlet's soliloquy in Act I Scene 2—"O that this too too sullied (or solid) flesh would melt, thaw, and *resolve itself into a dew*"—or in Sonnet 19—"What potions have I drunk from siren's tears, *distill'd from limbeks* foul as hell within"—or from the final scene in Act I of *Macbeth* where Lady Macbeth explains how to kill Duncan and blame it on his drunken servants—whose "memory, the warder of the brain, shall be a *fume* [a mist], and the receipt of reason a *limbec* only."

Then there's Ariel in *The Tempest*—"Safely in harbor is the King's ship, in the deep nook where once thou called'st me up at midnight to fetch *dew* from the *still*-vexed Bermoothes." Words like *dew* and *still* are clues that what Ariel fetched was moonshine created in a *still* in *The Bermoothes*—slang for a particular London slum.[42]

Or from *Venus and Adonis*—

Say, that the sense of feeling were bereft me,
And that I could not see, nor hear, nor touch,
And nothing but the very smell were left me,
Yet would my love to thee be still as much,
For from the *stillatory* of thy face excelling,
Comes breath perfumed that breedeth love by smelling.

Stillatory meant *distillery*. The first commercial laboratory in London was known as *The Stillatory*.

Shakespeare's Friar Laurence reveals his deep knowledge of Paracelsian medicine with the concoction he gives Juliet that will put her into a deathlike trance, thus saving her from marriage to the Count Paris. Paracelsus wrote—"Nothing is without poison—only the dose decides if it's poisonous." [43]

And as always, we have *the Sonnets*—with their constant theme of preserving the Fair Youth's beauty—

---

[42] Altrocchi "Bermoothes."

[43] Paracelsus was the first (westerner) to create a form of morphine (laudanum) by mixing poppy juice with wine.

Chapter II What Shakespeare Knew

From *Sonnet 5*

Then, were not summer's *distillation* left,
A liquid prisoner pent in walls of glass,
Beauty's effect with beauty were bereft,
Nor it nor no remembrance what it was,
But *flowers distill'd* though they with winter meet,
Lose but their show, their substance still lives sweet.

From *Sonnet 6*

Then let not winter's ragged hand deface
In thee thy summer, *ere thou be distill'd—*
Make sweet some vial, treasure thou some place
With beauty's treasure ere it be self kill'd.

In Shakespeare, distilling mostly appears as a metaphor—for making permanent a passing joy by capturing its essence in a poem—for acquiring understanding through experience—the process by which the turbulent events of life are distilled into wisdom; or—as in *The Sonnets*—for preserving the Fair Youth's beauty by distilling his essence in the alembic of a woman's womb.

Shakespeare's awareness of this process suggests that he was present often enough in such a laboratory that these images stayed with him as grist for his metaphorical mill. It also requires that he was either a believer in Paracelsian medicine himself, or was closely associated with those who were—because such metaphors suggest personal experience—not reading or conversation. Nor was such knowledge being taught then at the universities where 2nd-century Galen remained the ultimate authority on Medicine.

It also shows the connection between *distilling* and *alchemy*, the branch of the ancient Wisdom Tradition that in Shakespeare's time was itself on its way to becoming *chemistry*. With images like these he shows his understanding of the philosophy that lies at the heart of *alchemy*—whose processes may have had little or nothing to do with turning lead into gold, an impossibility—but were actually a coded manual for achieving spiritual awakening.

The vicious attacks launched at Paracelsus and his methods by continental physicians may have originated as professional jealousy

—but it may be that his plant based medicines threatened him and his followers with the kind of witch hunts that that at that time had other nations hanging and burning those who grew and dispensed plant medicines.

Shakespeare and gardening

Plant based medicine demands a knowledge of plants and how best to grow them, use them, and preserve them—a practice enshrined in the science of *horticulture*. As Caroline Spurgeon shows in her detailed study of *Shakespeare's Imagery* (one of the most important books ever written for those who would study the great poet in depth). Out of the dozens of categories into which she divides his images, Spurgeon finds that "one occupation, one point of view, above all others, is naturally his—that of *a gardener.*"

> This tendency to think of matters human as of growing plants and trees expresses itself in fullest detail in the central gardening scene in *Richard II*, but it is ever present in Shakespeare's thought and imagination, so that nearly all his characters share in it. . . . In moments of stress and emotion this tendency of Shakespeare's mind is very marked, and he betrays how constantly he visualizes human beings as the trees and plants he loved so well in orchard or garden. (86)

She discusses at length how Shakespeare uses imagery to provide a particular tone or color to a play—which she notes is "analogous to the action of a recurrent theme or motif in a musical fugue or sonata" —themes like *moon* and *night* in *A Midsummer Night's Dreame*, *music* in *Merchant of Venice*, *birds* in *Cymbeline*, *disease* in *Timon*, *sounds* in *The Tempest* (309), and that in the history plays—

> The most constant running metaphor and picture in Shakespeare's mind . . . is that of growth as seen in a garden and orchard, with the deterioration, decay and destruction brought about by ignorance and carelessness on the part of the gardener as shown by untended weeds, pests, lack of pruning and manuring, or on the other hand by the rash and untimely lopping or cutting of fine trees. (216)

Chapter II What Shakespeare Knew

Clearly Shakespeare's knowledge went well beyond what ordinary householders had to know to provide medicinal teas for the sickroom and salads for the dinner table. Most notable is his love of roses. Roses bloom whenever his thoughts turn to love, beauty or anything that delights him. The word *rose* appears in reference to the flower or its smell or color over 150 times in his plays and poems (Schmidt). Most notable is the rose imagery used to define the York-Lancaster feud, imagery that permeates the entire Lancastrian cycle.

As horticulturist Jules Janick puts it—"Shakespeare's allusions to gardens, gardening, botany, and plant lore are so abundant that it seems obvious that he was an expert gardener. His works contain allusions to almost 200 different plants and include descriptions of horticultural practices from grafting to breeding."

Plant lore, knowledge of their medical uses, was an essential element in the ancient Wisdom Tradition closely allied to astrology —where phases of the moon and its relation to the seasons dictate when to plant and harvest herbs for their greatest potency—a system adopted from the Arab physicians of the Middle East and southern Spain that was closely connected to their uses for distilling.

Sonnet 15

When I consider everything that grows
Holds in perfection but a little moment,
That this huge stage presenteth nought but shows
Whereon *the stars in secret influence* comment;
When I perceive that *men as plants* increase,
Cheered and cheque'd even by the self-same sky,
Vaunt in their *youthful sap*, at height decrease,
And wear their brave state out of memory,
Then the conceit of this inconstant stay
Sets you most rich in youth before my sight,
Where wasteful Time debateth with *Decay*,
To change your day of youth to sullied night;
And all in war with Time for love of you,
As he takes from you, I *engraft* you new.

So how did Shakespeare come by his knowledge of medicine, pharmacology, chemistry, astrology, and horticulture—much of it secret, most of it still buried in Latin, Greek, Italian, French, Arabic and German texts—knowledge that was so basic to his thinking that relevant metaphors seem to spring to his mind at every turn.

⸻ Shakespeare and Science ⸻

Science as a blanket term did not exist in Shakespeare's day—he used the word in the sense that it was used then—as a synonym for *knowledge*. Inherited from the Arabs and the ancient Greeks—the major sciences were based in beliefs that academics today regard as mysticism, superstition, or the occult. Chemistry now was *alchemy* then—a seemingly fruitless effort to turn lead into gold. Today's astronomy was known as *astrology* then—today's medicine as *physic*. What we call Physics, Anthropology, Botany, Biology, and Zoology, were lumped together as *natural philosophy*. Opposed to this ancient and medieval philosophical or theoretical approach to science, today's approach—based on hypothesis, experiment, and repeated testing—was still in its infancy.[44]

Around 60 BC—which is as far back as we can go in search of a western source—the Greek philosopher Pythagoras, based in southern Italy, was teaching the basic principles of mathematics, geometry, physics, astronomy, medicine, harmonics (music), and ethics—learned from wise men farther to the east—Egypt perhaps, or Damascus. Central to the Pythagorean system were beliefs in reincarnation and world origin—today labelled the *Orphic* or *Hermetic* tradition. Taken together with works from later thinkers, it represents what we call *the Wisdom Tradition*, embracing what Shakespeare's contemporaries generally meant by *Philosophy*.[45] Handed down over the centuries—possibly from prehistoric times—to the ancient Greeks through contacts with Egypt, Phoenicia, Chaldea, Mesopotamia, Palestine, India, etcetera—the teachings of Pythagoras survived through Plato, his students, his students'

---

[44] It would be promulgated in theory when Francis Bacon published his *Novum Organum* in 1620.

[45] From the Greek *philos* (love of) *sophia* (wisdom).

Chapter II What Shakespeare Knew

students, and on down to Shakespeare [46] and a few of his close contemporaries.

As the Greek culture and language spread throughout the Mediterranean and beyond following the 4th century BC Greek Empire created by Alexander of Macedon—himself a student of Aristotle, Plato's acolyte—this multi level conglomeration of science, philosophy and religion migrated from the intellectual élites of Greece to Rome, then—following Rome's collapse—through Byzantium to the Arabs of the Near and Middle East, for whom it fueled the scientific and technological advances of their Golden Age.

In the House of Wisdom—the library of the great university that evolved in Baghdad during the years before the rise of puritan Islam—texts by Plato, Aristotle, Hippocrates, Euclid, Plotinus and Galen were collected and translated into Arabic. On these and others from India and ancient Persia—Arab poets, humanists, and scientists based their own works and discoveries—which then spread to the West during the Middle Ages by way of the returning Crusaders—and from Arabic-speaking communities in Spain, Sicily and North Africa.

Western scholars were still in the process of translating these texts into Latin in Shakespeare's time. Since most of them were not yet available in English, academics have either refused to see the evidence of Shakespeare's awareness of such works, or—where it can't be ignored—have found ways to explain how it didn't require *knowing the languages* in which they were written. Most perplexing perhaps was his knowledge of *astrology*—central to The Tradition.

Shakespeare and Astrology

Most students of Shakespeare are aware of his references to astrology, but few see how deep it goes. References to being born under a dark or beneficent star or to political events as influenced by the stars are frequent enough in most Renaissance writers that the idea that his goes no deeper is common. But to professional astrologers—who hear in the conversations among his characters—not just the obvious and ordinary—but usage of the sort that only professionals will recognize.

---

[46] Shakespeare mentions Pythagoras three times.

Educating Shakespeare

As one such wrote in 1903—

> To the casual reader,.. quotations, shorn of the context... may appear of little moment; but the deduction is unavoidable that devotion to a science is necessary before it can be handled with such genial freedom and at the same time *never failing relevance and accuracy.*

Most of what's been published regarding Shakespeare's use of astrology is far too simplistic to be of any use. Those who know only the more commonplace externals see only things like the belief—expressed so often by his characters—that the stars guide their lives —or conversely, as with Hamlet and *Lear*'s Edmund—that they don't. Then there are those who clearly don't take astrology seriously—like Sir Toby, whose mocking of Sir Andrew's ignorance of what signs rule the various parts of the body seems little more than comedy relief. Doubtless based on what Shakespeare heard from persons who—ignorant themselves of the ancient science—relied on commonplace notions—but these do not reflect the author's own knowledge of the subject—which he reveals through phrasing.[47]

To those characters most often heard using astrological terms in Shakespeare "the stars" simply meant *luck* or *fortune,* while the planets represent qualities specific to each—like anger for Mars, love for Venus, benevolence for Jupiter, etc. But Shakespeare's own knowledge of astrology—and the ancient systems it once supported —goes well beyond what he put in the mouths of his characters.

When Shakespeare scholars argue over his personal belief system—was he a Catholic? A protestant? An atheist?—it's usually their ignorance of astrology that leaves the argument where they found it. In almost everything he writes Shakespeare reveals that it's the Wisdom Tradition that's central to his personal philosophy—as revealed most obviously in Ulysses's famous peroration on "the great chain of being" in Act III of *Troilus and Cressida*—or in Lorenzo's paean to the heavens in the last act of *Merchant of Venice.*

So comfortable was Shakespeare with the tenets of ancient

---

[47] Shakespeare uses the word *astronomy* for what today we call *astrology* because in his time the words were interchangeable, both derived from Greek.

Chapter II What Shakespeare Knew

Platonism—of which astrology, though central, is only a part—so basic to his thinking—that he gave it no emphasis. Like the knife and saucepan in the hands of a cook—or the harness and bridle in the hands of a horse trainer—it's simply there—unnoticed by everyone but professional astrologers. Where scores of examples could be cited, a few must suffice.

The Wheel of Fortune

Fortune portrayed as a fickle female is certainly not unique to Shakespeare—but he is unique in showing his awareness of its origins in astrology. In the old horoscopes there was usually a symbol that represents something called the *Part of Fortune,* one of several non-planetary "points" that ancient astrologers arrived at through celestial math. Connection of this point to an important planet in a natal chart was supposed to bring luck for everything related to that planet. Its use shows the emphasis placed upon Fortune by Renaissance astrologers because they earned their living "telling fortunes."[48]

Fortune is Shakespeare's subject in Act I of *The Tempest* when Prospero says—"I find my zenith [midheaven] doth depend upon a most auspicious star, whose influence, if now I court not, but omit, my fortunes will ever after droop." This may well have been a bow to some new patron, some Jove with deep pockets and/or influence at Court—but the one does not exclude the other. Shakespeare loves to conflate ideas with persons. Brutus provides another take on Fortune in Act IV of *Julius Caesar*—

> There is a tide in the affairs of men, which, taken at the flood, leads on to fortune; omitted, all the voyage of their life is bound in shallows and in miseries. On such a full sea are we now afloat, and we must take the current when it serves, or lose our ventures.

Sadly Brutus was wrong—evidently the tide of fortune was against him. Perhaps he was getting bad advice, or was himself an inept

---

[48] While historians consistently portray them as mathematicians and astronomers, most Renaissance stargazers like Copernicus, Kepler, and Galileo, were in fact astrologers whose business was "telling fortunes" to the wealthy and powerful.

astrologer. But what's important here is that he was displaying a belief in one of the basic tenets of astrology—which his author understood, whether or not he believed in it himself—that there is a current of energy that runs through the orbits of the planets—and that through their changing geometric (electromagnetic) relationships to each other—influence worldly events that can benefits those who keep an eye on the stars—as do farmers on the weather. Unfortunately it can also dash the unlucky to destruction—as it did Brutus. How the noble Brutus could so misread his stars may reveal Shakespeare's own belief—that while there is truth in astrology—it can be disastrously misinterpreted.

That Shakespeare didn't lose his interest in astrology as he matured is clear from how often it surfaces in what was probably his final play, *King Lear*, as shown from Lear's first speech which begins—"For, by the sacred radiance of the sun, the mysteries of Hecate and the night, by all the operations *of the orbs*[49] from whom we do exist and cease to be." Later in the same act Gloucester blames his good son's treacherous behavior on the stars—

> These late eclipses in the sun and moon portend no good to
> us—though the wisdom of nature can reason it thus and thus
> —yet nature finds itself scourged by the sequent effects—
> love cools, friendship falls off, brothers divide.

Following a list of these ill effects, his wicked son responds—

> This is the excellent foppery of the world, that, when we
> are sick in fortune, often the surfeit of our own behavior,
> we make guilty of our disasters the sun, the moon, and the
> stars, as if we were villains by necessity, fools by heavenly
> compulsion, knaves, thieves, and treachers [traitors] by
> spherical predominance—drunkards, liars, and adulterers
> by an enforced obedience of planetary influence—and all
> that we are evil in, by a divine thrusting on, an admirable
> evasion of whoremaster man, to lay his goatish
> disposition to the charge of a star!

---

[49] The OED lists the many uses of the word *orb*—some from astrology alone.

Chapter II What Shakespeare Knew

Gloucester may represent an older generation that looked to the stars for answers—while Edmund represents those who, having read Copernicus, were more inclined to be cynical. It should be noted, however, that it's the decent son who trusts in the stars and the evil son who does not.

The Seven Ages

Scholars have pondered the source of Jaques "Seven Ages of Man" speech in *As You Like It*—but few seem aware that, of all the various breakdowns into the various Ages from that time—four, five, seven, twelve—the division into seven comes from astrology—wherein each period is governed by a particular planet, there being at that time seven known planets[50] —each ruling a particular time of life.

According to astrology, life from birth to age four is influenced by the Moon, "the infant, mewling and puking in his nurse's arms." From four to 14 it's ruled by Mercury, "the whining schoolboy creeping like snail to school"—from 14 to 21 by Venus, "the lover, sighing like a furnace." From 21 to 35, the Sun takes over—something he skips—perhaps for political reasons[51] he moves on to Mars, the force that rules from age 35 to 56—"the soldier, jealous in honor, quick in quarrel." From 56 to 63 it's Jupiter—"the justice, with fair round belly, full of wise saws"—and from 63 to 70 and beyond —Saturn, which, as the last of the original seven, rules old age and death. Having skipped the Sun, Shakespeare divides this last into two—"the lean and slippered pantaloon"—and finally, senility— "sans teeth, sans eyes, sans taste, sans everything." This version of the seven ages—however misremembered—could not have come to him from anything but astrology.

The adherence to beliefs like "the great chain of being" and "the harmony of the spheres" that we see reflected in Shakespeare, and in astrology and all its derivatives—did not come to him from either of the two religions then at war in England. The Church—whether Catholic or protestant—did not see the material world as part of an

---

[50] In Shakespeare's time, Uranus, Neptune and Pluto had not yet been discovered.
[51] The easily offended Queen was often referred to as "the Sun."

integrated whole with the world of the spirit. All branches of Christianity saw life as a battlefield where good and evil, God and the Devil, battled for the souls of men. In Shakespeare, most of his characters represent one or the other—although an example of this battle within a soul can be seen when Claudius attempts to pray after Hamlet has caught his conscience in "The Mousetrap"—the play within a play. "My words fly up, my thoughts remain below—words without thoughts, never to Heaven go."

One of the central tenets of The Tradition is the concept of harmony or balance. In Shakespeare these show in his love of music as revealed in metaphors for harmony, happiness, and health. Music is an aspect of the Pythagorean Number Theory that lies at the heart of the Wisdom Tradition—as revealed through its intervals—the harmonious third, fifth, and octave, the empty, reaching fourth, the dissonant, yearning second and seventh—as demonstrated by the mathematics of the vibrations of a plucked string on musical instruments like the lute. Shakespeare shows that he knows these as fundamental to the Pythagorean world view—Ulysses's argument in *Troilus and Cressida*—that hierarchy determines from without and within, providing the balance from low to high—"take but degree away—*untune that string*—and hark what discord follows."

According to astrology—as the planets move through their orbits, their geometric angles relative to each other are continually sliding from harmonious to discordant (sweet to distressing) and back again—bringing about events pleasing or stressful according to the nature of the aspects (angles) thus formed—in the lives of persons, cultures and nations—as can be predicted (by astrologers) based on patterns present at their birth. In Caroline Spurgeon's discussion of Shakespeare she notes the platonic ideal of social harmony as expressed through music—something touched on by Sir Thomas Elyot in his *Boke Named the Governour* (1531)—in which he urges tutors to give the noble child some training in music. Elyot reflects the Pythagorean alliance of music with mathematics, in particular—

> how necessary it is for the better attaining the knowledge of a public weal, which . . . is made of an order of estates and degrees, and, by reason thereof, containeth in it a perfect harmony: which he [the student] shall afterward more

Chapter II What Shakespeare Knew

perfectly understand when he shall happen to read the books of Plato and Aristotle of public weals wherein be written divers examples of music and geometry.

Shakespeare's take on this is revealed in *Sonnet 14*—

> Not from the stars do I my *judgment* pluck,
> And yet methinks I have *astronomy*,
> But not to tell of good or evil luck,
> Of plagues, or dearths or seasons quality.
> Nor can I *fortune* to brief *minutes* tell
> Pointing to each his thunder, rain, and wind (pron. wined)
> Or say with princes if it shall go well,
> By oft *predict* that I in heaven find . . .

As is often the case, Shakespeare's only telling us what he doesn't or can't do—not what he does or believes. Words like *astronomy, fortune, predict(ion)* were used by astrologers, astronomers, and laymen alike, but there are two that he uses as only an astrologer would—*judgment* and *minutes*. What a novice calls a *reading*, an astrologer calls a *judgment*. As for the commonplace term *minutes*, each of the 360 degrees—points on the circle of the zodiac—is divided into sixty *minutes*. These are professional terms, used as a professional would use them. Other words that have particular meanings in astrology—words like *aspect, conjunction, meridian,, constellation, eclipse, mean, mundane, retrograde, zenith* and *orb*—are found in abundance—mostly used in the mundane way—but also with meanings peculiar to astrology.

There were no schools for astrologers in 16th-century England—no courses, no publicized lectures (such subjects were considered irreligious). What books there were would all have been in Greek or Latin. A poet could not have learned so much about astrology from anyone but a professional—or his books.

Shakespeare and Astronomy

The title of Copernicus's ground breaking book, *de Revolutionibus,* is itself a pun of cosmic dimensions. Although the title refers to the revolution of the planets—the book would cause one of the most

Educating Shakespeare

profound revolutions in the history of the West. The idea that it's the earth that circles the sun was a tremendous shock to the the 16th-century Europeans—whose vision of the universe—inherited from 2nd-century Greek Ptolemy—saw all the planets, including the sun, as circling the earth. As John Donne would put it—in the

> new philosophy that calls all in doubt,
> The element of fire is quite put out—
> The sun is lost, and th'earth, and no man's wit,
> Can well direct him where to look for it.[52]

Although the protestants had no more love for Copernicus than had the Catholics—they had even less love for the idea that Rome was the center of the universe. So while ideologues condemned the great Polish scientist as a heretic—the handful of thinkers who were aware of what Roger Bacon, Alhazen, or Hipparchus had theorized centuries earlier, were pleased that it had finally been touched on in print.

Thomas Digges and the Telescope

To most 16th-century English, the behavior of the planets was subordinate to more local issues—so little public attention was drawn to a theory so dangerously close to heresy and treason. According to Peter Usher, Professor Emeritus of Astronomy and Astrophysics at Penn State University[53]—the only persons paying serious attention to Copernicus then were Leonard Digges and his friend John Dee.

It was Digges's son Thomas—first taught by his father—then, following Leonard Sr.'s death—raised and taught by his father's dearest friend John Dee—who in 1576 opened the door to what would be the second and in many ways the greater awakening to our present reality. In a tract titled *A Perfit Description of the Celestial Orbs*, the youthful Digges urged that the fixed stars were *not* packed into a sort

---

[52] From "An Anatomy of the World" (1611).

[53] Usher received undergraduate degrees in mathematics and applied mathematics in South Africa and his graduate degree in Astronomy from Harvard, before becoming Professor of Astronomy at Penn State where he taught celestial mechanics, stellar structure, galaxies, quasars and cosmology and did research in perturbation theory, faint blue stars, and quasars.

Chapter II What Shakespeare Knew

of onion layer—as the ancient Ptolemaic model had it—but were in fact located at widely varying distances from each other in what he was the first to describe as *an infinite universe* ("Advances" 25).

History attributes the discovery of the telescope to Galileo sometime early in the 17th century, but as Usher explains—Digges had already come to this conclusion back in the 1570s by means of a telescope good enough to distinguish between nearby and distant stars. Only through a particular combination of lenses would he have been able to see that there's more to the Milky Way than the fuzzy horde that appears to the naked eye. As Usher explains, Thomas's father, Leonard Digges Sr.—

> was a keen experimentalist who is regarded as the inventor of the *perspective trunk*, a unique design comprising a planoconvex lens with a spherical mirror for an eyepiece. These devices were in use at least by 1570, as reported by John Dee in that year and by Leonard and Thomas Digges in 1571 in *Pantometria*. In the preface Thomas Digges refers to his father's "continual" use of *proportional glasses*.

In 1573 Digges published a treatise on the "New Star" in Cassiopeia —known today as the Supernova of 1572—which he dedicated to Lord Burghley. Usher reports that Burghley then "consigned to William Bourne the task of writing a treatise on a device known as a 'perspective glass' or a 'perspective trunk.'" In 1578 Bourne reported that the device enabled "a letter to be read at a quarter mile."

In 1576 Digges published *A Prognostication Everlasting*—into which he "tucked details" on the Copernican theory and his own theory of "the infinite universe." Ironically—according to Usher—he was so successful in disguising his advocacy of this alarming "New Astronomy"—as it came to be known—that not only did it go unnoticed by censors and potential Inquisitors at the time—but "the full impact of his shattering of the sphere of the stars has not been fully appreciated even to this day" (133). It was not until the second decade of the seventeenth century—when Galileo was able to support the Copernican theory with evidence obtained from bigger and more sophisticated telescopes—that the Catholic Inquisition realized the existential threat they posed to Rome—which, per their ancient belief, was not just the moral but the physical center of the Universe.

Digges's caution is understandable when considering the fate of scientists like Giordano Bruno, burnt at the stake in 1600 for openly promoting Copernicus—or Galileo, condemned in 1633 to a lifetime under house arrest. In England in the late 1580s, Thomas Digges's "second father"—as he called John Dee—came back from abroad to find that his laboratory had been ransacked by neighbors convinced that he was a Dr. Frankenstein. And there were also scientists like Thomas Harriot—whose discoveries lay unpublished due to his fear of dying at the end of a rope or tied to a burning stake.

Scholars have puzzled over the apparent fact that—despite Copernicus—Shakespeare still held with the old geocentric view. But as Usher has explained, he *did know* about the Copernican Sun. While he did not reveal it openly—he used his tricks of allusion to refer to it in bits of wordplay scattered throughout *Hamlet*—"caviar" for the "generals" among his readers on the lookout for such allusions—evidence that he was well aware of the way the world was now seen to be turning.

Did the Bard then choose this oblique tactic for the same reason that Copernicus presented his discoveries as no more than theory—or that Digges buried his equally ground breaking discoveries in a thicket of abstruse verbiage? Was it, perhaps, because—during this period when the Inquisition was at the height of its power—he preferred freedom to prison and life to death?

The clues begin very early. Tycho Brahe's *De nova stella*—published in Copenhagen in 1573—describes the supernova that had astonished the world the year before by its sudden appearance in the constellation Cassiopeia. By making careful measurements with a sextant, Tycho discovered that the new star *did not shift its position* with respect to the other stars—proof that Aristotle's fixed stars were not, as the Church claimed, little holes in the black sphere that hid the glories of Heaven from earth bound sinners. Though few copies were printed—Tycho's evidence was so convincing that his treatise marks the beginning of the end of the medieval concept of the heavens as a realm of light that lay beyond the sphere of worldly night.

Chapter II What Shakespeare Knew

Hamlet's "nutshell"

Lacking space to follow Usher's argument in detail—a few high points must do. As the play opens, after the watchmen, Bernardo and Marcellus, greet each other, Bernardo says to Horatio—"Last night of all, when *yond same star* that's westward from the pole . . . ."— that "yond same star" has been identified as the supernova of 1572, and *Bernardo* and *Marcellus* real astronomers.[54]

In Scene 2, per his mother's request, Hamlet gives up his plan to return to Wittenberg, remaining in Elsinore—as the English pronounced *Helsingor*, the castle the King of Denmark was just then renovating near the island observatory he had built for Tycho Brahe —where Tycho had begun making the observations that convinced him of the nature of the heavens.[55] Following his removal to Prague in 1599—he had passed these on to his assistant, Johannes Kepler, who would use them to reveal another astronomical milestone—the *Laws of Planetary Motion*.

The reader is then introduced to King *Claudius*, who, Usher suggests—when the play is plumbed for its references to Copernican theory—represents the old view, namely *geocentrism*—a term for the Universe the west had inherited from the ancient *Claudius* Ptolemy.[56] The King hints at the major problem with the Ptolemaic theory when he says that Hamlet's projected return to Wittenberg "is most *retrograde* to our desire." The word *retrograde*—unlike a more common term such as *opposed*—identifies the major problem with Ptolemy's model—the phenomenon known as *retrogradation*, that is, those periods—so confusing to the ancient astronomers—when all the the planets but the Sun and Moon appeared to stop and spend some time moving backwards in their orbits.

The elaborate mathematical schemes invented by astronomers over the centuries to account for this anomaly vanished when

---

[54] *Bernardo* suggests German astronomer Bernard Walther whose work led to discoveries by Copernicus, Kepler and Brahe.

[55] The last observatory to be built without telescopes—Tycho's observations were made with the naked eye.

[56] Particular names in Shakespeare almost always have an extra meaning that with a little extra effort can provide rich associations.

Copernicus moved the Sun, so that retrogradation was shown to be no more than an appearance due to the earth's motion relative to the other planets. Retrogradation appears when—from the earth's point of view—a planet appears to be *in opposition* to the Sun. Usher notes that the words *in opposition* precede the word *retrograde* by 14 lines. It would be hard to argue that Shakespeare's use of these terms was purely coincidental.

As the first to alert Horatio to the dangerous secret that Old Hamlet's death was murder—*Marcellus* may also be the first to alert the reader to the dangerous secret of the Sun's true position—to which Shakespeare, like Digges, may have been alerted by references in the *Zodiacus Vitae* by the astronomer poet *Palengenius*, whose first name was *Marcellus*.

While joking with Horatio about Yorick's skull—Shakespeare has Hamlet say, "Here's a fine *revolution* and we had the *trick* to see it." Apparently referring to Yorick's mutation to skull from laughing jester, it would seem that his substitution of the word *revolution* for something more common like *change* was also a revolution in usage. The OED sees this use of the word *revolution* as its second example under III.6 as "alteration, change, mutation"—a use it labels *rare*, dating it to 1600. First use of the next item, III.7—"A complete overthrow of the established government by those who were previously subject to it"—is also dated to 1600—both from shortly before the first quarto of *Hamlet* was published in 1603. Did Shakespeare *intend* to combine the two meanings? It would seem so —for "had we the *trick* to see it" suggests the use of a *device*—a word for which *trick* was a synonym—which does not fit the apparent meaning nearly so well as it does the revolution in science caused by the *device* the Diggeses termed a *perspective glass*.

Later—when Rosencrantz states that Denmark is "too narrow" for Hamlet—seemingly referring to the limitations of life at Elsinore, Hamlet responds—"O God, I could be *bounded in a nutshell* and count myself the king of *infinite space*." While this may suggest to readers—sitting in the "nutshell" of their study—that such books can open the mind to an undreamed of immensity—it could also refer to Digges's theory of "infinite space", as opposed to the little "nutshell" of the ancient view. While Claudius calls Hamlet's madness his

Chapter II What Shakespeare Knew

"transformation"—according to the OED it was Digges who first used the verb *transform* in a scientific sense in *Pantometria*—where he claims Copernican theory will *transform* astronomy.

Only a handful of men in England at that time could have taught Shakespeare—not only the tenets of astrology and astronomy—but the complicated mathematics required to understand the advances he hints at in *Hamlet*—the play most associated with Wittenberg and Science. Seeking the true author, we must seek as well such a teacher.

~~ Shakespeare and Literature ~~

Of course it's *Drama*—not just Literature *per se*—for which Shakespeare is best known—playscripts are not the same as novels or sermons—but however a work may enter the Elysium of the world's great classics—whether as playscript, poem, prayer, novel, sermon, speech, manifesto, biblical passage, eulogy or treatise—if it continues to linger in minds and hearts—eventually it will become *Literature.*

In tracking how much Shakespeare knew about the literature of his time—beyond authors and titles we have several areas to consider—among them his grammar, his style, and his most certain or likely sources. For the latter we have the eight volumes edited by Geoffrey Bullough (1964-1975) that provide lengthy quotes from what was believed by then to have been his major sources—meaning those that fit within the limits of the Stratford biography. Although Bullough claims that he purposely ignored the books and manuscripts that the Stratford Shakespeare could not possibly have read—he does, in fact, include some from outside these limits that are simply too compelling to ignore. These he fudges as "probable" or "possible."

It may strike us as bizarre that in that period of enthusiastic translating—of Greek-Latin polyglots and of references to Mount Parnassus" and the "Heliconian imps"—that Shakespeare should be limited to what had by then been translated into Latin—or that, due to a few words from Ben Jonson, John Dryden, et all—that his genius could not carry him so far as to learn how to read them in the languages in which they were originally written. Yet even without acknowledging that his debt to the ancient Greeks came directly from Greek—the fact that Bullough was not only able—but was forced for obvious reasons of space, cost and time, to limit his excerpts to *eight volumes*—should suggest the immensity of Shakespeare's knowledge of what was considered Literature back then.

Sources in English

From the 14th and 15th centuries came plot elements from Chaucer in Middle English. For *The Rape of Lucrece—A Midsummer Night's Dreame, As You Like It, Antony and Cleopatra, Two Noble Kinsmen* and *Troilus and Cressida*. From Gower, Chaucer's contemporary, came the *Confessio Amantis* which contributed references found in *Lucrece, Comedy of Errors* and *Pericles*. Bits of Lydgate's *Siege of Troy*—written in rhyming couplets—appear in *Troilus and Cressida*.

From the early sixteenth century came Sir Thomas Elyot's *Boke of the Governour* (1538), which provided him with elements for *Two Gentlemen of Verona*. Oberon, from *Dreame*, came from *Huon of Burdeaux*, translated by Lord Berners. He was provided with almost everything for *Romeo and Juliet* by Arthur Brooke's 1562 poem *The Tragical History of Romeus and Juliet*. From Arthur Golding's 1565-67 translation of *The Metamorphoses* came the plots and/or subplots for *A Midsummer Night's Dreame, Venus and Adonis, Merry Wives, Titus Andronicus, Othello, Winter's Tale,* and *The Tempest*. Ariosto's *I Suppositi* provided the subplot for *Taming of the Shrew*.

From English translations of Italian tales came *Painter's Palace of Pleasure,* published in 1566-67, which provided plot elements for *Lucrece, All's Well,* and *Timon of Athens*. From Thomas North's 1578 translation of Jacques Amyot's French version of Plutarch's *Lives of the Noble Greeks and Romans* came elements of *Dreame, Julius Caesar, Coriolanus, Timon, Winter's Tale* and *Antony and Cleopatra*. For *Antony and Cleopatra* there was also Surrey's English translation of Books 2 and 4 of Virgil's *Aeneid*. Barnabe Riche's *Farewell to the Militarie Profession* (1581) contributed to *Twelfth Night, Measure for Measure,* and *Merry Wives of Windsor*. Historians Edward Hall, Raphael Holinshed, Robert Fabyan, John Hardyng, Richard Grafton and John Foxe—either directly or through Holinshed's *Chronicles* —provided most of the material for his English history plays.

Chapter II What Shakespeare Knew

Sources in Latin

Few works considered *Literature* at that time were to be found in anything but Latin. Grammar school consisted almost entirely of learning to read and write in Latin in preparation for the University where students were expected not only to be able to read Latin, but also to converse in it with each other during their free time.

Despite the disclaimer by Ben Jonson that Shakespeare had only "small Latin" (a meaningless statement, either he could read it or he couldn't)—he had to have known enough to have read and understood *Amphitruo* and *The Menaechmi* by Plautus—the obvious source for *A Comedy of Errors*—the first not translated into English until 1595, the second not until 1769. From Ovid's *Fasti*—not translated into English until 1640—came the plot for *Lucrece*. From the *Gesta Romanorum*—not translated until 1838—came *The Merchant of Venice*. From either St. Augustine or the Geneva Bible came the title and the Angelo subplot in *Measure for Measure*. Tacitus—not translated into English until 1598—appears in *Henry V*. For *Julius Caesar* he used Titus Livius (Livy)—not translated until 1600—Suetonius, not until 1606—Sallust not until 1615.

For *Antony and Cleopatra,* there is evidence of Horace, of Lucan's *Pharsalia* (1627), of Josephus (1602), Lucius Florus (1619), and Dante. For *Troilus and Cressida* he turned to Homer's *Iliad*.[57] For *Hamlet* there's *Saxo Grammaticus*, Seneca's *Agamemnon*, Tacitus's *Annals*, and Paolo Giovio's *Eulogies* (1548). For *Othello*, Pliny—for *King Lear*, Geoffrey of Monmouth's *Historia Regium Britanniae* (1135)—for *Macbeth* the *Chronica Gestis Scotorum*, Boethius, *Scotorum Historiae*, and Seneca's *Medea* and *Agamemnon*. For *A Winter's Tale* there's the *Idylls* of Theocritus, Longus's *Daphnis and Chloe* (Englished by Angel Day in 1587) and *Amadis de Gaulle* (not until 1693.)[58]

According to John Vyvyan, it was from the ancient Roman playwright Terence that Shakespeare got the five-act formula found

---

[57] Parts of the *Iliad* had been translated into English by Arthur Hall at some point before 1581—but Hall's clumsy version seems an unlikely source.

[58] These are only the most obvious sources—hundreds more could be listed.

in all his plays. Although they were not divided into acts in his own time, Vyvyan shows how—based on scenes in both his comedies and tragedies—all move in a similar five-act arc with the conflict laid out in early scenes, crisis or turning point in mid-play, gains made by the Good in following scenes—often through some *deus ex machina* or other surprise element—to the final scene when Good triumphs in the comedies—Evil in the tragedies (*Rose* 12).

Latin Proverbs

One of the means by which the Reformation sought to instill ethics and morality was by having boys memorize Latin *sententiae*. It was thought that by having these tightly knit maxims (adages, aphorisms, parables) glued into his memory—they would remain with him for the rest of his life. Many are still with us. *Graculus graculo assidet*—"Birds of a feather flock together"—*Optime ridet qui ultimus ridet*—"He who laughs last laughs best."

By 1926 when Morris Palmer Tilley published *Elizabethan Proverb Lore*—still its standard text—he had some 13,500. Tilley's major sources are of interest. Most of his book provides—in alphabetical order by keyword—the 757 proverbs found in *The Petite Pallace of Pettie His Pleasure* by George Pettie and/or *Euphues: The Anatomy of Wit* by John Lyly—along with where they had appeared in works by Ovid, Pliny, Erasmus, Gosson, Francis Bacon, Robert Greene and others. Noting for each of the 700-plus proverbs where it was also used in some way by Shakespeare—Tilley devoted a final section of his *Special Index* to noting where in each of the plays a proverb appears. No one Shakespeare play or poem is devoid of a reference to one or more of these proverbs.

Sources in French and Italian

The so-called *romance languages*[59] of southern Europe—languages derived from Latin as spoken in the nations that lie along the northern

---

[59] Nothing "romantic" is meant by this use of the word *Romance*, which means only "derived from Rome."

Chapter II What Shakespeare Knew

shore of the Mediterranean—were not taught at the universities, but for those who knew Latin they were relatively easy to learn—or at least to read. That Shakespeare could read both French and Italian is evident from his plays—although the level of fluency and wit displayed, for instance, in the scenes in *Henry V* where the captured Princess and her governess banter in French—suggest he not only could read French—he could converse in it easily and with wit.

French: For *Love's Labour's Lost* he used elements from la Primaudaye's *The French Academie*, translated into English in 1586, and Enguerrand de Monstrelet's *French Chronicles*, not translated until 1810. For *The Merchant of Venice* he used elements from Alexandre Silvayn's *The Orator,* for which there was no English translation until Anthony Munday published his in 1595. For several of his English history plays, he used Monstrelet's *History of Burgundy*—Philippe de Comines's *Memoires* (translated 1596), and Froissart's *Chronicles*, available then only in manuscript. For *Troilus* he used Benoit de St. Maure's verse romance *Roman de Troie*. He used material from Belleforest's *Histoire Tragique* for *Pericles* and *Hamlet*. For *Cymbeline* he used Boccaccio's *Decameron*—which Bullough assumes he must have read in French since there would be no English version until 1620. Two French versions of *Antony and Cleopatra* preceded his—by playwrights Jodelle and Guarnier.

Italian: Most evident are comedies based on tales in Boccaccio, Bandello and Ariosto—some of which—like those published in translation in 1566 in *Painter's Palace* were available in English—but others came from works not yet translated. For instance, elements in *Love's Labour's Lost,* came from Book 8 of Arrigo Caterino Davila's *Storia delle guerre civil di Francia (History of the Civil Wars of France)*—first translated into English in *1647.* For *The Merchant of Venice he used* Masuccio's *Il Novelino*, the 14th Story (not translated until 1895), and Fiorentino's *Il Pecorone*—which he also used for *Merry Wives*. For *Much Ado*, he used Ariosto's *Orlando Furioso*, Book V, translated by John Harington in 1591, and Bandello of Lucca's *Novella XXII*, Italian, translated in 1554. For *Twelfth Night* he used *Gl'Ingannati (The Deceived)*—published in Italian in 1537 and 1554 and in French in 1543—there was as yet no published English version. For *Twelfth Night*, he used Nicolo Secchi's *L'Interesse (The Interest)*— published in Italian in 1581.

In *Measure for Measure* he used Cinthio's *Epitia* from the *Hecatommithi* (Decade 8, Novella 5) published in 1565—a French translation published in 1584— in English not until 1753. For *Antony and Cleopatra* he used Cinthio and Landi (1551). For *Troilus* he used Benoit's version in the Italian prose of Guido delle Colonne's *Historia Troina* (1287). For *Hamlet* he used Castiglione's *Il Cortegiano*, Guicciardini's *Historia Italia*, Paolo Giovio's *Eulogies of Men Famous for Warlike Virtue* (1554)—for *Othello* the *Description of Africa* by Leo Africanus, published in 1550, and Cinthio's *Hecatommithi*—no English version until 1753.

Sources in Greek

So crucial is Greek to our understanding of Shakespeare that the question of exactly what and how much he knew involves almost every aspect of his work. Aware that Greek was the key to so much of his knowledge of literature—if all that Ben Jonson accomplished in his introduction to the First Folio when he wrote that Shakespeare knew only "small Latin and less Greek" was to state what every educated reader in his time would have known had to be true—it apparently served his purpose. As any of these would understand far better than we can today—it would have been impossible then for the son of an illiterate ex-Burgess (Mayor) of a market town three days from London—to have known any more than that. Which is probably why Jonson's "small Latin and less Greek" was interpreted for over two centuries as *no* Latin and *no* Greek.

~~ **Shakespeare and Greek** ~~

In any case, as the curriculum created by Erasmus for Paul's grammar school at the turn of the sixteenth century continued to grow and spread throughout the nation's grammar schools and universities—by the late eighteenth to the early nineteenth centuries a cultural elite had formed—sufficiently conversant with the literatures of both ancient

Chapter II What Shakespeare Knew

Rome and Athens that an ever increasing community of university graduates began to realize the astonishing extent of Shakespeare's erudition. This must have gone on some time before the dam broke in 1857 with Delia Bacon's *Shakespeare Unfolded.*

John Churton Collins

First to broach the issue of Shakespeare's knowledge of the Classics in any lasting way was journalist and lecturer John Churton Collins (1848-1908)—whose book *Studies in Shakespeare,* published in 1904 —led with the chapter—"Shakespeare as a Classical Scholar."

Collins was a classicist with a passionate interest in seeing the study of Greek maintained at the universities. It was his unhappy fate to arrive on the scene just when the Oxbridge enthusiasm for the ancients had begun to flag. Having fallen in love with Greek during his student days at Oxford—when he failed to be hired by either university, he found himself on a career path similar in many ways to that of an earlier Shakespearean, Samuel Taylor Coleridge.

Over an energetic lifetime of lecturing and publishing—immensely prolific and—like Coleridge, gifted with a huge memory and compelling personality—Collins knew and communicated with all the leading scholars and literary lights of his time. His son would claim that he gave upwards of 10,000 lectures over the course of his life—sometimes as many as five in a single day (231).

Collins had stored in memory lengthy selections from Chaucer, Shakespeare, and other works in Greek and Latin, Italian and French, from which—also like Coleridge—he could recite whole passages spontaneously at short notice. Author of many books on a variety of subjects—he edited as many more. According to Prof. Laurie Maguire of Magdalen College Cambridge—it was largely due to his efforts that around the turn of the twentieth century his *alma mater* finally created a degree program in English Literature.

Consumed by the task he had set himself to awaken the world to the importance of classical Greek—the perception that Shakespeare had gotten so much from the Greeks was, for him, less about the Bard than about using his reputation to prod the University into retaining Greek in the curriculum. Said he—

Educating Shakespeare

> There are certain traditions which the world appears to have made up its mind to accept without inquiry, . . . a strange superstition seems to exempt them even from debate. . . . A very striking illustration of this is the tradition that Shakespeare's knowledge of the Greek and Roman classics was confined to English translations, that he had scarcely enough Latin to spell out a passage in Virgil or Cicero, and that in Greek it is doubtful whether he went beyond the alphabet (Maguire 35).

Detesting attempts to solve "the Shakespeare authorship problem" by attributing the canon to Francis Bacon—Collins hoped to explain Shakespeare's references to Greek literature by stretching Jonson's "small Latin" to cover Latin translations of Greek dramas. Said he (according to Maguire)—

> So far from Shakespeare having no pretension to classical scholarship, he could almost certainly read Latin with as much facility as a cultivated Englishman of our own time reads French; that with some at least of the principal Latin classics he was intimately acquainted; that through the Latin language he had access to the Greek classics, and that of the Greek classics *in the Latin versions* he had, in all probability, a remarkably extensive knowledge.[60]

First he had to show that Shakespeare had enough Latin to do even this much—so Collins spends his first thirty pages on Shakespeare's debt to the Roman playwrights—beginning with Seneca. Noting that "in his earlier plays, Shakespeare's style is often as near a counterpart in English of Seneca's style in Latin as can well be"—Shakespeare's

> familiarity with the Latin language is evident, first from the fact that he has, with minute particularity of detail, based a poem on Ovid [*Venus and Adonis*] and a play on a comedy of Plautus [*Comedy of Errors*], which he must have read in the original, as no English translations, so far as we know, existed at the time; secondly from the fact that he has adapted and

---

[60] Collins was mistaken about the availability of Latin versions—as will appear.

borrowed many passages from the classics which were almost certainly only accessible to him in the Latin language; and thirdly, from the fact that while he may have followed English translations, it is often quite evident that he had the original either by him or in his memory. (*Studies* 16)

Churton Collins goes into detail on Shakespeare's borrowings from Plautus in *Taming of the Shrew, Merry Wives of Windsor* and *A Midsummer Night's Dreame* (20-22). He notes the phrases from *The Tempest* and other plays that Shakespeare borrowed from the Golding translation of *The Metamorphoses*—including phrases that could only have come from the Latin original. As for the tragedies—he goes into similar detail with the influence of Seneca on *Titus Andronicus, Henry VI, Richard III, King John,* and *Macbeth*—as found in the original Latin—not the paltry English versions only available after 1581. Noting the errors in these early attempts in English—attempts that rather strangely Shakespeare got right—he also compares their differences in *tone*—something generally ignored by philologists.

As for Horace, he held that—"In Shakespeare's time there was no translation of the *Odes*, and yet his plays abound in what certainly appear to be reminiscences of them." Taking, as he says—"a very few from very many"—he shows close parallels from plays as divergent in period and theme as *Richard III* and *Much Ado*. Though Juvenal would not be translated into English until later—he finds quotes that crop up when something brings them to Shakespeare's mind—the same with *Persius* and *Lucretius*.

To Cicero's *De Republica* and St. Augustine's *De Civitate Dei*—neither available in English until later—he finds clear references in *Henry V*. As for the many Latin works for which there were English translations—Collins sees quotes from *The Metamorphoses* in plays like *The Tempest* and *Cymbeline* that prove that Shakespeare worked from the original Latin because he used words and phrases not found in the Golding version. "These are typical," he says—

> and the impression which they and scores of other passages make is that Shakespeare was writing, not with any direct or perhaps conscious intention of imitating, or even with the original before him, but with reminiscences of it recurring

more or less vividly to his memory.... Parallels swarm, and even if we resolve two-thirds of them into coincidence, are ... too remarkable to be the result of accident. (38-9)

Unlike today's critics who write only for each other and a handful of reviewers—Churton Collins's readers included a broad range of playwrights, poets, and educated laymen—so his message reached both academics and questioners. For the benefit of the academics he lambasts the "mischievous" heretics who purvey the "monstrous myth" that Shakespeare was Francis Bacon. Nevertheless—it's clear from the rest of the book that he was coming perilously close to joining ranks with the questioners. And how could it be otherwise—with the academics so adamantly opposed to the idea that Shakespeare was fluent in Greek—something that Collins's own education and his memorization of Shakespeare had convinced him was true.

Still, basic self-preservation and the need to protect his primary interests—the creation of an English Department at Oxford and the retention of Greek in its curriculum—required that he fudge his evidence with terms like "parallel illustrations" to which he claimed "no wish to attach undue weight."

> As a rule such illustrations belong rather to the *trifles and curiosities* of criticism, to its *tolerabiles nugae* [humorous tidbits] than to anything approaching importance. But, as the object of this paper was to establish a probability that reminiscences, more or less unconscious perhaps, of classical reading, not in English translations but in Latin and possibly in Greek, were constantly occurring to Shakespeare's memory, they could not be ignored. And, cumulatively, they are remarkable; for, let me repeat here, that so far from exhausting what I have collected I have chosen only such as are typical of whole groups. (vii-ix).

The academics were not fooled by Collins's "trifles and curiosities." This "whole groups" was dangerous stuff—threatening the sacred biography—cornerstone of the monolith just then rising at the Birthplace and on the shelves of libraries, publishers and bookstores. Churton Collins failed in both efforts. The universities continued to turn away from Greek—and to ignore Shakespeare's education.

Chapter II What Shakespeare Knew

Gilbert Highet

In *The Classical Tradition: Greek and Roman Influences on Western Literature* (published in 1949) Gilbert Highet shows how far the typical academic attitude towards Shakespeare's knowledge of Greek would develop in the forty years since Collins. Highet's opinion of Shakespeare's knowledge is of particular interest as an overview of the influence of the classic literatures of ancient Rome and Athens on the national literatures of Europe from 1200 on. A Scot—educated at Glasgow University, Balliol and St. John's College Oxford—Highet ended his long career as the Classics Chair at Columbia University in New York City (1938-71).

As he puts it at the start of his Shakespeare chapter—"There is no doubt whatever that Shakespeare was deeply and valuably influenced by Greek and Latin culture. The problem is to define how that influence reached him, and how it affected his poetry" (194). Unfortunately—for one in Highet's sensitive position, the simplest explanation—that he could read Greek—was impossible, due to the Academy's addiction to the Stratford story. In describing Shakespeare's style he notes—"intertwined with the Englishness of Shakespeare's characters . . . there is an all-pervading use of Greek and Latin imagery and decorative reference, which is sometimes superficial [a bow to the hardliners] *but more often incomparably effective*"—which he follows with examples.

It seems clear that Highet disagrees with Spurgeon that Shakespeare's imagery was limited to Nature and English country life—

> Shakespeare is fluent and happy in his classical allusions. No writer who dislikes the classics, who receives no real stimulus from them, who brings in Greek and Roman decorations merely to parade his learning or to satisfy convention, can create so many apt and beautiful classical symbols as Shakespeare. Except the simplest fools and yokels, all his characters—from Hamlet to Pistol, from Rosalind to Portia—can command Greek and Latin reminiscences to enhance the grace and emotion of their speech.

This, of course, must be followed by the mandatory caveat—

> It is of course clear that Shakespeare was not a bookman, . . .
> He knew more about mythology than about ancient history,
> he knew the classical myths far better than the Bible. . . he had
> far fewer classical symbols present to his mind than Marlowe.

If by "not a bookman" Highet means that Shakespeare was less committed to scholarship than he was to stories—what does stating the obvious do—either for him or for us? Shakespeare was not a scholar *by trade*—he was a story-teller! As for where he got these "Greek and Latin reminiscences," says Highet—

> Learning meant little to him unless he could translate it into living human terms. It is mostly his pedants who quote the classics by book and author, and such quotations are either weak or ridiculous, and almost always inappropriate.

What layman dares to ridicule pedants in their own terms if not one who knows, or believes he knows, as much or more than they do?

Much more could be said in a critique of this long and meaty chapter—but at the center of every one of Highet's examples lies the same unresolved issue—where and how did Shakespeare get the materials with which he wrought his literary magic? The fact remains that, with all his classical expertise, Highet has responded to only half the problem he outlined at the beginning of the chapter—that is, having asserted that Shakespeare was "deeply and valuably influenced" by Greek and Latin culture which "affected his poetry"—when faced with explaining how such an influence could have reached the ignorant Bard, he pulls the old "Jade's trick" typical of academics stuck in a logical fallacy—

> Jonson was literally correct: Shakespeare did not know much of the Latin language, he knew virtually no Greek, and he was *vague and unscholarly* in using what he did know. . , but he used it with the flair of a great imaginative artist. What Jonson could have added, and what we must not forget, is that Shakespeare loved Latin and Greek literature.

What does he mean by "virtually" no Greek? Either he knew Greek or he didn't. And how he could love something he couldn't read is yet another illusory puff to "the Shakespeare problem."

Chapter II What Shakespeare Knew

Rome vs. Athens

Considering the vast amount of material devoted to the question of Shakespeare's knowledge of the ancient classics as reported by Baldwin, Velz, Highet and others—few it seems have approached the issue from Shakespeare's point of view, that of a playwright whose purpose was to entertain a particular audience. Highet claims that Shakespeare

> feels much more sensitively about Rome than about Greece, with the single exception of the Greek myths which reached the modern world through Rome. The Roman plays, plus some anachronisms and some solidly English touches, are like Rome. The Greek plays are not like Greece.

According to Highet—"the spirit of his tragic plays is much less Greek than Roman," and although without the Greeks there would be no Roman drama—"the English Renaissance playwrights did not as a rule know Greek tragedy, and they did know Seneca"—whose "frenzied violence" was apparently more to Shakespeare's taste than the "Hellenic loftiness" of the Greeks. He acknowledges that Shakespeare's portrayal of the warriors in *Troilus and Cressida* show knowledge of the *Iliad*, which—due to the Stratford time limits—he's forced to attribute to Chapman's 1598 translation—"but even so, the whole play is not merely anti-heroic: it is a distant, ignorant, and unconvincing caricature of Greece." In general, the Roman plays are much better—with "few large misrepresentations and much deep insight into character."

It's certainly true that Shakespeare told more Roman stories than he did Greek. But was that due to ignorance or disinterest in Greek themes—or was it because Rome and its history were so much more important to his audience?

England and the Roman Empire

From the days of Chaucer, through the Augustan era, to its peak as a world Empire—the English saw ancient Rome as the leading example of what constituted an organized, forward-thinking, civilized, and above all, successful culture. Generations of British poets studied ancient Roman poetry. British statesmen and diplomats studied its history and the biographies of its emperors. British scientists studied ancient Roman discoveries. British architects studied ancient Roman architecture. In short, Shakespeare's educated audience—and those to follow over the next 200 years—were obsessed with ancient Rome.

For the 18th-century English, dreaming of an empire of their own, Gibbon's six-volume *Decline and Fall of the Roman Empire*, published 1776-1789, was required reading. Even the old mummer's play portrays Caesar in his bloody robe brought to life by The Doctor, with Alexander the Great and Robin Hood cheering him on.

In Shakespeare's time, the power of Rome loomed large as a source of anxiety for both his Court and his public audience. With Greece helpless after a century of domination by the Turks—whose navy still controlled the eastern half of the Mediterranean—protestant England struggled to maintain its hard-won freedom from the militant Roman Catholicism of Spain. Although the defeat of the Armada in 1588 was a giant step—it did not end the Spanish threat, which continued until the Treaty of London was signed in 1604 under King James. Even so, it would take centuries before protestant England could feel secure—as witness the fact that it wasn't until the mid-19th century that English Catholics were finally allowed the full rights of citizenship denied them so long ago by the Protestant Reformation.

As for Athens, although the humanist scholars who promoted the Reformation were aware of the role it played in the history of western civilization—and the religious reformers were certainly aware that the earliest of their most sacred texts were in Greek—the only thing the groundlings knew about Greece was the mummers version of Alexander the Great. Shakespeare knew that his audience was much more interested in stories about the Romans who headed west to conquer Britain than they were about the Greeks who followed Alexander to India.

There are also Shakespeare's personal reasons to consider. Why did he choose certain heroes and villains from history and literature, and not others? It seems clear he felt a sympathetic bond to most of his historical protagonists—four of them English—Richard II, Hotspur, Lear, and the Bastard Falconbridge—three ancient Romans

Chapter II What Shakespeare Knew

—Brutus, Coriolanus, and Antony. In his two Greek dramas—*Timon of Athens* and *Troilus and Cressida*, there is no hero in *Timon*, while the only truly heroic figure in *Troilus* is the Trojan Hector—the Greek Achilles portrayed as a petulant narcissist. Hamlet, Shakespeare's most fully developed protagonist, was Danish—another invader.

Why might Shakespeare—who as John Vyvyan shows, was steeped in the ideas and ideals of Plato—and as Earl Showerman has proven, in the Greek dramatists as well—why might he have been hesitant to portray a Greek hero?

It's well to keep in mind the effect Calvin's version of the Protestant Reformation had on everything that was written and published during the early days of the English Renaissance—and how the Greeks were regarded by the Calvinists as heretics whose gods were all too human in ways they considered sinful. Most heinous to these anti-sex reformers was the behavior of the Athenian power structure—in which men spent hours naked in each other's company at the baths and gymnasia—and where their relationships with each other appear to be sexual as well as political.

Much of the love poetry written by the ancient Greeks was written by mature men to youths—even by a woman (Sappho) to her girl students. Plato himself describes philosophy as having arisen from the homosexual culture of third century BC Athens. In 16th-century England—where the word *filth* was a much used synonym for sex—it's understandable that it wouldn't be wise to be showing too much delight in the ancient Greeks, or their philosophy.

Yet as his works suggest—and as Highet shows through examples—Shakespeare may also have felt it in the nature of a duty to pass on to his readers something of the glories of Greek literature —strewing hints throughout the pastorals and romances that recall quotes from the Greeks going back to Pindar, Homer and Hesiod.

John Velz

In his 1968 *Shakespeare and the Classical Tradition; A Critical Guide to Commentary*, John Velz provided an immense bibliography with which to summarize everything he could find in print that—up to that point—dealt with Shakespeare's knowledge of the Classics.

Born in New Jersey in 1930, Velz is another academic who preferred to ignore the authorship question. An Episcopalian with degrees from Michigan and Minnesota, he found his permanent niche at the University of Texas at Austin where he studied and taught until his death in 2008.

These single paragraph synopses—around 2500 altogether—are tremendously useful for anyone researching Shakespeare's knowledge of the Classics, particularly those in pursuit of a particular theme or aspect—all easily located through the voluminous cross listings by category located at the back of his book. The viewpoints thus provided show how the unlettered Bard has gradually given way over the centuries to an acceptance of his knowledge of the Classics, and—while apparently constitutionally unable to come down on the side of a direct influence from Greek—as opposed to the notion that he got everything from Latin translations—Velz at least provides readers with means by which they can reach their own conclusions.

After quoting Jonson's well known Preface, he remarks—"Virtually every aspect of Shakespeare study has concerned itself with the 'small Latin' question" (vii). He follows with a daunting list of the questions that this overarching issue affects, stating finally—"For three centuries, Shakespeare studies have been touched at all points by the question of Shakespeare's participation in the classical tradition. This bibliographical guide is an attempt to gather, classify, summarize, and appraise the commentary which has been written since 1660." It is indeed an amazingly thorough and useful piece of work—for which countless students, researchers, and literary anthropologists must continue to be grateful. As he explains—

> Studies of Shakespeare's direct use of classical sources constitute only a fraction of the entries. The devious paths by which the Renaissance found access to the classics have been explored and mapped in recent years, and studies which follow Shakespeare down those paths are included here. (ix)

Although it fails to appear what he meant by "devious paths"—more interesting is the Introduction in which he summarizes the argument over Shakespeare's learning from the Restoration to the mid-20th century—naming names along with brief descriptions of their varied

Chapter II What Shakespeare Knew

contributions to the controversy. He provides an overall view of the curve of the argument from Jonson's "small Latin" to Dryden's "no Latin" to Baldwin's "some Latin" up to his own time—the mid-1960s—where, as usual, the picture tends to fall apart. "Though there is still disagreement among scholars . . . the scholarship of the past three decades has provided a broad foundation of knowledge about Shakespeare's sources and generally about the legacy which came to the Elizabethans from Greece and Rome" (13).

That's it? *All* the Elizabethans? What about the Stratford entrepreneur with no education who couldn't write his own name? The best Velz can come up with is that "most scholars now believe that Shakespeare knew what most Elizabethans knew—most, that is, who were not university men"—which if taken literally would mean that he knew nothing.

In introducing Velz to readers it seemed useful to include a selection of his summaries of the other books treated here—that is, until it was apparent that Baldwin, for instance, has 90 numbered entries! And what in fact would such an effort produce in the long run? This is a big book, over an inch thick, with pages 8½" x 11"—printed in small type, two columns per page, in which numbered references to "Caesar" in the index fill over four columns—roughly 1500 entries—those to "Troilus" approximately 1300.

Velz soon reveals himself as heavily on the side of orthodoxy and consensus—the eternal enemies of independent thought. He likes the word *conservative*—always using it in a positive way. He disapproves of "private theories"—and in a footnote in his preface, treats the opinions of the Friedmans and Louis B. Wright as sufficient to dismiss the Authorship Question.

As with Baldwin and Spurgeon—an immense work of this sort is often undertaken as much to resolve the author's own questions as to inform others. If resolving "the Latin question"—as he puts it in his opening paragraph—was as personal as it was scholarly, it's unlikely that Velz ever arrived at anything close to certainty. Like so many academics—rather than allow himself to be influenced by his own native common sense—Velz seeks to arrive at a conclusion by averaging the opinions of hundreds of authorities.

Showerman and Werth

In an article published in *The Oxfordian* in 2002—Andrew Werth, then an undergraduate at Concordia University in Portland, Oregon—examined today's leading authorities on Shakespeare's Greek—J. A.K. Thomson's *Shakespeare and the Classics* (1966) and Charles and Michelle Martindale's *Shakespeare and the Uses of Antiquity* (1990). Werth suggests that Thomson's purpose at that time was to rescue Shakespeare from the disintegrators who were inclined to give anything that showed too much erudition to someone with university credentials. By proving that Shakespeare's Greek was limited to Baldwin's grammar school curriculum, Thomson hoped to keep the conventional authorship from disintegrating any further.

Yet, as Werth shows, Thomson must admit that Shakespeare reveals knowledge of Euripides's *Hecuba* in *Titus Andronicus*. In Act I, where Demetrius assures Tamara that "the selfsame gods that arm'd the Queen of Troy with opportunity of sharp revenge upon the Thracian tyrant in his tent"—will do the same for her—Thomson points out that

> One would have little hesitation in saying that the source of the English poet here is Ovid, were it not for the addition of the words "in his tent." Ovid says nothing about a tent, but it is in his tent that Polymestor is blinded in Euripides's play.

Werth notes—"Absent any known translation, the Martindales can only dismiss this as 'a slender peg.'"

Following Root, Thomson is forced to concede that Shakespeare knew Sophocles's *Ajax*—that in describing Ulysses, he ignores Ovid and follows the Greek—the two versions of Ulysses's motives being diametrically opposed. Says Werth, "Reflecting on these examples, Thomson equivocates, 'What it means I must leave to the experts to decide.'" To this, the Martindales sniff: "to argue that Shakespeare read the *Ajax* is to convict him of wasting his time, if that is all the fruit it bore,"—as if Shakespeare's concern was to provide future critics with evidence of his knowledge of Greek. "According to Churton Collins, it yielded a far greater harvest than this, since 'reminiscences of [the *Ajax*] seem to haunt his dramas.'"

Chapter II What Shakespeare Knew

Werth finds evidence of Homer in *Henry VI part three* and—in *Timon*—of Lucian, which did not exist in anything but Greek in Shakespeare's time. He goes on to note the words coined from Greek for which the OED gives Shakespeare "first use." Though fewer than the hundreds of Latin derived words for which he's been given first use—significant in their links to Greek literature are—*academe, dialogue, critic, metamorphosis, Olympian, ode,* and *mimic*—and that these tend to appear whenever Shakespeare deals with Greek themes.

Werth ends by proving that the final two *Sonnets—153* and *154*—were translations of Martial that Shakespeare must have read in Greek since there was no other way that he could have known them at that time (13-18). Since publishing this in 1997—no one on either side of the Authorship Question has questioned Werth's conclusions. Since then authorship scholar Earl Showerman of Ashland, Oregon, has dug deeply into Shakespeare's knowledge of Greek by providing exhaustive detail on the Greek sources as found in *Hamlet, Winter's Tale, Much Ado, Macbeth, and A Midsummer Night's Dreame.*

By now it should be obvious that Ben Jonson's "small Latin and less Greek" was nothing more than a flat out lie. There must be a reason why he felt it necessary to make such a point of it—or why poets and others who must have known the truth have continued to restate it ever since. The truth—like the body parts of Osiris severed by the evil Seth—remain scattered about in bits and pieces in the murky trough that is what has been left us by the Tudor historians who failed to see anything of interest in the creation and long life of the Elizabethan Stage than simply the fact that it happened.

~ Shakespeare and Mythology ~

Aware of the arguments that Churton Collins outlined in articles in leading journals throughout 1902 and 1903—articles that advocated Shakespeare's knowledge of Greek—academics at Yale University moved with lightening speed to publish an antidote before Collins could strike again. Someone at Yale saw to it that Robert Root's PhD thesis, *Classical Mythology in Shakespeare*—beat Churton Collins's book to the bookstores by a few months.

That someone was undoubtedly Root's editor—the philologist

Albert S. Cook, chairman of the Yale English Department. That dealing with Collins was the real reason for publishing Root's book seems clear from his opening statement that Greek influence on Shakespeare's conception of classical mythology was "all but nothing"—and that apart from The *Metamorphoses* and a bit from Virgil—"of any other Greek influence .. there is not ... a hint" —

> Mr. John Churton Collins, in a series of articles in the *Fortnightly* [*Review*] for 1903, has tried to show that Shakespeare was familiar with the Greek dramatists in Latin translation. At the time of going to press, the last article in the series has not yet appeared; but in the articles already published I find no evidence sufficient to overthrow my own belief that he was totally unacquainted with them. It is any rate certain that he nowhere alludes to any of the characters or episodes of the Greek drama; that they exerted no influence whatever on his conception of mythology. (6)

Having expressed at length his opinion of Shakespeare's limitations, Root finishes with—

> He did not know the great mythographers of Hellas, and was, in consequence, cut off from the sublimer aspects of their system; but from the mythology of Ovid and Virgil he was able to draw the poetic beauties which it offers, and while recognizing its limitations, to seek, not without success, for the deeper spiritual significance which it implies. (24)

How Shakespeare managed to draw "poetic beauties" from a mythology whose "sublimer aspects" he was denied because *he couldn't read them*, is yet another example of the kind of hocus pocus that—like the ink that an octopus emits when threatened—emerges from academia whenever some bit of truth comes a little too close to challenging the sacred Stratford scenario.

What is apparent is that Root was simply out to deny Shakespeare as much Greek influence as he possibly could—not surprising perhaps if—as seems likely—the book was his stepping stone into the *sanctum sanctorum americanum*—namely the English Department at Princeton—where in time he would come to reign as Dean of Faculty.

Chapter II What Shakespeare Knew

Uprooted

Since the book began as a dissertation, there must needs be a thesis, so what of that? What real value there is in Root's book lies in two alphabetized lists that take up its latter two thirds—the first the myths referenced by Shakespeare and the plays in which they occur—the second the myths in each play. While he misses—or ignores—a fair number—these at least provide researchers with a starting point. But as for Root's own thesis—the less than sensational idea that Shakespeare got most of his mythological references from Ovid's *Metamorphoses*—a theory long accepted by both academics and popularizers—he opines that of anything else there is simply not enough to bother about. Of Seneca, Horace and Martial—though he claims to have found suggestions—none are "conclusive."

Considering that Root was a medievalist whose focus was, and would continue to be, Chaucer—it's interesting that he found so few sources of Greek myths—apart from Ovid and Virgil—who, according to Henry Burrowes Lathrop—were "the two authors whom the Middle Ages enjoyed above all others"—and the only two that Caxton, England's first printer, had found it worthwhile to publish (25). In other words, like the drunk who looks for his lost car keys at night—not where he dropped them, but near the street lamp where there was sufficient light—undergraduate Root's "research" was limited to the little he himself knew about Greek mythology.

An "exceeding paucity"

Take what he has to say about Hecate, the ancient goddess mentioned by Shakespeare in several of the plays. For some reason he has her listed as an offshoot of Diana. It's true that Hecate was sometimes conflated with Diana—but as one of the many aspects of the Great Goddess of prehistory, no more so than a half dozen others. Her earliest mention comes from Hesiod's *Theogony*, while later she appears numerous times in all the Greek dramas—about which Root seems oblivious. His puzzlement over Shakespeare's reference to Hecate's role as a triple goddess and as "the light in the night" suggests the darkness of ignorance (5-6).

It seems that, to Root, only a proper noun, preferably the name of a divinity, qualifies as a genuine reference. In discussing *The Merchant of Venice* he notes that there were 28 allusions to myths—13 of them detailed—several "highly elaborate"—with three separate allusions to Jason and Medea. "It is to be noticed, however" says he—"that the divinities are seldom referred to" (10). Root states flatly that "The all but total disregard of the genealogies and family relationships of the divinities, which appear so prominently in Spenser and Milton, shows that Shakespeare could not have been familiar with Hesiod" (16-17). Why Shakespeare would have had to display an interest in the genealogies of the gods to prove his acquaintance with Hesiod's *Works and Days*, which—as Baldwin asserts two decades later—was standard grammar school fare in the sixteenth century—is not explained.

As a Chaucer scholar, one would think that *Troilus and Cressida*—which contains more allusions to the Greek myths than any of Shakespeare's other plays—would have given him pause—particularly when "in the course of the dialogue, the other myths of classical antiquity are referred to with remarkable frequency." Alas, nowhere near sufficient. Apart from these "remarkable" incidents in *Troilus*—Shakespeare's knowledge, which Root attributes solely to Chapman's 1616 translation of *The Iliad*—something William of Stratford would have to have read in manuscript since it wasn't published until the year he died—Root finds no hint of Homer.

Obvious parallels to Greek drama in style and form in plays like *Macbeth, Hamlet,* and *A Winter's Tale* (as detailed by Showerman)—whizzed right by him. If he sees no proper name, he either misses the allusion or brushes it off as "inconclusive." He's stymied by the 53 allusions in *Titus Andronicus*—among which are several that suggest an "acquaintance with the Greek drama"—as in Act I where Marcus says, "The Greeks upon advice did bury Ajax that slew himself, and wise Laertes's son did graciously plead for his funerals"—an allusion that, according to Root—who swears he searched through all the sources to which William had access—could only have come from the *Ajax* of Sophocles. This plus references to Hecuba and Prometheus causes him to conclude that someone else must have written *Titus Andronicus*.

Chapter II What Shakespeare Knew

"Substantially correct"

In general what value we get from Root comes less from his thesis than from its exceptions. Some of these he explains by attributing them to Chapman or some other contemporary of William of Stratford. Where he can't find a contemporary—he deals with it by dismissing his authorship. When forced to admit that Shakespeare knew what he was talking about—he relegates it to a footnote—

> An examination of the articles dealing with the several myths will show that Shakespeare's knowledge of the myths, though frequently scanty, is in general substantially correct. Only four instances of actual error have come to my notice: the confusion about Althaea's firebrand in *H4B*; the idea that Cerberus was killed by Hercules expressed in *LLL* 5.2; the use of the word *Hesperides* as the name of the garden where grew the golden apples with the idea that Hercules gathered them himself *LLL* 4.3, *Per* 1.1, *Cor.* 4.6; and the famous mention of "Juno's swans" in *AYLI* 1.3. To this may be added the mistaken form "Ariachne' of *T&C* 5.2. and the somewhat confused notions entertained of Lethe and Acheron. Other errors such as making Delphi an island, *WT* 3.1; considering the sun as Aurora's lover; and thinking of Perseus as mounted on the winged steed Pegasus, are hardly to be laid to Shakespeare's account, since they are all shared by his contemporaries. (7 fn)

Just for the heck of it, let's take a look at these errors. As we so often find with the academic mind, Shakespeare's humor escapes Root who appears to mistake a character's error for his author's. For instance, what Root calls "the confusion about Altheas's firebrand," a reference to the slap at Bardolph made by the Page during a teasing exchange between Hal and Poins in *Henry IV part two*. The page calls Bardolph "Althaea's dream"—meaning that as in the myth as told in Ovid—Bardolph was a firebrand (a rabble-rouser) like Althaea's son Meleager. Any confusion here is Root's. Why should the Page have gone into detail on a myth that he refers to only to tease Bardolph? How is it that Root fails to see the point of the boy's riposte—so

Educating Shakespeare

clever that Hal and Poins reward him for it with a tip?

The idea that Hercules killed Cerberus comes from Holofernes, who perhaps should have known better—but because he's a comic figure, this too may have been an intentional dig at some pompous pedagogue. This is certainly the case with the mistaken notion that it was Perseus who rode Pegasus—the mythical flying horse[61] as referred to by the Dauphin in *Henry V*—a vapid, preening aristocrat whose sole contribution to the conversation consists of praising his horse. Again, Root has missed the sarcasm. Perhaps it should be a given that critics of Shakespeare be tested in advance to determine if they have the necessary sense of humor.

Could Root (and his editor) be so blind to the likelihood of a 16th-century typographical error as to blame him for "Ariachne"—possibly a compositor's misreading of *Ariadne*—whose "woof" (thread) helped Theseus escape the Minotaur?—or else a misspelling of *Arachne*—the weaver so hated by Minerva for having portrayed the sins of the Olympians in her tapestries that she turned her into a spider? Had he no experience of the Secretary Hand and and its frequent misinterpretations by compositors working as fast as they could to get the book set in type, printed and into the bookstalls so they could get paid? Surely such a typographer would have been just as ignorant of these mythological weavers as was Robert Root.

As for the misuse of the *Hesperides*—is Root so oblivious to Shakespeare's love of metonymy that he can't see Antiochus's reference to "Hesperides" as conflating his daughter with the golden apples because *both were forbidden?* Is Menenius's reference to Hercules shaking down the "mellow fruit" a mistake made by Menenius—or was Shakespeare suggesting (nudge nudge wink wink) that Hercules was "shaking down" the Princess? Was Root so dull to rhyme and meter that he sees as a mistake the poetic phrasing when Berowne asks "is not Love a Hercu*lees*, still climbing *trees* in the Hesperi*dees*"? Or to Celia's reference to "Juno's swans," which certainly rolls off the tongue more nicely than would the hissing triple *sss* of "Venu*s's* swan*s*"—Juno being a more appropriate goddess for young girls than Venus—and Celia hardly a scholar? Is he so ignorant

---

[61] Perseus's horse was Bellerophon.

of the Bard's desire to penetrate to the heart of the myth that he reads him like any PhD candidate seeking to impress his dissertation committee—which is, after all, exactly what Root was when his professors used his dissertation to protect the sacred myth from the likes of the heretical Churton Collins.

As for the "isle" of Delphi—while mainland Greece is in fact a peninsula—to the English of Shakespeare's time, all of Greece, including the mainland, was frequently, if erroneously, referred to as "the Grecian Isles." And as for his reference to the Sun as Aurora's lover—as a personification of a feminine Dawn, what could be more natural, particularly to a sexy Renaissance poet, than to see her pursued and overtaken by the *rising* of the masculine sun? What Shakespeare's confusions over *Lethe* and *Acheron* might be he does not say—though it should be clear by now that Root simply had no sense of Shakespeare's free-wheeling use of terms and images. Why should ancient mythology be any more sacred to him than Medicine, the Law, or the Bible—all of which he treats with similar abandon?

Had Root been innocent of any ulterior motive—had he and his editor no academic axe to grind—he would surely have shown astonished delight that the uneducated Shakespeare knew as much about Greek mythology as he did. Missing the great forest for the few little saplings that he knew anything about—Root's scholarly details about Theseus and his marriage to the Queen of the Amazons are beside the point. To Shakespeare they represented the mixing together of two fiercely opposed cultures—creating civil harmony where before was only hatred and bloodshed. Most probably written for the Court wedding of a Catholic countess to a protestant knight[62]—it seems the poet knew his audience a great deal better than Robert Root knew anything about Greek mythology.

—∞— Shakespeare and Grammar —∞—

Sister Miriam Joseph (1898-1982), professor at St. Mary's College in Indiana from 1931 to 1960, in her book, *Shakespeare's Use of the*

---

[62] The most likely event for which it was written was the marriage in 1594 of the Catholic Countess of Southampton to the protestant Sir Thomas Heneage.

Arts of Language (1947), claims that "the extraordinary power, vitality, and richness of Shakespeare's language" are due in part to "those characteristics which differentiate it most from the language of today"—which she attributes to "the Renaissance theory of composition—which, as derived from an ancient tradition," she feels was "permeated with formal logic and rhetoric, while ours is not."

She quotes George Stuart Gordon (1928) on what he sees as the "experimental gusto" and "genuine and widespread feeling of word creation" during the 1590s." Shakespeare refers to this in *Much Ado* when Benedick complains how his love-struck friend Claudio—who "was wont to speak plain and to the purpose like an honest man and a soldier, and now is he turn'd *orthography*,[63] his words . . . a very fantastical banquet—just so many strange dishes."—As Gordon puts it, Shakespeare

> was, by every sign—indeed the evidence is overwhelming—in the first rank for the advance, and of all its members the most exuberant; an experimenter always. . . . For the first quality of Elizabethan, and therefore, of Shakespearean English, is its power of hospitality, its passion for free experiment, its willingness to use every form of verbal wealth, to try anything. (49-50)

While we may appreciate this today—there were complaints at the time about "inkhorn terms"—suggesting that not everyone then was on board with this freewheeling use of language. There was also a great deal of argument over what constituted genuine poetry.

While Shakespeare may have pushed this wordy adventure to its limits—none of it was really new—to him or to his immediate predecessors. While it may seem that he was casting tradition aside, what in fact he was casting aside were the gloomy affectations of what C.S. Lewis has termed the "drab era." In ignoring the restrictions of puritan gloom he was in fact returning to the "ornaments and lights" of the classical tradition. And as Sister Joseph shows—he did this in part by adhering to the ancient rules of rhetoric.

---

[63] In Shakespeare's time *orthography* covered all aspects of *linguistics* (37).

Chapter II What Shakespeare Knew

A "gleeful bandying of words"

These—however complex they may appear to us today—gave him leave to experiment with words from Greek and Latin, to trim prefixes, add English endings, turn verbs into nouns and adjectives, adjectives and nouns into verbs—anything to add movement, a little extra grace, an extra touch of meaning. From the Greeks, Aristotle and Isocrates—through the Romans, Cicero, Quintilian, and the anonymous author of the *ad Herennium*—the tradition passed, revived by Erasmus and Vives in the early days of the sixteenth century—in the 1530s by Sir Thomas Elyot—and yet again in the 1560s by Roger Ascham. As she shows, Shakespeare adhered to the classical schemes of grammar. These included figures of *comparison, compression, expansion, omission, transition, exchange, substitution,* and *repetition*. As Sister Joseph tells it—

> With figures of repetition, Shakespeare weaves a haunting harmony of sound; through the schemes of grammar he achieves such control over movement and rhythm that like a figure skater he may dart, poise, turn, plunge, go where he will, his words fraught with penetrating thought and deep feeling—and all this but an art subservient to the larger art . . . to plot construction, character creation, and profound insight into human nature and its problems. Yet this myriad-minded man has time for fun and nonsense, for parody and foolery, for mere gleeful bandying of words. (289)

Rhetoric was the third branch of the classical *trivium*, following Grammar and Logic. While grammar deals with fundamentals—the nuts-and-bolts of parts of speech and sentence structure—Logic and Rhetoric have to do with its uses—Logic with building reasoned exposition and argument—Rhetoric with persuasion—the former predominant with the Law and history—the latter with poetry, sermonizing and drama.

In the grammar schools of the early Reformation, students from ages ten to fourteen studied Grammar—from fifteen to eighteen, Logic and Rhetoric. Richard Rainolds—who taught Rhetoric at Oxford from the 1560s on, and who was responsible in his later years for compiling the majestic King James Bible—wrote that the purpose of Rhetoric was to "prove and defend by *the force and power of art,* things passing the compass and reach of our capacity and wit."

The Grammar of classical Logic and Rhetoric consisted of some 200 categories inherited from the Greeks. Within this array, both Logic and Rhetoric were primarily concerned with *schemes* and *figures*. S*chemes* are about style—"patterns of language which confer on it a character that distinguishes it from ordinary speech." *Figures* are specific patterns—each with a Greek term of its own. Although today we no longer use the elaborate system of cataloging that the Elizabethans inherited from Aristotle—we still use the forms, as we would had we never heard of *anadiplosis* or *hypozeuxis*.

Defenders of the uneducated Genius might argue that—because such schemes may simply be a natural development wherever poets play with language—so Shakespeare's use was "natural" in that it *just came to him*. Could he have used these tropes instinctively, as I—ignorant of their Greek sources, might use them? No, for instinct alone would not allow me to *name* them, which he does—often enough and correctly enough, that it's obvious he knows very well—not only their uses, but also their Greek names.

Just as he does with legal, medical, and astrological terms, Shakespeare plays with terms like *figure, sentence, device,* and *scheme*. He plays with the word *figures* in *Love's Labour's Lost,* in the first part *of Henry IV,* in *Henry V,* and *Sonnet 98*. He plays with the word *metaphor* in *Winter's Tale,* and with the word *simile* in *Winter's Tale, Troilus,* and *As You Like It,* with *comparison* in *Much Ado*—with *rhetoric* in *Love's Labour's Lost* and *Sonnet 82.* A similar list could be compiled of categories from Logic.

Schemes and figures

Shakespeare has been castigated by grammarians for misspelled words, improper usage, goofy syntax, wrong verb tenses, double negatives, bizarre metaphors, wordiness, incoherent sentences, and so forth. Once again, however, we learn from an expert that most of these so-called mistakes stem from the elements of style in vogue during succeeding phases of the sixteenth and early seventeenth centuries.

Chapter II What Shakespeare Knew

Of *schemes* (from the Greek *schemata*) there were two kinds, schemes of *words* and schemes of *construction*. Schemes of words covered variations from norms of spelling and pronunciation. Often interpreted as misspellings or compositor's typos—these were allowed where it was necessary to maintain the meter in a poem. Similarly schemes of construction allowed a poet to vary the syntax so that the meaning of a sentence could be fitted to the proper meter or rhyme scheme. While there were limits past which poets could not go without sounding absurd—this allowed them to bend or stretch a particular usage without violating it.

Understandably—as our approach to teaching language has changed—most of these ancient categories have fallen by the wayside—while the most necessary have acquired modern names, yet we still use many of these Greek terms today. Besides *idiom* there's *apostrophe, category, climax, chronology, ellipse, eulogy, hyperbole, metaphor, paradox, paradigm, rhyme, rhythm, parallel, parenthesis, parody, solecism, soliloquy, tautology*. Some that once had elaborate Greek names we've simplified for common usage—*pun, irony, malapropism, over-* or *understatement*. Apart from the standard tropes of poetry—*assonance, onomatopoeia, alliteration, meter, rhyme, rhythm*—there are hundreds of other figures with which pedants were concerned in Shakespeare's time. And however he may have teased them with characters like Nathaniel and Holofernes—Shakespeare not only knew them, but—as Sister Joseph informs us—he managed to use all 200!

In *Shakespeare's Use of the Arts of Language* she quotes some thousand examples from his works—each demonstrating his use of a particular Greek figure—showing how the internal debates of Hamlet, Brutus, and Macbeth that we distinguish by the Greek term *soliloquy*, are styled in the classical debate format as prescribed by Aristotle and Cicero—and as demonstrated by Mark Antony in his speech to the mob following the assassination of Julius Caesar.

Nor was this purely to make use of his own grammar school lessons—for many are sarcastic or ironic in tone. At least one of his comedies is based as much on jokes about grammar and rhetoric as it is about anything else. *Love's Labour's Lost*—aptly described as "that playground of the new language"—is one long verbal fencing match between the various characters, male and female, courtier and commoner, that may reflect—however exaggerated for effect—the kind of exchanges heard at that time at Court or in settings where educated folk amused themselves with similar verbal shenanigans had not some portion of his audience enjoyed such games themselves.

"Comparisons are odorous"

Most writers and English teachers know the painful feeling when a friend or family member violates a particular grammatical rule or misuses a word for the umpteenth time. In scene after scene in which two or three of the characters commit one rhetorical violation after another—what Sister calls "figurative vices"—*Love's Labour's Lost* can almost be seen as a demonstration of bad usage intended to entertain graduates of late 16th-century grammar schools. As pedants Nathaniel and Holofernes demonstrate a particular vice by mixing phrases from different tongues, Moth snickers, "They have been at a great feast of languages and stolen the scraps." Rewarding Costard for taking a letter to Jacquenetta, when Armado refers to the tip by the five-syllable word "remuneration"—Costard, stumped for a moment by the lengthy word, has to think a bit before regaining his composure—"Remuneration?" says he—"O, that's the Latin word for three farthings."

That Shakespeare knew what he was doing is clear from the fact that characters like Dogberry, Bottom and Launce—though they appear no more than once in the canon—are each guilty of regularly committing a particular category of figurative vice—as in the Italian Comedia where Braggadocio turns boasting into an art, as do Falstaff, Armado, and Glendower. Bottom gets his uses mixed up—he hears images and sees sounds. Dogberry has the astonishing gift of using words that mean the exact opposite of what he's trying to say. Launce persistently *misunderstands what he hears*—as with his response to Speed's question—"What news with your mastership?" to which he replies—"Why, it is at sea."

Some like Mistress Quickly are paragons of mispronunciation. Others, like the French Dr. Caius, the Welsh Sir Hugh Evans, Irish Macmorris and Spanish Armado—are masters of misunderstanding.

Chapter II What Shakespeare Knew

According to Sister Joseph there's even a Greek term for the tergiversations of Nurse as she shrugs off Juliet's demands for news of Romeo—another for her irrelevant asides.

As You Like it also has its share of such foolery—much of it coming from the word juggler Touchstone. He threatens Audrey's simple minded country suitor—not with bodily harm, but with the damage to his reputation that only the Spearshaker can wield with impunity. Touchstone's diatribe contains a pun that his audience will get—because they *hear* it *spoken*—while readers might not get it unless they hear it read out loud—"Then learn this of me," says Touchstone to the bumpkin—"to have is to have; for it is a figure in rhetoric that drink, being poured out of a cup into a glass, by filling the one doth empty the other, for all your writers do consent that *ipse* is *he*. Now you are not *ipse*, for *I* am *he*." Spoken, this becomes—"now you are *not tipsy*—for *I* am *he*." Doubtless Touchstone is meant to speak with glass and bottle in hand.

"Very like a whale"

Of all the figures used by Shakespeare, it's probably the schemes of comparison—the metaphors and similes—that most define him. If we include metaphorical adjectives and adverbs, what Caroline Spurgeon identifies as the sources of his imagery—he can hardly get through a sentence without a comparison of some sort. Love is compared to almost everything under the sun, while almost everything under the sun is compared to gardening. Who else would compare a girl's beauty at night to an Ethiopian's earring, or her death to the lust of "a lean abhorréd monster" who keeps her in the darkness of death as "his paramour"—or, as in *Henry V*—the mighty Alps to a disgusting old monarch spitting "his rheum" (melted snow) on the valleys (valets?) beneath—or the return of reason to the renegades in *The Tempest* to the kind of storm that will sweep away their "foul and muddy" notions. He's also fond of the implied metaphor—as in Hamlet's "I will speak daggers to her" (his mother)—or Antony on his and Cleopatra's military defeats—"We have kissed away kingdoms."

No writer has ever used metaphor to the extent that he does—whether obviously, as in "all the world's a stage"—subtly, as "in my *green* youth"—or by using nouns as verbs as in "Angelo *dukes* it well"—verbs as adjectives as in "cormorant *devouring* time," or the Egyptian Queen's fears that—should they lose the war—"some squeaking Cleopatra [will] *boy* my greatness" on the Roman stage.

Evidence of Shakespeare's knowledge of the Law, Medicine, Pharmacology and Astrology, comes as much or more from his use of their terms in figures of comparison as from direct references. Even plots can be metaphors—The title of *Measure for Measure*—from the Sermon on the Mount—sets up his audience for a sort of homily. Or *Taming of the Shrew*—where the means Petruchio uses to tame the willful Katherine are modeled on techniques prescribed for training falcons—hunters inclined to be skittish if not started young enough.[64]

Shakespeare both refers to and uses the other major figure of comparison, the *simile*—as in Imogen's "comes in my father and, like the tyrannous breathing of the North, shakes all our buds from growing." But with his penchant for compression, he can drop the comparative *like*—as with Sebastian's swipe at Gonzalo—"Look, he's winding up the watch of his wit—by-and-by it will strike"—or the Roman tribune's description of Coriolanus's manner of speaking —"his soaring insolence will be his fire to kindle their dry stubble."

Many of his most memorable speeches are based on metaphors —as when Ulysses compares hierarchy and tradition to musical harmony—Iago, the human body to a garden—Jaques, the world to a stage. Sister Joseph notes that the figure known as *catachresis*— technically "the wrenching of a word, most often a verb or adjective, from its proper application to another not proper"—as when one says that "the sword devours"—is "an implied metaphor . . . a vital instrument with which he forges sudden concentrations of meaning, and secures the compression, energy, and intensity which characterize great poetry" (146).

Some of Shakespeare's metaphors have left centuries of readers puzzled—for instance Prospero's "full fathom five my father lies, these are pearls that were his eyes." Nor is the reader the only one to be confused. What is Claudius to make of Hamlet's response to his

---

[64] Only females are used in falconry. Female peregrine falcons are their species' hunters—the males sit on the eggs and tend to the young.

Chapter II What Shakespeare Knew

efforts to locate Polonius—"Now Hamlet, where's Polonius?"—"At supper."—"At supper!" says Claudius, "Where?"—"Not where he eats," says Hamlet—"but where he is eaten. A certain convocation of politic worms are e'en at him."—And so forth in the delusional riposte with which the distracted Prince seems to be comparing the death of Polonius to the demise of the Protestant Reformation.

Earlier in the play he has Hamlet use a metaphor to confront his former schoolmate—whom he suspects of conniving with the King. Insisting that Guildenstern play the recorder, when his former friend explains that he doesn't know how, Hamlet compares it to his inability to "play" Hamlet himself—"S'blood, do you think I am easier to be played on than a pipe? Call me what instrument you will—though you can fret me, yet you cannot play upon me."

Among the various kinds of comparison, a favorite source of humor comes from someone comparing something to itself—as in Hugh Evans's absurd response to Shallow in the first scene in *Merry Wives*—"I do despise a liar as I do despise one that is false, or as I despise one that is not true!"—a silly use of *parallelism*. Parallelism is related to metaphor in that both enhance or extend a thing or an idea. It can be seen in his affection for both the phrase and the idea behind the frequent pairing of *shadow and substance*. It can be seen in his pairings of plot and subplot, often showing two versions of a particular theme—like the similar relationships between the couples in *Taming of the Shrew*, *Much Ado* and *As You Like it*—or the pairs of twins in *Comedy of Errors*. It can be seen in his poetic use of *hendiadys*—a technical term for two words connected with *and* that mean the same or almost the same thing—as "reek and smoke" or "shake and shudder." Parallelism is similar to *repetition*—another classical figure—whether for *euphony*, sweetness of sound—"beauty *itself* doth of *itself* persuade"—or *anaphora* for emphasis, the repetition of a word—"*still* he is sullen, *still* he lours and frets."

When figures like these are found in the early quartos we can be certain that they were not conceived by some unidentified predecessor—they can't be by anyone but Shakespeare himself.

"Set the word itself against the word"[65]

Second only to his love of metaphor, of comparison, is his love of *antithesis*, another form of parallelism. Not only as a rhetorical figure, repeated over and over—even, as Feuillerat complains, to a wearying extreme—antithesis is fundamental to his overall process, to the way his mind works. No sooner does an idea, a thesis, a premise, occur to him, than he must consider its opposite. Rather than a string of separate events—he sees history as a series of reactions to actions. While metaphor is used to deepen and enrich—antithesis is used to drive and dramatize. His plays, particularly the history plays, are like a tennis match in which statements are struck by one character to be struck back by another—the theme in one scene either repeating in the next with different characters—or followed by its antithesis—thus adding a sportive energy to the movement of the plot.

One might almost see antithesis in the very structure of his plays—the thesis as the initial action—the antithesis the reaction it brings about—such as Lear's opening decision to free himself from responsibility followed by his loss of power and its terrible results—or the bliss of Romeo's night with Juliet followed by the violent deaths of her cousin and his own best friend—or Colatine's brag to Tarquin of his wife's purity followed by her rape and suicide—or Beatrice and Benedick's verbal sparring as prologue to their romance.

It's as though the thesis—be it a word, a phrase, a theme, an action or an entire plot—inevitably calls forth a reaction—the *shadow* to which all *substance* is forever bound. His sonnets often consist of a statement reversed by the final couplet. He liked *stichomythia*—dialogue that consisted of brief statements that played off each other—that tends to consist of a series of reversals—as in the exchange between the masked Biron and Rosaline in *Love's Labour's Lost*—

> Biron: Your wit's too hot, it speeds too fast, 'twill tire.
> Rosa: Not till it leave the rider in the mire.
> Biron: What time o' day?
> Rosa: The hour that fools should ask.

---

[65] *Richard II*, Act V Scene 5.

Chapter II What Shakespeare Knew

Biron: Now fair befall your mask!
Rosa: Fair fall the face it covers!
Biron: And send you many lovers!
Rosa: Amen, so you be none.
Biron: Nay then will I be gone.

Sister Joseph alerts us to this aspect of Shakespeare's style—and that it appears to be based on patterns laid down ages before by the great stylists of Greek and Roman literature. No way could Shakespeare have acquired such expertise in the classical trivium—Grammar, Rhetoric and Logic—without having been trained by one who was himself a master of these things. Who was this master that history has either forgotten, or hasn't yet discovered?

Topics of Invention

In discussing this category, Sister Miriam writes—

> Shakespeare drew matter for his plays and poems from all the topics of invention . . . which were given an important place by the logicians and rhetoricians of his time. . . . The characters in his plays manifest a knowledge and practice of logical and rhetorical theory, lively, concrete, specific, displayed in parody as well as in serious application, which were expected to win a commensurate response from an audience . . . disciplined and practiced in the arts of logic and rhetoric. (172)

What audience would that have been? Surely not the illiterate public who paid their penny to see his plays at the Theatre or the Globe.

So when Ben Jonson described Shakespeare as having "small Latin" he was simply lying—or at best—obfuscating, equivocating—but to what end? It's simply not possible that Shakespeare could have acquired the expertise he shows with his uses of Grammar, Logic and Rhetoric without a thorough and early grounding in Latin—and the same for Greek. What purpose could Jonson have been serving with this blatantly obvious lie if not protecting the Stratford story.

~~ Shakespeare and Style ~~

As the mid 16th-century English poets struggled to free themselves from the turgid pseudo-Petrarchan style bequeathed by the Calvinists for whom the Devil lurked within every merry metaphor—arguments were fierce over what styles worked best in English. Having followed a developmental curve from the wildly varying meters of John Skelton (1500)—to the "lumbering" poulter's measure of Sir Thomas Wyatt (1540s)—and the "galloping fourteeners" of poets like George Gascoigne (1560s). But by the 1570s English versification had pretty much settled into a rhymed *iambic pentameter,* generally attributed to the influence of Christopher Marlowe, who used it to the exclusion of everything else.[66]

The handful of narrative poems attributed to Shakespeare are all in *iambic pentameter*—five two-syllable pairs per line, stress tending to fall on the second syllable of each pair—generally rhymed in an *aabb* pattern of couplet after couplet. Although the lines are always the same length—these could be varied by anything from six to twelve lines per verse, and by *abab* or other endings. As Albert Feuillerat notes, much more rhyming occurs in the early plays than would later—although he was always prone to ending a scene, or an important statement, with a rhyming couplet.

In general, dialogue between servants or comic characters is written in prose, with blank verse reserved for the nobility[67]—although occasionally a commoner will rise to a poetic level when impelled by noble feelings. As with everything he did—he sprinkled iambics with exceptions, varying it with pauses and disruptive beats that create a kind of syncopation in lines that—with Marlowe—tended to become monotonous. As Feuillerat tells it—

> In Shakespeare's day only two kinds of feet were used for such substitutions: the *trochee,* composed of an accented

---

[66] *Blank verse* consists of unrhymed iambics in which verse comes as close as it can to prose and still be considered verse. It is to the more insistent meters as, in opera, *recicitore* is to the *aria*—conveying the message in an easy flow without drawing undue attention to itself.

[67] Which makes the choice of blank verse for the monster Caliban most interesting.

Chapter II What Shakespeare Knew

> syllable followed by an unaccented one, and the *spondee*, composed of two accented syllables. These . . . produce different effects: the trochee, being the reverse of the iamb, dislocates the normal rhythm so that the ear, expecting the ascending movement of the iamb, is surprised; the spondee, on the other hand, with its two equally accented syllables, simply interrupts the ascending movement and holds it in suspense.
> . . . A great number of trochees renders the rhythm more agile and on the whole more lively, or even jerky, as of a man who staggers—a great number of spondees makes the rhythm sonorous, weighty, at time ponderous. (68)

Feuillerat's close examination of Shakespeare's rhyme schemes finds that, overall, he used the two equally. *Enjambment*—which ends a phrase or statement in the middle of a line rather than at the end—provides another means of adding variety. As Feuillerat notes, Shakespeare's verse

> is delicately organized to avoid monotony without destroying the specific quality of the iambic scheme. It is resonant without being strident, supple without being invertebrate. In a sense Shakespeare's versification in its avoidance of all excesses may seem banal, but it has an advantage which the dramatic author in Shakespeare instinctively discovered, of not differing essentially from the natural cadence of spoken English, which is unmistakably iambic. . . .[68] Shakespeare thus resolves the difficult problem posed by the use of verse in the drama. The theater seeks to give an exact image of life, but the question is how to reconcile the truth of this image with a means of expression that is admittedly artificial, for when man laughs or suffers he does not express himself in verse. (73-4)

True enough—but the theater itself provides the answer—for an audience that pays to be entertained expects to see—not simply a reflection of the life they know—but one heightened by drama, graced with music, richly costumed, expressed in a language sweeter to the ear, more polished than what they hear at home or on the street,

---

[68] Was it so naturally—or did Shakespeare make it so that others then followed?

Educating Shakespeare

and more amusing than what they hear in church.

> There is another characteristic of Shakespeare's verse which I have not yet mentioned, for it is difficult to classify. . . . I mean the art with which [he] combines vowels and consonants so that an ineffable impression of harmony results. This is a quality precious above all others in dramatic writing; it permits an actor to speak his lines without effort, leaving him complete liberty for the stage action. (74 fn)

It was a quality left over from the oral tradition—from a time when books were preciously few, the centuries-long habit of listening to something being read aloud that with cheaper books and greater educational opportunities would become solitary reading in private.

Feuillerat goes on to describe how he achieved this through phrasing his sentences so that the action of the organs of speech—the tongue and lips—moved smoothly and effortlessly. Surely this is the closest thing to a description of how beautiful language functions on the physical level—as opposed to the millions of written and spoken speeches that must fail that test—both for speakers and for readers speaking them aloud in private, the better to relish their poetry.

Yet that, of course, is only part of Shakespeare's technique, for with the surface meaning often go other, deeper meanings. It's for this—beautiful language, concisely expressing deep and powerful thought—that readers have always turned to literature for comfort as well as pleasure. Shakespeare couldn't do this with every line, nor should he—there must be the *recicitore* leading into the *aria*—but he did it often, and he did it very very well. He did it best of course in his masterworks, those he revised from time to time—as his style continued to develop—adding philosophic touches to the energies of youth—changing a scene's ending—perhaps even an entire play's.

Feuillerat shows how the archaisms so plentiful in his earlier plays gradually get replaced with modern usage. *For to go* turns into "to go"—*he thinketh* into "he thinks"—*doth* into "does"—*hath* into "has"—*thee* into "you"—*thine* into "yours." Sometimes in a single work—even in a single paragraph—we hear both the old and the new. This may be evidence of revision—but sometimes perhaps because a change would damage the meter. The six quartos of *Richard III*—

published every few years between 1597 and 1612—show how his mind worked when there was an opportunity for further polishing.

When eventually the concept of Shakespeare has been totally freed from bondage to the Stratford time frame—scholars will find his evolving usage a rich field for study. Was he reflecting changes in the way people talked? Did people change the way they talked because of what they were hearing in the theater? Did he change it for his own poetic purposes—responding to a classically inspired love of condensation—packing as much meaning into as few syllables as possible? In other words—as his audiences changed the way they talked to each other—he changed the way his actors spoke to each other—which would surely have changed the way his audiences spoke to each other—thus changing how they thought. Thus did Shakespeare educate his audience in ways both subtle and effective.

Inkhorn terms

As poets continued to reach to the ancients for new words, a backlash developed that ridiculed words derived from French or Latin as "inkhorn terms." The inkhorn was the badge of a scrivener, a scribe, a professional secretary who went from client to client, carrying pens in a bag and his ink in an "inkhorn," a container made from an animal horn—slung from his shoulder on a leather strap—as he carried in his head those Latin terms required for his business. Such men had a bad reputation with the citizens because they were used by authorities to deliver orders to show up in court—plus other disagreeable matters.

The Calvinist authorities who launched the Elizabethan era by condemning color and variety in clothing and furnishings as tricks of the Devil also condemned the use of color and variety in language— but if Shakespeare was bothered by this reaction to the plethora of newfangled terms in which he so freely indulged, he doesn't show it —though he does have fun with it—particularly in *Love's Labour's Lost*. Encouraged perhaps by the *de Copia* of Erasmus—aware that good poetry requires a large vocabulary for variety and to meet the demands of meter—the spear-shaker was the most active word creator of any writer who ever lived.

Shakespeare's imagery

The first thing that strikes the thoughtful reader is his use of images. All agree that he used them more widely, more freely, even more bizarrely, than anyone else. As English Professor Caroline Spurgeon proves in her painstakingly detailed study, the greater percentage of Shakespeare's images derive from

> the life of the English countryside, the weather and its changes, the seasons, the sky, sunrise and dawn, the clouds, rain and wind, sunshine and shadow; the garden, flowers, trees, growth and decay, pruning and grafting, manuring and weeding; the sea and ships, the river and its banks, weeds and grasses, pools and water, animals, birds and insects, sport and games, especially snaring birds, hunting and hawking, these are the things which chiefly occupy him . (44)

Spurgeon notes that while sympathetic to horses, deer, rabbits and birds, he was afraid of wolves and boars, and disgusted by dogs and toads. He saw plants as sources of medicines and poisons, and was familiar with the sport of hawking (falconry). The world of the kitchen and the hearth, herbs and cooking, provided him with many of his favorite comparisons. Most notable always is his love of action and movement—

> The more we study these main groups of images which constitute the greatest part of Shakespeare's imagery, the clearer it becomes that there is one quality or characteristic in them all which overpoweringly attracts him throughout, and that quality is *movement*: nature and natural objects *in motion*. In other words, it is *the life of things* which appeals to him, stimulates and enchants him, rather than beauty or colour or form or even significance. (50)

She notes how "movement also dominates his sense of color"—

> the color itself of less importance than its changeability, how it contrasts with another color, or changes due to circumstance, and these in two particular cases, the changing colors of the human face as they express emotions, and the

Chapter II What Shakespeare Knew

changing colors of the rising sun. These are often conveyed, not by the name of the color, but by the comparison with something of a particular color, as showing a face turned pale by fear by comparing it to white things, like paper, linen or whey.

Movement dominates imagery drawn from the human body. "No one of the other dramatists approaches Shakespeare in the number and vividness of his images drawn from quick nimble action"—

> how constantly in description it is the aspect of movement or life he seizes upon and portrays, so that many of his most memorable . . . lines are charged with this quality . . . His use of verbs of movement is a study in itself, . . . by introducing verbs of movement about things which are motionless, or rather which are abstractions . . . he gives life to the whole" as in "I *stole* all courtesy from heaven, and *dressed* myself in such humility, that I did *pluck* allegiance from men's hearts."

Spurgeon's purpose

Spurgeon claims in her introduction that it was primarily to put a stop to the questioning of Shakespeare's identity that she took on the immense task of naming and categorizing every image in the canon her final purpose to prove that his origins were in Stratford.[69]

Spurgeon held that his images from books "amount to curiously few among the mass which are derived from direct observation by the senses—facts learnt from books, or hearsay which he can never have seen or heard" (45). But what she missed is that Shakespeare's erudition is revealed through stories available only in Latin or Greek. As for his images, these were more likely to come from things his audiences will recognize—whatever their social class or setting.

However he uses them, whether directly, or metaphorically—they are simply the means by which he brings to life the evidence of

---

[69] As she explains, the purpose of her book was to put an end to efforts to give the authorship to Bacon or Marlowe. By making an issue of their differences, she was largely responsible for the defeat of both these theories (though Marlowe continues to be resurrected by the academically confused).

his erudition—the seduction of Adonis, the rape of Lucrece, the treasons of Brutus and Richard III. How better to create disgust for Crookback Dick than to compare him to spiders and toads—nasty things familiar to lords and groundlings alike? How better to express the effect of Juliet's beauty on Romeo than to compare it to the light of dawn after a long, dark night? Before electricity or gas lamps—nights at 50 degrees north latitude could seem very long and very dark—to everyone, lords and commoners alike.

It's this "aspect of movement or life" that gives the clue to Shakespeare's use of imagery—which is to bring to life for his 16th-century audiences stories buried in the Middle English of Chaucer, the Greek of Euripides, the Italian of Ariosto—stories enacted by men walking about on a platform whose only tools are their costumes, their gestures, and the words he's put in their mouths.

Spurgeon misses his references to literature for the same reason that so many academics miss them—not because they're not there—but because *they're not looking for them!*

Stylistic clues to Shakespeare's dates

We have seen how—by adhering to dates that support the Stratford biography—the Academy has eliminated those plays from the 1580s or earlier that bear the marks of his unique style—and in so doing have rejected what for any other author would be readily accepted as his *juvenilia*. A collection of these—*The Shakespeare Apocrypha*, published by Tucker Brooke in 1908—provides fourteen—since then others have been added. By allowing these seminal works to move to where their plots and characters connect to historical events and individuals—we can begin to examine them for genuine evidence of how his style continued to develop over time.

Clues that can help determine which of these early plays are his are—1) frequent disguisings of all sorts, such as girls disguised as youths or noble youths disguised as their servants—2) young people falling in love at first sight—3) love first felt and expressed silently through eye contact—4) legal, medical, and astrological puns, metaphors and proverbs—5) Italian names and locations—6) women compared to peregrine falcons—7) wit battles as a volley of rhyming

Chapter II What Shakespeare Knew

couplets—8) gentlemen and lords speaking rhythmically in meter while servants and yokels speak in prose—9) action verbs—10) scenes that end with rhyming couplets—11) internal debates (soliloquies)—12) two plots woven together—13) histories based on Holinshed's sources—14) plots from Greek romances, Golding's version of Ovid's *Metamorphoses, Painters Pallace of Pleasure,* or works attributed to John Lyly, Robert Greene, Thomas Lodge, Barnabe Riche, George Pettie, or George Gascoigne. Any of these 14 factors strongly suggests early Shakespeare. Only one or two? maybe not. More than that? probably. Over half—without a doubt!

What fostered this idiosyncratic style? First and foremost a great deal of reading. Although the basics of a grammar school education can't be discounted—what made Shakespeare unique had largely to do with the works that he read—either during his formative childhood years, spent—as Spurgeon's research suggests—in a country setting. Yet even these can't explain the important differences between his style and that of close contemporaries like Philip Sidney, Francis Bacon, Christopher Marlowe or Ben Jonson—the few whose reading would have been similar to his.[70]

~~ Shakespeare and Coleridge ~~

> The time . . . that a person requires . . . to penetrate a work of any depth is merely an epitome of the years, the centuries even, that must elapse before the public can begin to recognize a masterpiece . . . . a man of genius, to shelter himself . . . may say to himself that, since one's contemporaries are incapable of the necessary detachment, works written for posterity should be read by posterity alone.
>
> *Within a Budding Grove*

Proust continues to develop his point, namely that the public cannot comprehend the status of a genius upon first contact—they must be

---

[70] These are useful only where their styles have been properly defined. Many works have been wrongly ascribed to writers like Gascoigne and Marlowe because the academics have never bothered to define their native styles or concerns.

Educating Shakespeare

led to it gradually over generations. Thus there's no point in waiting until the public is ready—because it is the work itself, and only that—which will teach them why, and how, to appreciate it.

Despite the admiration of writers like Alexander Pope and Samuel Johnson—it was not until the dawn of the nineteenth century that a fellow poet introduced Shakespeare to the world as the icon of Literature that he remains to this day. This was Samuel Taylor Coleridge (1772-1834)—known to most as the author of *The Rime of the Ancient Mariner*. Where critics saw the plays as separate works, Coleridge saw them as an organic whole—each a branch of a single great work. As a poet himself, Coleridge took it as his major task to pass this vision on to his friends and fellow poets.

Coleridge was a harbinger for the next great epoch in English literature following the Augustans—roughly the last decade of the eighteenth century to the first of the nineteenth. In an arc that tends to repeat throughout literary history—(and that we can only pray will come again someday)—the *Age of Reason* under Pope and Swift gave way to the *Romantic Era* under Keats and Shelley—whose lives and personalities were almost as important to their readers as their poetry. Byron, Keats and Shelley were the heroes—or antiheroes—of their own works (and sometimes of each others works)—works that were the products, not of just their imaginations—but of lives lived wildly and creatively. Lives that tended to end early—and tragically.

Much as Mendelssohn—another genius from that era—would resurrect Bach for his colleagues and audiences—it was Coleridge's self-appointed task to use Shakespeare to inspire poets like Byron—who would quote him at every turn—to Keats, who clearly worshipped him—to Wordsworth and De Quincy—and also to the great romantic actors of the mid-to-late nineteenth century—who turned from the bowdlerized and sentimentalized Shakespeare of the eighteenth century to give the fullest possible expression to the passions inherent in his works as he first created them.

Because it was in the lecture hall that his genius blossomed, little remains of Coleridge beyond notes—scribbled to himself in advance and published post mortem by his nephew—or noted by listeners like John Payne Collier during his lectures. But clearly what he said—and how he said it—had a profound effect on the literary life

Chapter II What Shakespeare Knew

of London—and on how the world has seen Shakespeare ever since.

Psychologist Meg Harris Williams relates how Keats met the aging Coleridge by chance during the spring of 1819 while walking with a friend on Hampstead Heath. Noting that it was during the weeks following this encounter that Keats produced *La Belle Dame Sans Merci* and all but one of his Odes—she writes of the many accounts of the musical quality of Coleridge's voice, how it flowed like a river—and of the arresting nature of his expressive gaze—which caused contemporaries to compare him to his own Ancient Mariner. Coleridge seems to have held his audiences "spellbound"—whether in private or the lecture halls. As William Hazlitt would put it—"His mind was clothed with wings."

It may be that it was by means of this direct connection with a live audience that Coleridge was able to create a space somewhere between Page and Stage where his charismatic presence could move listeners past the dry distinctions of print. Drawing on ideas from Adam Smith and German philosophers Kant and Shlegel (Foakes 11)—he refused to judge his subject by any standards but those Shakespeare created for himself. In so doing he brought new dignity —not only to the great playwright—but to the entire Elizabethan era, which, to Samuel Johnson and the Augustans, had been "struggling to emerge from barbarity"—but which Coleridge and his successors saw as one of inspiring artistic advancement.

Coleridge was the first to propose that audiences contributed to the theater experience through "a willing suspension of disbelief." His instinct told him that *Love's Labour's Lost* was one of Shakespeare's earliest plays. Opposing the popular view that the "Swan of Avon" was uneducated—it was obvious to him that his hero was "well-read" and that his mockery of Holofernes was hardly that of an unlettered know-nothing. Recognizing the magnitude of Shakespeare's reading —Coleridge was so dismayed by the Stratford story that he accused early biographers Nicholas Rowe and Anthony á Wood of *lying!*

Until Coleridge—Shakespeare criticism resembled the way a man might describe one acquaintance to another—praise tempered by reality, his good points balanced by his faults. With Coleridge it became all right to sound like a lover. And this has been the great dichotomy ever since—the mere friends, Dryden and Johnson—the great lovers, Swinburne, Frank Harris, G. Wilson Knight, Harold Bloom, even Ben Jonson, who—for all his hedging, when push came to shove—cried out that he loved him—"this side idolatry!"

It was Coleridge's lot to raise Shakespeare to the stars while rooted himself to the dull and heavy earth. As Meg Williams puts it,

> Perhaps it was his fate to have been more of a prophet for poetry than a poet in himself (as he lamented); but one result of this was that he brought Shakespeare into the lives of subsequent generations in a way that has undoubtedly revolutionized our cultural perceptions. (4)

As day follows night—a romantic period like the one initiated by Coleridge has generally followed a period of cynicism and nitpicking. The Augustans had sought to tidy up the bad taste and gallimaufry of the Restoration by observing rules inherited from the ancients—chiefly in the arenas of subject and satire. What might be seen as the catchwork of the period—Alexander Pope's mock heroic *Rape of the Lock*—shows the spirit of his age by the very fact that Pope focused all his poetic intelligence, wit and style on a lock of hair! And although Dr. Johnson provided the world with a bigger and better Shakespeare—it was not without the quibbles that his time required.

With the coming of the Romantics—critiques like these were swept away by a great wave of emotion—a fascination with the lives of men like Byron, Keats, and Shelley—the dramas of their loves and deaths. Weary of drawing room conventionality and brittle wit, a new generation of readers craved tears and laughter. Thus—through the efforts of Coleridge, Hazlitt, Charles and Mary Lamb and the great actors of the day—once again the English were provided with the full range of Shakespeare's operatic emotions.

From the depths of Lear's and Othello's remorse to the ecstasies of Juliet and Cleopatra—the bawdy puns and double negatives that so distressed the Augustans were overwhelmed by the sheer panoply of life that was his art—demonstrated through the beauties of his language and his vast and sympathetic understanding of the human heart.

So we see that by ignoring the Stratford biography and all the limitations that it imposes—by dealing directly with those plays and

Chapter II What Shakespeare Knew

poems that from the start have been accepted as his by all but the most confused "experts"—the ignorant Shakespeare vanishes like an Arabian Nights genie back into the little black bottle kept tightly corked by the university philologists. What remains for those of the rest of us who care about truth and poetry is an individual with an astonishing knowledge of the Law, both English (Common) and Roman (Civil)—of Plato and the Greek dramatists—of English and Roman history and literature—of works in ancient Greek and Latin, contemporary French and Italian—of classical grammar, proverbs and sententiae—of scientific and medical knowledge.

But while these require the kind and number of books and years of study that's been so difficult to account for with the Stratford biography—there are other kinds of knowledge that are almost as challenging. This brings us to those areas of Shakespeare's learning determined less by the books he read than by his environment, the world that surrounded him—his audience, their pastimes, beliefs, and what they knew, or believed, about their contemporaries at home and abroad. How did he come to know so much about Italy, about the cities along the shores of the Mediterranean, about the wars being fought with the Turks by Christian states and cities hundreds of miles from England by sailors and soldiers speaking other languages than English? How did he come to know so much about the world beyond his homeland, a world known only to traders with access to sailing ships built to explore trade routes to and through the Mediterranean, and to to brave the Atlantic Ocean in search of fishing grounds in and around Newfoundland and—they dreamed—of the path through the upper reaches of the New World, near Newfoundland, that they hoped would be an easier passage to India than the present nightmare involved in sailing "around the Horn," the tip of South Africa.

Detail from Sandro Botticelli's famous painting "The Birth of Venus" which mythology places off the Italian coast of the Adriatic.

CHAPTER III

~~ Shakespeare in His Own Time ~~

Shakespeare was fascinated with Italy. Over half of his plays took place somewhere in Italy or are based on Italian stories. Because there is no evidence that the illiterate William ever travelled further from Stratford than Oxford and London, the Academy has been focussed for several hundred years on the mistakes he must have made in portraying Italy, but as two independent scholars have proven beyond all rational argument—all the mistakes so far have been made by the Academy. As Ernesto Grillo, professor of Italian Language and Literature at the University of Glasgow from 1925 to 1940 put it—

> The various scenes of *Othello* are no mere Venetian reminiscences, but pictures exhaling the very spirit of Venice. . . . the darkness of morning, the narrow and mysterious *calli* [streets], Brabantio's house with his heavy iron-barred doors, the *Sagittary*, the official residence of the commanders of the galleys, . . . the divine Desdemona, fair and beautiful as a Titian portrait. (*Shakespeare and Italy*)

And again—

> The plots of sixteen Shakespearean plays are to be found in Italian fiction; while others . . . contain much of the life, customs and art of Italy. The works translated into English were representative of all the best known Italian writers on every subject. . . . Of all foreign influences which contributed to the formation of taste and thought in the England of the glorious Elizabethan epoch, the Italian was undoubtedly the most conspicuous and far-reaching.

Most of the stories in *Painter's Palace* and other early anthologies that fed the imaginations of Shakespeare and his fellow poets and playwrights, were Italian in origin—ancient Roman historians like

Educating Shakespeare

Titus Livius and Quintus Curtius, poets and playwrights like Terence, recent playwrights like Machiavelli and Ariosto, storytellers like Boccaccio, Cinthio, and Bandello. Few of these were available in English (or French) in Elizabeth's time. All of which caused Grillo to ask in his final chapter—"Did Shakespeare know Italian?"

> It seems as if Shakespeare must somehow or other have learned enough Italian to read and understand our writers. Dramatic personae, like Mercutio for example, cannot avoid the Italian linguistic forms which Shakespeare employs with great ability and success. The greeting between Hortensio and Petruchio (*Shrew* I.2) is exchanged in two or three lines of pure Italian, Petruccio, "Signior Hortensio, come you to part the fray? *Con tutto il core, ben trovato,*' may I say. Hortensio, '*All nostra casa ben venuto, molto honorato signor mio, Petrucio.*'" (125-6)

Further questions arise from his familiarity with the Italian landscape, traditions, proverbs, colloquialisms, and cities—

> It has been argued that in Elizabethan England translations of Italian books abounded, but certainly Shakespeare's knowledge of life and customs in Italy was not entirely derived from them. In his lifetime some of the books to which he was indebted for much of his material had not been translated into English. In the collection of tales by Ser Giovanni Fiorentino entitled *Il Pecorone* we find the whole plot of the *Merchant of Venice* . . . in the *Hecatomithi* of Cinthio . . . the story of *Othello* . . . the adventures of Isabella . . in *Measure for Measure*. Many of Cinthio's novelle had been translated into French, but the tragic tale of *Othello* was to be found in neither French nor English.

Frequently whole lines are translated literally from Italian "without the slightest alteration." In *Two Gents* we hear "sound as a fish"—the phrase "'*sano come un pesce*' being an expression still in common use in his time in Italy." *Traghetto*—signifying an anchorage for gondolas—appears in *The Merchant of Venice* as "tranect."

Himself a descendant of the ancient Gonzago family, Grillo was

III Shakespeare in His Own Time

educated in Italy at a Catholic seminary before embarking on studies at the University of Bonn in Germany, and at St. John's Cambridge in England before he became Department Head of Italian Language and Literature at the University of Glasgow where he published scholarly works in Latin and created the first ever degree program in Comparative Lit at a northern European university. Grillo knew, as English-speaking academics did not (and still don't) that

> Italy with its public and private life, its laws and customs, its ceremonial and other characteristics, pulsates in every line of our dramatist, while the atmosphere of many scenes is Italian in the truest sense of the word. We cannot but wonder how Shakespeare obtained such accurate information, and we have no hesitation in affirming that . . . he must have visited Italy . . . . In *Taming of the Shrew, The Merchant of Venice, Measure for Measure, Twelfth Night* and *Othello* . . . we find such definite characteristics, such local color and such a wealth of precise and vigorous details that we are forced to conclude that Shakespeare must have visited Milan, Verona, Venice, Padua and Mantua. (132)

He could have added Florence from *All's Well that Ends Well*, Genoa from *Merchant of Venice*, and Messina from *The Winter's Tale*.

The local colour of *Taming of the Shrew* displays such an intimate acquaintance—not only with the manners and customs of Italy, but also with the minutest details of domestic life. "The description of Gremio's house and furnishings is striking because it represents an Italian villa of the sixteenth century with its comforts and luxury"—

> My hangings all of Tyrian tapestry;
> In ivory coffers I have stuffed my crowns;
> In cypress chests my arras, counterpoints,
> Costly apparel, tents, and canopies,
> Fine linen, Turkey cushions boss'd with pearl,
> Valance of Venice gold in needlework,
> Pewter and brass, and all things that belong
> To house or housekeeping.

Says Grillo—"these magnificent *objets d'art* were only to be found in Italy, in the palaces of the aristocracy of Milan, Genoa, Turin, Pavia, etc., since living conditions in England were very primitive and not even Elizabeth's courtiers could boast of possessing such refinements" (137). While England's trade with the East was just beginning—trade with India and China had been bringing goods for many years from all over the world to Genoa and Venice. Shakespeare did not learn this from books. The only way he could have known it was to have seen it for himself.

Says Grillo of *The Merchant of Venice*—"The topography is so precise and accurate that it must convince even the most superficial reader that the poet visited the country." He notes the exactitude of the distance between Monte Bello (Belmont) and Padua—20 miles according to Shakespeare—20 miles today (137). He notes how, like Portia, the lawyers and jurists of the Middle Ages and Renaissance would travel around the cities of Italy—putting their counsel at the disposal of the public, deciding lawsuits and giving judgments in commercial and civil cases.

As Grillo points out—"He knew that Padua with all its learning was under the protection of Venice and that Mantua was not." He knew that Pisa was renowned for her wealth, her avarice, and her "grave citizens"—and that Florence was known for her merchants and mathematicians. In *All's Well* he describes the long conflict between the Florentines and the Sienese with a phrase that's "pure Italian, namely that the Florentines are "by the ear" with the Sienese —"*si pigliano per gli orecchi.*"

Grillo was able to clarify Malvolio's comment in *Twelfth Night* when the foolish steward dreams of winning the heart of his mistress —for, after all, says Malvolio, "the Lady of the Stratchy married the yeoman of the wardrobe." Says Grillo, "Strachy" comes from the Italian *stracci*, meaning rags—thus "the Lady of the Strachy" is an English version of the Italian *la Signora degli Stracci*—"a sarcasm still common in many parts of Italy as an allusion to a lady poor but haughty." According to his editor, Grillo was alone

> in making the suggestion that Shakespearean drama displayed an acquaintance with the Italian scene and an insight into the Italian soul that could only have been gained from a personal

knowledge of the country, its people, and literature. There was at the time little concrete evidence to support this suggestion.

Enter Richard Roe

In the late 1990s the American lawyer, Richard Paul Roe, longtime resident of Pasadena, California and graduate of UC Berkeley—set out to prove to himself that Shakespeare must have known Italy at first hand. Roe carried with him a handful of maps and travel guides, a camera, and a dog-eared copy of the plays with place names underlined—as he sought to locate the actual scenes and places where Shakespeare based his stories. In 2011, his daughter, Hilary Roe Metternich, published a luxurious edition of her father's account—replete with maps, prints and photographs. Roe's feat of literary forensics proves (again) that the author must have seen these places, and that—unlike his critics—he knew what he was talking about.

Roe begins his book in "fair" Verona, where Romeo's mother, Lady Montague, asks Benvolio if he knows her son's whereabouts. Benvolio's answer—that just before dawn, driven by "a troubled mind" to take a walk—he'd seen his friend within "the grove of sycamores that westward rooteth from the city's side." On the wildest of chances that trees described 400 years ago might still be thriving in the genial Italian climate—Roe found his way to the western gate —saw sycamores in that very spot (10)—and took the pictures of them we see in his book—*Shakespeare Guide to Italy* (2011).

In Italian versions of the story—Juliet is ordered by her father to meet the County Paris at "Villafranca"—when translated means "Freetown"—which is what Arthur Brooke called it in his 1562 narrative poem (11)—long regarded as the major source for Shakespeare's version, and what Shakespeare calls it when he has Prince Escalus order the warring capos to appear before him at Court.

So what was "Freetown"—what was Villafranca—and who was Prince Escalus? All three are historical—Escalus is Latin for *della Scala*—in English, the Scaliger family, rulers of Verona and its surrounding territories during the Middle Ages—while Villafranca, or Freetown—three hours ride by horse from Verona—is the fortress that was once the administrative center of their domain.

Educating Shakespeare

Roe's efforts to track Romeo and Juliet were less complicated than many of his searches since both were real individuals whose story is still being told in Verona—so their homes were easily located. Also located without difficulty was Friar's Laurence's monastery, where important scenes take place, among them the lovers' marriage and deaths. Less easy to find was St. Peter's Church—where Juliet was supposed to marry Paris—but this too he was able to locate, not far from both her home and the Friar's monastery (18).

Two Gentlemen of Verona

While most of the places and characters in *Romeo and Juliet* are accepted as real, the same is not true of Valentine and Proteus—the two gents of the title. As Roe points out, "Critics say it has an absurd Italy, with seacoasts and harbors that never existed, and historical events that never happened." But Shakespeare knew better.

The first question has to do with how the young men get to Milan from Verona—both inland cities—located a distant 160 kilometers apart. As the play begins, Valentine is saying goodbye to his friend—"Once more adieu; my father at the road expects my coming, there to see me shipp'd." Roe points out that by "road," Valentine meant anchorage or port—while "shipped" meant *sent by water*. Today we use the term for transporting anything by any means—but the word *ship* shows its origin. According to Roe—

> Since Roman times, Verona was a city of major importance as a center to shipping, serving traffic, trade and travelers going through the Brenner Pass above it. By means of the Adige River, one could sail to and from it to many cities in Italy. One could also sail from Verona—through the mouth of the Adige, and reach the Adriatic arm of the Mediterranean Sea, and thence to the rest of the world. (38)

Clearly Valentine and later Proteus "shipped" from Verona by water —but how could this have taken them to Milan, located inland, with no connecting river? The place in Verona from which Valentine and later Proteus departed was easy—the vast quay just downstream from the great stone Ponte Navi (Ship Bridge), which—though destroyed

III Shakespeare in His Own Time

in World War II—had 'been captured on canvas by painters in the eighteenth century. But the river here flowed east—so how did they get to Milan—located many kilometers to the west? However they got there, they must have come by water—since Proteus, having just arrived in Act II Scene 4—greets Valentine, saying "Go on before. . . . I must unto the road [quay], to disembark some necessaries."

The problem for modern critics arises in large part from not understanding terms like *road* and *shipped*—partly from his mention of *tides*, which to travellers then meant more than just water levels—but mostly from the assumption that people travelled then as they do now—on land. In fact most people then preferred—whenever and wherever they could—to travel by water, whether on the sea, or inland, on rivers—and where there were no rivers, by barge on man made canals that then, and for another two centuries, were created to connect the major inland towns and cities of Europe—which is, of course, how the Two Gents got to Milan.

Another "mistake" that Roe investigated was the "Emperor's Court" to which—in Act I Scene 3—Panthino urges Antonio to send his son Proteus so that he may, like Valentine, who has gone before —"practice tilts and tournaments, hear sweet discourse, converse with noblemen, and be in the eye of every exercise worthy of his youth and nobleness of birth." The problem for the historians has been the fact that there was no "Emperor's Court" in Milan—where there was never a governor greater than a duke. Nevertheless, as Roe discovered with a little investigation—there was in fact an Emperor who just happened to be in Milan at the time depicted in the play.

It appears that in 1533, Holy Roman Emperor Charles V—having established his dominion over all of Italy—had accepted an invitation from Milan's Duke Francesco to receive his oath of fealty in the Duke's home city. Milan and all its surrounding towns prepared for a magnificent welcoming ceremony. Federico Gonzaga—Duke of Mantua (Shakespeare's inspiration for Old Hamlet)—had his Court artist, Julio Romano, design an imperial arch of triumph to welcome the Emperor and his retinue.

The Emperor arrived, accepted the Duke's oath, and enjoyed the welcoming festivities for three days. Setting out with his retinue on the morning of the fourth for what was understood would be a few

Educating Shakespeare

days of hunting—they never returned. It seems the Emperor and his company had simply continued heading back to their home in Spain—an embarrassment forgotten by everyone but the Milanese (64-71).

The bit that required some real digging was from Act V Scene 2, the mention of a "St. Gregory's Well"—to which Proteus directs Thurio, who is searching for his lover Silvia, for whom Proteus has conceived a naughty passion. Roe managed to locate where the church of St. Gregory once stood—on the verge of the immense lot outside the city that had been the site of the *lazzaretto* where the Milanese quarantined their plague victims.

But according to its priest, the church had never had a well, and, apart from one Italian, who recalled that the phrase "il pozzo di San Gregorio" was—according to her grandmother—"a synonym for Hell"—no one had any idea of what was meant by "St. Gregory's well." With time came the answer—by the "well" was meant the great hole dug in the churchyard of San Gregorio where the dead plague victims were dumped by the thousands during the sixteenth century plague—a hellish place—but just the sort where a malicious youth might send a rival for a pretty girl's affections (72-84).

Taming of the Shrew

After carefully tracing exactly how Lucentio got from Pisa to Padua by means of the rivers and canals in operation at that time—Roe hoped to locate where they disembarked. Clued by Lucentio's opening lines—"If, Biondello, thou wert come ashore, we could at once put us in readiness and take a lodging fit to entertain . . ." (94).

From the "at once" Roe suspected that the hostelry where they took rooms would have been somewhere close to the place where they disembarked. And since Baptista Minola and his daughters reveal that they too live nearby—Roe thought he might actually locate both. This became even more likely once he located St. Luke's—the church where Biondello tells us that Lucentio will marry Bianca. Since marriages then took place in the bride's parish church—this placed the hostelry and the Minola household within the same parish as the quay. The little Church lay just inside Padua's medieval wall—

Making my way through that arch, I found myself staring at

III Shakespeare in His Own Time

the setting of Act I Scene 1 of *The Taming of the Shrew*. . . . To this very day the entire layout before my eyes possesses all the elements that exactly fit the describing dialogues in that opening scene: a waterway (now narrowed by centuries of cast rubble); a landing place, quay, or road where a boat could tie up (now reduced to a narrow ledge); a bridge across that waterway, connecting both to a street with a Saint Luke's Church nearby and a wide space with a cluster of buildings.

As Roe puts it—"Still on that bridge, turning slowly, taking in the full circle sweep of the utter reality of all that the playwright described, I knew in a rush that I was standing exactly where the author of *Taming of the Shrew* had stood four centuries before me."

The Merchant of Venice

With *Merchant*, Roe began by investigating the "mistakes" noted by the experts who write the notes to editions of the play. Again, a single word caught Roe's attention. In Act II Scene 6, Gratiano and Salerio, disguised as maskers, are in the Ghetto discussing their plot to help Jessica rob her father so she can elope with Lorenzo. Says Gratiano— "This is the penthouse under which Lorenzo desired us make a stand." In Shakespeare's time, a *penthouse* was a small building appended to a larger building. As Roe discovered, there was only one such building in the Ghetto then—located next door to one of the loan banks that under Venetian law were restricted to the Jewish quarter —which was, of course, where Shylock would most likely to be found.[71] (139) "Eureka!" Roe had found it!

A Midsummer Night's Dreame

While on his way from Verona to Florence—Roe made a two-day stopover in Mantua to see the frescos and statues at the Palazzo de Te—designed by Julio Romano, mentioned by Shakespeare in *The*

---

[71] Lorenzo was forced to borrow from Shylock since usury—making money from lending money—was forbidden to Catholics.

Winter's Tale—and described by Lucrece in his "graver labour."[72] While there he was persuaded by another traveler to spend a day in the nearby town of *Sabbionetta*. Ruled in the sixteenth century by Vespasiano Gonzaga—a member of the same family that controlled Mantua (and that would inspire some of *Hamlet*[73])—Vespasiano was enamored of architecture based on the *de Architectura* by the ancient Roman architect Vitruvius—a book he kept with him at all times.

> Some of the buildings in Sabbionetta were originally commodious quarters for the duke's invited guests, his pleasure having been in inviting the erudite among both Italy's and other western Europe's nobility and intelligentsia for a visit to his model city. While there they would admire his rich collections of paintings and sculpture and take part in the festivities, salons, and scholarly lectures that he sponsored during his lifetime. (182)

After explaining what to the Duke and his friends was known as "Little Athens"—Roe's tour guide mentioned that the passageway through the great town gate was known as "il Quercia dei Duca," meaning, "the Duke's Oak." Roe was transfixed! Who but himself among the group would recall that in *A Midsummer Night's Dreame* it was "in the palace wood" at "the Duke's Oak" that Peter Quince instructs the rude mechanicals that they must rehearse *Pyramis and Thisbe!* The passageway with this interesting name led—not to a particular tree—but to an oak forest, the Duke's hunting preserve, where, in Shakespeare's imagination, Oberon will clash with Titania —and Bottom will have his comedic "translation."

Thus—through sheer serendipity—Roe found himself on the very spot where Shakespeare imagined his masterpiece taking place. It told him as well that the play was located—not in Greece, but in Italy—in Vespasiano Gonzaga's "little Athens."[74]

---

[72] Julio Romano is the only painter that Shakespeare mentions by name.
[73] And that in the 20th century produced Ernesto Grillo.
[74] Native Italian Noemi Magri provides more information on this in *Such Fruits out of Italy*.

III Shakespeare in His Own Time

All's Well that Ends Well

Though *All's Well* takes place mostly in France—Roe had reason to believe that the eight scenes in Florence were based on personal experience. His first clue was Bertram's response to the French King's command that he marry Helen, his father's ward, a commoner, to which he mutters—"I'll to the Tuscan wars and never bed her!" What Tuscan wars? The clue to that comes in Act I Scene 2, where the King comments to his companions—"The Florentines and Senoys (inhabitants of Siena, just south of Florence) . . . continue a braving war." At what point in these wars does the play take place? It couldn't be later than 1555, when Florence—after centuries of fighting—had finally conquered Siena. Since that occurred during the brief reign of Henri II—he must be the King who orders Bertram to marry Helen.

Act III Scene 5 provides the clues that make it certain that the author knew Florence at first hand. Helen—determined to get her man—has set out to track Bertram to his Italian lair. Disguised as a religious pilgrim—she has travelled on foot from one religious hostelry to another. Arriving in Florence at the same time that Bertram's company is announced with tuckets, she asks the Widow of the City and her friends, "Where do the palmers (pilgrims) lodge?" The Widow's response provides the necessary clue—"At the Saint Francis here beside the port"—doubtless a hostelry for religious pilgrims run by the Franciscans—possibly still in existence?

Having determined what was meant by "the port"—and by which gate to the city a company returning from the war with Siena would have entered—Roe figured their goal would have been the Fortezza da Basso, home for the Florentine military. Following Bertram's company's most likely route through the city to the place where the Widow and her friends must stand to see the troops pass—

> I positioned myself around the Piazza Goldoni and looked this way and that. Then I had it. All the elements fit. Were Widow to stand at the corner of the Piazza Goldoni and the Borgo Ognissanti, she could both view the oncoming parade and direct Helen. In that exact spot, by pointing her index finger, Widow could . . . inform her that the pilgrim lodge was "here beside the Port."

But where was the Saint Francis hostel—and could he actually hope to find it after the 400 years between Shakespeare and himself?

Before leaving America Roe had sought assistance from a Franciscan monk who provided him with a sketch of their traditional insignia. Long story short, he found it—right where Shakespeare said it would be—"a plain building with a large door"—and "embedded directly above it . . . the sign of Saint Francis—exactly where it had been ever since the building changed hands in the late sixteenth century" (211).

The Tempest

The Tempest is arguably Shakespeare's most important play—at least from a historical perspective. There must be a reason it was chosen to lead off the 1623 first edition—which, if its history is any clue, may mean it was the most popular of his plays during the rise to glory of the great Second Blackfriars Theater in the first decades of the seventeenth century. Rife with allusions to overseas discoveries by Europeans during the first burst of explorations—it seems to have been regularly updated with allusions to each as he heard the news.

Poised at the jumping off point on the verge of the Atlantic—a long history of ship building and fishing off Newfoundland had put England at the forefront of all the nations of Europe (but Portugal) when it came to such discoveries. Yet Shakespeare places his version in the Mediterranean at a time when Italy was the jumping off point for English vessels facing the Turks along the ancient trade routes to India and China. It's a jumping off point in Literature as well—beginning with Virgil's description of the return of Aeneas from the Trojan War—its opening scene a recreation of the nightmare faced by travellers heading west as they were forced to squeeze through the tiny passage between the toe of the Italian boot and the northern tip of Sicily.

It may be that nothing in Shakespeare Studies has aroused so much discussion and dispute as the question of what island Shakespeare had in mind when creating *The Tempest*. Roe believes it was *Vulcano*—the small volcanic island near Sicily where he found so many similarities to Shakespeare's descriptions that it's impossible to

III Shakespeare in His Own Time

dismiss it as having contributed at least some of its characteristics to Prospero's magical isle.

The southernmost of the eight tiny Aeolian islands—named by the Greeks for their God of the Winds—Vulcano is just west of the Straits of Messina where turbulent currents create the deadly whirlpool that the Greeks demonized as *Charybdis*. In attempting to avoid the monster who would suck ships fathoms deep, drowning all on board—those that chose to stick close to the rocky Italian shore risked being smashed to bits by the six-headed monster within its windy cliffs known as Scylla—as Virgil portrayed it centuries earlier in telling the story of how Aeneas returned from the Trojan War.

Clearly Shakespeare knew its deadly reputation when he opens his great fantasy with his most elaborately described shipwreck— soon revealed as nothing more than an illusion created by the great magician Prospero, former Duke of Milan, exiled to the island by his evil brother. Presented by Fate with a gang of his old enemies on their way home from a wedding in Tunis—he sets out to revenge himself on the conspirators who twelve years earlier had set him and his little daughter Miranda adrift on the sea.

Roe saw Vulcano as the original of the stinking bog described in Act II Scene 3 in which the drunken conspirators get mired. Described by Shakespeare as a "foul lake," a "filthy-mantled pool" that smells like horse piss—Roe sees this in the steaming mud pools he saw on Vulcano, covered with a foul-smelling sulphuric yellow crust—suggesting Ariel's description of its beaches made of "yellow sands." In Act I Scene 2, where Miranda's description of the sky— pouring down "stinking pitch" while the turbulent sea, "mounting to the welkins cheek, dashes the fire out"—perfectly describes the *fumeroles* that still send molten sulphur into the air, where, bursting into flame, they are immediately quenched by gushing waves.

The "noises" that "give delight and hurt not" he attributes to the volcano—noises Virgil long ago described as "groaning, hissing, pounding and panting." As for the name *Caliban*, it turns out that— in Catalan, an ancient language spoken in all the islands of the western Mediterranean—a *caliban* is an "outcast, or pariah," while *Ariel* means "mischievous air or water spirit."

Much Ado about Nothing

In bringing to life the romantic pairings of *Much Ado*, Shakespeare chose to place them at a particular place and a particular moment in history. Surely the prince who enters victorious from some great battle represents the famous Marcantonio Colonna who in 1571 commanded the Papal forces that helped to defeat the Turks at the historic Battle of Lepanto—the victory that brought security to Venice, and that—for England, opened the eastern half of the Mediterranean to trade with India, a trip that until then required sailing "around the Horn," the turbulent sea at the tip of South Africa.

Clearly it's this victory—historically the very moment when the Christian West stopped the Ottoman Turks in their westward surge—that Shakespeare's characters are celebrating in this joyous play. Colonna's importance is evident from the fact that it was in the harbor at Messina that the Christian army gathered the forces that would confront the Turkish fleet. That the history behind this play has never interested the Academy is no surprise. How could the ignorant Shakespeare have known or cared about events taking place at such a distance in time—from a home so far from the sea?

As one of the major turning points in European history, the Battle of Lepanto on October 1571 was the subject of hundreds of paintings and engravings now in the museums and archives of Italy.

All of Europe recognized, and continues to recognize, the hero of that battle, the masterful leader of the Christian forces, Don John of Austria. Like his half-brother Philip II, King of Spain, John was the son of the great and powerful Holy Roman Emperor Charles V—but unfortunately for the great Don, while his brother was the son of a Queen, which allowed his father to make him King of Spain—John's mother was only his father's mistress. This meant that unlike his rather unattractive brother, the Don was famously handsome, but it did nothing to guarantee him anything more important to do than command one of his father's armies. As King of Spain, his brother Philip saw to it that the Don never got any real opportunities for success. With all of Christian Europe blazoning his military might—his statue still dominates the central plaza in Messina in Sicily.

III Shakespeare in His Own Time

A small section of one of the many huge illustrations of the Battle of Lepanto. This by Martin Rota.

Don John of Austria, Mozart's Don Giovanni

Why does Shakespeare cast the great Don as the mean-spirited villain of *Much Ado About Nothing*? Surely it was because—following his great victory at Lepanto—he was sent by his father to strengthen the Spanish troops in the Lowlands War, where—had he prevailed—he would have taken the fight to England, made himself King, and married Queen Elizabeth—which, despite her fondness for handsome men—was simply out of the question. In the event it seems the Don died in his early thirties of a fever—leaving the world not only the

III Shakespeare in His Own Time

record of his military successes—but his even more famous record as a serial seducer of noblewomen—as would be memorialized centuries later by Mozart in the opera *Don Giovanni*.

Shakespeare's knowledge of the Mediterranean

It's fairly easy to track the path of Shakespeare's travels from the locations of his Italian plays. Taking off from Venice in a coastal galley, he would first have sailed north along the coast—past Trieste (then Bohemia)—then south down the coast of Dalmatia (Croatia) where Perdita is lost in *A Winter's Tale*—past Illyria where Viola and Sebastian are shipwrecked in *Twelfth Night*. Approaching the Gulf of Corinth where the battle of Lepanto had taken place—he would skirt Epidaurus—where Egeon seeks his lost family in *Comedy of Errors* —then on to Ephesus on the far eastern shore—where he finds them.

Stopping to explore Cyprus—where he will locate *Othello*—he must have turned to sail west to Sicily, where he will envision the characters in *Much Ado* celebrating their great victory. Rounding the Sicilian coast—after investigating Vulcano and heading north along the west coast of Italy—the long voyage comes to an end on the Italian mainland, where, through the mild Italian winter months he would explore the towns in Tuscany—Verona and Mantua, locations of *Romeo and Juliet* and *Two Gents*—Padua, location of *Taming of the Shrew*—to finally "End Well" in Florence.

~∞~ Shakespeare and Music ~∞~

Music dominates Shakespeare, partly by how musical references are woven throughout the plays, partly by the musicality of his poetry, and, for audiences today, by the great composers who have turned his stories into music over the centuries. A 1959 encyclopedia of concert music (Ewen) devotes more space to playwright Shakespeare than to most composers (418-420). The handful of other poets included—like Byron and Wordsworth—each get no more than a short paragraph, while Shakespeare gets *two full pages*—more than the author gives composers Handel or Haydn. He gets the same amount of space as Brahms, and only a little less than Mendelssohn. Only the greatest composers of our western culture—Bach, Beethoven, Schumann, Schubert and Mozart—rate more space in this concordance of concert music—yet it lists only the most significant of these, with no mention of the ballets or the over 200 operas—among them Verdi's *Macbeth, Falstaff, Otello,* Rossini's *Otello,* Gounod's *Roméo et Juliette,* Britten's *A Midsummer Nights Dream,* Tchaikovsky's *Hamlet.*

There are moments in Shakespeare—usually in the comedies —that are obviously meant for instrumental music—sometimes for dancing. In his *Shakespeare and Music,* 19th-century music historian Edward Naylor examines in detail the dances and masques in eight of his plays. Masques performed at Court were the precursors of today's ballets, operas, and Broadway musicals. As costumed extravaganzas created and led by professionals—the difference between these and those of today is that—in a masque—the audience is costumed to participate in the dancing. In some of his plays masquing is a part of the show. In *The Tempest* for instance it seems likely that—when performed for the Court—provided a full day's entertainment, with a break midway for a feast during the masque in Act IV.

As with all the great Renaissance Courts—music accompanied every activity. Every meal, every event was announced by flute or drum, to be accompanied by recorders and or lute where appropriate. Parsimonious to a fault in everything else, it's noteworthy that—in a household of 200 or so—the Queen housed and fed some 60 musicians. Youthful pages at Court and in noble households were often chosen for their ability to sing and play the lute—as we see in Act IV of *Julius Caesar,* where little Lucius—called in to sing Brutus to sleep—falls asleep himself.

Nor was this just at Court. There being as yet no means of recording music—all of life was accompanied by what today we call *live music.* Travellers on ships crossing the Channel heard the crew singing work songs. Travellers on the road heard farm workers in the fields. In London townsfolk were accustomed to the singing calls of street vendors—serenades to would be lovers—trios singing ballads for pennies on street corners and shillings in the taverns—carmen humming old favorites and new tunes made popular by solo performers in taverns and pubs. These filled the air—competing with the ringing of bells from the hundred or so parish churches—one for

III Shakespeare in His Own Time

almost every block in a city where the church steeples touched the sky, few rising more than three or four stories above the stony streets.

Everyone from barbers to lords sang rounds and catches—a collection of these is still extant that contains parts for anywhere from three to ten singers (Naylor 23). Men, women, even little pages—were expected to be able to play instruments and sight read notation. As Naylor—himself an organist and composer—quotes Thomas Morley's 1597 *Plain and Easy Introduction to Practical Music*—

> Here we read of a dinner-party, or "banket," at which the conversation was entirely about music. Also, after supper, according to custom, "parts" were handed round by the hostess. Philomathes [Lover-of-math] has to make many excuses as to his vocal inability, and finally is obliged to confess that he cannot sing at all. At this the rest of the company "wonder"—and some whisper to their neighbors, "How was he brought up?" Phil. is ashamed, and goes to seek Gnorimus the music master. The master is surprised to see him, as Phil. has heretofore distinguished himself by inveighing against music as a "corrupter of good manners, and an allurement to vices." Phil.'s experience of the supper party has so far changed his views that he wishes as soon as may be to change from *Stoic* for that of *Pythagorean*. Thereupon the master begins to teach him from the very beginning—"as though he were a child." (4-5)

At the opposite end of the critical scale—Naylor quotes Stephen Gosson's *School of Abuse*—"London is so full of unprofitable [poor] pipers and fiddlers that a man can no sooner enter a tavern than two or three cast of them hang at his heels to give him a dance before he depart." He quotes John Lyly—"Thou need no more send for a fiddler to a feast than a beggar to a fair." It could be easy to assume—based on his use of musical terms and metaphors—that Shakespeare himself was a player. Consider Hamlet's obvious challenge to his former schoolmate Guildenstern, whom he suspects of conspiring against him—"'Sblood, do you think I am easier to be played on than a pipe?" Stringed instruments consisted of lutes, citterns, and mandolins, which were strummed—and viols, which were bowed. These included the treble viol, which had the range of our violin—the tenor (viola), the bass or viol da gamba (cello)—the double bass (our bass). These came in sets—two trebles, two tenors, and two basses to a "case." We know from the wills of that time that men of status frequently owned "a case of viols, for"—for welcoming friends capable of putting them to use. Amateur players kept a "chest of viols" handy so when musical friends visited they could entertain themselves with what today we like to call chamber music. A group of instruments of the same type was known as a *consort*—a *broken consort* was a mixture of strings and "pipes"—flutes or recorders. Though largely consigned to school children today—the Recorder Consort was an important element at Court, ready for use at any time.

Brass consisted of trumpets and cornets of various sizes and shapes—required since ancient times for announcing visitors with a musical phrase known as a *tucket*.[75] A particular phrase associated with a nobleman would be passed down through the centuries as a means of alerting the inhabitants of a castle—or armies on a battlefield—whose armoured contingent was coming through the rye. In Shakespeare's time—three tuckets in a row, blasted from the tower atop the Theatre—announced that the show was about to begin.

The earliest keyboard instrument—the virginal—got its name from how it was chiefly played by the daughters of wealthy men to entertain their families and friends before they took on the full-time duties of wife, housekeeper and hostess—a tradition that lasted until the piano took its place in the nineteenth century.

"This music crept by me on the waters"

Naylor lists the many musical terms used by Shakespeare—both directly and as metaphors. According to him there are over 300 musical stage directions that occur in 36 out of the 37 plays in the First Folio—"out of his 37 plays, no less than 32" contain calls for music or references to music. In the 22 plays where Shakespeare gives the stage direction "music," "music plays," or "music within"—directors are on their own when it comes to choosing *what kind* of

---

[75] The military still has its traditional bugle calls like *Reveille* and *Taps*.

III Shakespeare in His Own Time

music—or how long it should last. Directions like these occur 41 times in 22 plays. "In eight cases we have music during a speech or dream of one of the characters—seven times as the symphony or the accompaniment to a song—seven times in wedding processions or pageants —six times for dancing—and five times during a banquet."

A musical light is cast in many of Shakespeare's plays by his use of musical terms as metaphors or jests suggesting the role music plays in romance. In Act III of *Taming of the Shrew*, Hortensio—disguised as a music teacher—woos Bianca, the Shrew's younger sister, with wordplay based on terms in *solfège*.

That Shakespeare was willing to risk the feeling of a scene for the sake of a quibble (a pun) was a famous criticism from Samuel Johnson. One such came in Act III of *Romeo and Juliet* when the lark—an offstage flute, began to "sing"—announcing the dawn that means that she and Romeo must part. Juliet responds with a play on the word *division*, in musical terms, meaning *variation* on a theme—"Some say the lark makes *sweet division*—this doth not so, for she *divideth* us." Where we say "keeping time"—they said "keeping *proportion*"—in Act V of *Richard II*, the King, hearing music played outside his prison cell, mourns—"How sweet our music is when time is broke and no *proportion* kept—so it is in the music of men's lives."

Shakespeare knows the Court dances of his time—as in *The Rape of Lucrece*—where the wretched lady mourns her violation in musical terms (a dump was a slow dance to a melancholy tune)—

> My restless discord loves no *stops* or *rests*,
> A woeful hostess brooks not merry guests.
> Relish your *nimble notes* to pleasing ears,
> Distress likes *dumps*, when *time is kept* with tears.

Naylor lists those places where Shakespeare refers to a popular song by name or by quoting the lyrics to the first line—many sadly lost. Where he gives the lyrics in full—lacking the music that accompanied it—others have provided tunes over the years for the merry-making that ends *A Winter's Tale*—or in *Twelfth Night,* when Sir Toby, Sir Andrew and Maria purposely annoy Malvolio with their loud and boisterous singing. In Act III of *The Tempest* the drunken conspirators march to a tune played by the invisible Ariel—while later Miranda's future husband Ferdinand explains how—

> Sitting on a bank,
> Weeping again the king my father's wreck,
> This music crept by me on the waters,
> Allaying both their fury and my passion
> With its sweet air—thence I have follow'd it,
> Or it hath drawn me rather. But 'tis gone—
> No—it begins again.

Ariel then sings—

> Full fathom five thy father lies—
> Of his bones are coral made—
> Those are pearls that were his eyes—
> Nothing of him that doth fade
> But doth suffer a sea-change
> Into something rich and strange.
> Sea-nymphs hourly ring his knell—

Ding dong bell. What wouldn't we give to hear this sung to the original melody! Shakespeare goes into similar detail with the songs in *Two Gentlemen of Verona, The Tempest, Cymbeline, Pericles, Othello, Henry IV, Henry VIII,* and *Troilus and Cressida.*

Beyond this obvious love of the Art there's a musical quality to Shakespeare's language that defies definition. His poetry has the power to rouse emotions much like music. Whenever the soul of the author lifts—whenever he reaches for images of harmony, spiritual uplift, emotional healing—his mind turns to music—referenced directly in some places, in others by imagery or metaphor. His musicality has inspired composers like Mendelssohn, Tchaikovsky, Verdi, Sibelius, Berlioz, Brahms, Debussy, and Stravinsky, inspired to compose music based on his stories.

As most are aware, the word *music* itself derives from ancient mythology, from the Nine Muses, the daughters of Jupiter/Zeus, each representing one of the nine Arts. Much of today's music theory originated with Plato—who taught mathematics by showing how sound ascends a scale by way of the mathematical wavelength of a vibrating lute string—a central theme of the Wisdom Tradition as he

III Shakespeare in His Own Time

learned it from Pythagoras—thence to philosophers, scholars and artists from Alexander the Great to Leonardo da Vinci.

The two figures in Greek mythology most directly connected to music are the god Apollo and his acolyte Orpheus—central figures in religious cults spread around the Mediterranean by the Greek empire. Apollo was earliest—with his emphasis on the quality of restraint—followed by Orpheus, embodiment of Dionysian rapture, both credited with bringing music to humanity. Shakespeare often reveals his knowledge of both, and their myths—most notably perhaps in *Merchant of Venice*—when Lorenzo describes to Jessica how music has the power to tame

> . . . a wild and wanton herd,
> Or race of youthful and unhandled colts,
> Fetching mad bounds, bellowing and neighing loud,
> Which is the hot condition of their blood.
> If they but hear perchance a trumpet sound,
> Or any air of music touch their ears,
> You shall perceive them make a mutual stand,
> Their savage eyes turn'd to a modest gaze
> By the sweet power of music—therefore the poet
> Did feign that Orpheus drew trees, stones and floods—
> Since nought so stockish, hard and full of rage—
> But music for the time doth change his nature.

Music is always Shakespeare's first thought when seeking a metaphor for harmony, as in Ulysses's famous comment—"untune that string, and hark what discord follows"—or *Sonnet #8* where he lectures the Fair Youth on his need to bring balance and harmony into his solitary life through marriage—"Mark how one string, sweet husband to another, strikes each in each by mutual ordering—resembling sire and child and happy mother—who all in one, one pleasing note do sing ." In the paeon of praise that Ben Jonson created to dedicate the First Folio to the poet he termed "Soul of the Age"—he calls him

> Sweet Swan of Avon! what a sight it were,
> To see thee in our waters yet appear,
> And make those flights upon the banks of Thames,
> that so did take Eliza and our James."

This suggests that Shakespeare not only arranged entertainments on the waters that passed the great palaces, Greenwich to the east, past Whitehall in Westminster, and on to Richmond Palace, perhaps even further past all the great houses on the bank of the river as it approaches Windsor Castle. Thus all the villages along the river, the great houses of the nobility and the wealthy, would be sweetly entertained along the way.

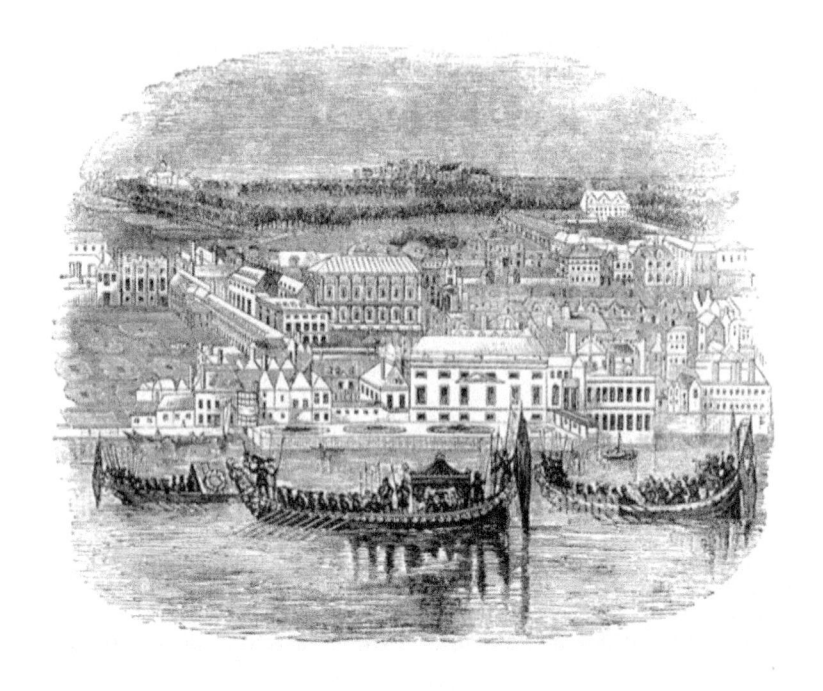

—∞— Shakespeare and History —∞—

If Shakespeare was one of England's greatest exponents of English Law, he was also one of her earliest and most effective historians. Before the Protestant Reformation, the history of their nation hardly existed for any but a handful of its people—mostly monks in monastic scriptoria. What little history apprentices to a trade may have acquired from their masters' idea of an education would have come from Bible stories based in the Middle East. In the old mummers' play—as it evolved over the centuries—St. George and Robin Hood traded slapstick routines with Julius Caesar, Alexander the Great, and

III Shakespeare in His Own Time

whatever local authority was deserving of some rowdy teasing.

With the Renaissance came the return of the ancient notion of history as a lesson—a "mirror for magistrates" that provided boys with stories of heroes to emulate and villainies to avoid. It was his knowledge of classical history that led to Machiavelli's conviction that "he who would foresee what is to happen should look to what has happened, for all that is has its counterpart in time past"—thus the Renaissance dictum: "Because man remains the same, history repeats itself"—as in Ecclesiastes 1.9: "What is it that hath been, that which shall be: and what is it that hath been done, that which shall be done: and there is no new thing under the sun"—or, as in *Sonnet 59*, "if there is nothing new that is but that which hath been before..."

The Protestant Reformation having done away with things like the mummers play, church ales, processions, and all the rest of the hundreds of Church related pleasures that took the English through the weeks of the years—the working classes in London were starved for entertainment.[76] To meet the Reformation demand for an educated polis—how better than plays that mixed history with comedy? As Robert Greene—quoting Horace—put it, *"omne tulit punctum qui miscuit utile dulci"*—"the Useful is most easily accepted when mixed with the Sweet." In 1592—when the London Stage was under attack as sinful and a waste of time—Tom Nashe, citing *Henry VI part one* —defended it with poetic energy—

> How would it have joyed brave Talbot, the terror of the French, to think that after he had lain two hundred years in his tomb, he should triumph again on the stage, and have his bones new embalmed with the tears of ten thousand spectators (at least)—who, in the tragedian that represents his person— imagine they behold him fresh bleeding. (Nicholl *Newes* 86-7)

In bringing their past to life on the Stage—Shakespeare showed his public audience how their ancestors responded when threatened with invasion. If the Church portrayed them as wicked sinners, dependent on God for salvation—the Stage reminded them of a valiant past.

---

[76] Those from distant rural areas could probably get away with some of their ancient "may games" in ways that Londoners could not.

Educating Shakespeare

Nor was Shakespeare alone in his interest in History. According to Lily Campbell, Shakespeare's "interest in history was shared by his age—the number of histories written, translated and printed under the Tudors is amazing, histories of England and of foreign countries, translations of the works of Greek, Roman, Jewish, and continental historians" (18). But these were books—and the men who would be facing the enemy were still largely illiterate. The best—in fact, the *only* way to reach them—was the Stage.

A half-century earlier and Shakespeare would have had few sources for his history plays. Until Henry VIII "dissolved" the monasteries—what records there were, were buried in manuscripts in monastic libraries. Written in insular script in everything from Anglo Saxon to Medieval Latin to Old French—none were in 16th-century English. Following the dismantling of Church properties for their stone and timber—cartloads of these old manuscripts were hauled away by junk dealers. Some of the aging parchments were worthless no doubt—but among them were accounts of events from as far back as the eighth century. From the late 1530s through the 1540s and 1550s, antiquarians like John Leland and John Bale worked to save what they could of these priceless accounts of England's early kings and their battles with invaders.[77]

Holinshed's Chronicles

Towards the end of Henry's reign, a consortium of antiquarians formed around the King's Printer, Reynar Wolfe who, over the years, had gathered much of this precious material with an eye to providing the English with a history of the world in a language they could read. Too busy himself with paying work to do right by this politically sensitive task—Wolfe hired Raphael Holinshed (pron. Holinshed) to

---

[77] Horror stories were told of precious documents baled and sold in bulk to traders who transported it to the continent to be turned into paper. Due to his zeal for eliminating papism, John Bale—who was as avid a reformer as he was an antiquarian—may have been responsible for some of this destruction—for as stated on the *Catholic Herald* website—"How many works as great as the Lindisfarne gospels must have been lost? Out of 600 books in the library of Worcester Priory—only six remain."

III Shakespeare in His Own Time

do the editing. This gave him and his team access to the official records in the Tower. Not all of his sources have survived—which has left the 1577 edition of *Holinshed's Chronicles* as the earliest extant record for some bits of English history.

When Wolfe died in 1573 with the book still unfinished—Holinshed did what he could to complete it—writing, editing, and patching together material by chronologist William Harrison, historian John Stowe and others—into a two-volume folio (2835 pages, 2.5 million words)—which finally got published in 1577 as *The Chronicles of England, Scotland and Ireland*. Few were satisfied with it—so planning soon began for a revised edition.

When Holinshed died in 1580 the project was taken on by a consortium led by Abraham Fleming and William Harrison, whose additions to the text were enhanced by borrowings from sources like Foxe, Buchanan, Guicciardini and Sir Thomas Smith. As the great history crept towards the present—inevitably it got mired in politics—the Crown wanting the protestant revolution portrayed as a sort of "Manifest Destiny"—while "the godly" wanted it shown as a series of showdowns between God and Satan.

Finally in 1587, a decade after the first edition—the version that all scholars agree was Shakespeare's primary source reached the bookstalls. Printed in three volumes in large folio format, both Harrison's "Historical description" and the "History of England" to 1066, were carried over from the 1577 edition. Signed and gathered independently, they comprise the entire first volume. Though present in the major libraries of the time—it's unlikely that grammar school students, or their teachers, would have had access to it. Its existence in print did not guarantee that its contents became known to more than a handful of scholars and antiquarians for many years.

Shakespeare's history sources

The centerpiece of Shakespeare's English history plays—the eight published in the First Folio—comprise the so-called *Lancastrian cycle* that begins with the fall of Richard II and ends with the death of Richard III.[78] As told by Shakespeare, from play to play the story moves through the century the Lancaster branch of the Plantagenet line battled with the York branch for control of the nation.

Shakespeare's major source for these was the elaborately titled *Union of the Two Noble and Illustrae Families of Lancastre and Yorke*. Written during the reign of Henry VIII by courtier Edward Hall—it was first published in 1542. A lawyer and parliamentarian, educated at Eton and King's College Cambridge—Hall (Halle) was active during the brief flowering of the Henrician Renaissance. Ambitious to provide the Court community with the kind of modern works being written by French historians like Froissart or Commines and the Italian Guicciardini—Hall drew on a variety of sources. His most important where Shakespeare is concerned are his descriptions of the historical personalities he had known personally—and the events he'd experienced himself.[79] Hall died shortly after Henry—so the final chapters of his book were added by his printer Richard Grafton—who then created his own version which he published in 1563, enlarging it in 1568.

For *Richard III,* Shakespeare got most of his material from Sir Thomas More's English biography. Published in 1543 by Grafton as a continuation of John Hardyng's rhyming *Chronicle*—Campbell emphasizes the importance of More's biography—both for its style and for its negative portrait of the king whose overthrow and murder by the Tudors called for justification.

There's no question but that these were the major sources for Shakespeare's English history plays—Hall (and Grafton) for the series of eight based on the consecutive reigns of the Lancaster Kings —Holinshed for the rest. Both were in English and both were sufficiently available so as not to cause too much trouble for future academics invested in the ignorant Shakespeare.

For his knowledge of things like the French chivalric code—or those bits about Edward III and Richard II that couldn't have come

---

[78] *Edward III* has been accepted into the canon in recent years, while hopefully *Thomas of Woodstock*, aka *Richard II part one* (Egan), will also someday.

[79] According to Bullough, Shakespeare got his hateful portrait of Joan of Arc from Hall, who got it from the 15th-century *Cronique de France* by Monstrelet—available at that time only in French.

III Shakespeare in His Own Time

from either of these sources—Shakespeare would have needed access to the not so available English version by Lord Berners of Froissart's eyewitness account in French. Even less available would have been Hardyng's verse chronicle in Middle English—published by Grafton in 1543—which provided eyewitness accounts of Harry Hotspur and Prince Hal. Having been Hotspur's page at the Battle of Shrewsbury —where the famous Percy was slain—Grafton's contribution had an authority provided by the fact that he had been personally involved in the events he describes.

As for Agincourt—Geoffrey Bullough, editor of the very useful 8-volume *Narrative and Dramatic Sources of Shakespeare* (1960)—limited by Stratford William's ignorance of French—thinks it unlikely that he could have known *The battaile of Agincourt*—which was not printed until later—nor, according to Bullough, would he have had access to the "many political ballads of the fifteenth century which remained in manuscript until modern times"—material he feels compelled to include, though only as "possible" sources.

Valued among these early historians was the Italian Polydore Vergil, who—having been hired by Henry VII to find historical support for his claim of descent from the semi-mythical King Arthur —stayed on after the monarch's death to become England's first humanist historian. All nine editions of Vergil's Latin *Anglica Historica* were published on the continent. A major source for students and later historians—the fact that Vergil's book wouldn't be translated into English until the nineteenth century has presented no problem for the "small Latin" academics—since any indication that Shakespeare acquired material or ideas from it could be said to have come from one of the historians who later used him as a source.
Of all the historians referenced by the Bard, John Stow (1525-1605) was the only one still alive during the period when Shakespeare and his actors "flourished." First published in 1561—Stow's *Summary of English Chronicles* was reprinted again and again during his lifetime.

A Londoner by birth—humbly housed in Lime Street Ward—Stow would have been well within reach of another writer located in London. Although there's no evidence that they were personally acquainted, it's most unlikely that—when working on a particular reign—the great playwright would not have been in touch with as

Educating Shakespeare

many living scholars as possible (Bullough 1.1, 3.372, 354). If so, Stowe—who mentioned so much—failed to mention it.

These were most of the historians whose works were available in English during the 1590s when the name *William Shakespeare* first began to appear on the title pages of plays published by the Lord Chamberlain's Men. Problems for academics mainly appear with sources that were only available in other languages. Though Bullough does not dwell on it, that there were such sources is clear from his opening statement in Volume III—

> Until recently editors underestimated his attention to authorities and assumed that he depended almost entirely on Holinshed. Those days are past, and there has grown among scholars an opposite tendency to regard the Histories as . . . creative research papers. If scholars cannot be great playwrights, at least there is some satisfaction in finding that the great playwright was himself a scholar with a liking for the rare, unprinted authority. Shakespeare may have consulted a few manuscripts, but he seems to have worked almost entirely from the printed sources popular in his days. (3.1)

Imagine how Bullough's eight volumes would have grown had he felt the need to quote the more arcane sources—which despite his scoffing, he does not deny.

Among the sources that he claims Shakespeare could *not* have used for *Richard II* were the Dieulacres Chronicle, Adam of Usk's Chronicle, the Chroniclers of St. Albans, plus the Parliamentary Rolls in Latin, Old French and Middle English. In French there was Froissart—whose obvious contributions he could ascribe to Lord Berner's translation—Jean Creton's *Histoire du Roy d'Angleterre Richard II*—an eyewitness account from Richard's time which Holinshed claimed was borrowed from John Dee—about which Bullough says—"The poignant narrative would certainly stimulate anyone's imagination, but there is no evidence that Shakespeare saw it"—and *La Chronique de la Traison et Mort de Richart Deux roy Dengleterre*, a problem for academics who can't allow him French.

Bullough spends several pages on the problems raised by *Richard II*—its sources as well as its authorship—finishing with, "In

III Shakespeare in His Own Time

the absence of more evidence and considering the skill shown in most of the play, we are justified in assuming that Shakespeare *planned and wrote Richard II himself*" (3.355). This rather astonishing remark brings us back to the issue of his identity—for if Bullough finds it necessary to justify *assuming* that Shakespeare was the author of one of his most famous plays—then how could he *not* have had questions about his identity?

"Substantially his own"

For those who still think the Shakespeare Authorship Question sprang fully matured from the head of Delia Bacon in 1857—it's worth quoting Bullough at some length on the subject of the authorship of the *Henry VI* triad. Here's a condensation of the "sketch" from his Introduction to "The Early History Plays" in Volume III—

> Many theories of multiple authorship have been evolved to explain the variety of style and the incoherencies in [*Henry VI part one*]. . . . Unfortunately scholars cannot agree on which collaborators wrote which parts of the plays. Thus H.C. Hart thought "Greene had a hand in the composition," and if he had collaborators, "Peele and Shakespeare formed the syndicate." Tucker Brooke dismissed Greene but included Peele with Shakespeare. Chambers saw four or five different hands, including Peele's and very little Shakespeare. Allison Gaw saw six authors—Marlowe, an unknown helper—Peele, possibly Nashe—Shakespeare, and another unknown. . . . J.D. Wilson argued that "Greene planned all the three parts of *Henry VI*, and was responsible for a good deal of the verse in all three plays"—but that "Nashe wrote most of Act I, while Shakespeare had a hand in thirteen or fourteen of the twenty-one scenes of the last four Acts, two of them being almost wholly his. . . ." A.W. Pollard was inclined to believe that the play was originally written by Shakespeare in collaboration with Peele. . . . Fleay and Allison Gaw believe that the varied spelling of proper names in F1 [First Folio] might be used to distinguish the presence of more than one author. (31-33)

Educating Shakespeare

Despite this dizzying lineup of ghost-writers—Bullough prefers to think that Shakespeare actually wrote *Henry VI part one* himself—for "despite many weak moments, repetitions, incoherencies of style—the play shows the emergence of a historical idea and a vigorous, if unsustained, power of construction and characterization" (35).

Thus—in a demonstration of what has rendered so much of the official scholarship tiresome beyond enduring—problems stemming from the limitations imposed by the Stratford dates force Bullough to spend endless paragraphs on the possibility that so many sources *might* suggest multiple authors and who they *might* have been. His solution to this should stand as one of the most original and most absurd of all—that Shakespeare was *just as clever at imitating other writers* as he was at everything else he did (34)—

> H.C. Hart and J.D. Wilson have demonstrated remarkable parallels to Greene, and Wilson has also cited many resemblances to Nashe. But Shakespeare may have read and echoed Greene's work and he may also have read Cornelius Agrippa and Henry Howard's *A Defensative against the poyson of supposed Prophecies*, which are reflected in *1 Henry VI*, and which Nashe drew on later. . . . —for this and other reasons I incline to believe that if in *Henry VI part one* [Shakespeare] worked over ground already covered *inadequately* by Greene or others—he rewrote what he found in the light of a full consultation of the Chronicles . . . largely remaking the old play (if such there was) so that as we have it—it is *substantially his own* in outline and in conduct." (40)

So as Bullough would have it, it was *Robert Greene*—remember him?—author of what Henry Burrowes Lathrop labelled "England's first great translation of Greek poetry into English"?—who conceived of the original *Henry VI part one*—Shakespeare merely a reviser.

Feuillerat differs only in that—while Bullough names Greene, Feuillerat keeps to himself any notions he may have on the identity of the hypothetical originator—commenting with regard to *Richard III*—"There is *no conclusive evidence* that parts of the play were written by other authors such as Peele, Marlowe, or Kyd."

III Shakespeare in His Own Time

The "all-pervading" intruders

Thus we see that confusions over who or what was meant by *Shakespeare* were endemic long before Delia Bacon suggested replacing William of Stratford with a handful of courtiers. Together with Bullough's dismissal—there's the vicious if silent monster lurking beneath the podium—namely the long and ongoing uncertainty over *who wrote the canon*—not the whole thing—Heaven forfend!—but some bits and pieces of it—so many bits, so many pieces, so many minor authors possessed by occasional flashes of genius!

> At the end of the last century the idea that the Shakespearean canon was not entirely authentic was so firmly established that it was generally admitted that *Titus Andronicus* and the three parts of *Henry VI* contained [only] traces of Shakespeare's hand—that in *Henry VIII* one must acknowledge Fletcher's collaboration—and that in *Richard III, Hamlet, The Two Gentlemen of Verona, The Taming of the Shrew* and others, there appear some remnants of older plays . . . that "it was difficult to see what remained of Shakespeare, so numerous and all-pervading were the intruders."[80]

Thus, Bullough and colleagues continued to tiptoe around what is probably their biggest problem of all—the relationship between these anonymous quartos and the plays that bear the famous name. With titles like *The Troublesome Raigne of King John, The Famous Victories of Henry the Fifth, The True Tragedy of Richard Duke of York, The First Part of the Contention between York and Lancaster, The Second part of the Contention,* and *The True Tragedy of Richard III*—they cover Shakespeare's entire Lancastrian cycle—plot for plot, character for character, even speech for speech.

Published anonymously throughout the 1590s—if it were not

---

[80] There's no end to this malarkey. The current "authorized" edition of Shakespeare's plays—published in four volumes by Oxford University Press in 2016—has him sharing the authorship of the three Henry VI plays with Christopher Marlowe! It seems that the 23 philologists (from five different countries) that so courageously put their names to this nonsense, see "other hands" in seventeen of the thirty-nine plays!

for the dating limits imposed by the Stratford biography, these—certainly, absolutely, without the shadow of a doubt—would be taken for Shakespeare's own early versions. But because the Academy insists on seeing the author as a prodigy who emerges from total obscurity as a fully fledged professional playwright at age twenty-nine—albeit one who has written nothing original, only revising the works of earlier playwrights—deaf, dumb and blind to the history of the repressive politics limiting creative or lyrical works—no amount of research that shows that upwards of half of his sources came to him in ways that William could not possibly have known—has ever forced them to see this conjuring trick for what it was then—and still is—four centuries later.

For whatever reason they continue to strain after "early sources," "bad quartos," and "memorial reconstructions." At one point—with the help of fashionable abstractionists such as Noam Chomsky and Jacques Derrida—they found a toehold with the notion that—in the grand scheme of things—*all that matters is the text*—who wrote it, why they wrote it—of no real or lasting importance.

Shakespeare's religion

What we have examined so far of Shakespeare's fund of knowledge about the Law, Medicine, Science, Italy, Literature and Music—however unusual in quality and abundance—were not such that would invite any great trouble with the authorities. Religion was a different matter—one that would have affected all of the above. Religion lay at the angry center of the continental wars and the rebellions that sprang up every few years in the north and west of England—as the protestants battled to change a people that were still very Catholic at heart into protestants. Wrong beliefs could get a person imprisoned for life, hanged, drawn and quartered or burnt at the stake as audiences of hundreds found it entertaining to see how well or poorly they met their deaths—a genuine *Grand Guignol*.

The dangers during that time for anyone dealing with religion in any way other than whatever the Crown was prescribing at the moment may explain why scholars have found so little in Shakespeare that testifies to his own beliefs. He must after all have been raised in

III Shakespeare in His Own Time

a particular religion. Academic curiosity—unwilling to focus on *who* he was—has been obsessed with *what* he was—Catholic or protestant—evangelical or moderate—recusant or Church of England—agnostic or atheist?—When no obvious bias could be discerned from his works, they sought answers in his references to the Bible.

Bibles were immensely important in Shakespeare's time. The Protestant Reformation was based on bible translations. To turn the word of God—up to then accessible only through hearing it chanted in Latin—into something that could be read by ordinary people—was the impulse driving reform throughout Germany, Scandinavia, parts of France and the low countries—and those parts of England closest to the continent. From Erasmus to Luther to Calvin—from John Bale to John Knox and John Foxe, the cry went out—"Give the people the Word of God in a language they can understand and they will see how far the Roman Church has drifted from its origins!"

Early English translators—rising to the challenge—paid the ultimate price. Though Wycliff managed to die on his own without help from the authorities, his corpse was not so lucky. In 1428 his critics had it dug up, burnt, and thrown in the Thames. In 1536 Tyndale was burnt at the stake by papists. In 1556—in one of the century's crowning events—Archbishop Cranmer, creator of the Book of Common Prayer—the established cornerstone of today's Church of England—was burnt at the stake as hundreds watched to see with what impressive style he performed his blazing finale.

If we can understand to what extent governments then were instruments of religion—and to what extent different sects relied on particular versions of the Bible—we can begin to understand why translating it into the vernacular was so necessary to the reformers—and so dangerous to those who actually did it.

"Death be not proud"

Most educated folk today base their world views on science—but in a world in which death was a constant for all humans—rich or poor, wellborn or low—what happened after death mattered more than anything science had yet to offer. Well might the poet John Donne, who spent his life pondering such things, proclaim—"Death, thou shalt die." Most Elizabethans could not imagine a life lived outside the shadow of *the Reaper*—summer to winter, childhood to old age. Those who survived birth and childhood tended to marry at least twice, if they lived long enough, even three times—not from divorce, which was illegal—but from the deaths of their mates. Despite the fact that childbirth was the leading cause of death for women—many women would give birth to as many as ten or twelve in hopes that two or three might live to maturity. As Lawrence Stone explains in *Family, Sex and Marriage*—

> In London in 1764, forty-nine percent of all recorded children were dead by the age of two, and sixty percent by the age of five. . . . Between a quarter and a third of all children of English peers and peasants were dead before they reached the age of fifteen. (68)

Pause for a minute and let that sink in. Nor were children more vulnerable than any other group. In France—comparable to England in most respects—"death rates were four or five times as high as they are today"—and statistics show that "the actual numbers who died in their twenties was about the same as the numbers who died in their sixties. . . . Death was at the center of life—just as the cemetery was at the center of the village."

As a result, the Elizabethans were intensely concerned about "that bourne from whence no traveller returns." Where were their mothers, their husbands, wives, sisters, brothers, their beloved friends, their precious babes? The Bible was the raft to which these lost souls clung. Not that it was anything they could read themselves or even hold in their hands—until the Reformation it was against the law for anyone but an ordained priest to own a bible—just words read to them in a language they couldn't understand by a priest whose importance was emphasized by his elegant vestments, or sung to them in echoing churches and cathedrals by boys who looked and sounded like the angels they so fervently hoped were making the afterlife pleasant for the dear ones gone on before.

To most Elizabethans—more even than their own salvation, Heaven held the hope of reunion with their loved ones—and so the question of who was to be admitted—by what earthly means could they, poor sinners, children of Adam, be allowed within the realms of the saints—was a matter of overwhelming concern. Rejecting the cynicism of the Catholic prelates who had sunk to selling tickets to Heaven (known as *indulgences*)—protestants were torn between the Calvinists—who believed that only the Elect, the chosen few who knew themselves and each other purely by Faith, were allowed into Heaven—and those who, in hopes that good works were sufficient, demonstrated their value to God by endowing grammar schools and university chairs, building hospitals and almshouses, repairing roads and bridges, and showing up for whatever form of communion the government was endorsing at the time.

The Reformation

Today's Academy—preoccupied with Shakespeare's use of feminine endings—pays little attention to the fact that he appeared in English history at a midpoint in this great spiritual battle. Literary criticism —largely concerned with the effects on their works by what's going on around them—treats Shakespeare as uniquely untouched by the events of his time—something of a literary Saint. Well might he say "We are the stuff that dreams are made of"—for many English, they were more the stuff of what we'd call nightmares today.

With the success (however shaky) of the Elizabethan regime —the struggle that had begun with reformers versus papists having shifted to Calvinists versus Lutherans—then, with the success (however shaky) of the Anglican Establishment, having shifted to Church of England versus dissenters (Presbyterians, Methodists, Baptists, Congregationalists, Quakers, etc.) the turmoil finally led— to the war between the Parliamentarians (formerly Dissenters)—the Crown (Church of England)—and the shameful execution of a King! Is it so strange that—in this tempest of religious upheaval—that scholars have found it difficult to locate the great Poet's beliefs? The better question might be—could he have accomplished all he did if he'd been more specific?

Educating Shakespeare

The battle over the Bible

When seeking where to begin with the religious issues of that time it makes sense to begin with Henry VIII, whose desperate need for an heir drove him to break with Catholic Rome because the Pope refused to grant him a divorce. Intolerant of anything that stood in the way of getting what he wanted—"Robin the Bobbin the big-bellied Ben" broke with the Pope and all of Catholic Europe[81]—which enabled him—or forced him—to declare himself head of the English Church. When that led to the beheading of his most dependable supporters[82] he was left at the end with none to support him but the sort of reformers he detested—chief among them Archbishop Cranmer.

Henry appointed Thomas Cranmer Archbishop of Canterbury, the top religious post in the nation, because the youthful prelate had come up with a (sort of) legal way out of the corner into which the King had painted himself in his search for a way to get rid of the wife who wasn't providing him with an heir. Desirous of keeping his own head—Cranmer kept to himself how involved he was becoming in the religious revolution launched by Martin Luther—whom Henry would have hanged or burnt at the stake had he had the opportunity.

As Cranmer and his friends saw it—maybe now was the time, not just for a reformed Catholic Church, but for a *new* Church—one stripped of its Catholic flummery and returned to the principles on which it had originally been founded by Christ and his disciples. While continuing to give the King whatever he wanted on a day by day basis—Cranmer found himself slipping ever more deeply into a leadership role within the European reform community—and with his kind and loving heart—just as securely into the heart of Henry's sick and frightened little heir, the future Edward VI.

Thus with the King's death in 1547, control of the nation and its religion passed into the hands of a nine-year-old—a perilous moment for a government reeling from the insanities of Henry's final years. Cranmer now found himself largely in control of what would happen

---

[81] This was Pope Clement VII, who was dependent on the Holy Roman Emperor Charles V, uncle of the very Queen Henry was attempting to divorce.

[82] Cardinal Wolsey, Thomas Cromwell, Sir Thomas More, among others.

III Shakespeare in His Own Time

next—for little Edward, now King, was determined to help his friend make the world a better and safer place for kings and little boys. In 1549—only two years after Henry's death—together with Edward's uncle Duke of Somerset and his secretary, the Cambridge scholar and parliamentarian Sir Thomas Smith—they saw to it that Cranmer's Service—so beautifully described in his Book of Common Prayer—was made the law of the land. Thus did the English religion change from Catholic to protestant—seemingly overnight.

Somerset—who had risen as a military leader during Henry's interminable wars—seemed taken by surprise when the summer of 1549 the nation erupted in riots and rebellions against this sudden change to their ancient habits of worship. Somerset's failure to respond led to his overthrow by John Dudley, now self-titled Duke of Northumberland—who put Somerset and his staff in the Tower—releasing them only when he felt himself sufficiently secure as the nation's head of State. When the consumptive little King died three years later—and Henry's Catholic daughter became Queen, Dudley/Northumberland left his head beside the Tower block.

During the ensuing five years that Mary and her Catholic husband Philip II of Spain held the throne—before she too succumbed to mortality—they had overseen the slaughter of several hundred protestants, many hundreds more having fled to one or another of the various protestant strongholds on the Continent. Among those they consigned to the flames during this period was the great Archbishop.

With Mary's death in November 1558—the protestants who had survived the Marian holocaust looked—with William Cecil's help, to Mary's younger sister Elizabeth—to establish what Somerset, Cranmer, Smith and her brother had initiated a decade earlier.

Survivor of a brutal and uncertain childhood similar to that endured by her little brother—by the time Elizabeth took the throne at twenty-five she was the battle-hardened, tough-minded survivor of one of the most dangerous childhoods and early adult lives in history. For Elizabeth, publicly displayed religious feeling was a purely political concern—neither a philosophy nor an escape. For escape she preferred the Stage. For years the series of holiday plays from December 26 through Shrovetide (Carneval) were known to her supporters as "the Queen's solace."

Shakespeare's Bible

After a few cursory efforts over the years to track Shakespeare's beliefs through his use of biblical quotations—at the beginning of the twentieth century Richmond Noble [83]—apparently with the support of the universities of Glasgow and Liverpool—set out to run the elusive fox to ground. In *Shakespeare's Biblical Knowledge and Use of the Book of Common Prayer*, published in 1935, Noble provided the first thoroughgoing examination of his knowledge of the Bible.

As he makes clear—the one Shakespeare knew best, that he referred to again and again—was the Geneva Bible. First published in 1560, it's still considered by many today as the backbone of the Protestant Reformation.[84] In a chapter titled "General Considerations of Shakespeare's Biblical Knowledge," he quotes Dr. Wordsworth, Bishop of St. Andrews, who claims in *Shakespeare's Use and Knowledge of the Bible* (1864) that he was "in a more than ordinary degree, a diligent and a devout reader of the Word of God."

Although Noble was troubled by William's biography—"Close and continuous study demands an academic training that Shakespeare affords no evidence of having possessed"—yet, he "definitely made identifiable quotations from or allusions to at least 42 books of the Bible, 18 each from the Old and New Testaments and 6 from the Apocrypha . . . indicating a remarkably wide range of quotation" (2021, 41-42, 43). In a definitive review of Naseeb Shaheen's *Biblical References in Shakespeare's comedies*—American Roger Stritmatter of Coppin State University notes—

> In his three books, Shaheen finds more than 1300 Biblical references, an average of almost 40 per play. In the 12 comedies, Shaheen finds 371 biblical or liturgical references. These references are established by locating key phrases or idioms of a distinctively biblical origin. Because such phrases often recur in more than one biblical verse, the references

---

[83] Richmond Samuel Howe Noble (1877-1940) also wrote *Shakespeare's Use of Song* which provides the lyrics to all the songs in his plays.

[84] Those who choose to see Shakespeare as a Catholic would do well to consider why he would prefer the Geneva over the Rheims—the English Catholic Bible.

III Shakespeare in His Own Time

yield a total of 1202 potential source listings in Shaheen's appendices. (62)

Noble tackled the question of exactly where in his works Shakespeare quoted the Bible—which bible he used—and how often he quoted it. He disdains the impression given by dissenters that the only evidence of Shakespeare's biblical knowledge was his use of proper names. "This is far from the fact. Shakespeare often alludes to or makes use of a biblical incident in some way or other without mentioning any proper name at all." He refutes the popular image of Shakespeare as uneducated—"The truth is that he was no exception to the race of great poets; he was an avid reader of books. By no other means could he have acquired his remarkably extensive vocabulary." According to Noble, Shakespeare

> displays such a familiarity with Job, Proverbs and Ecclesiasticus and in later years with Isaiah, as can only have been acquired by reading. . . . Job had been read by Falstaff (he knew that life was as a weaver's shuttle), by Duke Vincentio (it furnished the burden of his counsel to Claudio), and by Constance (it gave tone to her cursing). . . . As for Ecclesiasticus, it served Constance in her welcome of death, Portia in her great Court speech, Hamlet's uncle in his reproof of his nephew's mourning, and is apparent in numbers of other places. (43)

For the Reformation English, it was dangerous *not* to be seen by the authorities as taking communion—so while Shakespeare might use references from Greek drama or Roman history that only university graduates or Inns of Court lawyers would understand—he knew that *everyone in the audience* would get his Bible references.

In giving examples of the means by which he worked these into his plays, Noble notes that they "only comprise a selection, but they are sufficient in quantity to warn anyone that allusions to biblical incidents are more numerous than might appear at first sight." He suggests that this is why "so many of Shakespeare's uses of scripture are overlooked," to lie "undetected even by the eyes of experts."[85]

Among those things most easily missed are the sort of unusual word combination that could only have come from the Bible—such as Caesar's "the valiant never *taste of death* but once," the phrase "taste of death" coming from the Greek Gospels—or Bolingbroke's "*bitter bread* of banishment"—from "bread of affliction"—Kings 22:27. The phrase "heart's desire" is so common now that few realize that before using it in *Much Ado*, Shakespeare remembered it from Psalms 20 and 37—"Delight thou in the Lord and he shall give thee thy *heart's desire*." Such references may be missed because Shakespeare was so fond of combining bits from two sources into a single sentence or phrase—which tends to fudge both as sources. Above all, as Noble notes, it's well to keep in mind that—

> The dramatist . . . must not divert attention from [his] main purpose; we may forgive ordinary writers if they take us down an occasional side alley, but if the dramatist does it he may find his diversion fatal. His points must be comprehensible to his audience, and if he aims over their heads so that they fail to grasp his intent he will miss success as a writer for the stage. . . . If the audience caught the allusion, so much greater their enjoyment, but if they failed, they yet had something.

Some plays contain more allusions than others. Those that contain the most are *Henry VI parts one* and *two*—particularly quotes from Cranmer's Prayer Book—those with the least, *Shrew, Two Gents* (few, but remarkable), and *Cymbeline*. The histories are rich in such references—notably those in the *Henry VI* triad, wherein the pious King "quotes scripture on every convenient opportunity"—and whose "references to the Psalter are especially numerous."

Some plays appear to be based on biblical themes—for instance *Richard III* is surely the incarnation of the Devil who can and does "cite scripture for his purpose." *Measure for Measure* takes its theme from Matthew 7:2: "with what measure ye mete, it shall be measured

---

[85] Since then Shaheen, in three books, has added to this, while Stritmatter has added more in his *Marginalia of the Geneva Bible* (2001).

III Shakespeare in His Own Time

to you again," and *King Lear* which dramatizes Ecclesiasticus 18:20

> Give not thy son and wife, thy brother and friend, power over thee while thou livest; and give not away thy substance and goods to another, lest it repent thee and thou be fain to ask of them again.... For better it is thy children to pray thee than that thou shouldest be fain to look in their hands.

Noble feels that Shakespeare must have read Isaiah while writing *Coriolanus*—while of *Richard II* he notes—

> In his prosperity he is gay, light-hearted and profane. As his mind darkens with grief he becomes more and more scriptural, until finally his heaviness of soul overwhelms him. At the first stroke of misfortune his mind appears to occupy itself with Job.

Berowne's well-known complaint—"Why, all delights are vain, but that most vain, which with pain purchas'd, doth inherit pain, as painfully to pour upon a book to seek the light of truth"—a reference to Ecclesiastes 12:9-12—"All is but vanity (saith the preacher) ... for to make many books it is an endless work; and too much study wearieth the body." And so on for over 100 pages of allusions.

Noble's classifications

"For the sake of convenience"—Noble divides these allusions into three classes—*certain, probable,* and *possible.* He understands that some of these may seem weak if taken singly—but when seen as pieces of a whole are convincing by their sheer quantity and by how subtly they add a religious tone to the text—

> It is only when we assemble all the references to Adam and Eve that we realize how intimately he knew that narrative; the isolated references do not impress at all, but when they are gathered together, it is borne in on the collector that there is hardly a phase of the story as narrated in the first three chapters of Genesis that has been missed. (42)

To the first group he assigns those passages in the plays "which can positively be stated to contain biblical quotations or allusions."

Passages with *probable* references, "which would commend themselves as such to any reasonable person conversant with the Bible and with the plays" he puts in the second class—while the third is reserved for those "about which no one could be dogmatic one way or the other"—but which "must be considered if it is desired to estimate the probable extent of Shakespeare's indebtedness to the Bible and Prayer Book" (24).

While the first examples are interesting in revealing what he recalled word for word—the second reveal his process—how he would paraphrase, or otherwise make use of a word, an image, or the meaning of a passage, without quoting it directly.

Yet it's the third group that most claims our attention, as it demonstrates how ideas, images and phrasing heard repeatedly in chapel could sink so deeply into his psyche that they appear in a variety of situations far from spiritual in nature. Among these Noble gives Hamlet's "O shame, where is thy blush?" as a variation on the phrase from the Burial Service—"O death, where is thy sting?"

Shakespeare and The Psalter

The Book of Common Prayer—Cranmer's majestic replacement for the Catholic Mass—was probably better known to the English then than most of the Bible—for those parts of the Bible that Cranmer included in its sermons, offices and ceremonies would have been read aloud and recited in turn by the audience, word for word, at church on Sunday, where all parishioners were required by law to be present. At every christening, wedding, funeral, and communion—where Elizabethans heard the same texts repeatedly from childhood on until they became permanently lodged in their minds.

Phrases from the Bible, the Psalms, and the letters of St. Paul were embedded in ceremonies whose wording has lasted through the centuries, even into our secular age. In films and television we hear phrases from the marriage ceremony—"Dearly Beloved, we are gathered together in the sight of God and this company. . . in sickness and in health . . . so long as ye both shall live"—at funerals, "ashes to ashes and dust to dust . . . the Lord giveth and the Lord taketh away, blessed be the name of the Lord."

III Shakespeare in His Own Time

Noble notes that Shakespeare "quoted more from Cranmer's Psalter than from any other biblical work. There is no doubt that a large proportion of such quotations can be identified as according more with the version in the Prayer Book than with any other" (76-86). For instance—from Act V of *Comedy of Errors*, Antipholus of Syracuse spurns his brother's courtesan—"Sathan, *avoid!* I charge thee, tempt me not!"—while from *Henry IV part two* Bolingbroke sends away the spirit he's called forth—"False fiend, *avoid!*" The bibles use other terms, but in the Communion Service for the First Sunday in Lent it's "*Avant Satan!*"

Typical also is the use of the phrase—"amendment of life" in Act I of *Henry IV part one* where the Prince says to Falstaff, "I see a good amendment of life in thee"—a phrase borrowed from the Communion Service—"confess yourselves to Almighty God, with full purpose of *amendment of life.*"

In Act II of *Richard III*, the Queen says—"Uncle, for God's sake, speak *comfortable words*—also from the Communion Service —"Hear what *comfortable words* our Savior Christ saith unto all that truly turn to him." And when Richard prods Aumerle for attempting to dissuade him from taking a dangerous course with the phrase "Discomfortable cousin!"—he echoes from both the Geneva and the Bishops Bible the phrase—"*discomfortable* words."

According to Noble: "From first to last there is not a play in the Folio entirely free from a suggestion of a use of the Psalms. In two plays, *Henry VI part two* and *Henry VIII*, the allusions to the Psalms run into double figures. Even *the Sonnets* are not devoid of such quotations" (48). From Psalm 125—"even as Mount Sion, which may not be removed" is echoed by Mortimer in *Henry VI part one*, who describes the House of Lancaster as "like a mountain, *not to be remov'd.*" From Psalm 94—"That thou mayest give him patience *in time of adversity*" is echoed in *Comedy of Errors* by Dromio of Ephesus—"'tis for me to be patient, for I am *in adversity.*" And from Psalm 8 of the Geneva Bible—

> When I behold thine heavens, even the works of thy fingers, the moon and the stars which thou hast ordained, what is man, say I, that thou art mindful of him, and the son of man, that thou visitest him? For thou hast made him a little lower

165

Educating Shakespeare

> than God, and crowned him with glory and worship. Thou hast made him to have dominion in the works of thine hands: thou hast put all things under his feet.

—suggesting Hamlet's—"What a piece of work is Man?!"

Noble feels that Shakespeare's knowledge exceeds what he would have recalled only from hearing them read in church. He feels that only reading them on his own—or participating in a service with repeating responses, could have left him with such lasting memories. As Sidney Lee, author of a 1905 biography and the original DNB bio put it—"His use of scriptural phraseology, as of scriptural history, suggests youthful reminiscence and the assimilative tendency of the mind in a stage of early development. . . ."

Cranmer's Book of Common Prayer reflects the best of the best of protestant theological thinking—rendered in Renaissance terms in English for those who understood how great the need for clarity, as in Miles Coverdale's version of the 100th psalm, *Jubilate Deo*—

> O be joyful in the lord, all ye lands; serve the Lord with
> gladness, and come before his presence with a song.
> Be ye sure that the Lord he is God; it is He that hath made
> us, and not we ourselves.
> We are his people, and the sheep of his pasture.
> O, go your way into his gates with thanksgiving,
> and into his courts with praise—
> Be thankful unto him, and speak good of his Name,
> for the Lord is gracious, his mercy is everlasting,
> And his truth endureth from generation to generation.

This is truly magisterial prose. With examples like this, how could Shakespeare fail to be inspired? The Psalms, Sermons and Lessons as given in the Prayer Book—heard from the pulpit and possibly recited—were one of the major streams that fed not only his style, but also his thinking and his beliefs. If a belief in a great central spirit, in a life after death, and the power of Good over Evil, are evidence of religious feeling—Shakespeare was a believer.

Nevertheless the question remains—what brand of believer?

III Shakespeare in His Own Time

A little innocent mischief

One thing we can be sure that he believed in was laughter. There's a time and a place for everything—and in Elizabethan England—up against the brutality, the poverty, the disease, the religious dissention and the dismal attitude of the puritans that believed it was sinful to "make merry"—you might say there was a crying need for laughter.

However Shakespeare might use Scripture to add weight to his tragedies—neither could he resist having fun with it. One charming example is Bottom's reaction to his idyll with Titania—"The eye of man hath not heard, the ear of man hath not seen, man's hand is not able to taste, his tongue to conceive, nor his heart to report, what my dream was"—which must have been amusing even to the few who didn't catch it as a play on the Geneva Bible's version of First Corinthians 2.9—"The eye hath not seen, and the ear hath not heard, neither have entered into the heart of man the things which God hath prepared for them that love him."

Another occurs when Jaques comments on the couples as they arrive for the great wedding that ends *As You Like It*—"There is sure another flood toward, and these couples are coming to the Ark"—then, as Touchstone and Audrey approach—"Here comes a pair of very strange beasts." As Noble notes—"the point would be more obvious to those who remembered that, according to Genesis 7:2, the beasts that entered the Ark in pairs were unclean, while 'those that were clean entered by sevens'"—which suggests that Touchstone and Audrey are "beastly"—or at least that's how Jaques sees them.

Noble quotes Carter—"not that [Shakespeare] always quotes with a religious object in view; on the contrary, he becomes so daring . . . that he shocks the sensitive mind. He may be said to use Scripture on any and every occasion—to dignify the thought of a king, point the jest of a wit, or brighten the dullness of a clown. . . ."

> The impression made on my mind by these sallies of Shakespeare is not that he favoured this or that doctrine, or that he was hostile to some other, but that he regarded the contents of the Bible *dispassionately*. If he was guilty of profanity, he was unaware that a little innocent mischief did anyone any harm or that he had committed any offence. (51)

Noble notes how, on the other hand, he also uses scripture to heighten the emotional effect of moments like Othello's reference to Judas—how "like the base Judean" he threw a pearl away "richer than all his tribe"—or how, like Judas "I kiss'd thee, ere I kill'd thee"—or by Bolingbroke in *Henry IV part one* who craved to walk where "walk'd those blessed feet which fourteen hundred years ago were nail'd for our advantage on the bitter cross."

> It has often been said of Shakespeare that he failed to give the world a single religious character. It might have been said in reply that King Henry VI exhibited all the attributes of a deeply religious character.... If that was not satisfactory then it might be said that the failure to discover a religious character was due to the fact that the critics in question had lifted their eyes to heaven and had not peered among the damned in Shakespeare's hell. (54)

Noble notes that it is in his "ability to apply *aptly* rather than in *extensiveness of knowledge* that Shakespeare's excellence in Biblical allusion must be sought"—which can also be said of all aspects of his incredible education.

> Perhaps no greater tribute can be paid to Shakespeare's use of the Bible than the comparative paucity of the mistakes it has been possible to trace in the plays. No effort has been spared in the quest; in fact, it must be confessed that the search has been keen with a desire to establish errors; yet the total bag is small, and about any one item there would not be general consent. (99)

More than just another form of literature to be plumbed for stories and metaphors—what did the Bible mean to Shakespeare? And if he was as "dispassionate" about it as Noble claims—then what *did* he believe in? He was certainly not a "dispassionate" writer—cool and detached like the Augustans. Passion surges through his works. In fact, one of his most understanding interpreters sees passion itself as the ground in which his true belief system was founded.

III Shakespeare in His Own Time

Shakespeare's Philosophy

According to John Vyvyan, writing in the 1960s—it was neither Calvinism, nor Catholicism, nor evangelical Protestantism that gave Shakespeare his central core of belief. Though it's obvious he knew them all—none plays the sort of defining role in his works that it would were he a devotee. According to Vyvyan,[86] Shakespeare's true religion was *Love*. Nor is he being cute. Vyvyan is entirely serious—explaining his thesis in three important books.[87]

> In all Shakespeare's work, love is the star by which his characters must set their course; when they do not, their power and their learning only assist the storm that drives them to disaster. And however lightly Shakespeare seems to be writing, he is illustrating this philosophy. (*Rose* 23)

Having traced the theme through all the plays, Vyvyan shows—with insights into half a dozen—how he became aware that *all* of Shakespeare reveals the same obsession. And although personal experience must have played a part—as he explains in *Shakespeare and the Rose of Love*—he drew continually on three great traditions—*Agape*, "the redemptive love of the Gospels"—*Courtly Love*, "the mystical associations that gathered round the Rose"—and *Platonic love* as prescribed by Plato (13). The first was available to all who could read the Bible and the Prayer Book—but where did he find the others?

Shakespeare and Courtly Love

Courtly Love has been credited with civilizing Europe in the Middle Ages. The all-male Trinity of the early Church having displaced the Great Goddess of prehistory, She—without whom men become desolate—was resurrected at the medieval Courts of Europe by troubadours who enshrined Her in some living female of beauty, high degree and spotless reputation. "As if invested with the aura of the

---

[86] Vyvyan (1908-1975) was known as an archaeologist and an activist for animal rights (Wikipedia).

[87] *The Shakespearean Ethic; Shakespeare and the Rose of Love; Shakespeare and Platonic Beauty* (1960-61).

vanished goddess—she becomes the means to a mystical revelation —a radiant avenue to God." In Shakespeare she appears as Portia, Olivia, Pauline, the Princess in *Love's Labour's Lost* and the Abbess in *Comedy of Errors*. For Romeo she was Juliet, for Benedick she was Beatrice, for Antony she was Cleopatra.[88]

The pilgrimage—the mystical journey described by the 13th-century Persian poet and mystic Rumi, who saw music, poetry and dance as ways of approaching God—or the early 14th-century poet Hafiz, who—like Dante, having fallen in love with a woman with whom he couldn't be intimate—experienced his love as a form of religion. Troubadours sang that love could lead to enlightenment. Says Vyvyan,

> Ideally this should culminate in the mystic vision, or philosophic conclusion, or the unity of being, which other explorers . . . have arrived at by different roads. That Shakespeare chose the path of love must be partly for reasons of temperament, but mainly because . . . Neo-Platonism and the Gospels had prepared his way. (148)

And perhaps also because he and his entire community—oppressed by Calvin's view of life as a stinking cesspool of Sin—were so desperately in need of a little happiness.

The romance of restraint

The version of this worship of the Feminine that worked best in a European context was where the protagonist gives his heart to a beautiful woman who will not or cannot reciprocate—who may not be conscious of his love—or even of his existence—as with Hafiz's Shakh-e Nabat, Dante's Beatrice, Petrarch's Laura—even, however satirically, Don Quixote's Dulcinea. While the version prescribed by Christian chivalry allowed *desire* to flourish between a knight and his prince's mistress—this was only so long as they kept their hands to

---

[88] We may see something of this in da Vinci's *Mona Lisa*, which it seems he kept with him until he died. Whoever she was, she was his Beatrice, his Laura.

themselves—"*Honi soit qui mal y pense.*"[89] Should they yield to their passion—tragedy was inevitable—as with the mythical lovers Tristan and Isolde, the semi historical Lancelot and Guinevere, or the real Héloise and Abelard.

Passions stirred by this philosophy would have been intense at the Elizabethan Court where it seems some men were given high place and perquisites as much for their good looks as for their wisdom or experience and where maidens were perpetually garbed in virginal white as chorus for a Queen adorned like a peacock with brilliant colors, gold fabrics, yards of lace and great strings of pearls.

Male courtiers, hopeful of advancement, scrambled to play Tristan to the Queen's Isolde—but however intriguing to outsiders— Elizabeth's romances were nothing more than elaborate "may games" played largely for political ends. Should the game get too serious for a pair of her courtiers—which of course it would (and did)—she saw to it that they were quickly and permanently separated—such was how she chose to use the power she'd inherited from her father

From long acquaintance with the romances of chivalry—such roles were familiar to her courtiers. As their wills testify, next to prayer books and missals, Arthurian romances were the most popular reading for literate aristocrats of the fourteenth and fifteenth centuries (McFarlane 236 fn 5). Works like Spenser's *Faerie Queene*, Sidney's *Arcadia* and Shakespeare's *Sonnets* hint at unrequited passions.

This fascination with Courtly Love—with the love songs and poems that occupy the thoughts of youth and that with most tend to fade with the responsibilities of adulthood—lasted long at the Court of the unfulfilled Virgin Queen, and her constant appetite for the paraphernalia of romance. However deeply felt by Shakespeare, in his youth at least, as a personal as well as poetic testimonial—it may have been his use of the tropes of Courtly Love that first endeared him to his royal mistress, who—in that cold climate where everybody slept with someone—was forced by the situation into which she had been born—to sleep alone.

When Elizabeth said she was married to her people, she spoke the simple truth. Well aware through hard experience that the love of

---

[89] "Shame be to those who think it" was the motto of the Knights of the Garter.

courtiers came and went with the political tides—she was just as aware that her strongest and most dependable support was the very real love of her people.[90] Not only did knowing this give her courage, it also helped to keep her enemies at bay. Since there were no newspapers then, no photographs or videos to expose how the passage of time had turned her hair gray and blackened her teeth—so long as she remained unmarried she remained in their minds the golden haired princess who survived a cruel beginning to reign as their ageless vestal.[91]

However their representatives in Parliament may have called for her to marry—she knew that marriage would inevitably have changed how her people felt about her—as must have been all too clear from the fates of fellow queens like Mary Queen of Scots, displaced by her baby son—or Elizabeth Valois, died in childbirth attempting to provide Philip II with the requisite heir—or, not least, her own mother.

Some have seen the hysterical overreaction to an erring favorite in terms of myths like Diana and Actaeon—but the transgressions of official lovers like Leicester, Oxford, Raleigh or Essex were not the sort that would have outraged an ancient goddess. Driven by a full measure of raw female jealousy—Elizabeth was angry because they had allowed their sexuality to tarnish the fantasy she fostered, and that she herself so wished to believe—that her official lovers willingly gave up the satisfactions of the flesh out of their pure and genuine love for their (untouchable) Faerie Queene.

Forced by political necessity to a life without sexual fulfillment, she demanded that in exchange for the perquisites they enjoyed—prestigious offices, lucrative monopolies, grand estates—they be happily reconciled to the same self denial that was forced on her. And when they fell short—as all (but Christopher Hatton) eventually did—her fury was truly goddess-like. Although she never totally abandoned any (but Essex)—for a fallen favorite there would be no

---

[90] There's no doubt that she was greatly loved, as the many nursery rhymes about Eliza, Liza, Betty and Bess testify.

[91] The word *virgin* meant something different to the ancients than it does to us today. To them it had nothing to do with sex, it simply meant a woman who could live on her own, without having to depend upon one or more men.

more lavish gifts, monopolies, or sinecures. From then on they had to make do with what they'd already been given—nor were any of them ever raised any higher than Knighthood. Over the forty years of her reign, Elizabeth, uniquely, allowed the creation of only one dynasty.[92]

The *Roman de la Rose*

Shakespeare's fondness for rose imagery suggests that his primary source for this was the immensely popular medieval poem, the French *Roman de la Rose,* in which Dan Cupid causes trouble by instigating illicit attractions. So popular was the elaborate *Roman* that some 300 manuscript copies remain. As the *Ars Amatoria*—the love manual of the Middle Ages—it shows via a complex allegory how a lover might bypass the "walled garden" with which society and family protects the innocence of a maiden whose name was *Rose* (nudge nudge wink wink).[93]

Shakespeare's most immediate access to the *Roman* would have been Chaucer's translation of some part of it into Middle English—published in 1532. While Vyvyan can't see how the uneducated William could possibly have read it in French—he notes that *somehow* he became acquainted with a section Chaucer had left out of his English version (84). As Vyvyan states—

> In Dante, for whom love takes on a mystical significance . . . this subtle meaning becomes more evident. I am not affirming that Shakespeare was directly influenced by Dante, but that both of them—together with Guillaume de Loris, Chaucer and many more—were nourished by a common tradition, virtually a *faith*, to which each made a unique contribution. They share the idea that falling in love is something more than a romantic experience—it is also a rite of initiation into a new life. (40)

---

[92] This was Baron Burghley, and that was only so that his daughter was worthy of marriage to the Earl of Oxford. For political reasons she made Robert Dudley Earl of Leicester, but because he was her own official lover, he didn't dare marry anyone else until it was too late to start a dynasty of his own.

[93] However flattering, the rose is a not very subtle symbol for a maiden's vagina, reminding us that seducing a virgin was frequently described as her *deflowering*.

Lover's eyes

The notion that love first arises through eye contact is such a favorite with Shakespeare that its very presence can help determine him as author. Once alerted we find this reference to eyes and their power everywhere throughout the canon. Vyvyan speaks of the "gradual deepening of the ideas of love and learning with which Berowne is merely toying in *Love's Labour's Lost*. So disturbed does he become by gazing into Rosaline's eyes

> that he tries to defend himself from them by denigration—"two pitch-balls stuck in her face . . . !" But nothing can save him from Shakespeare's decision that his understanding is due to be quickened. . . . We might fairly say that, in the religion of love, the lady's eyes represent the baptismal font.

That love could be expressed and inspired merely by the exchange of glances would have been a popular notion at Elizabeth's Court where this was just about all the contact lovers were allowed—and even that was dangerous. As one maiden put it in a poem to her beloved—

> Thou seest we live amongst the lynx's eyes,
> That pries and spies each privy thought of mind;
> Thou knowest right well what sorrows may arise
> If once they chance my settled looks to find.

Love as a pilgrimage

A pilgrimage is Shakespeare's primary metaphor for the awakening that can come from falling in love. After his first meeting with Juliet, Romeo is more than just "in love"—he has been spiritually altered. Vyvyan suggests that the idea of a religious pilgrimage—a favorite pastime in medieval Europe—comes to both by their mutual response to the overwhelming sensation that has just come over them—when Juliet, not yet ready to kiss his lips, takes his hand, saying "Saints have hands that pilgrims' hands do touch—and palm to palm is holy palmers' kiss." Ophelia, trapped, driven mad by conflicting loyalties to her father and Hamlet—sings that a girl knows her true love by his pilgrim's paraphernalia—his "hat and staff and his sandal shoon."

III Shakespeare in His Own Time

Three more girls in his early plays take to pilgrimages to find their men—Imogen for Posthumous, Julia for Proteus, and Helena for Bertram. As for the men—Berowne and his pals are only the earliest of Shakespeare's protagonists to find themselves embarked upon this pilgrimage—later to be followed by Romeo, Valentine, Benedick, Demetrius, Lysander, Lucentio and Lorenzo. For Romeo, Lear, and Othello—all of whom loved "not wisely but too well"—awakening comes too late—for Leontes and Claudius—better late than never.

The lover in the *Roman de la Rose* and in Dante's *Comedia* both embark upon just such a pilgrimage. As Vyvyan notes, the final chapters of Dante's *Comedia* are "saturated" with conceptions of pilgrimage and spiritual vision (141). In Shakespeare, the pilgrimage takes both men and women to the wilderness of exile—the "naked hermitage" to which the Princess sends the King at the end of *Love's Labour's Lost*—the forest in *Two Gents* where Valentine is captured by bandits—the forest to which Imogen and Belarius escape in *Cymbeline*—the "life removed" from which the Duke emerges in the last act of *Measure for Measure*—the chapel of penitence in *Winter's Tale*—the desolate beach where Perdita is abandoned—the magical island where Prospero is stranded—the forest in *Midsummer Night's Dreame* where Bottom is transformed. All represent the "wild wood" —the wilderness where Nature awaits those in need of awakening.

"O brawling love"

With detailed comparisons—Vyvyan proves that the primary source for *Love's Labour's Lost* was the *Roman de la Rose*. Shakespeare's Dan Cupid reflects the role played there by Cupid as does his fondness for the antitheses for the conflicting emotions created by the wicked infant. Romeo's passionate—"O brawling love! O loving hate! . . . Feather of lead, bright smoke, cold fire, sick health"—are tropes from the medieval original—

> Love is hateful peace, love is hate in love. It is disloyal loyalty, it is loyal disloyalty; it is fear that is completely confident; it is hope in despair. . . reason completely mad, it is reasonable madness. . . laughter filled with tears and weeping.

In *Two Gents*, Valentine's Sylvia—who, according to Vyvyan, is an early version of Shakespeare's goddess of love—has, like Rose in the *Roman,* been imprisoned in a tower by her jealous guardian—with Proteus as the envious and scheming *False Semblant*—the villain of the *Roman*—who purposely and maliciously reveals his friend's efforts to rescue her to the very man who has imprisoned her—and again, when he sends his rival to the poisonous hell represented by St. Gregory's Well. It's clear that Proteus was seriously in need of redemption—as was the caddish Bertram of *All's Well*—suggesting that the original versions of these plays may have been revised by a wiser author for a later, more mature, private audience.

Vyvyan comments that authors of works closer in time to Shakespeare than Chaucer also reflect the theme—among them the Italian Castiglione, whose 1508 *Il Cortegiano* (*The Courtier*) was written in the Courtly Love tradition for the Estense Court of Ferrara —and in the love poetry written by the Earl of Surrey at the Court of the young and still gallant Henry VIII. Yet although the woman is important in these—she is still an object, the receiver of man's love. With Shakespeare she's become his transformation. It's *her* love, not his, that will open first his heart, then his mind.

Unlike Castiglione's Emilia Pia or Surrey's Fair Geraldine— characters like the French Princess in *Love's Labour's Lost*, Portia in *Merchant*, Paulina in *Winter's Tale*, and to some extent Hippolyta in *Dreame*—are more than mere passive receivers of men's worship, they are priestesses of divine wisdom, who will transform their lovers' animal desire into divine understanding. In Valentine's words,

> What light is light, if Sylvia be not seen?
> What joy is joy, if Sylvia be not by?
> Unless it be to think that she *is* by,
> And feed upon the shadow of perfection.
> Except I be by Sylvia in the night,
> There is no music in the nightingale.
> Unless I look on Sylvia in the day,
> There is no day for me to look upon.
> She is my essence, and I leave to be
> If I be not by her fair influence
> Foster'd, illumin'd, cherish'd, kept alive. (Act III Sce. 1)

Thus "love's labour" is *not* their effort to woo the ladies—it is the sometimes wearisome pilgrimage that brings them to the wisdom they thought they were seeking by escaping women to bury themselves in books—but that was actually to be found in the eyes and hearts of these same women—a message that must have been some solace to the Virgin Queen and her corps of cautious ladies.

"If this is not nonsense it must be philosophy"

All of which brings us to Vyvyan's third source—Plato's doctrine of love as described in his dialogues—*the Phaedo* and *the Symposium*—and what is most obvious to those in search of the basis for Shakespeare's beliefs—the ground from which his own faith grew.

Vyvyan, a Platonist himself, sees evidence of this throughout Shakespeare. As a primary instrument through which the European Renaissance found its impetus—it's also far more likely than any of the religions of the time. It was the ancient phrase "Know thyself"—carved in the stones of the temple of Apollo at Delphi—that became the watchword of the Renaissance—as quoted by Marsilio Ficino in one of his letters—"Know thyself as a [spiritual] race clothed with a mortal garment!"

The idea that humanity is a divine species—that the human soul is immortal, and that the path to spiritual enlightenment is through self-knowledge—is what gave the great Italian artists and writers of the fifteenth and sixteenth centuries the freedom to raise their eyes from the grim business of preparing for death to creating the visions of truth and beauty that remain today in the works of Donatello, Brunelleschi, da Vinci, Michelangelo, and Raphael. Mindful of Shakespeare's role in educating his public audience—we might expect that those who purport to study him would finally come to see him—not as a collection of mediocre poets—but as *the single means* by which the light of the Renaissance came to free the English from the gloom and doom of Calvin's kind of Reformation.

None of the university academics who've made it their life's work to study Shakespeare are themselves poets, actors, scientists, inventors, or any sort of genius. That they are none of these suggests that they are simply not equipped—not only to explain, but even to understand—what it means to be a genius. Shakespeare was as far above and beyond his contemporaries as have Newton, Pasteur and Einstein been above theirs. His genius had no need for the styles of the lesser, later writers the dull-witted claim to locate in his works.

Shakespeare's awareness of Plato and his belief in the immortality of the soul is clear from remarks made in passing by his characters—by Poins in the first act of *Henry IV part two* where he comments on Falstaff's illness, "Marry, *the immortal part* needs a physician, but that moves not him [because] though that be sick, *it dies not*"—or Sebastian in *Twelfth Night*, where the half drowned twin assures his sister—who thinks he may be a ghost, that he's alive in every sense —"A spirit I am indeed, but am *in that dimension* grossly clad, which from the womb I did *participate*"[94]—or Lorenzo, in *Merchant of Venice*, while gazing at the night sky with Jessica—

> There's not the smallest orb which thou behold'st
> But in his motion like an angel sings,
> Still choiring to the young-eyed cherubim;
> Such harmony is in immortal souls;
> *But whilst this muddy vesture of decay*
> *Doth grossly close it in, we cannot hear it.*

Quoting Berowne on women's eyes—"They sparkle still the right Promethean fire. They are the books, the arts, the *academes*, that show, contain and nourish all the world." On this Vyvyan comments —"We are certainly not in the sphere of ordinary lovemaking. If this is not nonsense, it must be philosophy."

Far from nonsense, as both philosophy *and* mythology, Lorenzo has touched on both Plato and the myth of Prometheus—known only to those who knew Plato—or Aeschylus, Pindar, Homer or Hesiod— and by his use of the word *academe*, which, according to the OED, was the first time it was ever used in English—a word he got from the *Academy*—the name Plato had given the school he based on the teachings and beliefs of Socrates—known ever since as *Platonism*.

---

[94] The verb *participate*—which makes no sense as used here—may be a compositor's error for *precipitate*—meaning the condensation of matter from a liquid or a gas—a term from distilling with which the typesetter was not familiar.

III Shakespeare in His Own Time

Plato's cave

No reader can miss Shakespeare's fondness for the phrase "shadow and substance"—his favorite metaphor for illusion versus reality." He uses it continually—in *Lucrece*, "Love like a shadow flies when substance love pursues"—Helena in *All's Well*— "Tis but the shadow of a wife you see, the name and not the thing"—Macbeth, "Life's but a walking shadow, a poor player . . ."—Hamlet, "The very substance of the ambitious is merely the shadow of a dream." [95] The word *shadow* is filled with meaning for Shakespeare. In *Dreame*, Puck calls Oberon "King of Shadows"—referring in the epilogue to his power over London's *actors*—"If we shadows have offended . . ."

Another expression of Shakespeare's fascination with *shadow* as *illusion*—is Narcissus who—as described by Ovid—upon seeing his reflection in a pond, falls in love with it and bending to kiss it, literally *falls into himself* and drowns—a perfect metaphor for those who mistake illusion for reality.

Disguise—frequently used by Shakespeare, particularly where girls masquerade as boys—is another kind of shadow—one he turns to farce in *Merry Wives* when he has Falstaff escape trouble disguised as a woman. According to Vyvyan, when Shakespeare has Proteus fail to recognize Julia because she's in male garb—he shows how easy it is to fool humans with a flimsy disguise. Shakespeare often uses the image of a *cloud* for something that hides the truth as clouds hide the sun—as with characters named *Claudio* who fail to see the truth about the noble nature of a wife or sister.

No one can deny his source for this substance/shadow metaphor was *Plato's Cave*—a philosophical construct from *The Republic* where the only things that humans can see—submerged in the darkness of the material world—are the shadows cast on the walls of their earthly prison by the timeless spiritual realities that blaze without. Thus human ideas, policies, dogmas, are only the unstable reflections, wavering and distorted, of eternal verities—"moonshine on the water," as Rosaline puts it in *Love's Labour's Lost*.

---

[95] Samuel Johnson noted that Shakespeare "accidentally" inverted an expression from Pindar—who wrote that human life is but the dream of a shadow.

"Call it what you like"

Nearly all Renaissance theorizing on Love and Beauty stems from conversations between Socrates and the youths gathered to hear his philosophy on the steps of the Forum in 4th century BC Athens—as recalled by Plato years later. From *the Symposium* comes the idea that Love begins as a quest for Beauty—a notion that, according to Socrates, was explained to him by the priestess Diotima, a process that begins with the desire for a beautiful companion that leads first to love, and then to the Greek equivalent of an *epiphany*. Says she—

> And now, Socrates, there bursts upon him that wondrous vision which is the very soul of the beauty he has toiled so long for. It is an everlasting loveliness which neither comes nor goes, which neither flowers nor fades, for such beauty is the same on every hand, the same then as now, here as there, this way as that way, the same to every worshipper as it is to every other . . . while every lovely thing partakes of it in such sort that however much the parts may wax and wane, it will be neither more nor less, but still the same inviolable whole. (trans. B. Jowett).

Vyvyan explains how the transformation takes place—

> This is the way, the only way, he must approach, or be led towards, the sanctuary of Love: starting from individual beauties, the quest of the universal beauty must find him ever mounting the heavenly ladder, stepping from rung to rung . . . from bodily beauty to the beauty of institutions— from institutions to learning, and from learning . . . to the special lore that pertains to nothing but the beautiful itself: until at last he comes to know *what beauty is*. . . .

Having quoted Diotima at some length, Socrates explains—

> This, Phaedrus, this, gentlemen, was the doctrine of Diotima. I was convinced, and in that conviction I try to bring others to the same creed, and to convince them that, if we are to make this gift our own, Love will help our mortal nature more than all the world. And this is why . . . all my life I shall pay *the*

III Shakespeare in His Own Time

power and the might of Love such homage as I can. So you may call this my eulogy of Love, Phaedrus, if you choose—if not, well, call it what you like.

In other words, once an individual has experienced such love, they will continue to seek it in everything.

Socrates seems to have held a fascination for Shakespeare. Numerous commentators have pointed out the similarity of the death of Falstaff—as related by Mistress Quickly in Act II of *Henry V*—to the death of Socrates as related by Plato in the *Phaedo*. By conflating Falstaff with Socrates, surely Shakespeare was sending a message to some part of his audience—although exactly what is anyone's guess. But what matters is that *Shakespeare knew the story*—though academics needs must claim that—being ignorant of Greek he would have read it in some Latin translation. Unfortunately, according to Sears Jayne, for the English at that time, access to Plato was limited.

~ "Small Latin and less Greek" ~

While scholars of the Medieval period were chiefly focussed on Latin translations of Aristotle, we're told that Plato was all but forgotten. For one thing—for the Europeans who sought to understand him—it was necessary to know either Arabic or Greek, and both were difficult for Europeans, Greek in particular was difficult for the English. While most European languages share their alphabet and root words with Latin—Greek has a totally different alphabet—belonging as it does to an altogether different branch of the Indo European language tree. While modern Italian, French, Spanish and even German derive from Latin—a reflection of the vast reach of the Roman Empire—Greece, further east,[96] was more like the Middle East. And because Greek relied on pitch[97]—without the guidance of a native speaker—most Europeans were at something of a loss as to how to pronounce it.

Anyone who has attempted to translate a known language into

---

[96] Maps of the Sea show how the Mediterranean is divided in half by the Italian peninsula, which defines everything to its left as Europe and "the West"—and everything to its right as "the Middle East."

[97] Variations in pitch can cause variations in meaning.

Educating Shakespeare

a learned language knows how difficult it is to recreate the mindset of one in another—even more, to reproduce its charm. Imagine then the problems faced by the English when attempting to express in their homegrown local language the profound thoughts and delights—not only of Plato, but of all the ancient philosophers as well.

Nevertheless—English scholars were among the earliest to study Greek at the University of Padua. Having studied under Politian (Politiano)—Thomas Linacre and William Grocyn brought their love of Greek back with them to Oxford University—and to households like that of Sir Thomas More and Cardinal Wolsey—where youths were being trained for service to the nation. If not pervasive—Greek was certainly not unknown—but it was expensive.

Back in the fifteenth century, when the scholarly Venetian craftsman Aldus Manutius set about to use a recently invented printing press to provide his wealthy patrons with masterworks in Greek—it was at a price that only they could afford. For the first years of print publishing—printed books of any kind were only slightly less expensive than the handwritten, elaborately hand painted manuscripts they were meant to replace.

Books like those published by the Aldine Press at the turn of the sixteenth century were produced at first in small numbers for this same community of wealthy buyers. They were expensive, they were precious—and as such they were not to be shared with any but the most trusted associates. If this was true of books in Latin, it was doubly, triply true of books in Greek. While the same font could be used for books in English that was used for books in Latin—Greek required a totally different font—adding considerably to the cost of its publication (Febvre 266). Added to these was the need to find and pay compositors fluent in Greek[98]—and all in addition to the cost of publishing all books in England where—until 1587 when the English got their first paper mill—even the paper had to come from overseas.

For these reasons, the European's knowledge of Greek and their ownership of books in Greek remained the purview of two groups dependent on wealthy patrons—scholars, primarily theologians, who

---

[98] These were relatively easy to find in Venice at that time as scholars of all faiths were fleeing the spreading Ottoman Empire.

III Shakespeare in His Own Time

were connected with the universities—and poets, most of whom were supported by wealthy Italians—the Medici, Farnese and Borgia.

Greek comes to the universities

Literary historians are inclined to descant on the glories of Renaissance Humanism and its appetite for learning—as do the authors of *The Coming of the Book* (1958), Febvre and Martin—whose study, though focused primarily on France, includes all of Europe, the Slavic nations, Russia and the New World. According to F&M—"From about 1525 the study of Greek became, outside Italy, *almost a craze*—at Oxford and Louvain in 1517, at Alcala in 1528, Paris in 1529, and in several German towns where it began to be studied and taught in a university" (268)—a craze? Hardly!

The numbers they supply may sound impressive—in 1530 a work in Greek sold 500 copies in a few days, with 40 Greek authors published in France that year, 32 in Greek, compared with 33 editions of Latin authors. In 1549, 33 more Greek works came out in Paris compared with 40 in Latin, not counting translations (268). Yet if we consider the actual size of this community, these numbers are a good deal less impressive. According to Febvre—"To become a *homo trilinguist*—i.e. to know Latin, Greek, and Hebrew—was the aim of many of the humanists, and many of them managed it."—That was in France. How many whose native language was English?

It's clear from their history of the European printing and publishing industries as outlined by F&M—the numbers of books, printers, and buyers were barely enough to support an arcane study like Greek. Not until the eighteenth century was the study of Greek at the English universities fully supported by works published in Greek or their translations (192).—So while "the triumph of the humanist spirit" may have been working its way through Europe, the audience for the classics published in Italy remained a "fairly restricted public." In fact, "complete books in Greek do not . . . appear to have been printed outside Italy until the second decade of the sixteenth century."

In England the total was zero.

England's place in the book trade

Despite the fact that a handful of English scholars had been among the first western Europeans to take a serious interest in Greek—when it came to publishing, or even to buying the classics—England was decades behind the continent. While the Europeans were having their Renaissance in the fourteenth and fifteenth centuries, England was at war with itself. With the arrival of the Tudors, support for the classics, never very profound, appears to have waxed and waned in tandem with their religious struggles. But with the Reformation in the sixteenth century, the Inquisition began hanging and burning printers of anti-Catholic doctrine—and those who could were fleeing to protestant England—the balance began to slip towards those ancient works which appeared to support the Reformation.

As Queen Elizabeth's Secretary of State, it was Sir William Cecil's duty to establish a press that conformed to Crown policy. In an effort to prevent the publication of anything that smacked of papism or dissent—he established censors—required that printers be licensed—and kept the number of licensed presses as few as possible with none allowed outside London.

Eventually classics in Latin began to emerge—but those that failed to conform to Crown policy continued to remain in short supply. This is not to say that English scholars and poets were unable to get Plato—it's just that getting them was a good deal more difficult than it was for their counterparts on the continent. Orders had to be made through dealers with agents in trade centers like Paris, Lyons or Frankfurt. Letters to friends living or travelling abroad are filled with requests to send or bring them particular books they can't get at home.

It was "all Greek" to Casca

Those members of Shakespeare's audience who knew something about Roman history would have understood that when Casca reports Caesar's comment in Act I Scene 2 of *Julius Caesar*—where he claims to have missed what Caesar said because "it's all Greek to me"—he was speaking as a plebeian. Educated auditors would recall from their studies of Roman history that Casca was a tribune at the

III Shakespeare in His Own Time

Forum in what was still the Roman Republic—where he represented a class of Romans who had no knowledge of Greek—that being a purview of the aristocracy—to which Cicero belonged, but not Casca.

The European Renaissance was a trickle down phenomenon. The knowledge it sought in ancient Greek and Roman texts had been transmitted for a good 200 years to a very small handful of aristocrats and the writers they patronized. And how was this knowledge transmitted—Greek being so difficult for Europeans? Erasmus—aware of the problem—sought to provide a solution when in 1515—in his long awaited translation of the New Testament into Latin—the Latin text was presented side by side with its Greek translation—providing readers who knew Latin with the means to learn Greek.[99]

Around the turn of the sixteenth century, Aldus Manutius, creator of the Aldine Press in Venice—driven by his desire to awaken the world to the literary wonders of the Old World—having acquired certain ancient texts from immigrants from Greece and Byzantium, had Greek fonts created with which he produced translations of the Greek dramatists and an edition of Plato (1513). These were followed by later editions from other publishers. According to Henry Burrows Lathrop, author of *Translations of the Classics into English*—[100]

> The public of Erasmus was the international body of educated people who read Latin and who were accustomed to reflection and deliberate thought . . . he has in mind the well-to-do, the leaders, as an important part of his public, and the main subject of his educational program. For this view, he had Greek and Roman precedent, education in classical times being essentially aristocratic. (35-6)

That this was also the case in England is confirmed by Sears Jayne, English professor at Brown University and author of *Plato in Renaissance England* (1995). "The revival of Plato in pre-Tudor England was . . . the work of members of the aristocracy, lords of the realm, both temporal and spiritual, but above all, men of wealth" (13).

---

[99] Such a book was known as a *polyglot*.

[100] A product of Harvard and the University of Wisconsin—Lathrop provides what information he can on the publishing history of Greek translation c. 1477-1620.

As the appetite for Humanism spread from the Courts of princes to local communities and from the theologians to their congregations —inevitably translators began translating Greek into Latin, and Latin into their own vernacular languages. With this as with everything else—England lagged behind the continent. Tudor England under Mary and the Henries saw few Latin works translated directly into English. While Chairs in Greek had been established at Cambridge and Oxford c.1540-41—according to Lathrop, towards the end of Henry's reign there is nothing to show that even the best poets of that time—Sir Thomas Wyatt and the Earl of Surrey—could read Greek, or that their Latin went beyond those old favorites—Ovid, Horace and Virgil (97). Lathrop documents the growth of English interest—

> While translations of classical authors grew increasingly numerous in France from the beginning of the 16th century. . . . In England, which had a smaller population . . . book sellers only seem to have found it easy to sell translations in *the second half of the century*—there were 43 editions of classics in English translations before 1550, and 119 between 1550 and 1600. (272)

No masterpieces

A little over 100 published English translations isn't much for a span of 50 years—minuscule when compared with similar records from France and Germany. According to Lathrop, these translations were "vulgar and clumsy" because there were as yet "no masterpieces to suggest the possibilities of the language, or to create any standard of style, . . . no abundant body of metrical achievement to guide the translator to a worthy form"—in other words—no Shakespeare.

More to the point perhaps, is the fact that translating Latin into English is considerably more difficult than translating it into Italian, French or Spanish. Since English, despite its abundance of French words, is rooted in Anglo Saxon—finding appropriate equivalents to Latin terms and syntax was daunting even for the educated. In addition—English translations were hampered for centuries by the lack of a standardized spelling. As a result, most of the Latin works translated into English during this period came by way of French translations—while the handful of translations from Greek came at third hand from French (or Spanish) translations of Latin translations. Thus it's hardly surprising that—apart from one or two notable exceptions—little of value could have been transmitted from ancient Greek to 16th-century English readers via translation.

The reign it reigneth every day

Language barriers were not the only problem faced by Early Modern English translators. An even greater problem was the Protestant Reformation. For the major patrons of such translations—Secretary of State William Cecil and his friend Matthew Parker, Archbishop of Canterbury—it seems that any touch of sensuality or humor based on human frailty or the humanity of officials was considered "lewd" (bawdy or seditious). This put a serious damper on the kind of translating that was popular at the French and Italian Courts. As a result, the first period during which English poets attempted to respond to the Renaissance urge for self-expression was cramped in the extreme. Dubbed the "drab era" by C.S. Lewis—it represents one of the lowest periods in all of English literature.

Lathrop doesn't conceal his contempt for the translations from the Tudor period which he divides between what he terms the "literature of instruction"—strictly informative or grimly protestant—and the "literature of delight"—things meant purely to entertain.

Where's the delight?

While Lathrop has no problem with the *literature of instruction*—with the *literature of delight* he seems overwhelmed with confusion. *Delight*, in his view, begins with two translations to which he gives several pages each—*The Golden Ass* by William Adlington, from the Latin of Apuleius, published in 1566—and *Theagenes and Chariclea* by a T. Underdowne—from the Greek *Aethiopica*, published in 1569—works he terms "minor masterpieces" (158). According to Lathrop, Adlington substitutes

> for the abrupt . . . rhythm of Apuleius an ample and flowing manner, using connectives and filling up omissions and

balancing large groups unostentatiously but harmoniously. His diction is habitually raised above prose without being extreme and strange, and now and then flowers into an imaginatively exquisite phrase. (161)

Underdowne too outperforms the Greek original. Although the style of Heliodorus's Greek is "full of ingenious conceits"—according to Lathrop it "lacks color and various rhythm [and] is poor and thin" while Underdowne's translation is "rich and full-bodied." Like Adlington, Underdowne has the gift of "an ample rhythm. . . . Having a tamely written original, he heightens and gives spirit to the diction." But who were William Adlington and T. Underdowne?[101]—Their themes suggest Court over University—but it's hard to say, since neither has left anything in the record but their names.

For poetry, who most arouses Lathrop's admiration is Robert Greene, whose madrigal, "Rest Thee Desire"—based on an ancient Greek poem—"first made the magic union of Italian or French grace . . . with the blithe and brisk rural and sylvan tradition of English life" (157). But who was Robert Greene?

Equally perplexing are those translators that Lathrop forgets or ignores—among them the teenaged Lady Jane Lumley—whose 1550-1553 translation of Euripides's *Iphigenia at Aulis* was the very first English translation (to survive) made directly from Greek. Most peculiar of all is Lathrop's apparent ignorance of *Thomas Watson*—who, having translated Petrarch's *Canzoniere* from Italian to Latin in the late 1570s, in 1581 published what was probably Europe's first translation from Greek to Latin of Sophocles's *Antigone*, and in 1582 his *Hekatompathia or Passionate Century of Love*—which, according to Arber (1870), shows him "at home with the entire body of Greek and Latin poets." Perplexed by these mysteries—Lathrop either ignores them or gives them nothing more than a passing mention.

---

[101] Lathrop gets *William Adlington's* name wrong twice, calling him *Thomas* in the text and *John* in the index, nor does Adlington have a biography in the DNB, though Wikipedia holds that his translation was a favorite of Shakespeare's. *Underdowne* is included in the DNB, but only as the author of this one work.

III Shakespeare in His Own Time

Plato's "fervent welcome"

It's been obvious for centuries that the ideas and ideals expressed in Plato's dialogues represent the driving spirit of the Renaissance—but while this is assumed it's not all that easy to find an account of how it happened. One thing, however, is clear—it was far from overnight. During the so called Dark Ages, Europe lost its awareness of Plato, as scholiasts turned their focus to translations of Aristotle. It wasn't until the first Greek codices reached Italy in about 1400, when—according to the author of *The First Cambridge Press in its European Setting*—Plato "gained a fervent welcome from the humanists" (24).

Sometime towards the end of the fourteenth century, Cosimo de Medici, banker and philosophical leader of Republican Florence, created what he called *The Academy*—meant to function on principles outlined centuries before by Plato—with whom Cosimo apparently became acquainted through conversations with a wise man from the East while taking a brief political time-out in Venice. As Goldschmidt tells it—"By 1477 the Florentine Platonist Marsilio Ficino—a scholar supported by Cosimo—completed his translation of the whole corpus of Plato's writings—and by April 1485, the first Latin edition of Plato's works was published at Florence, in two volumes—with a second edition six years later." As for Plato in the original Greek—that had to wait until Aldus Manutius of the Aldine Press published his edition in 1513. Again—"no second Greek edition came out in Italy for centuries" (24).

Clearly the revolution inspired by Plato—however important—was limited from the start to a very small community, and took a very long time to spread beyond it. And no sooner did it spread to France and Spain than politics ended it in Italy. Per Goldschmidt—

> It is a strange thing to realize that this magnificent effort was the end, not the beginning, of humanism in Italy. They are the culmination of the endeavors and wishes of a whole century—but their sequel is negligible in Italy. They bear their fruit beyond the Alps. (29)

The baton of Greek studies then passed to southern Spain, where enough scholars from the Golden Age of Islam remained to facilitate the translation of Arabic versions of the ancient Greeks into Latin. "Despite the fact that Spain was still cut off from the rest of Europe, important works made it across the mighty Pyrenees to assist with the process of enlightening the rest of Europe" (31). According to Goldschmidt, the small number of copies that have survived the centuries suggest that not all that many actually made the trip.

England and Greek

During the Renaissance—the cultural revolution in which Platonism played such a crucial role—a handful of English scholars were involved from the beginning in establishing the traditions that would lead to Shakespeare. While Oxford University remained stuck in the medievalisms of its founders—Cambridge followed the humanism of Bishop John Fisher, who brought Erasmus to Cambridge in 1510 as its first Greek reader.

Goldschmidt notes that in 1525—of the five press correctors used by Aldus for his first edition of Galen in Greek—four were English, including Thomas Lupset, Colet's student at St. Paul's who, along with Thomas Starkey, had studied at the University of Padua. So—despite its seeming later decline—it's clear that Platonism and Greek were embraced by English scholars early on.

No books entirely in Greek were printed in England until 1590 when one was published by George Bishop—with whom Richard Field of Stratford first apprenticed in 1579—the same Richard Field who would print Shakespeare's *Venus and Adonis* in 1593, and who would also publish a number of Shakespeare's most important sources, among them the 1587 edition of Holinshed's Chronicles and the 1589 Latin edition of *The Metamorphoses*, plus a number of other works connected to the truth about Shakespeare.

Plato the heretical pagan

In an effort to provide the Academy with some hard facts with regard to England's awareness of Plato—Prof. Sears Jayne of Brown University spent part of the twentieth century delving through every possible archive and text to locate what by or about Plato had been

III Shakespeare in His Own Time

published or sold in England from his complete works in Greek to the mere mention of his name.[102] According to Jayne—while Plato was popular on the continent—at Oxford, Greek scholars Linacre and Grocyn were more focused on Aristotle. He claims that at St. Paul's grammar school—while Colet was interested in Ficino's works—he seems not to have mentioned translations of Plato (83). Here we see the orthodox mind at work. Just because these scholars failed to mention Plato in print, doesn't mean they hadn't read it.

Knowing the importance of Plato to the Europeans during their Renaissance—why the seeming lack of interest by the English? Nor was it just Plato that they resisted—but, according to some—all study of Greek. During England's brief Renaissance under the youthful Henry VIII—it seems that his attempt to introduce Greek at Oxford led to a "violent" controversy between the *Grecians*—who wanted it, and the *Trojans*[103]—who thought it was "un-English."

Henry tried to resolve the controversy by issuing injunctions requiring both universities to teach it—though without effect[104] until Wolsey created colleges in the early 1540s at both universities, where he it nailed into the curriculum. After studying at Oxford and Paris, John Redman set up a Greek course at Cambridge by which means he passed his enthusiasm on to students John Cheke and Thomas Smith—who would push the university to use the Erasmian pronunciation. Yet, according to Jayne, Elizabeth's tutor, Roger Ascham, educated at Cambridge, shows "little knowledge of Plato."

The Tudor "blackout"

"Why was there so little interest in Plato in England during the Tudor era?" asks Jayne. He believes this was due to the fact that "the Tudor monarchs controlled what was thought in England," and "they were not interested in Plato" (137). Of course not—Plato's belief that

---

[102] To date, Jayne's results remain unpublished in six volumes of typescript in two archives at Brown University.

[103] The medieval English considered themselves descended from Brut (Brutus) a mythical Trojan who supposedly had escaped the burning of Troy.

[104] Due to Henry's efforts, it seems the dons allowed Plato to be read at Oxford—but not in class—and only during holidays.

souls were divine and therefore transcended earthly death was totally out of line with Adam's fall, when they "sinned all"—threatening an eternity in Hell if they didn't repent while alive. If humans were *born* divine—why bother to seek salvation?

As for the reformers, Plato's philosophy of love, embracing as it did—or at least tolerating—the sexual behavior of the Athenians where it was apparently born—was anathema to the evangelical hardliners, focused as they were on sin and damnation. Aware of the prejudice—if not its cause—Jayne notes that

> The tightness of the Tudor grip on the thought of the English population is often underestimated.... Because England was an island, the Tudors were able to mold their small population into an extraordinarily homogeneous society. They did this primarily by religious education, catechizing from infancy every soul at every level of the social hierarchy, to accept the authority of the regime.... But the Tudors did not rely on religious education alone. They also used their control of the printing press and import licenses to dictate what books the English people were allowed to read. Nor was that all. Whenever an unruly citizen stepped out of line, the regime swiftly whipped him back into position, using any method that seemed appropriate: confiscation of property, imprisonment, exile, torture, public maiming . . . public execution. (136-7)

Jayne follows this with a convincing argument—"The proof that it was the regime itself that was primarily responsible for the 'blackout' of Plato during the Tudor era is that during the Stuart dynasty that followed—English interest in Plato immediately burgeoned." What's likely is that the English were just as interested in Plato as the Europeans—they were simply more careful about revealing it.

What then are we to think of Jayne's dismissal of Sir Thomas Elyot's knowledge of Plato—knowing as we do, how in his *Boke of the Governour*—Elyot encouraged tutors to teach their students to read the Greeks in their own language, or his policy as he states in that important book that by seventeen a boy should be reading philosophy, Plato in particular! In an article published in the online *Literature Compass* in 2007—Oxford scholar Kirsty Milne writes—

III Shakespeare in His Own Time

Modern scholarship continues to present Elizabethan England as a culturally deprived backwater . . . where the study of Greek authors had decayed since the time of Ascham and John Cheke. The teaching of Greek is described as "patchy and intermittent," while collections of scholarly books were "mostly all imported."

Aware of the appreciation of Greek that somehow escaped Jayne—Milne discovered a previously unmentioned trove of some 21 works listed in the *Short Title Catalogue*—published in the 1580s and '90s—all or mostly all in Greek. She questions why these books have escaped notice for so long—suggesting several possibilities—but finally concluding that the

> best explanation for the invisibility of these books is the dominance of *a historical model that precluded their existence.* Now that Renaissance studies tend to be focused on vernacular rather than classical texts, the idea of the Elizabethan Greek "blank" has been allowed to pass unchallenged. (687)

Surely by this unidentified "historical model" she means the Stratford authorship, extending its potent if unnamed influence from its center within the university *sanctorum*. Here we are then—back where we began—with the First Folio and the "small Latin and less Greek" that was Jonson's effort to dismiss with a wave of his editorial hand the vastness of Shakespeare's classical learning. Knowledge of Greek—however difficult to acquire—was the only means by which *Platonism*, the Pierian spring that fed his creative genius—could possibly have reached him. The only question is through what, or whom, was Shakespeare introduced to Plato and to Greek.

—⁓— Poetry vs. the Reformation —⁓—

However the English Reformation may have embraced and reinforced the Renaissance enthusiasm for Learning, where they clashed was in their attitudes towards Art. For Art—that is, the pursuit of the Beautiful—so admired and sought after at the 15th-century Courts of the southern European princes—in 16th-century Northern Europe ran into the all-consuming fear of Sin and the Devil that were possessing so many former Catholics. To followers of John Calvin—Beauty was a snare and a delusion—a tool of Satan in his appetite for souls. How the Devil got such a grip on the English—and how Shakespeare—the greatest poet of all, managed to ignore Him, keep writing and getting published—is not only an important question—it may be *the most important question!*

Having taken control of the English Church under Edward VI, some evangelicals who had made modest advances under Henry VIII— went to extremes. In their campaign to cleanse the Church of flummery and eliminate what they regarded as pagan idolatry—gangs of extremists smashed the precious stained glass windows in the churches—stole and melted down the gold and silver candlesticks, chalices and crucifixes from the altars—and with the painted wooden statues of saints and elaborately carved rood screens made bonfires in the streets outside. During this period, most of England's publicly shared art was lost, stolen, or destroyed.[105]

At the same time the art of portraiture—the only means then of recording the faces and figures of family members—of social and political leaders—declined into stiffly stylized icons. Perhaps it was the Queen's pleasure that caused the exaggeration of height in portraits where some appear to be ten to twelve feet tall.[106] After the works of the great Hans Holbein during Henry's reign—there would be almost no portraiture of genuine artistic value until Gainsborough and Reynolds in the eighteenth century.

Literature managed to survive this purge of the Arts, but it was not without a struggle. Details of the long ongoing battle between the Reformation and the Stage as found in Book IV of E.K. Chambers's *Elizabethan Stage* under "Documents of Criticism" and "Documents of Control." As for the Press—while less obvious (the censorship that

---

[105] In October 2014 the Tate Britain mounted an exhibit labelled "Art under Attack: Histories of British Iconoclasm . . . the first such exhibit to explore the history of the attacks on Art in Britain during the 16th century" in which examples of paintings, stained glass windows and sculptures damaged by the Calvinists were displayed. Sadly, England has very little undamaged art from this period.

[106] Portraits of Robert Devereaux, Earl of Essex, are typical.

III Shakespeare in His Own Time

prevented works from being published having left fewer examples)—it's more crucial, since publishing is our most precious means of analyzing the past. While historians may mention this in passing—due to the gulf that separates History from Literature—little attention has been paid to the effect such censorship had on the literary Arts.

One who did notice, the respected Shakespearean, English Professor Lily B. Campbell of UCLA—made it the subject of Chapter IX in her *Shakespeare's Histories* (1945). In "History versus Poetry in Renaissance England" she begins—

> [T]o understand the place of history in the English Renaissance we must turn to the attacks made upon poetry ... first by the adherents of the Reformation and later by the Puritans. ... These attacks on poetry are not today so well known as are the *defenses* of poetry and particularly the great defense offered by Sidney.[107] Nevertheless, the defenses of poetry cannot be fully comprehended unless we remind ourselves that defense is always organized *to resist attack*. ... Any consideration of literary criticism during the Renaissance must ... recognize the compelling necessity which made it primarily a *defender* of poetry. (85)

Campbell is one of the few who have grasped the significance of the fact that—uniquely among the nations of Europe—the Reformation was upon the English before they'd had their Renaissance. She explains how the reformers enlisted Plato in their war against the Stage. Plato's argument against poetry in *The Republic* had long since been countered by Aristotle—who explains how laughter and pity can heal through catharsis—but this meant nothing to the evangelicals whose wary eyes were on the Fiend.

"A vain jarring of words"

In pamphlets published and distributed by officials—whether City, Church, or Crown isn't known—former playwright Stephen Gosson lashed out at his erstwhile colleagues as "crocodiles" and their little

---

[107] *An Apologie for Poesie*—published in 1580 in response to Gosson's diatribe.

stage in the Liberty of Blackfriars as "the Nest of the Devil and the sink of all Sin." Preachers railed from the pulpit. Mayors bombarded the Privy Council with demands that the theaters be "plucked down." From the late 1560s on—every riot, every visitation of the plague, was blamed on the theaters, the actors, and, of course, the authors of their plays—so it should be obvious that the identity of an author of a particular play—or series of plays—would have been as much a matter of concern for the actors as it was for the authorities. One of the earliest attacks came in 1569 when James Sanford's translation of Agrippa's 1530 *Vanity and Uncertainty of the Arts and Sciences* was published as an attack on Poetry and the Stage,

> Poetry, as Quintilian writeth, is another part of grammar, not a little proud in this thing only, that in times past the theaters and amphitheaters, the goodliest buildings of men, were erected not by philosophers, not by lawyers, . . . but with exceeding great expense by *the fables of poets*, an art that was devised to no other end but to please the ears of foolish men with wanton rhythms, with measures, and weightiness of syllables, and with *a vain jarring of words* . . . to deceive men's minds with the delectation of fables. . . . Wherefore it doth deserve to be called *the principal author of lies, and the maintainer of perverse opinions.* (Campbell 88)

Poets and storytellers fought back—most notably Thomas Lodge in 1578, Philip Sidney in 1581 (both against Gosson), and Thomas Nashe (against Sanford) in 1593—but to no avail—the Crown itself having shifted from the humanism of the Lutherans to the evangelism of the "Elect." From "the most direct attack upon poetry as lying" with which Campbell was familiar, she quotes the translation by Sir Edward Hoby of a French diatribe titled *Politic Discourses upon Truth and Lying*, published in 1586 and dedicated to Hoby's uncle, William Cecil Lord Burghley, who apparently continued to be the final authority regarding what got published. She comments—

> The description of poetry as poison mixed with honey, the emphasis upon pleasure derived from poetry as suspect, the reiteration of Plato's contention [in the *Laws*] that passion and vice are replenished by poetry, are all familiar—but it must be

III Shakespeare in His Own Time

noted that all other charges are made subordinate to the main thesis of the chapter, *that poetry is lying*. (92)

She notes that all of Hoby's Chapter 36 is dedicated to condemning the "backbiters, mockers, and evil speakers, and why the comedians, stage players and jugglers have [always] been rejected," and how plays "infecteth more the spirits and wrappeth them in passions then drunkenness itself." She quotes Hoby—

> As touching plays, they are full of *filthy words*, which would not become . . . lacqueys and courtesans and have sundry inventions which infect the spirit and replenish it with *unchaste, whorish, cosening, deceitful, wanton and mischievous passions*. . . . And besides all these inconveniences, comedians and stage players do often times envy and gnaw at the honor of another, and to please the vulgar people, set before them sundry lies and teach much dissoluteness and deceit . . . cities . . . would never . . . entertain them. (92-3)

Written in 1586 when England was suffering the increasing severity of Burghley's war on dissidents and Catholicism—six years after his brutal capture, torture, trial and execution of Saint Edmund Campion—nine years before his son's equally brutal execution of the Jesuit poet Robert Southwell—we should consider that perhaps it was less the poets' "filthy" language that had inspired this from Burghley's nephew than how they did "envy and gnaw" at the honor of the Cecils.

"Beautified is a vile phrase"

Though Burghley may have encouraged the Stage back in the 1560s when Philip II blamed him for satires defaming his Spanish Majesty (Read *Secretary* 133)—it seems that, by the mid-1580s the Lord Treasurer was preparing to restrict the Stage and the commercial Press—perhaps uproot them entirely.

It's Polonius—universally accepted as Burghley—who sneers at Hamlet's poem to Ophelia as he reads—"To the beautified Ophelia —That's an ill phrase," says Polonius, "a vile phrase— *beautified* is a vile phrase." To describe *beautified* as *vile*—which according to the dictionary means "highly offensive, repulsive, disgusting, morally debased, depraved, or despicable"—might seem a bit extreme. (On the other hand, Ophelia *was* his daughter.)

"Who doth not wonder . . . ?"

As Sidney, Lodge, Nashe, and other defenders would emphasize—*without Poetry* there would be no History, for all human knowledge, all records from the dawn of Time to the Elizabethan present—came in meter and usually also with rhyme and other poetic effects. Long before humans discovered how to keep records through inscribed symbols they preserved their sacred stories and beliefs by passing them directly from one mind to another during the centuries covered by *the Oral Tradition*.

Since humans first maintained cultures purely by memorizing texts passed from one mind to another solely by word of mouth—they were forced to use verbal tricks like *alliteration, repetition* and *rhyme* (*mnemonics* in Greek) for the message to stick exactly as given without alteration. Thus what we call poetry today developed as the primary means of maintaining and transmitting culture—its beliefs and its laws. Since the ancient Celts has left us nothing in writing—this was their only means of maintaining a culture whose existence has left us its effects only in designs on swords, shields, and helmets.

It may be that written messages tend to appear for the first time when governing elders are faced with some devastating threat—fearing that all whose task it was to know and remember the important chants, hymns, epics, mantras, prayers, etc., may not survive—leaving no other means with which to transmit them to the future[108]—they were forced to create a written language. Labelled as by Homer, Confucius, Lao Tsu, etc., the anonymous authors of the Vedas and Upanishads, the Scandinavian Eddas, the Irish Mabinogion, the theorems of Pythagoras and the Hebrew Old Testament—were put into forms that came as close as possible to what, till then, had been transmitted orally.

---

[108] The discovery of the Dead Sea Scrolls in 1946-1956 in jars buried in the sand in the Judean desert—suggests an attempt to preserve them from some great threat.

III Shakespeare in His Own Time

As Philip Sidney explained in his *Apologie for Poetry*—this is why the oldest works of wisdom and religion come framed in verse—and as Thomas Lodge cried out in furious response to Gosson's diatribe—"Who then doth not wonder at Poetry? Who thinketh not that it procedeth from above?"

Not all such ancient versification was confined serious matters—much Greek and Roman verse was meant to entertain, to woo or praise a lover—some salacious. To the Calvinists such works were not only sinful and a waste of time—they were dangerous—encouraging the young to focus too much on their feelings, leading them to indulge in illicit love, thence to lust, thence to narcissism, melancholia and eventually to madness.[109]

Happily for the merry English—by the time the full force of Calvin's regime had gained control, they were protected to some extent by the Erasmian curriculum, which—based largely on Italian humanist literature—was already in place. To students indoctrinated by the Church into fears of sin and damnation—grammar school, with its studies of the poetry of the ancient Romans, much of it based on Greek models—provided them with a glimpse into the life-affirming Platonism that was being stamped out by dirty-minded officials for whom the word *love* could only mean *sex*.

Not that sex wasn't a problem when it came to teaching Greek. Unfortunately for the tutors—it was often these same great poets who wrote the more explicitly sexual poetry. Ovid in particular was a problem—particularly his *Ars Amatoria* (*The Art of Love-making*)—but so were Lucian, Catullus, and Martial.

Thus—right from the start—we can see how, for Reformation pedagogues from Erasmus to Vives to Elyot to Ascham—teaching boys through reading and translating the ancient poets could be a Catch-22. They all deal with it—advising how and where to edit the ancient masters so as to protect their students from infection. But boys will be boys—and having learned to translate—it wouldn't take long before they found, and shared, the more explicit texts. Most dangerous of all were the Greek love poems, since these were often

---

[109] According to Polonius, Hamlet first "fell into a sadness, then into a fast, thence to a watch, thence into a weakness, thence to a lightness, and, by this declension, into the madness wherein now he raves and we all mourn for."

Educating Shakespeare

addressed to some member of the poet's own sex. Generations of boys raised in males-only boarding schools where lonely hearts and developing libidos had nothing to focus on but each other.

When the Renaissance in Art that had captivated Italy two centuries earlier finally burst into bloom under Queen Elizabeth—with visual expressions like sculpture and painting frowned upon by puritans—it was only in arenas like music, poetry and stories where they found an outlet in what Lathrop would term "the literature of delight." Even scholarly studies were limited by the reformers' fears. As Nashe would snarl—

> As there be those that rail at all men, so there be those that rail at all Arts, as Cornelius Agrippa [in his] *De vanitate scientarium,* and a treatise that I have seen in dispraise of learning, where he [Hugh Sanford[110]] saith, it is the corrupter of the simple, the schoolmaster of sin, the storehouse of treachery, the reviver of vices, and mother of cowardice, alleging many examples, how there was never man egregiously evil but he was a scholar; that when the use of letters was first invented, the Golden World ceased, . . . how study doth effeminate a man, dim his sight, weaken his brain, and engender a thousand diseases.

Thus the English Renaissance—when finally it arrived from foreign shores—had somehow to find its way past Satan—so for those who could read, books offered an alternative. Within rows of little black marks, romantic, even sexy narratives could lurk unseen. Ambiguous texts, disingenuous titles, ridiculous claims of utility—suggest that these pamphlets did all they could to slip past Burghley's censors. It's also the major reason for the hiding of the identities of all but two of the most important writers of that time. The first, Sir Philip Sidney—was saved from shame only because he was dead by the time his sister had his poetry published. For the other— Christopher Marlowe, the motto on his portrait says it all—not for him alone, but for all the poets and playwrights of the English Renaissance—"*ce qui me nourrit me détruit*"—"that which nourishes me destroys me"—in

---

[110] Secretary to the Earl of Pembroke and tutor to his children by Mary Sidney.

III Shakespeare in His Own Time

Marlowe's case, quite literally.

For gifted poets born at this time, particularly courtiers, Catholics, or educated women who felt the irresistible urge to publish things that Burghley might think "vile"—there was no other choice —it was either anonymity or a pseudonym. The Tudor-Stuart period is unlike any other in the number of works signed only with initials.

As it was in the beginning . . .

The Courts of Europe were the nurseries of the Arts and Sciences of the Renaissance. Fostered by recent discoveries of the arts of ancient Rome and Athens, few besides courtiers had the leisure to pursue these themselves. With the resurgence of interest in ancient Roman playwrights like Plautus and Terence—whose works were performed for the the Dukes of Ferrara, Gilbert Highet notes—"like the original pastoral Greek and Roman idylls, the Renaissance pastorals and pastoral romances were nearly all written by courtiers" (168).

This would probably have been just as true in England as it was in France and Italy had not the Reformation blocked it. During Elizabeth's reign—no courtier who allowed a work of poetry or fiction to be known as his was ever given office. Simply writing it was not the issue, since many at Court, wrote occasional verse, just as they sight-sang madrigals, conversed in French, Spanish and Italian, and played musical instruments. What was *verboten* was to take it too seriously. Worst of all was allowing it to be published, where it lay in the bookstalls next to jokebooks and almanacs.

Courtiers driven to write and publish but who also had ambition for important offices were forced to stop—as did Thomas Sackville, a poet of great promise, who, having inherited his father's title as Baron Buckhurst—bid farewell to his youthful folly (in a poem)— after which, so far as we know, he never published anything else.

"Stop a stream from running and it will rage"

Renaissance Courts were generally sinkholes of sin, but as Europe's Queen of the Protestant Reformation—vilified by Catholic Courts as the Great Whore of Babylon come back—Elizabeth was determined to show the world that a Royal Court could be glamorous, even romantic, whilst adhering to the highest principles of morality.

Beyond the insult to her prerogative—it was the necessity to maintain the myth of her supernatural powers that sent the Queen into such rages when one of her favorites fell victim to their lower instincts. One of her "maids of honor"—having lost her virtue to one of Elizbeth's courtiers, explained how it was for women at Court—

> Thou seest we live amongst the lynx's eyes,[111]
> That pries and spies each privy thought of mind;
> Thou knowest right well what sorrows may arise
> If once they chance my settled looks to find....
>
> And let me seem, although I be not coy,
> To cloak my sad conceits with smiling cheer.
> Let not my gestures show wherein I joy,
> Nor by my looks let not my love appear.
>
> We [helpless] dames, that false suspect do fear,
> And live within the mouth of envy's lake,
> Must in our hearts a secret meaning bear,
> Far from the show that outwardly we make....
>
> So where I like, I list not vaunt my love;
> Where I desire, there must I feign debate.
> One hath my hand, another hath my glove,
> But he my heart whom most I seem to hate.
>
> Thus farewell, friend—I will continue strange.
> Thou shalt not hear by word or writing aught,
> Let it suffice, my vow shall never change.
> As for the rest, I leave it to thy thought.

In short, the gentlemen pensioners and ladies-in-waiting—those who knew what was good for them—learned to hide their feelings for each other. In such a climate—mere glances were open to interpretation, gossip, and—if the man wasn't careful—punishment in the form of assignments that could take him to the far corners of the Queen's

---

[111] The lynx was thought to have superior eyesight.

diplomatic service. Pent up in bored and restless hearts—courtiers with no other outlet than pen, ink, paper, and anonymity—spent their nights pondering rhymes and metaphors. Unable to express them directly—lovers and romantics poured their feelings into verse. Out of such a climate arose some very beautiful literature.

Thus damned to hell, dammed up and discouraged—Dan Cupid used the Stage and the Press to burst past the Reformation controls to flood the bookstalls—where readers flocked to buy their anonymous sonnet cycles—and in so doing, helped create the periodical press.

Original Sin

At the heart of Calvin's anti-sex campaign lurks an unpleasant truth that must be understood for this attitude towards sex to be seen in perspective. Sin was a concern from the beginning—"In Adam's fall we sinnéd all." By the third century BC the "Seven Deadly Sins" were already hardwired into the Christian Creed. What was new in the mid-sixteenth century was Calvin's emphasis on *Lust*—which until then was among the lesser sins. Replacing spiritual sins like *Pride* and *Greed*, something must have happened to move *Lust* to the forefront —as is clear from the sudden predominance of terms like *filth* and *filthy*—buzzwords for sex. To Calvin—all pleasure, even between husband and wife—was soul destroying lust.[112]

How on earth did these reformers manage to persuade their followers that sexual desire either should or could be eliminated? Not only is sexual climax one of the sweetest (and easiest and least expensive) of pleasures offered by life to the suffering human animal––but as the very force that brings life into existence, it should be considered sacred—as it *was* considered back when humanity was much more concerned with surviving as a species.

How did the puritans succeed in getting so many to join Calvin's anti-sex crusade? More to the point—what led them to this

---

[112] Here begins the hysterical revulsion towards same sex love that would culminate in the vicious brutalities of England's 19th-century epidemic of homophobia (Crompton). Here begins the notion perpetrated on generations of children that masturbation will lead to blindness and insanity. Here begins the emotional (as opposed to the merely legal) prejudice against persons born out of wedlock.

bizarre, even dangerous, position?—dangerous because if sex could be eliminated—there would be no more puritans to protest.

Throughout the centuries dominated by the Catholic Church, unmarried men and women were segregated into communities of monks and nuns—or bound into couples by marriages that could not be legally sundered. This did not prevent illicit relations—but it did make consummation more challenging. The Church was largely willing to accept the children born of illegal liaisons—allowing their parents to find places for them in society—raising others in orphanages maintained by nuns. But once the evangelicals got hold of sex as an issue—any understanding or forgiveness was damned as well. Unlucky infants who died before they were baptized (by a protestant minister) went straight to hell. As Calvin explained—

> Original sin, therefore, seems to be a hereditary depravity and corruption of our nature, diffused into all parts of the soul . . . [which] brings forth in us those works which Scripture calls "works of the flesh" (Gal 5:19). And that is properly what Paul often calls sin. The works that come forth from it—such as adulteries, fornications, thefts, hatreds, murders, carousings —he accordingly calls "fruits of sin" (Gal 5:19-21).

Note the order of these evil manifestations—while *adulteries* and *fornications* head the list, *murders* come second to the last, only slightly more terrible than *carousings*—drinking, dancing (and of course creating and watching plays). Hoby's 1586 adjectives shows the same order—*"unchaste"* and *"whorish"* lead his list.

Nor was the Reformation the sole purveyor of this far reaching anti-lovemaking campaign—for it was about this same time that the Catholic Inquisition—instituted to weed out heresy—erupted in its anti-witch program. Charges of practicing witchcraft or pagan rituals, or simply of "misleading their children" were sufficient in the Catholic nations to give the locals a thrill as they watched unpopular women get burned to death. According to historians—over the 160 years from 1500 to 1660—Europeans saw between 40,000 and 80,000 human beings, chiefly women, executed for practising witchcraft in Germany and France (a mere 1,000 in England).

So what—beside the wrath of God—was the reason for the

III Shakespeare in His Own Time

success of these brutal anti-sex, anti-female, anti-pleasure, anti-poetry, anti-laughter campaigns? While there have always been "preachers of asceticism"—there must have been a reason why so many at this time chose to adopt the grim mandates of Calvinism—more generally referred to by historians as *puritanism*.

Enter "the Great Pox"

So far the best, in fact the only sensible answer comes to us from *sociology*—that branch of history (institutionalized by Karl Marx) that seeks to expand our understanding of historical events beyond human politics to include natural disasters and epidemics—among the latter the sudden appearance of syphilis, a disease spread by sex of a more virulent nature than anything known until then.

In 1989, Stanislav Andreski, professor of Comparative Sociology at the Polish University in London published *Syphilis, Puritanism and Witch Hunts,* in which he proposed that "the importation of syphilis into Europe had . . . profound effects on civilization" affecting most directly religion and economic development. He held this opinion, said he, "on three grounds—chronological congruence, psychological plausibility," and what may be most convincing of all—"the complete inadequacy of alternative explanations" (4).

Known in Shakespeare's time as *the Pox*—due to the pitted scars it left on the face and body (or *the Great Pox*—as opposed to the *small*pox, potentially disfiguring but nowhere near as deadly —syphilis was first reported in Naples in 1495, spreading rapidly thenceforth throughout Europe from port towns to brothels to the Courts of kings like Henry VIII. Among STDs—even comparing it with the terrible epidemic of HIV that hit the West in the 1980s (and is still rampant in Africa)—syphilis remains among the most horrific due to its apparent disappearance after the first trimester, later reappearing as incurable sores on various body parts—then in the final trimester destroying both mind and body. Perhaps most horrible is how it infects partners, infecting the fetus in a mother's womb.

As Andreski puts it—"With a little bit of bad luck, one sinful act by either spouse could cause both of them to rot alive, become paralysed or mad, and their offspring be born diseased or dead" (7).

Although his discomforting thesis has been largely ignored by historians—it's hard to deny that the Protestant Reformation in Europe was influenced by this fear. As Andreski put it—

> Causation of great historical processes is always bafflingly complex, and clearly many other factors were involved. But this seems to me less uncertain than any other explanation—puritanism would not have had the appeal which helped it to find adherents so quickly and widely without the spread of syphilis. (5)

Andreski notes how it ravaged the royal houses of Europe. The tendency of kings and princes to sexual profligacy resulted in the "degeneration and dying out of noble families," among them the Borgias, and though he doesn't dwell on it—the Tudors.

Henry's "Great Matter"

Among the kings whose "bizarre behavior" suggests syphilis—Andreski names Ivan the Terrible and Henry VIII (77). If the great King's history is examined with an unprejudiced eye—that he was infected with syphilis during the profligate years of his youth explains as nothing else can the litany of sorrows that accompanied his efforts to acquire a legitimate heir. The deaths of his wives in childbirth—the stillbirths of their children—the details of the deaths of those of his children who survived birth but died in the their teens—all testify to what has simply been too ugly to accept.

Unwilling to admit what must have been clear at the time to his courtiers, who—not yet saved by antibiotics—would certainly have been well aware of its symptoms. They would also have known the political dangers of discussing or writing about it—so the historians who deny that the King had syphilis because nobody mentioned it at the time—are simply clueless about life at Henry's Court, and the dangers posed to anyone who dared to speak the deadly word.

Every few years someone comes up with yet another arcane disease that they claim had caused Henry's symptoms. Relying on the fact that people died frequently of diseases that had some similar symptoms, historians have simply ignored the evidence in the score of deaths that followed Henry, his partners, his children, and himself.

~∞~ Shakespeare and Divine Right ~∞~

From Jack Cade to Bolingbroke—Shakespeare portrays rebellion in the terms repeated over and over in the Homilies. In play after play he reinforces the idea that monarchs rule because God has willed it. Whether kings—or in England's case, queens—be right or wrong, no matter by what means they had achieved the throne—to rebel against "God's anointed" was an unpardonable sin, sending all who attempted it—or even considered it—to eternal damnation. Put in the mouths of rhetoricians like Sir Thomas More in the play of that name[113]—Mark Antony in *Julius Caesar*—or Ulysses in *Troilus and Cressida*—Alfred Hart shows, point by point, how Shakespeare's characters repeat the language, and certainly the political intent, of the homily.

Through protagonists like Henry V and Ulysses and even satiric characters like Armado—Shakespeare reaffirms doctrines familiar to his audience from the pulpit, through his use of terms like "the Lord's anointed," "God's officials," and the adjectives *sacred* and *divine*. So prevalent is this theme that chaos of any kind is described in the language of the Homilies—language with which Mark Antony threatens Caesar's assassins, Carlisle threatens Bolingbroke, and Prospero threatens Caliban.

By portraying what happens to rebels in plays like *Julius Caesar, Coriolanus,* and *Henry V,* Shakespeare demonstrates that acts of rebellion, though they may succeed for a time, inevitably lead to the rebel's destruction—nor does it make any difference whether or not they were justified. What God wants for his people is that they bear up under tyranny until He gets around to fixing it. The only path open to those suffering under a cruel or wicked monarch is patience––their only recourse prayer—which must not be that said monarch will suffer any sort of physical or material harm—only that he (or she) will somehow find their way to a just course.

---

[113] Evidently Hart attributes "The Play of Sir Thomas More" to Shakespeare.

Shakespeare was not the only Tudor playwright to promote this, nor was he the first. According to Hart, that honor goes to John Bale, that harbinger of the Reformation, in whose play *King Johan*, performed before the Queen and Court in 1561, Verity states—

> For God's sake obey, like as doth you befall;
> For in his own realm a king is judge over all,
> By God's appointment; and none may him judge again
> But the Lord Himself; in this the Scripture is plain. (23)

Hart finds such use of the term "sacred majesty" for royalty in Shakespeare's immediate predecessors—Lyly, Nashe, Bacon, Peele and Greene—and in anonymous plays like *The Troublesome Raign of King John, The True Tragedy of Richard III, Selimus, Mucedorus, A Knack to Know a Knave, Edward III* and *Sir Thomas More*. He finds plentiful use of the term "anointed" in all three plays about Richard II, including the anonymous *Jack Straw* and *Thomas of Woodstock*. "Though most occur in the plays on English history, they are also to be found in comedies of his early and middle period, in the . . . tragedies, and . . . romances like *Pericles* and *The Winter's Tale.*"

> Were thirty or forty allusions of this type all that were present in Shakespeare's plays, he would not, in his language about royalty, exhibit any important difference from his predecessors and contemporaries except in the greater number of such allusions . . . . What is peculiar to Shakespeare is that he treats the politico-theological doctrines of divine right, non-resistance, passive obedience and the sin of rebellion as the accepted and immutable law of almost every land in every age. (28)

As Hart explains—this has no basis in history—nor has he found any trace of such a doctrine in any of the chronicles or other sources that gave Shakespeare and his fellows their plots and themes (70). Shakespeare expresses it most frequently and emphatically in *Richard II*—but nothing in history shows that either the real Richard or any of his chroniclers ever said anything of the sort. Whatever their despotic behaviors—an English king in Richard's time wasn't considered *divine*. He was considered—as were kings throughout the feudal period—as *primus inter pares*, "first among equals"—which perhaps was why the historical Bolingbroke felt no qualms about dethroning the cousin he thought less capable of leadership than himself.

In fact, although the doctrine of *Divine Right* would increase in authority up to and through the reigns of James and Charles I, the origin of the notion that—however an ordinary mortal may have managed to get on the English throne—once on it, that he—or in the Tudors' case, she—were thenceforth to be regarded as semi-divine—can be traced no further back than Henry VIII. Following the fright he experienced during the uprising known as the Pilgrimage of Grace, Hart claims that Henry saw to it that wording to that effect was added to an earlier tract[114] which Cranmer then expanded in his first version of the *Homilies* into an edict handed down by the Almighty.

Such "fundamental articles of the Tudor State religion"—created to protect the later Tudors from their political enemies and promoted by playwrights like John Bale and Shakespeare—were relatively ordinary instruments of governmental control.

But why the Stage?

Cranmer and Bale were well aware that pamphlets like John Cheke's 1549 *Hurt of Sedition*—published after Ket's Rebellion—or Sir Richard Morrison's 1556 *Remedy for Sedition*, published after Wyatt's Rebellion—reached only that small segment of the public that could read. To get the message across to the rest they needed the Stage to put forth the message that Shakespeare hammered home from Henry IV to Hotspur, from Brutus to Mark Antony—that no matter how desperately desired by a downtrodden citizenry, rebellion always brings destruction—not just to those who rebel, but eventually to the entire nation.

With the assassinations of one continental leader after another—in 1572 the French Huguenot de Coligny—in 1584 the Dutch William of Nassau and Orange—in 1588 the French Duc de Guise and shortly after, Henri III—with riots a never-ending concern—with military threats from Catholic Spain without and angry dissidents

---

[114] Known as the Bishops Book.

within—all were in agreement that something had to be done to maintain public order. Lacking a militia or a real police force—if the Stage could help—why not use it?

Unfortunately, in politics, as in physics—a pendulum held too long at one extreme—when released—rather than at a comfortable midpoint—will swing first to the opposite extreme. Here it swung from the violence of the Wars of the Roses to the rigid controls of the Tudors. Hart's final words ring true—"Perhaps in his insistence on the doctrine of divine right, with its corollary the sanctity of the Queen, Shakespeare was trying to do the State some service" (76). For us the better question would be—just how tightly bound was Shakespeare to the Crown? With no clear answer from history—English Lit fails even to ask the question.[115]

Hamlet and the Reformation

Hamlet is universally held to be Shakespeare's greatest play. Harold Bloom—Sterling Professor of Humanities at Yale University and Berg Professor of English at New York University after 1955—credits Shakespeare with "the invention of the human"—his most famous character as "the secular Christ." Like da Vinci's *Mona Lisa,* or Michelangelo's *David*—hallmarks of the Art of the Italian Renaissance—*Hamlet* is the hallmark of the English Renaissance.

Less understood is how Shakespeare embodied in his play all the issues that tormented thinkers in that time—including, one might suppose, the playwright himself. It is a given of criticism that Hamlet's one fault lies in how long it takes him to exact revenge on his father's murderer—"Oh, what a rogue and peasant slave am I?" What's rarely noted is that Hamlet is trapped between the clashing codes of the feudal culture which he inherited with his title and the Christian culture that is tying his hands—the first urging him to avenge his father with "an eye for an eye and a tooth for a tooth"—

---

[115] Hart shows more courage than most academics who've addressed his attitude towards politics. As with so many of the most important Shakespeare scholars, 16th-century English Literature was only Hart's avocation. Perhaps for this reason, and because he was an Australian (1870-1950), he may have been less concerned with Oxbridge politics.

III Shakespeare in His Own Time

the second warning, "vengeance is mine sayeth the Lord!"

Also not seen is how Shakespeare himself was constrained by the policy that would not allow any staging of the overthrow of an "anointed" monarch. Thus, Hamlet—while justified for exacting revenge on his father's murderer—must also die. On the Tudor stage a regicide must not survive the final act.

Also missed are the Reformation themes that emerge from the dialogue. For instance, in Act IV Scene 3, when pressed by the King to tell where he's left the body of Polonius, Hamlet responds with seemingly pointless wordplay—

> KING: Now, Hamlet, where's Polonius?
> HAM: At *supper*.
> KING: At *supper!* Where?
> HAM: Not where he eats, but where he is eaten. A certain *convocation* of *politic worms* are e'en at him. Your worm is your only emperor for diet: we fat all creatures else to fat us, and we fat ourselves for maggots. Your fat king and your lean beggar is but *variable service*, two dishes, but to one *table: that's the end.*

The King deplores Hamlet's lunatic response—but is Hamlet really crazy?—or is he faking it, like the *Amleth* of Danish history who, like Shakespeare's Hamlet, faked insanity to escape the vengeance of his father's killer.[116] Hamlet's responses may seem inappropriate—but perhaps they have a meaning that his audience understood, even if today's critics can't. By *worms* surely he means the maggots who are "e'en at" Polonius—but why *convocation?* Why *politic?*

Most critics are agreed that Polonius is based on William Cecil Lord Burghley—England's primary instrument of religious and political reform, who was known to boast that he was born in 1521, the year the Ecclesiastical Conference known as the *Diet of Worms*[117] gathered in the German Cathedral town of that name where they convicted Martin Luther of heresy—the event that, according to history, launched the Protestant Reformation.

---

[116] From Shakespeare's source—the *Gesta Danorum* by Saxo Grammaticus.
[117] A pun only on paper—Germans pronounce it *Vayrms*.

Although the Reformation began as a religious movement—by the time it reached Denmark it had evolved into a full-blown political revolution—one Burghley/Polonius believed could be established in England. Denmark—which then included a much greater area than it does today—was in the lead at that time in bringing the Reformation to Northern Europe.

Academics tend to smile at the thought of Lord Burghley—that "well-meaning old gentleman"—shrugging off this satire—another example of the determined failure to take either history or human nature into account. There is no evidence of any public performance or print version of *Hamlet* until after Burghley's death.[118]

Surely *Hamlet* was written for the lawyers and parliamentarians of the Westminster community—men whose responsibility it was to turn religious tenets into law. Certainly it could *not* have been written to entertain the Court—for the depiction of Gertrude as implicit in the murder of her husband was not the sort of thing with which an intelligent playwright would attempt to entertain a hypersensitive Queen[119]—nor would Elizabeth have enjoyed the depiction of Claudius as a murderer—for the plot of *Hamlet* comes too close to rumors rampant in the 1580s that her favorite—the Earl of Leicester, was responsible for the death of his rival, the Earl of Sussex, Lord Chamberlain of the Household (and patron of the Court Stage).

What then is the meaning of Hamlet's remarks as directed to members of one or all of Elizabeth's three parliaments in the 1580s? Is it pure coincidence that in this absurdly tasteless fashion he uses terms from the ongoing dispute between conservatives and reformers over the proper observance of holy communion in which terms like *supper, variable service,* and *table* were hot buttons?

It was at the *Last Supper* that for centuries it was believed that Christ told the apostles that in eating the bread and drinking the wine they were eating his body and drinking his blood. Known as *the Real Presence*—it was this that was the major block to establishing a universally accepted version of communion, for the raising by the

---

[118] That Nashe mentioned it in 1589 is no proof that it was the same version as the one published in 1604, when both Burghley and Elizabeth were dead.

[119] There is no evidence of a published version of *Hamlet* until 1603—the year Elizabeth died.

III Shakespeare in His Own Time

priest above his head of the chalice holding the blessed wine—to Catholics the "Elevation of the Host"—was anathema to reformers.

Evangelicals were also demanding that the altar be moved from its ancient location at the upper end of the chancel and replaced by an ordinary *table* in the center of the nave. *Variable service* reflects their attempt to provide elements of both Catholic and protestant versions of communion in one ceremony—while "that's the end" reminds—even as it negates—the traditional "world without end."

Thus Hamlet seems to be describing the death of Polonius/Burghley as another, grosser, sort of communion, the form of which was always the major sticking point among the various reform movements striving for control of the Church and thereby of the State. Was he claiming that—with Burghley's death, the last vestiges of those forms of worship created by Cranmer were making way for what—under Bishops Whitgift and Bancroft—was becoming the almost but not quite Catholic service towards which—by the end of the century—the Church of England had either drifted or been maneuvered by Elizabeth and her bishops.

Shakespeare's propaganda

Shortly before Richmond Noble published on Shakespeare's debt to The Book of Common Prayer in 1934—the Australian Alfred Hart provided an equally detailed account of Shakespeare's debt to its immediate precursor—Cranmer's Book of Homilies. While both were created by the Archbishop for much the same purpose—to provide protestant ministers with sermons in English—what Shakespeare seems to have recalled from the Homilies was rather different from what he remembered from the Prayer Book.

What Hart tells us about the Homilies gives the lie to the Stratford notion that Shakespeare was "above" politics. Cranmer's first edition—*Certain Sermons or Homilies, appointed by the King's Majesty to be declared and read by all Parsons, Vicars, or Curates every Sunday in their Churches*—had been published towards the end of Henry VIII's reign. Following his death it was printed again and distributed to the bishops. Suppressed under Mary—with Elizabeth's accession reformist clerics began preaching again from what remained of Cranmer's edition until a revised version, with some new sermons, was published in 1563.

For the most part these sermons focus on issues of faith—how to live a Christian life while avoiding the Devil's temptations. Though all show their Reformation nature by their frequent references to false doctrines from Rome—that the basic motivation behind these ready-made sermons was political can be seen by their history and even more obviously by the two that Hart dwells on—the first, "#10"—added by Cranmer in 1547 to the original collection from 1542—the second added in 1573 following the Papal bull of 1572—absolving of sin anyone who would rid the world of the Queen of England.

The one added shortly before Henry's death in 1547—a nine page "Exhortation concerning good order and obedience to Rulers and Magistrates"—required that it be read aloud once a year, on three consecutive Sundays, to parishioners who were compelled by law to be present. The one from 1572, following the Papal bull—filled *forty-six* folio pages—and was required to be read once a year on *six* consecutive Sundays. Evidently a mere nine pages over three Sundays was no longer sufficient. In any case—it was through these harangues that phrases like "divine right," "nonresistance to authority," "passive obedience" and "the wickedness of rebellion," were familiarized—both from the pulpit and the Stage.

Shakespeare and politics

Unlike his religion, which, however misinterpreted over the centuries, has at least been considered—Shakespeare's politics hasn't been discussed all that often. This may seem odd, since religion and politics were so bound together then that they could hardly be seen as separate subjects—but the Stratford myth has made it impossible to correlate the politics of the plays with the events that otherwise would so obviously have inspired them—such as *Henry V* to the threat of the 1588 showdown with Spain—or *Much Ado* following the defeat of the Turks at Lepanto—both far too early for William of Stratford, whose dates force everything into the nineties.

Whether or not she ever married—by the 1590s Queen Elizabeth was simply too old to provide the nation with a male heir

—so the focus of attention had switched from her marriage to *the Succession*—that is, to who would rule the nation following her death—an issue that in earlier times might have launched a bloody civil war. With this in view, Secretary of State Robert Cecil and his cohort Lord Henry Howard were making furtive promises to James VI of Scotland—furtive because most English weren't enthusiastic about handing their nation over to their frequent enemy to the north.

The Queen's politics

Elizabeth's virginity was as political as it was personal—not that it wasn't true—just that she had learned to use it as a means of staving off foreign attack. A master tactician, she understood that so long as she remained unmarried—and could continue to play the game of seeking a husband—France and Spain would hold off on attacking as they continued to wait and see, which, if any, she would choose, since her choice of husband would determine a great deal about the course of European politics from then on. Why invest men and money in acquiring England by force so long as there was a chance of acquiring it through marriage? Having taken the throne at twenty-five—Elizabeth had a good twenty years to play the marriage card.

If her statements to Parliament are taken seriously, it should be clear that she did actually tell them in so many words that she *did not intend to marry* (Neale *Parliament*)—that is, of course, unless she found the right man (which, of course, she never did)—though she could put on a most convincing act. Her first Parliament lasted for four years simply because she refused to tell the MPs when she was going to marry and to whom—causing them to stall on voting her the subsidy she needed to run the Court. Having had a great deal of practice at putting a good face on penury—she simply outlasted them. Her final performance in this marriage game was with the youngest son of Queen Marie di Medici of France—an unprepossessing little chap to whom she became quite attached. Because they were officially courting, she could be alone with him as she never could with any other man.[120]

---

[120] To do so would have caused an avalanche of gossip.

Educating Shakespeare

Although she did her best to keep these courtships going—by the late 1580s Secretary of State Walsingham was faced with having to warn her that time was running out on preparing for the attack he knew was coming from Catholic Spain. Alas for Walsingham, as always when faced with any kind of extra expense, Elizabeth simply ignored him. It may be that the stress of facing the coming storm without the help of the Queen's exchequer caused the good Secretary the ulcers that eventually killed him.

Walsingham has been been portrayed by Cecil's historians as a dour puritan who hated Mary Queen of Scots because she was a Catholic—but his dislike of Mary had less to do with her religion than with to her refusal to acknowledge Elizabeth as the nation's rightful Queen—her pleasure at being considered by her fellow Catholics to be the true Queen of England—and the relentless plotting focussed on her by papist plotters like Henry Howard and the crazy 2nd Earl of Southampton. As Elizabeth's Ambassador to France at the time, Walsingham had experienced the St. Bartholomew's Day Massacre in Paris when the Huguenots were butchered by the hundreds and thrown in the Seine by militant Catholics. He knew all too well what could happen if the Spanish got their feet on English soil.

Orthodox historians are wont to claim that Walsingham had no interest in the Stage—which they must know is a patent absurdity since it's a matter of historical fact that it it was he who created the acting company known as the Queen's Men, the first royal acting company, and also the company first known to perform works by Shakespeare—most notably the early versions of his history plays (McMillin). In *King John*—"Everyman" Falconbridge urges the audience to fight all invaders. In *Henry V*, the focus is on how the English King dealt with the threatening French.

Created as a touring company that would not play in London except during the winter holidays (a bow to the Mayor and Aldermen who hated the Stage)—the declared purpose of the Queen's Men was to travel from one city to another, up one coast and down the other, performing plays meant to rally the public audience for its support in keeping the nation English. As the nations of Europe drifted towards war—Walsingham worked with Lord Admiral Charles Howard and the Earl of Leicester to prepare for what they knew was coming.

III Shakespeare in His Own Time

None of this matters to the university academics whose Shakespeare has no interest in politics. According to historian A.F. Pollard,

> No period of English literature has less to do with politics than that during which English letters reached their zenith. . . . Shakespeare himself . . . shuns the problems of contemporary politics. The literature of his age was not political . . . and its political writings . . . were not literature.

In the days when men held office for life—when any other means than a natural death meant war or murder—how is it possible that Shakespeare alone never used his craft as centuries of playwrights have done—before and since? Of course he did. And once we start connecting the plays with the events that inspired them—we will be well on our way to establishing dependable dates for their creation.

Back when people *expected* to see political commentary from the Stage—when a comedian's popularity rested on his ability to amuse the audience by satirizing authority figures (as on *Saturday Night Live* on American TV)—how is it that while other playwrights were haled into court for offending authority—Shakespeare alone "'scapes calumny"? When his actors were publicly questioned for performing *Richard II* for Essex and his friends—on trial for rebellion—why is it that the man who *wrote the play*—not only wasn't examined during that trial—his name wasn't even mentioned?

Provoking Authority

It's not hard to understand why the academics are so inclined to ignore Theater history, since it would so clearly show how out of sync with the general trend of theater history from all times before and since is their version of how it developed under the Tudors.

Ever since the playwrights of 5th-century BC Athens had contributed to the rise of the first political democracy that we know anything about—playwrights have been recognized as the *vox populi*, the *popular* voice, whereby advocates of particular policies spoke most directly to the plebians, the commoners, the uneducated *people*.

From Aristophanes, who's been credited with bringing down

Socrates—to Mikhail Bulgakov, the Russian playwright who faced off against Stalin—Bertolt Brecht, the German Jew who escaped Hitler—Garcia Lorca, executed by a Nazi firing squad—Vaclav Havel, repeatedly imprisoned in Czechoslovakia by Stalin's regime—Arthur Miller, blacklisted for refusing to name names at the Army-McCarthy hearings during the 1950s Red Scare scare in America—playwrights have endured exile, the rack, the hangman and the stake. As Alec Wilder puts it in his Introduction to *American Popular Song* (1968)—"*Theater has always dared.* It has troubled princes and prelates alike. . . . Possibly no other art has so consistently taken such extravagant chances in provoking authority."

How then can it be then that—as A.F. Pollard and so many other academics have solemnly testified—that the greatest playwright of them all "shunned" the political upheavals of his time? How can it be that as a commentator from 1927 would have it—

> Shakespeare was "no partisan, or satirist, no reformer or propagandist—he stays his hand, lets things be; . . . he betrays no bias in affairs of church or state. . . . Theories and questions, creeds, problems, parties, these were not for him."[121]

Alfred Hart, despite his wisdom about his politics, tried to squeeze Shakespeare into the Stratford mold—"He was not a playwright with a purpose or a mission; he had no wish to reform the world or to force his ideals of life, conduct or art upon his public" (10). Thus to the ignorant Shakespeare of the 17th and 18th centuries was added the politically deaf and dumb Shakespeare of the 19th and 20th.

While able to accept that Shakespeare modeled Polonius on Lord Burghley, England's ruling politician for forty years—Hamlet's statement that the actors were the "abstract and brief chronicles of the time" zip right past our friends in the universities. So subtly did Shakespeare dress policy statements in his plays in classical garb—in aristocratic and folk themes enhanced with romance, poetry and humor—that those whose task it has been for over a century to solve the mysteries of their creation have been just as hoodwinked, as seems

---

[121] Stoll, E.E. *Shakespeare Studies.* New York, 1927 (12-13).

III Shakespeare in His Own Time

to have been the censors of the great playwright's own time.

Not all have been so wide of the mark. Among the handful who've seen the forest for the trees has been the oft-quoted Lily B. Campbell—whose 1947 opus, *Shakespeare's Histories: Mirrors of Elizabethan Policy*—focuses on what should be the obvious fact that although the professed purpose of his plays was entertainment—they were all—particularly the history plays—rife with political commentary. Born in 1883, Campbell got degrees at the Universities of Texas and Wisconsin before beginning her reign in the English Department at UCLA (1922-1950). Having studied Tudor history as well as its literature—she knew her subject. Aware that the Stage has *always* been an instrument of policy, she knew—despite being hampered by the Stratford dates—that there had to be a connection.

She opens Part One—"History, Historiography, and Politics—with sarcasm, quoting H. H. Furness, editor of the recent New Variorum edition of *King John*—"I can't reconcile myself to the opinion that Shakespeare never made use of his dramatic art for the purpose of instructing, or as a means of enforcing his own views, any more than I believe that his poetic inspiration was dependent on his personal experiences." "Comforting thoughts!" snorts Campbell—

> I do not believe that a poet exists in a vacuum, or even that he exists solely in the minds and hearts of his interpreters. I do not believe that he can write great poetry without conviction and without passion. I do not believe that his reflection of his period is casual and fragmentary. . . . Rather it seems to me the poet must be reckoned a man among men, *a man who can be understood only against the background of his own time*. His ideas and his experiences are conditioned by the time and the place in which he lives. (6)

This of course, requires that his works be accurately matched to the events of his time—not that history be mined for incidents to be fitted to some preconception passed down from a handful of 17th-century propagandists—

> If however he is not merely a poet but a *great* poet, the particulars of his experience are linked in meaning to the universal of which they are a representative part. If he is a

great poet, his feeling becomes an intense passion. It is not that he does not write out of the experience that sets him as a man apart; it is rather that he penetrates through experience to *the meaning of experience.* . . . It is not lack of feeling but a passion for universal truth that takes his hatred and his love out of the realm of the petty and into the realm of the significant. *In this sense, and in this sense only, is he impersonal.* (7)

Bloom and Jaffa

Allan Bloom, professor of philosophy at post WWII universities in France, Canada and the US, is another who sees the politics in Shakespeare. A Platonist (his translation of Plato's *Republic* was published in 1968)—Bloom's career focused on the classics and— separately, on theories of democratic government—a topic of great interest to postwar thinkers seeking ways to prevent another world war. In his *Shakespeare's Politics*, published in 1964, he explores the political structures of *Merchant of Venice, Julius Caesar,* and *Othello*, while his colleague—Harry V. Jaffa, a noted Lincoln scholar—examines *King Lear*. He claims that he and Jaffa are "professors of political philosophy" —

> We contend that Shakespeare is not the preserve of any single department in the modern university. . . . We believe that political philosophy is the proper beginning for the elaboration of the comprehensive framework within which the problems of the Shakespearean heroes can be viewed . . . [that is] that Shakespeare was *an eminently political author.* (4)

It boggles the mind to realize that someone like A.F. Pollard—or for that matter, any educated person who ever read or saw *Julius Caesar, Coriolanus or King Lear*—could truly believe that Shakespeare "shuns the problems of contemporary politics"—or that "the literature of his age was not political, its political writings . . . not literature."
—As Bloom puts it—

> The man who could write *Macbeth* so convincingly that a Lincoln believed it to be the perfect illustration of the

problems of tyranny and murder must have known about politics; otherwise, however charming its language, the play would not have attracted a man who admittedly did know. (5)

Jaffa's dissection of the politics of *King Lear* is utterly convincing as step by step—from the opening scene—he reveals the scaffolding of *realpolitik* behind the King's every move as he sets up the situation that then—due to the clash between the political realities of rulership and the demands of his own immortal soul—he brings the whole carefully planned edifice down on himself. It's impossible to summarize, since every point relies on the one preceding, and all are required for it to be seen as a completed whole.

Reading Jaffa's essay brings an increase in respect—not only for Shakespeare, but for the audience for whom he created the play —or at least that part of it that he knew would get his fuller purpose. For the rest—that they too might get his point—if not on a conscious or intellectual level, then on the emotional level where he was always so effective. An intellectually thrilling piece of exegesis—Jaffa's chapter reveals *King Lear* as a masterpiece of political theory.

Politics and the Queen

Elizabeth loved the Stage—of that we have no doubt—but that she loved it when it promoted policies other than those she favored is unlikely. The first (recorded) play to offer hope for a Renaissance English Stage was *Gorboduc*—a dual effort by two young Court regulars, Thomas Sackville and Thomas Norton, who produced it sometime between 1560 and 1565.[122] Based on a bit of very early English history—Lily Campbell sees it as a discourse on policy directed at the recently-crowned Queen and her ministers (111). Each act of the play teaches a lesson—the first, the dangers of a divided rule—the second, the poison of flattering counsel—the third, the calamities brought about by the dissension of royal brethren.

How the Queen responded to this rather stodgy polemic is not recorded—but what is evident is that neither author ever wrote another play. As for Sackville—as soon as his father's death made

---

[122] Norton's contribution has been questioned in recent years.

Educating Shakespeare

him a Baron—the thirty-one-year-old poet—among the best at Court—made a formal exit bow from "the paper stage" with what he claimed would be his last poem. As Lord Buckhurst—Sackville was destined to become one of the most politically—and economically—successful of the nation's officials—with great offices to show for his willingness to leave such "trifles" to those who didn't care how they were spoiling their chances for advancement.[123]

Norton—who in his youth had turned Calvin's quotations from Virgil into fourteeners—turned away from such "toys" as soon as he became eligible for roles like counsel to the Stationers, the Queen's representative in Parliament—and finally, her personal watchdog, prison warden, and her chief interrogator of suspected traitors.

However much Elizabeth may have been entertained by their creations—no courtier who wrote or published poetry, stories or plays past his early twenties was ever given a place on her Privy Council.

King John and *The Troublesome Raigne*

Although it was the first English play to be seen as in any way a work of the English Renaissance, *Gorboduc* was not the first to ply the Queen with a political message. In 1561, when the first summer progress of her reign passed through Ipswich in East Anglia—she was treated by the 16th Earl of Oxford to John Bale's *King Johan*—written in the old-fashioned style with characters named for their functions. Bale's was the first of three plays about John's reign produced during the early Elizabethan period—each crafted to promote a particular policy on relations with the Pope. Shakespeare's *King John*—dated by academics to 1596, though clearly written decades earlier as it's all in verse—was based, as most agree, on an even earlier play—the anonymous *Troublesome Raigne of King John*.[124] Written at some point in the 1580s for the Queen's Men (McMillin 91)—its politics suggests the period when Walsingham was so intent on warning the English along the southern coasts.

---

[123] This doubtless at his father's instigation—Sir Richard Sackville had been greatly enriched by the Dissolution of the Monasteries. A financial wizard—he was Elizabeth's cousin on her mother's side.

[124] Provided by Bullough in its entirety.

III Shakespeare in His Own Time

Campbell holds that *The Troublesome Raigne* was produced primarily in response to Marlowe's *Tamburlaine*. She quotes the opening address "To the Gentlemen Readers" from the 1591 quarto, doubtless written closer to 1587 when first performed as England approached the 1588 showdown—

> You that with friendly grace of smoothéd brow
> Have entertained the Scythian Tamburlaine,
> And given applause unto an infidel—
> Vouchsafe to welcome (with like courtesy)
> A warlike Christian and your countryman.
> For Christ's true faith indur'd he many a storm
> And set himself against the Man of Rome [the Pope]
> Until base treason by a damnéd wight
> Did all his former triumphs put to flight.

Campbell likes to quote Richard Simpson—a 19th-century Catholic who saw the connection between Shakespeare's histories and Crown politics. In his article for the New Shakspere Society (1874)—Simpson notes that in *Troublesome Raigne*—Shakespeare "entirely" suppressed its political message—

> The clearly expressed design of the old play is to show the precursorship of [King] John to the reforming Messiahship of Henry VIII. John was like David, unworthy to build the temple because his "hands with murder were attaint." But a Solomon should succeed who should put down monks and their cells. . . . This leading idea of the old play is utterly excluded from the new, where the points brought out are those connected with the tenure of the Crown. . . . practically a discussion of whether John shall remain King. (397)

Simpson lists eight points where Shakespeare deserts the chronicles—"Every one of these points . . . is so turned as to contain allusions to contemporary politics, or to events which had a decisive influence on them." What were these "contemporary politics"?

> It was not the legitimacy of John's title that was the real object of interest to Shakespeare or his audience. Hecuba was nought to them. Elizabeth's title, and the succession to her Crown,

were the great questions of the day. (26)

Up to the year 1569 the doubts of Elizabeth's title were all connected with the validity of her mother's marriage, and the force of her father's testament (that she was illegitimate). In that year Dr. Morton was sent over from Rome to announce to the northern Earls the impending sentence of excommunication . . . published against her in 1570. From this time she was declared to have forfeited the crown as a heretic. Dr. Allen in publishing the Pope's plenary indulgence to all Englishmen who should favour the Spanish invasion of 1588 exhorted "any person public or private . . . to arrest, put in hold, and deliver up unto the Catholic part the said usurper [Elizabeth], or any of her complices." (401). These "complices" were, of course, William Cecil Lord Burghley and the rest of the Queen's Privy Council. Simpson continues—

> From a princess's prison to her grave is no long journey. . . Shakespeare altered the facts of John's interdict to make them fit the contemporary history of Elizabeth's excommunication. After the execution of the Queen of Scots, Elizabeth's situation was exactly parallel to that of John after the death of Arthur, as (unhistorically) represented by Shakespeare. (401)

In comparing the Queen's situation to this portrayal of King John—Simpson notes that Shakespeare's changes involved—not only "a reconstruction of the facts" which might be laid to the demands of the stage—but more significantly "a reconstruction of the motives of history. . . . To what end were these liberties taken with the chronicles?"

Point by point, event by event, he shows how Shakespeare uses his version of the story to exhort the English to steer clear of foreign intervention by demonstrating how it led to grief under King John, and would do so again should they look to France or Spain for support. He has his youthful protagonist end the play with—"This England never did and never shall lie at the proud feet of a conqueror!" (Not true, but it sounded good.)

Described as a commoner and a "natural" (bastard) son of the great Lionheart—Shakespeare's Falconbridge speaks as a voice from the past—most immediately and directly to the youths in his public

III Shakespeare in His Own Time

audience—urging them to see themselves less as defenders of the Faith than as patriots of a proud nation. As Simpson puts it—Shakespeare seems to be saying to them—whatever you think about the justice of your cause or the crimes of your opponents, whatever outrages you have to endure, whatever the merits of the losers or the faults of the winners, settle your quarrels amongst yourselves—and above all things—beware of inviting foreign intervention! Thunders Falconbridge—facing the youths in his male audience, fist in air—"Naught shall make us rue—if England to herself do rest but true!" —bringing them—shouting and cheering—to their feet! This may have been Shakespeare's personal view—but it was also that of the Privy Council—and most notably that of Secretary Walsingham.

If we agree with Simpson's interpretation—we must date *The Troublesome Raigne* to shortly after the Pope excommunicated Elizabeth—and *King John* to sometime between the trial and conviction of the Queen of Scots in 1586 and the 1588 battle with the Armada. To separate *King John* from what is obviously its natural place in English history is to allow the English Department to falsify both Literature and History.

Shakespeare and the Crown

When the literature of the period is matched to its history it becomes apparent that the playwright known as Shakespeare was an arm, a necessary arm, of the Crown—at least until the nineties, when the connection begins to fail. For at least fifteen years—from the final decade of Elizabeth's reign into the first two of King James—he seems to have written exclusively for a company patronized by a ranking member of the Privy Council. To suggest that such a playwright would be ignorant of Crown policy, that such policy played no part in his choice of subject, and that, particularly in his Lancastrian plays, his handling of history was utterly innocent of all political intent—is the kind of thinking—rather *lack* of thinking— that comes from an English Department intent on acknowledging the realities of history only if and when it suits their departmental politics.

When the name "Shake-speare" appeared for the first time on a play in 1598, it was the playwright's patron—Henry Hunsdon, Lord

Chamberlain of the Household—second only to England's Secretary of State as top ranking member of the Privy Council—whose job it was to provide the kind of entertainment that would please, but—even more important—*not annoy*—the Queen or any of her visiting foreign dignitaries. This means that Hunsdon had to have at his right hand a playwright who could amuse members of this political hotbed without offending—an exceedingly tall order.

The Lord Chamberlain was also in charge of the Queen's appointments—which means that Hunsdon had the power to decide who could see Her Majesty in person. That he was also the one who established and had control over the theater company for which Shakespeare was the primary playwright for thirty years suggests that they were necessarily in accord where issues of government policy were concerned—in particular what was acceptable to show the public. Since importing the first printing press in the late fifteenth century[125]—the Crown had exercised close to total control over the Press—the number of print shops allowed, who ran them, and what they were allowed to publish. Why would it have been any less concerned with the influence wielded by the Stage?

Theater is expensive—it is now and it always has been. Raising money to pay for dozens of actors, stagehands, costumers, rehearsal space and rooms in which to perform has always been the province of patrons—"angels" in Broadway parlance—persons of substance, persons with enough disposable income to support something they love. There's no way there could have been a London Stage without influential patrons, whose motives were always, as was true in the days of the ancient Greeks and Romans—far more purposeful than simply to entertain their friends or distract the *hoi polloi*.

For roughly thirty years—from before June 1594 when the Lord Chamberlain's Men first began publishing his plays in quarto—to 1623, when his collected works were made available to future readers—Shakespeare's plays were the mainstay of this royal team. So popular was his company that—during their second decade they became one of the more successful of the commercial enterprises of

---

[125] Caxton's biography makes it clear that in establishing the first print shop in England in 1476 it was with the full support of the Crown.

the period. Years after the earliest sharers were dead and gone, lawsuits were still being fought over ownership of their shares.

The official silence

The silence that surrounds the relationship between the London Stage and the Crown stems largely from the fact that—apart from the occasional order to close the theaters due to increases in plague deaths—there is almost nothing in the minutes of the Privy Council that reflects their discussion of issues related to the Stage. This despite the obvious fact that at least four of the leading members of Elizabeth's Privy Council—the Earls of Leicester and Sussex, Lord Hunsdon and his son-in-law Charles Howard—were patrons of London's top two theater companies. Did they never discuss such issues? If they did, as they must have, these were either not included in the minutes, or if they were, someone got rid of them later.

Although it's been proven by Scott McMillin that during Walsingham's time as Secretary of State—the Queen's Men, the company he created to spread Crown policy to the provinces—had in their repertory early versions of *King John, Richard III,* and *King Lear*—no academic so far as we know has extrapolated from this anything that suggests that Walsingham might have been working with Shakespeare, or *even that he knew him*. No one has suggested that it was the Crown's intention to provide the as yet mostly illiterate English with a history of their nation that accorded with Crown policy. In fact, if anything is said at all along these lines, it's always to deny—with a peculiar intensity—that Walsingham had any interest in the Stage—which might suggest to the suspicious that evidence of his obvious advocacy was erased—like the relevant minutes in the records of the Privy Council—a theory that sorts well with the fact that immediately following his death—all of his papers vanished.

The politics of *Henry IV*

While adjectives like *divine* or *sacred* or phrases like "the lord's anointed" were easy enough to include in a speech or two—when it came to portraying some of the more problematic bits of English history—Shakespeare was presented with a much more complicated task. This is most apparent with the transition from *Richard II* to *Henry IV*. As is fairly obvious from the plays themselves—what remains of those that deal with Richard were written long before he got around to dealing with Bolingbroke.

While versions of *Richard II* are clearly among the earliest of his plays—there was no way that Shakespeare could finesse the fact that Henry Bolingbroke (pron. Bullenbrook), Duke of Hereford—son of the Duke of Lancaster (*aka* John of Gaunt)—got the crown by brutally and illegally deposing his cousin Richard. Too recent in time to be lied about or glossed over, Henry IV could hardly be portrayed as the patsy of a powerful Archbishop—a theory proposed by historian Terry Jones in *Who Murdered Chaucer* (2003). Neither could he be portrayed as a villain—since he was the founder of the Lancaster line that included the Tudors, of which Queen Elizabeth would obviously be the last.[126]

Finding himself between ye olde rock and a hard place—it's not surprising that when he finally got around to writing *Henry IV*, Shakespeare pulled another "Jade's trick"[127]—squeezing history into a few short scenes while giving the bulk of the plays to Falstaff—thus shifting the burden of the story from a problematic regicide to something that Will Kempe, the City's most popular comedian, could use to get the audience roaring with laughter.

Richard II probably began as one of his earlier plays, one that he revised, perhaps more than once, over the years as it evolved from a mere history play into a classical tragedy—in which, as with ancient works like *The Oresteia* of Aeschylus—the audience, most of them aware how it will end, watches in suspended anxiety while Richard preens like a gilded rooster—vaunting it over his older and wiser advisors—until he finds that Bolingbroke—rebelliously returned

---

[126] Elizabeth was often compared to Richard—as she was obviously aware. In 1601 when shown documents bearing on the reign of Richard II by William Lambarde, Keeper of the Tower Records, she commented, "I am Richard, know ye not that?—this tragedie was fortie times plaied in open streetes & howses."

[127] As Beatrice complains in *Much Ado,* Benedick is wont to "slip the collar" like a "Jade" (a naughty mare) attempting to escape her rider—because he is tiring of a wit battle that she seems to be winning.

from exile—has won Parliament's backing. This is history, pure and simple, written from a particular—and fascinating—point of view.

The politics of *Edward III*

Edward III may be the Shakespeare play most questioned over the years regarding its authorship—partly over its style, and partly for the curious fact that it was left out of the First Folio. It has another mark of special importance because it's the first in the so-called Lancastrian cycle, the ten plays that follow the lives and rivalries of that King's sons and grandsons—up to and ending with Richard III. The play also reveals a connection between Lord Chamberlain Hunsdon—the Queen's cousin Henry Carey (possibly her own half-brother)—and the playwright—from before June of 1594 when Hunsdon first went public with the Lord Chamberlain's Men as a royal company and a handful of their plays were first registered with the Stationers—plays that within a few years would be attributed to someone who called himself *Shakespeare*.

In 1991, in an article in *Connotations*, Roger Prior, of the University of Belfast, compared *Edward III* to notes jotted in the margins of Hunsdon's copy of Froissart's original French version of his *Chronicles of France* (now in the British Library)—a book known (in its English translation) as the major source for the play. As Prior notes, it must have been one of Hunsdon's favorite books, since he used its blank pages to note the dates of his family's births and deaths.

That the future creator and patron of the Lord Chamberlain's Men was interested in the same "small section" of Froissart's tome that Shakespeare used for his *Edward III* is evident from these notes and from other bits of marginalia written in what Prior describes as Hunsdon's "firm and elegant hand" (245). As Prior notes, Hunsdon begins his notations at the same point in Chapter 24 that Shakespeare began his borrowings from Berner's translation[128]—

> The marginal notes vary in importance. Some consist of a word or two, and are little more than signposts, but others are

---

[128] Hunsdon's notes end at Chapter 123—Shakespeare's continue for another 50 chapters.

> longer and indicate a greater interest. When we compare these longer annotations with *Edward III* we find again and again that what Hunsdon thought worth recording is reflected in the play. What makes these parallels especially significant is that both Hunsdon and the dramatist are highly selective. . . . In fifty chapters of Froissart . . . Hunsdon may make as few as ten marginal notes, and the dramatist, of course, is equally selective. (245)

Most notably—Shakespeare uses words that are found in Hunsdon's annotated copy of the Froissart's original, but not in Berners's English version—suggesting that Shakespeare got his information as much from Froissart as he did from its English translation—and, not least—directly from Hunsdon.

In addition, as Prior shows—a substantial amount of material in Shakespeare can be traced to Hunsdon's marginalia, including—though Prior says nothing of it—that "The king falls in love with the Countess of Salisbury"—something that happens in the play but is nowhere in Froissart or any other account.[129] Even more interesting is how he emphasizes Edward's wars with the Scots—which reflects Hunsdon's military career on the Scottish border. As Prior relates—

> Hunsdon and his sons were professional soldiers; war was their occupation and their pride, and the front on which they saw most service was the Scottish border. . . . The border was the most vulnerable and unreliable part of Elizabeth's realm; she therefore entrusted it to her most reliable subjects—*the Carey cousins who were her nearest kin*[130]. . . . Both Hunsdon himself and his eldest son George made their military reputations here. . . . Hunsdon held military command on the border from 1568 until the end of his life. (249)

Hunsdon detested the Scots—an attitude Shakespeare reflects in

---

[129] Georgio Melchiori (1998) gives "Novel 49" in *Painter's Palace* as the source for this romance.

[130] Hunsdon's mother, Mary Boleyn, was the older sister of Anne Boleyn, Elizabeth's mother. They may also have shared a father if, as rumor had it, Hunsdon was born of an early liaison between his mother and Henry VIII.

III Shakespeare in His Own Time

Edward III. In describing the raids that went unpunished he emphasizes the need for garrisons, an issue of major importance to Hunsdon, who, while governor of Berwick, was responsible for maintaining law and order on the border. In some points Shakespeare ignores Froissart, who says nothing of the Scots taking Berwick and Newcastle—while Hunsdon was in continual suspense over just such a possibility. Hunsdon often described fights with the Scots in terms of hunting, like the King does in the play, scorning their braggadocio—something that also irritated Hunsdon.

The play begins and ends with military ceremonies invented by Shakespeare—

> The giving of arms is not in Froissart at all; nor is the knighting at Crécy. It is true that Edward did knight the Black Prince, but not at Crécy, nor for valor in battle. . . . Froissart has only a brief reference to the Prince being allowed "to win his spurs" at Crécy. He spends more time on Edward's refusal to rescue his son, but even this . . . is easily explained, since the refusal to rescue creates a highly dramatic situation. But the emphasis on the knighthood is neither necessary nor particularly dramatic. Why then did the dramatist invent it, and build his account of the battle of Crécy around it?

Perhaps because Lord Chamberlain Hunsdon had four sons who had all been knighted by their commanders on the field of battle.

Lord Hunsdon functioned as patron of one of London's top acting companies ever since he and his son-in-law, Charles Howard, were appointed Vice-chamberlains in 1572 by the Earl of Sussex, shortly after Sussex was appointed Lord Chamberlain by Elizabeth. Sussex, Hunsdon, and Howard had formed something of an elite corps while fighting the Scots along the border—which may explain why—when Sussex was called away from Court by military duties—he would ask Hunsdon or Howard to fill in.

Who wrote *Edward III*

As with the early quarto versions of other history plays, the authorship of *Edward III* has been questioned largely because of what Prior calls "its mixture of the crude and the sophisticated—

> While the scenes between Edward and the Countess take a complex and subtle view of human relationships, the battle scenes are excessively simple. In these scenes war is viewed with almost unqualified approval, and the value of military honor is never questioned. War is good . . . because it is the only arena where honor can be won. In the words of the Black Prince, war is the "school of honor," and the tumult of war is therefore "as cheerful sounding to my youthful spleen" as "the joyful clamours of the people" at a coronation. (255)

While most commentators tend to resolve this by attributing the crude stuff to a ghostwriter—Prior sees it as Shakespeare's desire to please Hunsdon, who was known for his blunt speech and adherence to a military code of honor. A more likely explanation for this would be *revision*. The crudely simple scenes are left from versions written by the author in his youth—when honor and the thrill of battle were most appealing—while the more sophisticated scenes dealing with human relationships are the result of mature revision.

As Prior notes, there seem to be references to the Armada fight which suggest that the play as we have it is a version from the early 1590s when Shakespeare revised a number of his early plays for Lord Chamberlain Hunsdon's new company, the Lord Chamberlain's Men. Prior also acknowledges the suggestion by MacDonald Jackson that there are echoes of *Edward III* in early quartos like *The Contentions* and *True Tragedies* (264).

Obviously, considering how roughly the play portrays the Scots —an attitude too central to its plot to be modified or eliminated when the plays were published as a collection in 1623—that there was a hypersensitive Scot on the throne just then should suggest at least one reason why *Edward III* was left out of the First Folio.

—∞— Politics and the London Stage —∞—

With the 1590s we come to the period that the Academy sees as the beginning of Shakespeare's career because that's when the plays as we know them first begin showing up in the record. That these were

III Shakespeare in His Own Time

published—or at least registered—in anonymous batches, beginning in May of 1594—that it took four more years and more anonymous batches before an author's name appeared on any of their title pages—an anomaly unlike anything else then or later—would seem to require an explanation—which of course has not been forthcoming.

Also, what should be obvious is the fact that the London Stage—which by then had been functioning relatively smoothly for almost 20 years as London's primary source of public entertainment—was now in serious trouble—and that this trouble was due to politics at the highest level, has also been ignored, and continues to be ignored.

Back to the Nineties

As previously noted—beginning in 1590, companies that had been performing regularly at Court for decades begin disappearing from the record. First to go were the Children's companies, most notably Paul's Boys, Elizabeth's favorite actors since the earliest entries in the Revels Record—their final Court performance took place the winter of 1590-1591. Next to go was the first Crown company, the Queen's Men—for ten years a constant supplier of as many as three or four plays a season. Their final Court appearance was recorded the following December. Again—no explanation.

With their company disbanded—some of the actors from the Queen's Men found work with "new" companies like Sussex's Men or Pembroke's Men [131]—others sought work abroad. When an outbreak of the plague in the summer of 1592 closed all the theaters through most of 1593—government agents went after Christopher Marlowe, London's most popular playwright at that time. On May 30, 1593—while awaiting further interrogation by the Star Chamber on a charge of atheism—he was taken to the port town of Deptford by three of these agents where he was stabbed to death (in the brain (through the eye) by one of them. The one who confessed to the stabbing escaped charges when all three swore that it was Marlowe who started the fight. (Nicholl *Reckoning*).

Not only does the Academy and those who slavishly follow its

---

[131] New patrons, but the same actors.

lead continue to report these incidents without comment or concern about possible political factors—it fails to see anything unusual in the fact that the winter following Marlowe's murder—after a decade when anywhere from eight to ten plays would normally be performed at Court by the three top London companies, including Marlowe's—the record for the winter of 1593-1594 shows only a single play performed at Court in January, by the Queen's Men—their last to be recorded after ten years of producing as many as four per season.

The disappearance of Paul's Boys continues to be attributed (without a shred of evidence) to their having performed anti-Church satires—while the Queen's Men supposedly failed because—without Richard Tarleton, who died in 1588, the public "had tired of them" —an explanation that may make sense to an academic who may see a play every now and then—but would hardly make sense to anyone closely involved in show business. Performers who achieve stardom *never* lose their audiences—and certainly not to *boredom*.

The "Duopoly"

In a series of moves *obviously* intended to save what any intelligent reader would see as an attack by a government agency turned hostile —Lord Hunsdon and his son-in-law Lord Admiral Charles Howard, doubtless with Elizabeth's support, set about to create what Andrew Gurr has termed the "duopoly" that would remain in place for the next few years. While Gurr's reasons for this are vague, it should be clear just from the facts that Hunsdon, the Lord Admiral, and doubtless the Queen herself—were doing what they could to save the Stage.

Managed by Hunsdon and his son-in-law—theater assets were divided between the two companies. Marlowe's old team, the Lord Admiral's Men, got Richard Henslowe for their manager and his public theater in Southwark for their stage, where the by then famous tragedian Edward Alleyn continued as London's first dramatic star.[132] As for a playwright—Henslowe hoped that by hiring a passel of stringers they could make up for the loss of Marlowe.

---

[132] All star performers up to then had been comedians. Edward Alleyn was the first actor to achieve fame as a tragedian, beginning with his portrayal of Hieronymo in *The Spanish Tragedy*, who goes mad over the murder of his son.

III Shakespeare in His Own Time

The Lord Chamberlain's Men had Shakespeare as playwright, Burbage as manager, and Burbage's *Theatre* in Norton Folgate as their stage. Burbage made up for the loss of Alleyn with his 27-year-old son Richard. The companies also divided between them the top actors from the now dissolved Queen's, Lord Strange's (Admirals), and Pembroke's Men. These two companies were to be the only companies allowed to play within or near central London for the foreseeable future.

While the spear-shaker's name would not appear on a published play for another four years—the Lord Chamberlain's Men began performing the plays that would eventually be published as by him, while the Lord Admiral's Men continued to perform Marlowe's plays at the Rose, along with those of a handful of newcomers, among them the aspiring young Ben Jonson.

The Parliament Chamber

With the establishment of these two officially licensed companies, entertainment returned to the Court and the City—though not for long. Two years after creating the *duopoly*—Hunsdon's company, the Lord Chamberlain's Men, found themselves in trouble again—this time from threats to the big public stage in Shoreditch.

After twenty years of almost daily traffic, the great *Theatre*—the first of its kind in England and perhaps all of Northern Europe—had fallen into disrepair. Its lease was up and the landlord was dodgy about renewing it. The Curtain, the smaller theater nearby, was either in trouble itself, or it simply wasn't big enough for the audiences its neighbor was created to accommodate.[133] So early in 1596 James Burbage—surely with financial backing (probably Hunsdon's)[134]—acquired the old Parliament Chamber at Blackfriars and began the

---

[133] We still have much to learn about the Curtain. Recent excavations have revealed its location near the Theatre and that it was rectangular in shape, but so far nothing more. Was it created by Burbage as a place to rehearse? Was it to make more entertainment available to greater crowds? Was it intended to entertain a more select audience at higher ticket prices? At this point we can only guess.

[134] Although history credits Burbage with building the Theatre, he could not possibly have paid for it without help from someone with real money.

Educating Shakespeare

work of turning it into a year-round indoor theater.[135]

The Revels complex at Blackfriars was comprised of roughly two-thirds of the western wing of the huge quadrangle that until the Dissolution of the Monasteries had been the London base of the Dominican Friars. Known as the Black Friars—due to the color of their habit—they had been given (by Edward I) a whopping eight acres on the south slope of Ludgate Hill on the northern shore of the Thames—just inside the southwestern corner of the City Wall.

Largely due to its magnificent hammerbeam ceiling, the great Parliament Chamber has been dated to the time of Richard II, who also oversaw the building of Westminster Hall—the architectural jewel of London's government center which has a similar ceiling. Built towards the southwest corner of the Blackfriar's complex, where the land plunged over a full story down to the river's edge—the building went from two to four stories near the river where there remained a landing capable of accommodating the boats bringing the MPs for meetings of Parliament—for which earlier kings had used the great Chamber—among them Henry VIII. Across the Fleet River that bordered the west wing of the old monastery, the young King built the palace he named Bridewell in honor of his marriage to his dead brother's widow.

At some point in the 1530s it seems that Henry lost interest in that section of the riverbank. Having used the Parliament Chamber to destroy the reputation of his brother's queen, Katherine of Aragon—and the life and reputation of the great Cardinal Wolsey—Henry moved his center of operations up the river to Whitehall—turning what was left of the old Blackfriars monastery over to Sir Thomas Cawarden, his Revel's Master—to whom he eventually bequeathed

---

[135] A letter of January 9, 1596, from Hunsdon to landlord Sir William More, seemingly miffed that More had not given him first option on the purchase of the Parliament Chamber—"understanding that you have already parted with part of your house to some that had means to make a playhouse in it"—he offers More as much as he wants for another Blackfriars property that he's heard he wants to sell (Wallace *Evolution* 195-6 fn 7). This would suggest that Hunsdon had no part in the deal to create the new theater. That Hunsdon, a man with great wealth and credit, already heavily invested in the area surrounding the Blackfriars theaters, had no part in providing the company he had helped to create with the theater they so badly needed—is most unlikely.

III Shakespeare in His Own Time

the entire western half—the rest having already been sold or given to supporters as he drained the nation of its wealth to fund his many wars and battles with the Pope, at home and abroad.

As Cawarden dismantled the old monastery for the lead and stone with which to create residences for wealthy courtiers—he kept intact the Old Parliament Chamber—and that half of the western wing of the monastery which he continued to use as storage and places to rehearse shows for the Revels that Henry now held further up the river. When Cawarden died in 1559—his widow sold what remained of his holdings in Blackfriars—including the revels complex—to her neighbor, Sir William More of Losely (Smith 122).

The First Blackfriars Theater

Thus it was in this western wing of the Blackfriars monastery that the properties and activities related to Court entertainment were stored and maintained—and where, in 1576, was created the school for choristers known to history as the First Blackfriars Theater. Promoted as a school where the boys who sang in the Queen's Greenwich Chapel could study and rehearse close to her palace in Whitehall—it included a rehearsal stage plus seating for an audience of some 250.

According to Irwin Smith, author of the massively researched *Shakespeare's Blackfriars Playhouse* (1964)—the apartment that contained the school was located in that part of the west wing of the old monastery closest to the river. Partly due to its classy neighbors,[136] and partly to the fact that Henry VIII had modernized it for the visit of his imperial brother-in-law—we can be certain that the little stage required little more than the addition of a few partitions and benches to turn it into an indoor theater. Irwin Smith goes into detail on the configuration of this stage, largely based on *The Arraignment of Paris*—the only play known to have been performed on it.

In an effort to turn the huge Parliament Chamber into a rental, Cawarden had it divided into two long apartments down the middle. Having leased the western half to the Court's dance master Richard

---

[136] Earlier it had housed John Cheke, tutor to Edward VI (119). More recently it had been leased to courtier Sir Henry Neville, Lord Abergaveny (120). .

Educating Shakespeare

Frith, whose access must have been via the great outside staircase that once brought MPs up from the river landing—More leased the Eastern half—plus a section of the old monastery—to Richard Farrant—formerly Master of the boys choir at Windsor Castle.

Although Smith has a different take on the layout, what makes the most sense is that the boys lived and studied in the old monastery section, while the theater occupied the eastern half of the Parliament Chamber. With the dance academy next to it—a fencing academy on the floor beneath it—with a short walk outside to the Queen's Wardrobe where a collection of old skirts, slops, bodices, cloaks, jackets, and other items of clothing provided material for costumes —it was an ideal location for training and rehearsing the Queen's little favorites—known to history as Paul's Boys.

As history has it, the school and its rehearsal stage functioned for eight years—from 1576 until shut down (by court order) in 1584. Eight years is a long time in the history of the early stage—but since there's no record of anyone else purchasing or leasing this choice bit of property until its leases (to John Lyly and the Earl of Oxford) came due in 1589 and 1590 (Smith 156)—it's entirely possible that William More and Lord Hunsdon came to an (unrecorded) agreement that allowed it to continue until the leases were up in 1590.[137] Although Chambers reiterates that the school came to an end with More's legal victory in 1584—he gives no evidence for how or by whom the apartment was used between 1584 and 1590—when everything but the Parliament Chamber was sold to a pharmacist, one Dr. William de Laune (156).

Further evidence lies in the fact that it wasn't until 1591 that the Parliament Chamber—previously home to the little theater school and Frith's dance studio—became the "Pipe Office"—where the "pipes," the rolls of Exchequer parchments—were henceforth to be stored under authority of the newly appointed Chamberlain of the

---

[137] It's clear from his later history that—despite his legal victory, More's ambition for Court office may have made him flexible with influential courtiers like Oxford and Hunsdon. Shakespeare scholar Andrew Gurr states flatly in *The Shakespeare Company* that the First Blackfriars Theater lasted for 14 years (4), which, with 1576 still in mind, puts its end date at 1590. E. K. Chambers too, in his chapters on the Children of the Chapel and the First Blackfriars Theater—gives the same dates.

III Shakespeare in His Own Time

Exchequer—the Honorable *Sir William More!*[138]

Parliament and the London Stage

Early in 1596—faced with the loss of their aging public theater—the Burbages and their patrons began making arrangements with More to purchase both halves of the Parliament Chamber for the whopping sum of £600 (millions in today's money). The plan was to create a great indoor stage the likes of which had never yet been seen in England—possibly in all of Europe. Based on its size and the design of similar structures from the same period—Smith describes it as two stories tall topped by an immense hammerbeam ceiling.

To turn it into a theater, they would only have had to remove the interior wall with which Cawarden had divided it—build a stage across the back wall, create seating on the floor and galleries along the walls. At the same time Burbage also purchased space on the floors beneath the great Chamber where he put the machinery that raised actors and props through a trap door in the stage floor (141-2).

As for audience access—what makes the most sense is that playgoers ascended by means of the original stone staircase—built against the outer side of its western wall, so that back in the days when it was Parliament's meeting place, the MPs—having arrived at the original river landing—would climb the hill and go directly up to the outer door and into the great chamber. Smith discusses an outside stair created by Henry Neville, who had leased the apartment that became the First Blackfriars Theater under Farrant—but in Elizabeth's time it's much more likely that—with the renovation of the entire hall—many would have preferred to come to it by way of the river so as to avoid the traffic in the narrow streets surrounding Ludgate.

Trouble comes to the Stage

As the eighties became the nineties, Baron Hunsdon's patronage was crucial to the Lord Chamberlain's Men and the success of their posh

---

[138] More appears in a number of roles in this story, another example of the limited numbers in question.

Educating Shakespeare

new indoor theater. Not only was he the second most influential member of the Privy Council by then—he was commonly believed to be the Queen's own half-brother—born of Henry VIII's affair with Mary Boleyn before he married her sister, Elizabeth's mother. With Sussex and Walsingham gone, it was Hunsdon and his son-in-law

What the second Blackfriars Theater in the old Parliament Chamber may have looked like. From page 307 of *Shakespeare's Blackfriars Playhouse* by Irwin Smith.

III Shakespeare in His Own Time

Charles Howard she now relied upon for her holiday "solace." [139]

Hunsdon had long been purchasing and leasing properties in Blackfriars for years[140]—so it may have been his goal all along to see the great room made into an indoor theater a short walk from the nation's policy centers where Shakespeare could "entertain" the MPs every three or four years. Burbage's immediate goal would have been to have it ready for that year's winter holidays—while Hunsdon's would have been to have it ready for the next meeting of Parliament, projected for the fall of 1597, when upwards of 500 men of importance (and their wives) from all over England would be gathered nearby—hungry for the kind of sophisticated entertainment they rarely got to see back home.

Another "reckoning"?

What a shock it must have been that July when the actors and their patrons learned that Hunsdon was dead. He was no longer young—but he had been well enough to attend a Council meeting a few weeks earlier. Most suspicious is the fact that he left no will, which—for someone with heirs and a great deal of lucrative property to bequeath—strongly suggests that he was not living in fear of any sort of death.

In any case—whatever the truth about how he died—there's no doubt that it took Robert Cecil a step closer to total control of the Crown. The final step was taken two weeks later when the Queen appointed Cecil's father-in-law—William Brooke Lord Cobham—to Hunsdon's office—Lord Chamberlain of the Household. With the Cecils now in control of the Privy Council—the term *regnum cecilianum* begins to appear in the record.

Elizabeth had always been adept at maintaining the balance of power among her supporters. Why she lost her political savvy at this crucial juncture has troubled her biographers, but the fact is that she

---

[139] Hunsdon's DNB biography is silent regarding his life long involvement with both the Court and London Stage, a lacunae typical of all DNB biographies of the wealthy and highly placed patrons of the London Stage.

[140] By 1583 he was already in possession of the lease to the nearby Mansion House and garden (Irwin Smith, 155; the Blackfriars Record BR 17:21; Malone Society Collections, Vol II, Part I.).

may have felt she had no choice, with so many of her trusted servants gone by then—Rutland in 1587, Leicester in 1588, Walsingham in 1590, Hatton in 1591. Burghley was against appointing men like Francis Bacon to offices he wanted for his son. Elizabeth owed her throne to Burghley. With only seven years left in her own long life—perhaps something within her was beginning to fail—perhaps she was no longer fit to "take arms" against the "sea of troubles" assailing the nation just then—the bad weather, failed crops and inflation—the starving vagrants on her doorstep, the wounded back from the war, unpaid, homeless, sleeping in the streets.

Falstaff and "the great reckoning"

A third shock, almost as devastating as the death of Hunsdon and the appointment of Robert Cecil to Secretary of State came four months later. Just as the Company was preparing to open its grand new Blackfriars Theater for the winter season came an edict from the Privy Council ordering that it remain closed. It seems that Lady Russell—Burghley's daughter, Robert's aunt Elizabeth, whose properties in Blackfriars lay directly adjacent to those of the Brooke Cobhams—had talked her neighbors into signing a petition to the Privy Council that it stop the theater from opening—due to the noise and discomfort it would cause respectable residents of the Blackfriars community.[141] This meant that the only way the Company could entertain the MPs in the middle of a bitterly cold winter would be the outdoor theaters in Shoreditch and Southwark—or at one of the equally inadequate theater inns.

According to the Revels record, the six plays performed at Court over the winter holidays of 1596-97 were all by the Lord Chamberlain's Men.[142] Given the time constraints of history—it must have been that one of these was the version of *Henry IV* in which Sir John Oldcastle is portrayed as a drunken clown. As all at Court would

---

[141] In his recent book, *Shakespeare and the Countesse* (2014), Chris Laoutaris attributes the circulation of the petition entirely to Lady Russell.

[142] These would have been *Richard II, Richard III, Merchant of Venice,* both parts of *Henry IV*, and a comedy, probably the version of *Love's Labour's Lost* that portrays Armado as a caricature of Antonio Pérez (Dumaurier *Lads*, 94-135).

III Shakespeare in His Own Time

have been aware, Oldcastle was an ancestor of Robert Cecil's father-in-law, William Brooke-Cobham—whom the Queen had just picked to replace Hunsdon as her Lord Chamberlain.

Literary forensics analyst Alice-Lyle Scoufos has demonstrated scholarly courage by addressing the *realpolitik* behind the creation of Falstaff. In *Shakespeare's Typological Satire* (1979) she points to the descriptions of Sir John Oldcastle that suggest that the Company's new Lord Chamberlain was Shakespeare's inspiration for his first version of Falstaff.

Although the real Oldcastle had been a friend and supporter of Henry IV and his son the future Henry V—once the latter was crowned it was Oldcastle who turned on the young King—not, as Shakespeare has it, the King on his friend. According to history—it was Oldcastle who fomented the rebellion that led to the Battle of Shrewsbury where—captured and wrapped in chains so he couldn't escape—the historic Oldcastle was burnt alive.[143]

The Brooke family

William Brooke Lord Cobham's wealth and status at Court was all Burghley's doing (we're told they were distantly related). While building his power base during early years as Secretary of State—Cecil had need of a Lord Warden of the Cinque Ports who would look the other way when his agents robbed foreign couriers from overseas —so he could make copies of their papers. With the power this gave Brooke Cobham—and the wealth he could squeeze from business flowing into and out of England—William Brooke Cobham was as valuable to William Cecil as Cecil was to Cobham.

Back in 1562—on a desolate stretch of road between Dover and London known as Gads Hill—two of Brooke's younger brothers—disguised as highwaymen—had held up couriers headed for Spain so that Cecil could have transcripts made of the papers they carried (Scoufos 87, 93). The information thus acquired had resulted in the incrimination of several peers of Norman descent—a maneuver that

---

[143] Labeled a traitor by earlier historians, defamed by Catholics as a Lollard, Oldcastle had been recast by 16th-century reformers like John Bale and John Foxe as a harbinger of the Reformation.

gained Brooke (and Cecil) the hatred of the ancient Catholic nobility.

When Brooke was arrested in 1571 for complicity in the Ridolfi plot (according to evidence detailed by Scoufos, though ignored by Read and winked at by Hume)—because he had conspired for a substantial payoff to open the ports to the Spanish invader—Master Brooke would have been hanged as a traitor had not Cecil saved him—thus earning his eternal gratitude and a great willingness to look the other way when couriers were detained and their papers taken.

It's unlikely the public had an inkling of these matters—but the *Henry IV* plays contained material meant for the Court and the legal Inns where such things were not likely to be forgotten and where the reputation of the current Lord Chamberlain was always a concern.[144]

Thus, as Scoufos shows—both the *Henry IV* and *Henry VI* plays are compounded of political slurs directed at various members of the Brooke Cobham clan, present and past. Combining references to their ancestors in the rudest possible way—they're thick with these and an assortment of other Cobham family scandals.[145]

By combining Oldcastle's treachery with dirt on the Brooke family, with Brooke's daughter now Robert Cecil's wife—with Henry Brooke Jr.'s dishonorable behavior with the Maids of Honor thrown in for good measure [146] (202-03), it would seem that Shakespeare's attacks on the Brooke Cobham family may well have dominated the 1596 winter season. Intriguing to outsiders, uproarious to insiders, infuriating to the Brooke Cobhams—this it seems was the sort of challenge that the nation's new Secretary of State could not allow to pass without retaliating.[147]

Grievously—whatever sense of poetic justice may have

---

[144] Also performed that winter was *Henry VI part two* in which Shakespeare dramatizes how in 1442, an earlier Brooke, Eleanor Cobham, had been condemned to public shame and a life behind bars for interfering in royal politics.

[145] Brooke had more than the usual trove of scandals ripe for mining. His aunt Elizabeth, while married to Sir Thomas Wyatt, had lived in adultery with a paramour. His sister had lived adulterously with William Parr, the Marquess of Northampton, now married to Anne Bourchier, who had also lived in adultery.

[146] The Court was already disgusted with Brooke Jr. for how he toyed with the affections of the beautiful and much loved Margaret Radcliffe (Scoufas 202-03).

[147] Scoufos makes no attempt to explain how William of Stratford could have dared, or even known about these Court scandals.

III Shakespeare in His Own Time

animated the actors and their playwright while performing these satires over the winter of 1595-1596—their pleasure must surely have been darkened by the loss of James Burbage, who died, cause unknown, sometime in January. Having struggled halfway through the holiday season without his grand new indoor theater, the founder of the London Stage, creator of the first commercially successful, purpose-built theater in history, left his company without any obvious support beyond whatever his working-class sons, Richard and Cuthbert, both only in their early thirties, were able to muster from patrons.[148] It must have seemed that someone was digging the ground out from under the Lord Chamberlain's Men—and it's not likely they were confused about who it was.

Even when relief came a month later with the death of the aging William Brooke—whose Blackfriars property then passed to his son Henry—the Company could not rest in anything like security, since the major contenders for the office of Lord Chamberlain were the sons of the previous Lords Chamberlain. Should the Queen in her wisdom give the office to Brooke, they would be no better off than they had been under his father—worse in fact—for while Henry was a dissipated rake, he was, by then, also brother-in-law to Robert Cecil, the nation's new Secretary of State.

On this occasion, however, the Queen could not afford to take her usual time about choosing, since a new Chamberlain had to be in place by April 23rd, St. George's Day, the traditional date for the Garter Assembly—a gathering which would require a patron with a substantial purse. Because the Company would be called upon to perform—the actors may have been in something of a quandary over what direction to take—and because writing a play for the Court and getting it rehearsed takes time—with only a month and a half until the Garter Assembly—they couldn't wait for the Queen to decide.

Both history and common sense see this as the moment when Shakespeare wrote the comedy that—as Scoufos notes—combines in the character of Falstaff something of the nature of the recent Lord Chamberlain with the peccadilloes of his son. If Carey got the office

---

[148] This was when the brilliant John Hemmings, who would act as their company manager for the next forty years, first enters the picture.

245

he would not object to the embarrassment of his rival while if Brooke got it he would be warned of what to expect from the angry and rebellious company he was supposed to manage.

Thus did *Merry Wives of Windsor* appear to cheer the Queen and her Court, if not in the fourteen days assigned it by hearsay, certainly under some pressure of time—during which the Company, outraged and grieving the loss of their Privy Council patron, their father-manager, and their beautiful new theater—would show their opinion of the flunky who had just been foisted off on them as their Privy Council patron.

In *Merry Wives*, Shakespeare demonstrated his power to defame—something he would soon be using more directly on a far more dangerous enemy. Nor would changing the buffoon's name from *Oldcastle* to *Falstaff* make much difference to the Court—for by then everyone must have been fully aware of who were the current victims of their impresario's spleen. To make it as clear as he could —he named one of his characters *Master Brooke*.

Although George Carey, Hunsdon's son and heir—now owned or held the leases to so many of the properties surrounding the Second Blackfriars Theater—there's no evidence (so far) that as patron of the Company he did much of anything to help the actors get back the use of it. Having inherited the apartment that lay directly beneath the Parliament Chamber—this seeming lack of effort may be less political than simply because he didn't want the kind of noise and activity that any theater will generate going on over his head.

Nevertheless—in 1600 George did allow, or apparently did nothing to prevent—a new commercial children's company from leasing the great stage. Suffering from some illness, dying in 1603— it's possible that towards the end of Elizabeth's reign he was too sick to care what happened to his father's dangerous legacy. He was less experienced in power politics than his father—he hadn't his seniority or his close relationship with Elizabeth—and he also had more than one reason to be afraid of Robert Cecil.

Not only did Lord Hunsdon's death follow suspiciously "hard

III Shakespeare in His Own Time

upon" the Cecils' recent series of power plays[149]—two years earlier —when Ferdinando Stanley Lord Strange died suddenly at the age of thirty-six shortly after having become Fifth Earl of Derby—it was George Carey's wife's sister, George's sister-in-law, who was widowed by his death. In a letter George wrote his wife six days later, he revealed his belief that Derby had been murdered (Wilson 474-5).

Carey would certainly have been aware of the rumors—some claiming the Cecils had murdered Stanley because he had the blood royal[150]—others because Burghley wanted the Derby title for his granddaughter (Oxford's daughter Elizabeth) (176). Historical truth emerges less from what personalities say than from what they do. On January 26, 1595—nine months after Stanley's death—his younger brother William, now 6th Earl of Derby, was married to that same Cecil granddaughter in an elaborate Court ceremony that raised the Cecil family to their present place in the upper peerage—something that—according to David Cecil[151]—their 20th-century descendant—was Burghley's goal from the start (58).

~~ Enter Shakespeare stage left ~~

It was in 1598 that the name *Shakespeare* was first spread throughout England's green and pleasant land. Over the final months of 1597—sometime between October and the end of December—first editions of his *King Richard the Third* (and *King Richard the Second*) were published anonymously by someone acting in behalf of the Lord Chamberlain's Men. The timing suggests that these were made available on purpose so that the upwards of 500 members of Queen Elizabeth's ninth Parliament— congregating just then in Westminster—had time to read them before seeing them performed over the Christmas holiday.

Either because these had sold out immediately or for some other

---

[149] According to history, only George, whose father had died in his arms, was in a position to know his final wishes (DNB).

[150] What the historians don't mention is that Lord Strange, 5th Earl of Derby, was also, at that time, the official patron of Christopher Marlowe's acting company.

[151] David Cecil, *The Cecils of Hatfield House: An English Ruling Family* (1973).

reason—second editions of both of these plays were published the following year—the only difference between these and their earlier editions that the legend "by *William Shake-speare*" had been added to the title page. At almost exactly the same time the name was broadcast by the publication of a pamphlet titled *Wit's Treasury* (aka *Palladis Tamia*)—in which its author—an otherwise unknown individual named Francis Meres—listed twelve currently popular plays by a *William Shakespeare*. In this way, at almost the same time, was the author of plays that had been entertaining the public for over twenty years named for the first time. Why now? Why then? When history fails to solve a mystery, we must propose a likely answer.

The Showdown

While on the road during the summer of 1597—faced by the fact that they had no theater in which to perform for the coming Parliament—both their manager and their Privy Council patron dead and gone—it may be that the Lord Chamberlain's Men turned to the only thing they had left—their playwright. Taking up his *spear* (his pen)—he may have turned his old *True Tragedy* into a vicious portrait of the man causing the trouble, Robert Cecil, England's new Secretary of State.

Enemies of the Cecils would have been willing to provide the actors with a private hall where—over the three weeks of the Christmas break, it may be that upwards of 500 MPs saw Richard Burbage perform the role for which he would forever after be most fondly remembered. Dressed all in black, imitating Cecil's voice and mannerisms, his "wry neck" and lurching gait—surely this was how he struck the blow that Cecil, disdaining as beneath his dignity to acknowledge in any way an attack through something as déclassé as the Stage, was helpless to prevent—even to acknowledge.

With the first edition of the play in their pockets and their minds, did the members of Parliament—who seeing Cecil perform before them by day in Parliament, having seen with their own eyes Burbage's imitation on the Stage—take back to their home counties the astounding news that the Royal Company's holiday play was a vicious portrait of England's new Secretary of State? Because there is nothing in either published version of *Richard III* that points

III Shakespeare in His Own Time

directly to Cecil—only those MPs who were seeing him perform daily as the Queen's advocate in Parliament and *who had also seen the play performed* with Richard Burbage as the evil king, costumed and performing in imitation of Cecil—could have made the connection.

Nor was this something that could be openly discussed. Fearful lest one of Cecil's agents get wind of it and get them in trouble[152]—those who had seen it would have spoken of it only to their closest friends and family members—who would have spoken of it only to their own closest friends and family members. Thus silently may have, could have, been spread *through the nation* the rumor that the Crown's own Company had portrayed England's new Secretary of State as history's most evil King.[153]

Cecil was stymied. While the satire did nothing to displace him or prevent him from consolidating his power it does seem to have stopped him from direct attempts to destroy the Lord Chamberlain's Men. That the fight between the actors and the Cecils went no further at that time suggests that the Queen put a stop to it.

As for the Company—forced to travel—their great City Stage given over to a new company of "little eyases"[154]—they managed to get by for the next few years with only the Globe, their old outdoor theater—until 1609 when King James finally returned to them the use of the great indoor theater created by their father and Lord Hunsdon back in 1596. After repairing the damages caused by recent renters —when Richard and Cuthbert Burbage were finally able to open the doors of the great Second Blackfriars Theater to the public in 1610 (Irwin Smith 247)—their fortunes and those of all involved were assured, and their playwright—"the man *Shake-speare*"—became permanently and unalterably fixed in the minds of the public as the

---

[152] This fear of Cecil—which Handover describes as a "near pathological hatred" (230)—is evident from the slanders that continued to erupt long after he was dead.

[153] While there is no direct evidence of such a ploy, there must be a reason why the role for which Richard Burbage, who would have played dozens of roles over his lifetime, was most famous for his portrayal of Richard III.

[154] Hamlet's famous slap at the boys was at the commercial company that was renting the theater beginning at some point in or around 1600. The timing here is crucial to dating the version of *Hamlet* published in 1603. Irwin Smith devotes all of Chapter 9 to this issue (175-209).

author of plays they had been enjoying for decades.

The evidence

Three scholars, respected academics, have put this identification of the model for Shakespeare's evil King beyond argument—Margaret Hotine in 1991, Pauline Croft in 1999, and Mark Aune in 2006. Hotine argues that the first five quarto publications of Shakespeare's *Richard III* were—as Aune puts it—"connected to or caused by Cecil's ambitions and his regular promotions" (27).[155] Croft details the foul nature of the libels against Cecil that poured forth following his death in 1612—many of them cast in the same terms used by Shakespeare in the play. Aune quotes several of Cecil biographer P.M. Handover's description of the anti-Cecil sentiment generated in 1601 by the Essex trial when someone scratched on Robert Cecil's bedchamber door—"Here lieth the toad"—an image used *six times* by Shakespeare to describe the King. As one such limerick put it—

> Here lieth Robin Crooktback, unjustly reckoned
> a Richard the Third, he was Judas the Second . . .
> Richard or Robert, which is the worse?
> A Crooktback great in state is England's curse. (16).

Although most of the play's imagery came from earlier works by Sir Thomas More and More's mentor Cardinal Morton—who hated the Yorkshire branch of the sons of John of Gaunt—the weak legs described by Shakespeare—"crippled and graceless in movement," walking "so lamely . . . that dogs bark at me as I halt by them"—could only have described Robert Cecil. No one before Shakespeare had ever described Richard III as crippled or lame.

If not this then something similar must have happened to cause the question of who was responsible for writing their plays rise to a

---

[155] Margaret Hotine, in her 1991 essay in *Notes and Queries*; "*Richard III* and *Macbeth*: Studies in Tudor Tyranny"; Pauline Croft, Professor of Early Modern History at Royal Holloway, University of London, in her article in TRHS: "The Reputation of Robert Cecil: Libels, Political opinion, and popular awareness in the early seventeenth century" (1991); and Mark Aune, Associate Professor of English at the California University of Pennsylvania in "The Uses of *Richard III*: From Robert Cecil to Richard Nixon" in *The Shakespeare Bulletin* (2006).

III Shakespeare in His Own Time

level that forced the Lord Chamberlain's Men to put an author's name on a new edition of *Richard III*. It had to have been something like this that forced the Company to come up with a stand-in for the author—someone without attachments to anyone of importance, someone whose name would not be damaged by the association. If hiring William of Stratford for the use of his punnable name did not satisfy everyone involved, it did succeed in putting the authorship question on ice—where it has remained ever since.

However popular with audiences over the centuries, *Richard III* has never been a favorite with critics. Its lack of polish, ornament, or comic relief, its crude drive—are not "good" Shakespeare. Most damning, it lacks a single sympathetic character—everyone in *Richard III* is either weak or evil. Shakespeare was in a hurry, they say. He was in a bad mood.

Indeed he was! Contemplating the loss of his theater, the deaths of his patrons, the hardships dealt his actors, perhaps even the potential threat to his own life, certainly to his life's work—the great author called on his "Muse of Fire" to demonstrate to Cecil and the rest of the Court the power of his pen—the immense size and power of the audience he'd created—and more to the point where History is concerned—the clear and undeniable power of the London Stage.

Francis Bacon and the Periodical Press

History, however controlled over the centuries by the Salisburys (Robert Cecil would be dubbed First Earl of Salisbury by King James) there were many at Court and within the print community who feared their increasing power in the 1590s—concerned about the cruelty with which the Crown was dealing with the families being thrown off the land, the rising prices for food, the diminishing provisions of necessities like flour and butter, and—not least, the herds of wounded and starving soldiers returning from the continental wars. There would surely have been many who saw the actors as a force for justice, many who would have done what they could to help get *Richard III* performed in 1597, and—what should be most worthy of notice—had something to do with the fact that the play got published again *with the Shakespeare name on it*—not just once, but *six times* over the coming decade!

Among those involved we can be certain were the Bacon brothers—Francis and Anthony—who, like Robert Cecil himself, were descended from Sir Anthony Cooke through their mothers—and who—also like Cecil, were the offspring of one of Elizabeth's earliest and most honored officials—her original Lord Keeper, Sir Nicolas Bacon. Like Robert, the Bacon brothers had been raised at Court and as children had lived in York House, formerly the City palace of the Bishops of Durham, now the official home of the Lord Keeper of the Privy Seal. Like so many others, the Bacon brothers were bitter about the way they were being denied positions at Court that were being given to Cecil toadies. While history can be silent on many things—it's very clear on how deeply Francis Bacon resented being shut out of his nation's government by his Cecil cousins.

"An idle pen or two"

By the nineties, Francis was still occupying the rooms at Gray's Inn he'd been assigned by Burghley—which he was putting to good use. Situated in the heart of the Holborn community where graduates of the universities made a living penning fair copies of handwritten originals from the nearby Inns of Court—he appears to have made use of his reputation to become something of a freelance private secretary to a wide circle of clients, something that contributed a great deal to his fund of inside information. His relationship with Bishop Whitgift, his tutor for several years, was a valued alliance.

With the return in 1592 of his brother Anthony from the Court of Henry I of Navarre, it seems that together the brothers created something of a secretarial service at Gray's Inn where they gave the "scribbling rascality" work making copies for the nearby Inns of Court. In her 1975 biography of the Bacon brothers, *Golden Lads*, their descendant Daphne du Maurier quotes a footnote added by Francis to a letter to his brother—"I have here an idle pen or two . . . I pray send me somewhat else for them to write out besides your Irish collection, which is almost done."

In cases where more than one or two copies were needed, it was quicker and easier just to have them printed. Run off in a few sheets

III Shakespeare in His Own Time

by a local startup print shop looking for work, if the Cecils could shut down the theaters—the Bacons' ability to get writers work and their works published was creating something that would prove to be just as troublesome as *The Stage*—that thing we now call *The Press*. Once having embraced a startup printer, Francis may have felt it something of a duty to keep providing him with paying work.

The Northumberland Manuscript

In 1867, in the archives of Northumberland House, located on the Strand right next door to York House (Bacon's birthplace and his home again when Lord Chancellor under King James)—was found a folder covered with pen marks, that had obviously belonged to him in 1596 and '97. Scribbled at random on its cover are several famous titles—apparently a list of the manuscripts it had once contained, perhaps holding them in advance of getting them printed. Also scribbled on its cover was the title "Richard the Third"—and also, several times, "William Shakespeare"—a good two years before the name would appear on the title page of *Richard the Third*.

Academics tend to ignore the *Northumberland Manuscript*. It does the Stratford scenario no good—and it's been appropriated by the Baconians to support their claim that Francis was Shakespeare. Wikipedia ignores it. Nevertheless, it demands a place in the inquiry.

As the Northumberland Manuscript makes clear to anyone with eyes to see and ears to hear—Francis Bacon was involved in the publication of the two editions of *Richard III*—the first in 1597—without *William Shake-speare* on the title page—and the second in 1598—*with* the name on the title page—these the first appearances of the name anywhere in the record.. If this doesn't qualify as a "smoking gun"—it's hard to think what would.

Who was it then that in 1597 had dared to portray the powerful Secretary of State as the evil *Richard the Third?* Who was it who had such prestige that when one of his actors was called to testify at the trial regarding the request by the Earl of Essex and his friends to have *Richard the Second* performed for them privately the day before the Essex rebellion in 1601—the play's author was not only *not* called to testify—he wasn't even mentioned during the trial?

One of the many portraits of Richard III painted during his brief life.

The truth about Richard III

How evil was the historic King Richard III? Not only was he not evil, as those who have since formed the Richard III Society have attested in numerous books on the subject—he was one of England's best and most highly educated monarchs. Sold out by the Earl of Derby at the Battle of Barnet's Field—where he was not simply taken prisoner but was hacked to death by those determined to put a Tudor on the throne, Richard was blamed by his Tudor enemies for crimes that he had no reason to commit, and for which there is no evidence. The Tudors

III Shakespeare in His Own Time

needed a scapegoat—and Shakespeare needed a villain.

Who published the two editions of *Richard the Third*?

In seeking the source of the first mentions of the name *Shakespeare*, the first would be whoever had them published. The simple answer to this is *Andrew Wise*, whose name appears as publisher on the title pages of both editions of *Richard the Third* and *Richard the Second*. But according to Lukas Erne, Wise is so ephemeral that he can't be considered a professional publisher at all (88).[156] Another dead end?

The first to name him as publisher was Thomas Nashe in 1593 on his *Christ's Tears Over Jerusalem*. Not until late August 1597 would Wise appear again as a publisher when he registered *The Tragedy of King Richard the Second*, then again in October with *Richard the Third*. He registered *Henry IV part one* the following February, *part two* in 1600 along with *Much Ado About Nothing*—the last to be registered under his name. According to Lukas Erne—after having transferred the copyrights for these in 1603 to "someone else"—"Wise was not heard of again."

Erne suggests—"If some time in 1597, Shakespeare and his fellows, willing to sell the manuscripts of *Richard II* and *Richard III*, asked [James] Roberts for advice and if Roberts *was* unwilling to take the risks of purchasing the manuscripts himself—he would have good reasons to recommend Andrew Wise" (88).

Why Erne thinks Roberts, a fixture among publishers of almanacs and the like, might think it "risky" to publish these plays he doesn't say—nor why he should have had "good reasons" for recommending Wise. As for who *printed* the plays, their title pages assign the first and second editions of both to Valentine Simmes[157] —of whom, as with Wise—nothing is known beyond the fact that his name appears on some equally questionable works from that period.

It's true that the more literate members of the reading audience

---

[156] Andrew Wise is another name without a DNB biography.

[157] Simmes also printed the first and third quartos of both parts of *Henry IV*, the second quarto of *Henry VI part two*, the 1603 quarto of *Hamlet, Taming of A Shrew, Much Ado about Nothing,* and *The Troublesome Raigne of King John*, plus works by Jonson, Marlowe and Dekker. Like Wise—Simmes has no DNB bio.

would have been aware that the name *William Shakespeare* had recently appeared on an inside page of *Venus & Adonis*—but this would have been the same small group of poets and their admirers who already knew the author's identity and why it was a secret.

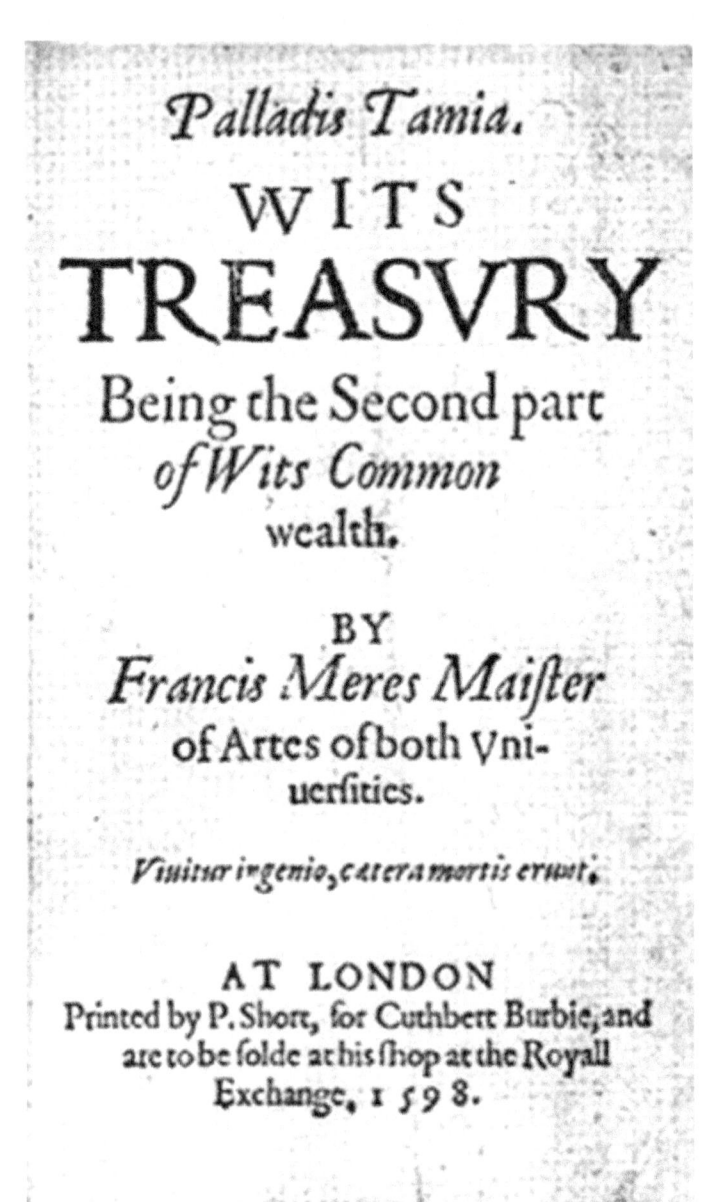

Palladis Tamia.
WITS
TRESVRY
Being the Second part of *Wits Common wealth.*

BY
Francis Meres Maister
of Artes of both Vniuersities.

Viuitur ingenio, cætera mortis erunt.

AT LONDON
Printed by P. Short, for Cuthbert Burbie, and are to be folde at his shop at the Royall Exchange, 1598.

III Shakespeare in His Own Time

These second editions of *Richard III* and *Richard II* are only the first of several dead ends. Also published that year was the second time that the name *Shakespeare* appeared in public—*twice in one year!* The second was in a handbook titled *Wit's Treasury*, apparently one of a series produced by a group of writers, printers and publishers who had set up as something of a consortium in the brave new world of commercial publishing. Cautious about using their full names, these included R.A., thought to be Robert Allot—N.L., thought to be Nicholas Ling—A.M., Anthony Munday—A.B., Anthony Bacon.

Francis Meres, named as author of *Wit's Treasury*, seems not to have been one of these, or not for long. A sizar[158] at Pembroke College Cambridge, he got his MA in 1591 after which he apparently joined the consortium in an effort to make a living in London. Failing to secure a patron by means of his translations of Spanish sermons—he left the world of publishing to become rector (minister) of a small vicarage in the Midlands. That he was actually the author of *Wit's Treasury* seems most unlikely.

In any case, in a section of the book devoted to comparing famous writers of the past to their present counterparts, Shakespeare is compared to Plautus and Seneca, along with the titles of twelve of his plays including "Richard the 2" and "Richard the 3." Also mentioned are his "sugar'd sonnets"— shared among his private friends.

Known to the Academy for some reason by its Greek-sounding subtitle—"Palladis Tamia," a phrase located above the actual title—it purported to be second in a series titled "Wit's Commonwealth" after the first, published in 1597. *Wit's Treasury* was followed by *Wits Theater* in 1599 and *Wisdoms Palace* in 1604. Supposedly written by one "Francis Meres Maister of Artes of both Universities"—graced by a Latin quote from Aquinas—*Wit's Treasury* was printed by Peter Short, a small one-press printer like those frequently used by Francis Bacon.

---

[158] Sizars were poor students who got by by working for the university. As such they were more likely than other students to do whatever they could to get by—such as sell the use of their name to writers or publishers in need of a cover.

Prospero and Miranda on Shakespeare's imagined magical isle.

CHAPTER IV

~ Shakespeare in Our Time ~

> Whenever any human practice refuses to die in spite of centuries of assault from theory, there must be something wrong with the theory.
> Wayne Booth, *The Company we Keep*

As Shakespeare Studies spread from enthusiasts in the eighteenth century to self-ordained experts in the nineteenth—attempts to deal with the still unresolved anomalies created by the Stratford scenario led to one group effort after another. Each achieved temporary fame, publishing tracts, articles and books paid for by wealthy patrons. When one set of theories gave way to new theories that were partly outgrowths—partly rejections of the previous theories—frustration led once again to confusion—and all eventually failed. Though none had yet found footing at one of the universities—where the vulgar Shakespeare was still beneath their classical dignities—all were driven by energetic, well-positioned university graduates—each with an idea with which to give the question another try.

The Shakespeare Society

The first to acquire historical notice—*The Shakespeare Society*—was founded in 1840 by the news reporter and fledgling lawyer John Payne Collier. Collier's enthusiasm led to a paid position as librarian for William Cavendish, 6th Duke of Devonshire, whose role as Queen Victoria's Lord Chamberlain of the Household (1830-1834) was fueled by his family's long interest in the London Stage. This gave Collier access to the Duke's considerable collection of early plays—and to that of his friend, the Earl of Ellesmere.

In partnership with that indefatigable collector and publisher of

Educating Shakespeare

Shakespeare material, James O. Halliwell-Phillipps, the Shakespeare Society published a journal and a number of important works before it came to an abrupt halt in the 1850s with the unhappy revelation that their number one investigator had forged some of his "discoveries."[159] Collier it seems was only a genuine scholar by half—the other half a journalist out to get a story—by hook or by crook. Pressured by his patrons to get results—baffled by the lack of evidence that's largely what this book is about—rather than admit that he could find no more than what had already been found—eager to keep his place with the Duke, now and then Collier would "discover" a well placed forgery.

The New Shakspere Society

Stunned into mortified silence by the notoriety that attended Collier's fall—it was almost 20 years before a new set of enthusiasts formed another group. Though still not formally connected to a university, the New Shakespeare Society initiated the trend to change the focus on the Bard's language from its artistry to its structure—the path that would eventually be taken by the universities.[160] Driven largely by their reaction to Delia Bacon's group theory—the book that opened the way for the Baconians' claim that Francis was Shakespeare—they retreated into what they claimed was *Science*—where immeasurable factors like love and beauty could be ignored.

Founders Frederick Furnival (1825-1910), a graduate of Cambridge University, together with the Reverend Frederick Fleay (1831-1909), graduate of Kings College London, and Trinity College Cambridge—possibly in response to the enthusiasm created by Darwin's *Origin of Species*—must have figured that if Darwin could unlock the secrets of human evolution with biology—surely something just as scientific could unlock the secrets of a few old plays. Members included biologist Thomas Huxley, art critic John Ruskin, playwright George Bernard Shaw, poet Robert Browning,

---

[159] Though certainly not all. Determining whether or not something Collier published is genuine or a forgery remains an issue.

[160] So eager were they to distance themselves from the previous Shakespeare Society that they changed the way they spelled his name. Where a quote spells it *Shakspere*—it's fair to assume the author was a member of this group.

IV Shakespeare in Our Time

another Duke of Devonshire, plus a lineup of other heavyweights. Furnival, a philologist with a math background, was also editor and co-founder of the OED—the Oxford English Dictionary—in which so many first uses are given to Shakespeare. Fleay—whose training, like Furnival's, was primarily in math—believed that metrical testing would succeed where earlier approaches had failed. By examining the texts at a subatomic level—taking sentences apart, counting beats, noting instances where rhymes occurred and where they didn't, adding up the numbers and creating verbal "equations"—Fleay was certain he could solve what E.K. Chambers would dub the "Shakespeare problem." Anything that in Fleay's view didn't fit the profile of their version of the Bard was discarded as by some nameless other.

Enter the University Wits

It's in this way that the so called *University Wits*[161] first appear as players in these ventures into purely intellectual critique. Introduced towards the end of the nineteenth century, Furnival and Fleay found in these cheaply produced 16th-century pamphlets—language and themes with Shakespearean overtones. Thus it was that names like *Robert Greene, Thomas Nashe, George Peele, Thomas Watson, Thomas Kyd,* and half a dozen others were introduced by Fleay and company as the likely authors of the originals which the Stratford Shakespeare—having arrived so late to the London theater scene—would then perfect. Their frequent mentions by each other in the dedications they wrote for their publication of these works gave the Wits a collective reality missing from their individual biographies. Since the only thing they appeared to have in common was that most of them had attended—however briefly—either Cambridge or Oxford—they were dubbed the "University Wits."

This assignment of Shakespeare's works to ghostwriters roused the wrath of E. K. Chambers, who—in a lecture to the Academy angrily labeled it *disintegration*—Furnival and Fleay *disintegrators*. He accused Fleay of disintegrating and redistributing parts of *"Henry VI, Richard III,* and *Titus Andronicus* among Marlowe, Greene, Peele,

---

[161] As dubbed by George Saintsbury in 1887.

Lodge, and Kyd"—of finding Lodge and Drayton in *Taming of the Shrew*—traces of Peele in *Romeo and Juliet*—Kyd in *Hamlet*—Dekker and Chettle in *Troilus and Cressida*"—and so forth. Fleay may have been the first to broadcast such theories through the Shakspere Society—but, as Chambers noted, he was not the first—

> You find the substantial Shakespearean authorship of *Comedy of Errors, Love's Labour's Lost*, and oddly enough *Winter's Tale*, doubted by Pope (1725), of *Henry V* by Theobald (1734), of *Two Gentlemen of Verona* by Hanmer (1743), of *Richard II* by Johnson (1765), of *Taming of the Shrew* by Farmer (1767), Coleridge, who questioned much of *Richard III* . . . and *Love's Labour's Lost*. . . . Charles Knight (c. 1843) suggested that Shakespeare was only a reviser of *Timon of Athens*; James Spedding and Alfred Tennyson (c. 1850) fixed the second hand in *Henry VIII* as that of Fletcher; and William George Clark and William Aldis Wright (1874) elaborated Coleridge's heresy about *Macbeth* by ascribing substantial interpolations in that play to Middleton. (*Disintegration* 5-6)

Yet even Chambers could not avoid the temptation to do some disintegrating himself. Apparently it was only losing whole plays that troubled him—for in *Facts and Problems,* he questions scenes in *Henry VI part one,* allowing Shakespeare only three-fifths of *Taming of the Shrew*—"The other writer is responsible for the subplot of Bianca's wooers. *I do not know who he was.*"[162]

"Above all—chemical analysis"

As Prof. Laurie Maguire of Magdalen College Oxford has explained —the study of English Lit in the nineteenth century was "egregiously philological. . . . Literature *per se* played no part." In other words, it was about everything *but* the story. Impressed by the success of Jean

---

[162] Theater historian William Ingram—focused on finding what history he could in the factual desert left by the Tudors—refers to Chambers's "dispassionate, leaden prose," his instincts as "agglutinative rather than analytical," his work as an example of "Tory empiricism" and "a tribute more to accumulation than to insight" (32)—and his sentiments as more like the puritans than the players.

IV Shakespeare in Our Time

François Champollion, who had recently succeeded in deciphering Egyptian hieroglyphics by way of the Rosetta Stone (1824)—partners Furnival and Fleay felt they already had all the tools they needed to solve any and all problems relevant to Shakespeare—er, Shakspere. As Terence Hawkes has put it since—they hoped "to get his life and times straight, his plays accurately edited and classified, to align the one exactly with the other, to fix the shape of both irretrievably, and to weld them together forever as a single, comprehensible, and coherent unity" (118-19).

According to Fleay—if they were to succeed, Shakespeare scholars must have "a thorough training in the Natural Sciences, in mineralogy, classificatory botany, and above all, chemical analysis," because "the methods of all these sciences are applicable to this kind of criticism, which, indeed, can scarcely be understood without them." You can stop laughing because this in fact is where Shakespeare criticism began at the universities—nor is it all that far from where it continues to malinger to this day.[163]

Despite the importance of their many contribution to Shakespeare Studies through the plays and other early works they got published—the effort by these early Shakespeare societies to establish a reliable order and set of dates was inevitably skewed by that potent if invisible Charybdis—the Stratford biography—with its exceedingly narrow time factor. Nor did it help that—while self righteously condemning the "impressionism" of their predecessors—they too were prone to a little bourgeois fantasy—as in Furnival's "Introductory Address" to the Society's first session—

> Thus, added to the use of that revised order for the purpose of studying the progress and meaning of Shakespeare's mind, the passage of it from the fun and wordplay, the lightness, the passion, of the Comedies of Youth, through the patriotism . . . of the Histories of Middle Age, to the great Tragedies dealing with the deepest questions of man in Later Life; and then at

---

[163] As I write, notice is broadcast that in the current edition of Shakespeare's works recently published by the Oxford University Press—a cohort of so-called experts now officially credit parts of the three Henry VI plays to *Christopher Marlowe!* The world's response to this seems to have been a great yawn.

Educating Shakespeare

> last to the poet's peaceful and quiet home life again in Stratford, where he ends with his Prospero and Miranda, his Leontes finding again his wife and daughter in Hermione and Perdita. (qtd by Sawyer, 3)

So began the great division that continues to this day, with the academics—descendants of the philologists who were the first university men[164] to address the Shakespeare authorship problem—as opposed to the "impressionism" of poets, novelists, playwrights, and psychologists who have had their own ideas about how great literature gets created—ideas they have not been hesitant to share. Critic and poet Charles Swinburne was merciless in his ridicule of the scientific approach, claiming that—

> a person who counts the number of times of occurrence of a certain word in a certain poem or play is a harmless but pressingly deserving candidate for Bedlam, and that a whole society of gentlemen who spend their time in allotting to their own satisfaction separate scenes and acts of Shakespeare to different authors among his contemporaries must be a candidate of the same class. (Sawyer online)

When this kind of dissension provoked public battles between founders Furnival and Fleay—the Shakspere Society more or less discredited itself—and after plodding along for another decade, disappeared at the approach of a new and hopefully better century.

The New Bibliographers

But Shakespeare Studies was far from done with performing autopsies on their golden goose—for waiting in the wings at the British Museum where copies of these early versions had been gathering—Alfred W. Pollard, the Museum's Keeper of Printed Books, alarmed by threats to the holy of holies—was about to enter the lists in defense of the miraculous William.

It would be Pollard's book—*Shakespeare Folios and Quartos:*

---

[164] English universities did not give women graduates accredited status until 1948 at Cambridge, 1974 at Oxford.

IV Shakespeare in Our Time

A Study in the Bibliography of Shakespeare's Plays (published in 1909)—that would launch the career of Walter Wilson Greg—England's most vocal and durable Shakespeare authority throughout the first half of the twentieth century. Though not affiliated with a university, Greg was positioned to take the "Shakespeare problem" roaring off into the weeds of pseudoscience where it soon stalled and has languished ever since. By making it his life's work—by having a long life (1875-1959) with no need to do much of anything else—and by using (and misusing) his mentor's terminology—Greg was perfectly positioned to lay the foundation for the circular direction about to be taken by the fledgling English departments.

Greg's grandfather—James Wilson, creator of *The Economist*—had seen to it that his grandson got the standard upmarket education at Harrow and Trinity College Cambridge. When this was followed by a gift of stock in *The Economist*—the young enthusiast found himself free to spend his postgraduate days at the British Museum, perusing their collections of Early Modern works and introducing other eager young beavers to Shakespeare. Jumping on his mentor's ideas—Greg rode them for decades, churning out books, articles and reviews that so cemented terms like "bad quartos" and "memorial reconstruction" into the minds of the early English Departments that they remain permanently imbedded in the academic psyche.

In her book—*Shakespearean Suspect Texts: The Bad Quartos and their Contexts* (1996)—Prof. Laurie Maguire, later at Magdalen College Oxford—documents the history of the "New Bibliography"—Pollard and Greg's effort to get Shakespeare Studies established as a science. Science was achieving marvels in philosophy (dialectical materialism), biology (evolution), medicine (penicillin and quinine), astronomy (the planets Uranus and Neptune), transportation (steam and gasoline engines) and so forth—so why not Shakespeare Studies? Just because Furnival and Fleay had failed didn't mean it couldn't be done, if approached by the right team with enough scientific rigor.

Pollard provided the rigor—Greg provided the team. Calling themselves the "New Bibliographers"—they consisted of Greg, his friend from Cambridge days Ronald B. McKerrow, founder and first editor of the *Review of English Studies,* launching pad for their theories—plus the prolific John Dover Wilson, and the Scottish outlier, Peter Alexander. Much like Furnival and Fleay—Greg and McKerrow also shared a fundamental interest in math and science. While McKerrow preferred medical metaphors, Greg would compare questions of style to equations. While McKerrow—educated at Harrow, Kings College London and Trinity College Cambridge—is known today for his edition of the Thomas Nashe canon—Greg dealt with everything else. By sharing ideas and continually referencing each other's work—they endowed their efforts with the gravitas of collaboration while avoiding the kind of public brawls that wrecked the Shakspere Society.

The early quartos vs. the First Folio

By the time Greg found his way to the British Museum it had become the main recipient of donations from collectors of important literary incunabula[165]—among them the Early Modern manuscript and rare books collections of Steevens, Malone, Halliwell-Phillipps, the Earl of Bridgewater, and the Dukes of Devonshire. As these early works continued to accumulate at the BM—the New Bibs basked in the certainty that their approach would yield results.

How, for instance, was an anonymous play like *The Famous Victories of Henry the Fifth* related to Shakespeare's *Henry V*—in which so many bits and hints of the latter's plot and language appear —or the *First Part of the Contention between the Two Famous Houses of York and Lancaster* to *Henry VI part two*—or the *True Tragedy of Richard Duke of York* to *Henry VI part three*—all so similar to the plays as published in the First Folio?

Yet, however similar in story, plot, characters, and language to these masterpieces—the early quartos were all over the place in style —some oddly archaic, some with unusual verse patterns—while others varied only slightly from their First Folio versions. Weak versions continued to appear in the Stationers' Register both late and early. Stymied, the team turned to what they were pleased to call the science of *Bibliography*.

According to Wikipedia there are two forms of bibliography—

---

[165] Since 1998 these have been located at the British Library.

analytical bibliography—which is "concerned with the objective physical analysis and history of a book"—while "*descriptive bibliography* employs all data that analytical bibliography furnishes, and then codifies it with a view to identifying the ideal copy or form of a book that . . . represents the printer's initial conception."

Although the first would have made sense—it must have been the second that led Pollard and Greg to fasten onto the notion that the versions that best fitted the "ideal copy or form" of Shakespeare's plays were those published in 1623. Thus the various "incompetent" versions must have been created by the "injurious impostors" mentioned by Hemmings and Condell in their Preface to the First Folio—the rascals who had "stolen . . . surreptitious copies" by "frauds and stealths."

In defense of what he termed a "reliable and scientific text"— Greg tore into his predecessors for sloppy thinking, ignorance of facts, and lack of editorial principles—which they dared to publish, as he claimed—"for the sole purpose of displaying their own astounding ignorance" (Maguire 40). To rectify this would require Pollard's field—Bibliography, which Greg defined as "a science by which we coordinate facts and trace the operation of constant causes." (He neglected to mention chemical analysis.)

"Bad quartos" and "memorial reconstruction"

Greg and company offered two possible sources for these supposed knockoffs. Some were the product of the faulty memory of an actor who had performed a particular role in the Folio version—others of a scrivener who, seated in the audience during a performance of the 1623 version, managed to scribble enough on a hidden notepad that he was able to sell it to one of the piratical printers that so densely populated the imaginations of these 20th-century Bibliographers.

While some quartos were much closer in style to the First Folio version than others—this meant relegating each to one of two scrap heaps—"bad quartos"—those created by someone other than the author, someone with a bad memory or poor transcription skills —and "good quartos," those produced by someone other than the author, but who had a good memory and/or good transcription skills.

Educating Shakespeare

None, in their view, could possibly have been created by Shakespeare himself—whose versions had to have been, as they saw it, limited to those published in the First Folio—a conclusion only marginally more bizarre than the Stratford theory—but based upon the same old uncertain ground on which this new house of cards was being so enthusiastically constructed, the Stratford dating scheme.

Three possible theories

Maguire explains—"The enthusiasm with which the theory of memorial reconstruction was accepted can best be understood in relation to earlier theories held to account for suspect texts." She lists three such theories—1) they were Shakespeare's *source plays*, meaning they had been written earlier by someone else—2) they were Shakespeare's *own early drafts*—or 3) they were *the product of actors with bad memories* who transcribed them in shorthand as they sat in the audience (7).

Maguire's response shows intelligence—If #1 was true and the quarto was a *source*—then "there existed early on a dramatist with Shakespeare's ability in plotting, gift for characterization, and interest in poetical experimentation, who has left no other trace of his work" —something she sees as "improbable."

As for #2—his own *early drafts*—she notes the 1941 objection "to the notion of a playwright who graduated very rapidly from 'quite miserable ineptitude in his early days to complete perfection' within comparatively few years." If the brilliant but unnamed precursors of #1 were the New Bibliographer's Scylla, the early drafts of #2 were their Charybdis—since the short time span allowed by the Stratford biography required much too steep a curve to account for Stratford William's leap from ineptitude to perfection. Thus the most obvious and most likely choice had to be rejected for the same reason that every other aspect of the "Shakespeare problem" has failed—because the Stratford biography won't allow enough time for it. Only this can explain why the New Bibs would choose #3.

Since both #1 and #2 demand attention to the integrity and availability of the original author—only a great unwillingness to take the author into account can explain the fact that it was the least likely

IV Shakespeare in Our Time

of the three options—"forgetful actors and reportorial thieves"—that became their preference. For the Bibs, what #3 had going for it that the others didn't was that it allowed them to state, *a priori*—without any justification and despite common sense and all evidence to the contrary—that the Folio version was Shakespeare's original—so that every other version, no matter how early, must have come from the play as it was published in 1623—in some cases 40 years later. The absurdity of this notion—particularly where an ephemeral medium like Theater is concerned—boggles the rational mind.

The real advantage of #3 was that it provided the Bibs with a great straw man—or more particularly, a whole gang of straw men—the University Wits—that they could buffet at length for their archaic terms and un-Shakespearean style. By thus moving the discourse from questions regarding the authorship of the canon to the authorship of the quartos—like Tweedledum and Tweedledee—Greg and company could engage in a seemingly endless and pointless skirmish that achieved at least one good result—it distracted readers from that "Giant Crow as big as a tar barrel"—the author's identity![166]

None of the ideas put forth by the New Bibs were really new—all had been suggested by earlier scholars. Alexander Pope had questioned the authenticity of parts of several of Shakespeare's plays—so had Samuel Johnson, so had Malone. Most active in such questioning "the disintegrator" Frederick Fleay. Then—at about the same time that Greg was beginning his studies—one J.M. Robertson, journalist, parliamentarian and controversialist—launched the most enduring and informed attack on the integrity of the canon—claiming to see *all of it* by one or another of the various University Wits.—According to Robertson, there simply *was no such person as William Shakespeare!*[167]

This is not to say that the production of poor copies was never

---

[166] As a mathematician, Lewis Carroll's targets were his colleagues at Oxford who just then were engaged in flights of mathematical fancy known as "the New Math," which departs from Euclid in ways that outraged Dodgson. According to Melanie Bayley, the Oxford graduate who noted this in 2009, failing to get attention from a po-faced media, Dodgson added mathematical elements to a story he'd written originally to entertain the little daughter of his Dean.

[167] His other target was the historical Jesus, supposedly another myth.

anything but a fantasy or that transcribing and memorization were impossible. The corruption of printed works—originally distributed via hand-copied manuscripts—was a problem for all writers then and earlier. So how likely is it that these supposed knockoffs were the product of somebody's bad memory?

Memorization—once upon a time humanity's only means of record-keeping—was still very much a necessary skill in the sixteenth century, and not just for actors. Lawyers were required to know by heart vast stretches of legal language. Grammar school and University students were tested by oral examination (it would be another century before printing would provide the means for learning and testing directly from a text).[168] In addition, memorizing text accurately is one of the most necessary skills for any actor. Why should these actors happen to be so bad at it? In several cases the quarto version was the equal to its Folio version—even, as some worthy to express an opinion have urged—more truly Shakespearean. As Maguire notes—

> New Bibliography is least satisfactory, because least equipped, when dealing with the subject of multiple texts. Bibliography can assess variants due to corruption because that is what it is designed to do. Present it with two readings which may possess equal validity and it cannot cope. The bibliographic mindset is trained to think in terms of good and bad, right and wrong. Faced with two sheep, it is all too easy to insist that one must be a goat. (52)

Maguire quotes A.E. Housman—

> If Providence permitted two MSS to be equal, the editor would have to choose between their readings by considerations of intrinsic merit and in order to do that he would need to acquire intelligence and impartiality and willingness to take pains, and all sorts of things which he neither has nor wishes for; and he feels sure that God, who tempers the wind to the shorn lamb, can never have meant to lay upon his shoulders such a burden as this.

Why were some quartos registered with the Stationers while others

---

[168] The oldest continental universities still rely on oral exams.

IV Shakespeare in Our Time

were not? Why had half the plays in the First Folio been published many years earlier in quarto, some in multiple editions, while the other half remained unpublished until 1623? Why was *Titus Andronicus* so different from plays like *Othello* or *Julius Caesar*?

What could account for their bizarre publishing history—four plays published anonymously in 1594—twelve identified in 1598 as by *William Shakespeare*—five published in 1600—seven more published over the following years—until 1609, after which (almost) nothing was published for 14 years until all (but *Edward III*) were published in the First Folio in 1623, in what appears to have been something of a rushed job.

Greg, McKerrow, Wilson *et al* egged each other on as they labeled one quarto after another good, bad, stolen, badly copied, misreported, poorly memorized—everything, that is, but the most obvious explanation—that it was *the author's own early version*—his *juvenilia*. Shakespeare's lack of juvenilia is one of the great weaknesses of the Stratford thesis. He seems to have emerged, fully matured, out of nowhere. Surely they knew this. Why did they ignore it? Why do they still ignore it?

Page versus Stage

Focused on the minutiae of editorial process and typesetting—the Bibs also ignored the processes by which plays are created for an audience. While it's important to know how a play may have moved from pen to print—that's only half the story. The first and more important half has to do with what is obviously its original function—that it was intended for a particular audience, and just who that audience might have been. As Maguire puts it—

> Greg is everywhere anxious to protect the standards and methods of professional Elizabethan performance, but, since we do not know the standards and methods of professional Elizabethan performance, Greg is merely protecting his own assumptions. This results in some extraordinary contradictions.

It's also ignoring the not insignificant matter of artistry. Maguire quotes statements by Greg such as—"To the bibliographer the literary contents of a book is irrelevant," and "critical bibliography is the science of the material transmission of literary texts . . . its interests are not 'artistic' [but are] 'governed by methods of scientific enquiry'" (32)—which would seem to equate the Shakespeare canon with the London phone directory.

No doubt the New Bibs did yeoman work in deciphering the issues surrounding 16th-century publishing—but their lack of focus on the content and its purpose led them into far more reckless treatments of the authorship issue than anything produced by the old Shakspere Societies or the Baconians. These at least show some respect for the author's genius—while the Bibs, like Seth dismembering Osiris—cheerfully slash whatever bits and pieces don't suit their ideas of what "sounds like Shakespeare"—distributing them willy-nilly to various University Wits—about whom they knew little or nothing—whilst arguing at impressive length over whether a particular play or scene was written by the mysterious Robert Greene or the even more mysterious Thomas Watson.

Enter the English Department

What may be missed in other treatments of this subject is the fact that the English Departments that now hold the high ground in any discussion of Shakespeare are newcomers to Shakespeare Studies—having emerged only a little more than a century ago, long after scholars like Steevens, Malone, and Halliwell-Phillipps laid the groundwork—and half a century after the authorship question first became public. In fact, as Maguire informs us—"When Greg and McKerrow studied at Cambridge, there was no separate school of English; English Literature came under the aegis of the School of Medieval and Modern Languages . . . it was 1926 before one could read for a degree purely in English Literature at Cambridge" (32-3).

Following Churton Collins's campaign—"in 1884-85, after protracted and heated debate, Oxford inaugurated its Merton Chair for English Language and Literature, and then promptly negated this progress by appointing a philologist to the post" (35). It seems that what Maguire calls *philology*—Greg called *bibliography*. Philology is defined by Wikipedia as "the study of literary texts and written records, the establishment of their authenticity and their original form, and the determination of their meaning."

Maguire suggests that it was concern over how to teach literature more seriously than just as a matter of taste that caused the English departments to cleave to philology. In *philology*, and its cousin *linguistics*, the sciences of how languages are formed—the purpose of particular texts are not the major concern. Put plainly, while Greg and friends were interested in the plays as published texts—they seem unconcerned with what common sense would assign as their primary purpose—*live entertainment*. For whom? By whom? About what?

With English drama still a parvenu at the universities—the New Bibs, like the drunk looking for his keys under the street lamp—stuck to what they could see with this approach rather than to any one of a number of paths—such as History or Psychology—that might have led—if not directly to the truth, then a little closer to it—but not, as has been the case—in an entirely wrong direction.

"Memorial reconstruction"

As time went by, Greg's adherence to the First Folio as ultimate source forced him to dismiss the work of scholars who dared to look anywhere else. Maguire notes his response to Madeleine Doran's credible suggestion in 1930 that the comparison of the quarto of *King Lear* to its Folio version shows Shakespeare working through problems of composition. Maguire quotes Greg—"That Shakespeare evolved the seemingly inevitable expression of passage after passage" by "fumbling after his expression, and even after his meaning . . . is hard to believe."—Says Maguire—

> Greg therefore rejects the question of revision, even though his monumental collection of manuscripts meant that he was all too familiar with authorial palimpsest and second thought. Such empirical evidence is blithely dismissed: "the revised type is probably not found in Shakespeare's plays, though it is well known elsewhere." Shakespeare strikes gold at once, his expression is "inevitable." (55)

The uneducated genius produces perfection right off the bat. Unlike Darwin's God, he has no need ever to revise or tweak, nor do his actors ever require it of him over thirty years of language evolution and audience development. The true reason—why authorial revision is so repugnant to the English Department—is that it threatens the Stratford story because of the time required for such changes—time the sacred biography can't provide.

Bent on deconstructing—Maguire shows how, in work after work—Greg violates his own precepts by departing from strictures he demands in theory. It's rather touching that—towards the end of his career, after arranging the facts about a particular title page in the manner that he continually preached would lead to understanding—he comments, "Those are the facts, and they do not make sense" (44).

The philological Ice Age

Neither Pollard nor Greg were the first to suggest "memorial reconstruction" as an explanation for the early quartos. As far back as the 1840s John Payne Collier had suggested that it explains the first quartos of *Hamlet,* and *Romeo and Juliet*. The New Shakespeareans followed suit. But it was Pollard and Greg who set it in stone—promoting it through articles in McKerrow's *Review of English Studies* as the ultimate explanation for the vagaries and problems of the early quartos. Greg's support from the Shakespeare establishment, his unflagging energy and long life, gave him—much like William Davenant's eight children—the power to flood the field with his opinions for so long that he left Shakespeare Studies with a permanently altered shoreline.

Due to the size and duration of the wave of influence thus raised within the Academy—and to the generations of students who got their Shakespeare from Greg and his followers—*memorial reconstruction* has remained ever since the standard explanation for the existence of the early quartos. You'll find it all over Wikipedia—where Stratford defenders continue to promote its gnarly old rubric. Interest may have shifted from the bibliographers to the linguists—and from the linguists to the theater historians—but all this has done has been to shift the focus from Page to Stage without altering in any substantial way the unending repetitions of these notions in everything published.

Why should something so obviously flawed have caught and held the attention of the Shakespeare community for so long? According to Maguire—"Much of New Bibliography's appeal comes from the narrative charm of the chase." It's "an academic detective story in which textual sleuths follow stationers and compositors, identify type and press corrections, and triumphantly distinguish the 'good' from the 'bad.'" And—quoting academic Gary Taylor—because it offered a literary community hungry for solid answers "a promise of science and the promise of finality" (42). It seems the promise alone has been enough for Taylor and company—still buzzing like bees around the same old rotten Malvolian apple.

It's also because the New Bibs gave Shakespeare Studies some of their most valuable research materials—among them Pollard and Redgrave's *Short Title Catalogue,* Greg and Jackson's *Records of the Court of the Stationer's Company*, Greg's *Bibliography of the English Printed Drama,* his *Dramatic Documents from the Elizabethan Playhouse,* his edition of *Henslowe's Diary*—the Malone Society reprints, and the inspiration for E. K. Chambers's monumental four volume cornerstone of the Shakespeare edifice, *The Elizabethan Stage*—fundamental to all Shakespeare research ever since.

Still—since it has become obvious that they were incapable of fulfilling that promise of "science and finality"—why did/does the Academy continue to adhere to ideas of "bad quartos" and to the First Folio as the original text? Is it because that's what they were taught as undergraduates, so it remains the platform on which they continue to base their own work, no matter how badly it sags from a century of malfunction? Or could it be because it gives evidence of what appears to be exemplary scholarly activity without ever having to deal with the crucial matter of its origins?

With eyes firmly fixed on the text, all those ghostly actors and scribes who supposedly misreported Shakespeare's originals never have to be identified. Mingling with the University Wits—whose biographies haven't even confirmed some of them as anything more than names—the peevish actors, careless reporters and profligate printers create an imaginary crowd that surrounds and hides from cool scrutiny the cartoon with the Page Boy bob and wispy goatee.

Noting their "reluctance to contemplate" revision as an explanation for the quartos—Maguire traces it to the result of earlier theories, suggesting that, in academia, one theory tends to lead to another in a sort of Darwinian process where ideas duplicate and mutate in a continuum that never will, perhaps never can, return to a basic original—and so inevitably must part altogether from a too long spurned reality. Jonathan Swift spoofs this in *Gulliver's Travels* where the Holofernes of his day is followed by a servant whose job is to keep him from falling to his death off the brink of the floating island of Laputia—Swift's naughty spoof of 18th-century Oxbridge.

The New Bibs were forever sneering—at the inept reporter who couldn't get the lines right, the ignorant typesetter, the dull-witted editor, the piratical printer—never for a minute entertaining the most plausible explanation for the wide spectrum of language styles—some from as early as the 1560s—of a genius revealed in succeeding stages of his development. Obviously Shakespeare was a genius—why don't they try to see him from this perspective? Are they so ignorant about what it means to be a genius?

Maguire quotes Kirschbaum in noting that although in the first quartos of *Hamlet, Romeo,* and *A Shrew* there is

> clear evidence of a second hand contributing new writing, this "new writing" is never conceptualized as "authorship," even when the "reporter" is behaving suspiciously like a playwright. When Shakespeare or other known authors perform such activities they are "using sources"—when a nameless other does it, he is mindlessly copying. (87-8)

What the Bibs see as evidence of reporting works just as well as evidence of revision by an author as he strives to keep pace with his actors and their audience—all changing in their usage of language as they grow in literacy and perhaps as they adopt what they're hearing in the Theater.

"A revival with alterations"

Albert Feuillerat, Professor of French at Yale from 1927 to 1954, argues sensibly that revision was in fact a standard means for

IV Shakespeare in Our Time

managers like Burbage and Henslowe to maintain audience interest and a financially healthy box office. Feuillerat's book, *Shakespeare in Composition*, published in 1953, is the result of thirty years of study. He began his research in the early 1920s, right about the time that Robertson was eliminating Shakespeare from the canon and Greg's team were eliminating him from the quartos.

Confronted by the differences between the early quartos and the First Folio versions—Feuillerat committed to a rigorous examination of the most problematic texts—to which he gave the literary equivalent of a DNA analysis far more sophisticated than Pollard's. After demolishing memorial reconstruction with a few refreshing blasts of common sense—he argues for *revision* as the most likely explanation for the variations in question. He claims that revision—whether by the author or a later editor—was used and advertised by acting companies and theater managers as "an easy way of economizing in the purchase of plays."

Pointing to the evidence of the many title pages that proclaim a play as "newly corrected, augmented and amended"—he explains how revising an old play with a proven track record was more cost effective than investing in something new and untried. A company's playbook was its most precious investment. Stagehands and carpenters could always be replaced and new actors trained, but skillful playwrights—the kind who could bring an audience back to see a play again and again—are not a dime a dozen, then or now. If, as seems logical, the frequently noted "*ne*" in Henslowe's Diary refers to a play that's been "*N*ewly *E*mended"—the greater receipts for those performances marked "*ne*"[169] add proof to Feuillerat's contention that creating new plays out of old was good for business.

What writer doesn't revise? All writing for publication is half creation, half revision. There are instances where poems and short stories have appeared, fully-formed, in the mind of an author[170]—sometimes bent on something longer and more complex—yet almost everything from poetry to Thomas Wolfe has required editing—i.e.,

---

[169] For evidence that by "ne" Henslowe meant *Newly Emended,* see Appendix E.

[170] As we're told occurred with Robert Frost's "Stopping by Woods on a Snowy Evening"—or with Coleridge's "Kublai Khan."

revision. But not the Shakespeare of the Oxbridge Academy or the Birthplace Trust. As Lily Campbell puts it—

> The first mistake was to take for granted and postulate that the folio text, being longer and better, was the first and only authentic text, and that the quarto text, being shorter and often inferior, was consequently a truncated and corrupted form of the folio text. It is difficult to believe that plays which in certain cases were in the possession of Shakespeare's company for thirty years, remained untouched at a time when the practice was to refurbish the repertoire constantly. (41-2)

Nor are Campbell and Feuillerat alone. John Vyvyan notes places in the plays where Shakespeare adds or changes the text to amplify his theories. He quotes Dover Wilson who "saw *Love's Labour's Lost* as a play 'written on the threshold of Shakespeare's career and *twice rehandled*.'" As Vyvyan puts it—

> The title page of *Love's Labour's Lost*'s quarto describes it as "newly corrected and augmented." There must then have been *two versions*. We may assume that the first of these was, at least, a very early work, and that important additions were made to it—possibly some years later. The augmentations show an evolution of thought, which is not the product of mere polishing, but of time. (*Rose* 14)

Vyvyan suggests that originally the play ended with the Princess's embassy fulfilled—as suggested by the line "for my great suit so easily obtained" (Act V Scene 2). Since in the play—as published in the First Folio—the Princess's suit was *not* obtained, nor was it even mentioned again, Vyvyan notes—"Shakespeare was notably careless in such matters, he often does not bother to delete an earlier line, but he could not have made her say such a thing in the first place without warrant." (46)

As Roslyn L. Knutson reports in an article in *Theatre Research International*—in "Henslowe's Diary and the Economics of Play Revision for Revival"—Greg fudged his stand against revisions—

> Defending the sign "ne" as the mark of new plays, he offered as an exception a play "new in the sense that it was *a revival*

IV Shakespeare in Our Time

with alterations." In the Cambridge editions of Shakespeare's plays, J. Dover Wilson systematically identified textual variants and cruxes in the early plays as evidence of revisions. ... Over the years, editions of and monographs on plays with more than one textual version have reinforced the association of major alterations with a play's return to the stage after some period of retirement. For such an apparently widespread playhouse practice, G.E. Bentley developed a "rule of thumb"—"almost any play . . . kept in active repertory by the company which owned it, is most likely to contain *later revisions by the author* or . . . another playwright . . . for the same company."

In *Facts and Problems*, Chambers stated that "the problem of revision is more complicated" (than that of working with a collaborator), although he doesn't say why—

> Plays which had been laid aside were often revived. A stock favorite was called a "get-penny". . . . Conceivably three or four plays marked "ne" in Henslowe's accounts for 1594-97 may have been revived and so were not strictly new; the significance of "ne" is not quite clear. (215).

And so on and so forth—maybe this maybe that—for five pages listing every recorded instance in which it's obvious that a play was altered with no effort to discriminate between authorial revision and "play-patching"—ending with the obligatory bow to tradition—that Shakespeare *never revised his own work!*

Feuillerat dwells at some length on revision and how necessary it was to the repertory companies that inaugurated the London Stage. Just about every one of the dozens of symptoms of reporting as listed by Maguire work equally well as evidence of revision by an original author—experimenting as he develops what—by the 1590s—had matured into his famous style.

Unfortunately, because Feuillerat was forced to fit his scenario to the Stratford dates, his is as skewed as every other. Forced to create imaginary writers to take the place of the author himself—he conjures up authors A, B, and C—to whom he gives credit for what is most precious to authors—their ability to create something uniquely meaningful out of their own personal experience and reading.

Feuillerat's scheme forces him to assign to Shakespeare an even lowlier role than Bullough's plagiarizer—that of "play-patcher"—a hack called in to spiff up old plots. This is hardly how any gifted author would wish to be seen—nor is it what Shakespeare's inventive genius would suggest. What it does suggest is that once again an intelligent academic has been forced by the Stratford biography to trade a solid insight for a piece of the author's identity. Feuillerat may have preserved William's name and biography (and not least his own career)—but only by denying Shakespeare his originality.

Pristine examples of the styles of the 1580s—the early quartos of Shakespeare's history plays—show how these changes occurred from the mid-1580s—when most were first created—to the mid-1590s when they were revised. To the eight of the First Folio can now be added *Edward III*—left out, no doubt, because a tetchy Scot was on the throne—and *Thomas of Woodstock*—from the same period as the *True Tragedies* and the *Contentions*—but never revised.[171]

As Scott McMillin affirms in *The Queen's Men and their Plays* (1998)—the first royal company had four of these early anonymous plays in their repertory—*The Famous Victories of Henry the Fifth*, *The Troublesome Raigne of King John*, *The True Tragedy of Richard III*, and *King Leir* (189-91). If we accept McMillin's (proven) thesis that Walsingham created the Queen's Men as primarily a road company meant to spread policy in the provinces—there's every reason to see the first two of these plays as written to do this by an author who would later revise them for the Lord Chamberlain's Men.

Moving forward

In the land of the blind the one eyed man is king. In spite of the problems created by the Stratford biography—where scholars have ignored it and worked directly from the plays, there have been results. In *The Case for Shakespeare's Authorship of the Famous Victories* (1961), English professor Seymour Pitcher provided the first modern

---

[171] In 2006, Michael Egan, then a professor at the University of Hawaii, published a four volume exegesis on *Richard II part one*, (aka *Thomas of Woodstock*) in which he proves in detail its relationship as a precursor to *Richard II*.

era publication of what certainly appears to be the first version of Shakespeare's *Henry V*—with over 30 pages of comparisons to the later play. Shrugging off stuff like memorial reconstruction by actors or derivation from a missing original—Pitcher gives several pages of sources. As for *The Famous Victories*—we relish the following—

> It seems impossible that it was his mere source for the later three [*Henry V* and *Henry IV parts one and two*]. He used it ingeniously, as he used his sources, but more than that he used it instinctively as if it were his own. He knew it by heart, by total assimilation. Presumably not a first draft by intention, it served him as such, and by the tedious—and devious—ways of art, it at last evolved into the trilogy. A source, to be sure, may offer a second writer fresh motivation, stores for plunder, materials to cast anew, but in contrast a first draft grows, sometimes with abrupt mutations here and there, from what it has been to what it can, and perhaps must, become; the development that it undergoes is largely internal and organic. And it was thus, I believe that *The Famous Victories* became the ultimate trilogy. (6)

As historian and authorship scholar Ramon Jiménez has since proven beyond all rational argument—the anonymous *Troublesome Reign* became *King John,* the anonymous *True Tragedy of Richard Duke of York* became *Henry the Sixth parts one and two,* and the anonymous *True Tragedy of Richard III* became *Richard III*. Once again comes Ockham's razor—wielded by Jiménez, cutting to the clean and lovely truth—eliminating centuries of elaborately misconceived hogwash.

Edmund Ironside

In 1965, E.B. Everitt presented the case for six early plays that he recognized as nothing other than Shakespeare's juvenilia—among them *Edmund Ironside, The Troublesome Reign, Edward III,* and *Thomas of Woodstock*. Twenty years later, Eric Sams took up where Everitt left off with *Edmund Ironside: Shakespeare's Lost Play.* In his Introduction to the second edition (1986) Sams attacks with vigor the academics' defenses against logic and common sense. Pouncing on a particularly absurd suggestion, he purrs—"His analysis persuaded him to postulate, admittedly on no evidence at all, an additional actor-playwright attached to Shakespeare's own theater company, . . . well placed to plagiarize all their performances." Among the results—

> an enormous lot of parallel passages, similarities in structure, the sources the same . . . . a great many similarities in terms of verbal parallels, images, the actual political situation which is presented in the play, . . . an intimate knowledge in detail of these plays. . . . intimately familiar with Shakespeare's chronicle writing . . . a tremendous excitement . . . so there's a feeling the language is sort of creating and generating itself very prolifically in the very act of writing . . . (x)

After which Everitt comments drily—"Only a Shakespeare specialist could fail to see which actor-playwright in Shakespeare's own company is being described here. There would be only a very small number of them—such as *one!*"

Those questioners who have not already read his book will find the introduction to his second edition as rich in laughs as groans over the depths to which academic malfeasance will sink when confronted with the Blatant Beast of Early Modern English Lit—the *Shakespeare Authorship Question!*

Stage versus Page

With their training in philology and bibliography—and their scorn for the "vernacular stage"—Oxbridge Shakespeareans have always been far more comfortable dealing with Shakespeare and his fellows as writers of books than creators of performance art. Per Maguire—

> Rather than be caught wrong footed by applying material rules to an immaterial art form, Greg redefines Elizabethan drama. Shakespeare, he says, must always have written with one eye on publication; that is why his plays are so long. The material text is therefore more important than the immaterial performance. (56)

More important to Greg perhaps—hardly more important to the actors

IV Shakespeare in Our Time

and audiences for whom they were created. As the Oxbridge English Departments drifted ever more deeply into an airless iconosphere—a brief burst of humanism in the 1970s saw the Bard's return to the theater—and to films and television, high school stages and reading groups. Leaving his text to speak for itself—experiments in staging began reaching in every possible direction—entertaining audiences with films like Kenneth Branagh's beautifully filmed and scored *Henry V*—and his *Much Ado About Nothing*—Trevor Nunn's *Twelfth Night*—Baz Luhrmann's dazzling *Romeo & Juliet*—and Kurosawa's stunning *Ran (King Lear)*. With little thought for either his mechanics or his identity—university theater departments leapt to the forefront of Shakespeare Studies with books and articles on how to produce him, how to pronounce him, how to interpret him.

Just as a pendulum held too long at one extreme will swing when released to the opposite extreme—Drama Departments—disgusted perhaps with the pomposities of the English Departments—began treating the published versions of the plays as little more than theatrical prompt books—that is, if Shakespeare overwrote it was merely to offer the actors more choices. But most directors were happy to begin with the play—ignoring its history and eliminating its ambiguities with cuts. Most still are.

Shakespeare, of course, wrote for *both* Page *and* Stage—each or a different purpose—neither a spinoff or a lesser version of the other. Lukas Erne has written an entire book[172] to prove what simple common sense would suggest. The published play, in Shakespeare's case at least, was never, or almost never, just the actors' prompt book —but a version specifically intended for readers—who, with time to pause and absorb what would have been wrong for the Stage—either because it was too involved, too erudite, or because it would have slowed the action—required a different version of the story for the reader who did not have the advantage of seeing it performed—or who wanted more than just the one afternoon's pleasure. The Lord Chamberlain's Men had no need to refer to any published version. As a repertory company, they knew what worked for their audience, and when change was required, they had the author—so long as he lived

---

[172] *Shakespeare as Literary Dramatist* (2003).

—to make what changes he—or they—felt were needed.

We don't know exactly what Shakespeare's audiences saw—we can't know. It may be that some of the quartos were based on prompt books, as has been argued. In any case what his audiences craved were his stories. Where this was the largely uneducated public it would make sense that the platonic soliloquies and legal arguments would be trimmed from scenes written specifically for the educated audiences at the Court or the Inns of Court. We know for a fact that the deposition scene in *Richard II*—where the King is forced to hand the crown over to Bolingbroke—was eliminated in the early quartos, as also doubtless it was when produced at Court. What monarch would willingly tolerate an enactment of her own worst nightmare?

Perhaps the biggest advantage with accepting the quartos as Shakespeare's own early works are the insights it gives into his development—how he self-edited, changing the order of words, crafting the language into something more powerful, more beautiful, and ever more deeply meaningful—a process revealed by the first six quartos of *Richard III*—each separated from the next by no more than a year or two—which reveal as nothing else does his habit of revision. He would not have bothered had he not regarded the result of these revisions as anything but genuine literature—aimed at standards set by Sophocles and Euripides, Terence and Plautus, Machiavelli and Ariosto.

So, did Shakespeare write Shakespeare?

Indeed he did; that is, Shakespeare *the genius* wrote all of the plays that bear his name—*and* their early versions—*and* a great many other works—among them the published translations into English of some of the more important sources for which he's not yet acknowledged—since they were published under someone else's name. The early works may vary widely in quality—but there should be no argument that they were written by the same mind and hand over the various succeeding stages in his—and his audiences'—development.

Even had the plots and characters of some not been almost identical to those in the First Folio versions—differing hardly at all except in style and details—there are just too many other things about

IV Shakespeare in Our Time

these quartos—the "bad" as well as the "good"—that foreshadow what was on its way to becoming the iconic Shakespeare of the First Folio. To imagine that there could have been a second (earlier) writer, or writers—his equals in creating stories and inventing language—is no less absurd than the idea that he was capable of going in the three years allotted him by the Stratford biography from "ineptitude" to "perfection." Stretch those three years to three decades and we've got a plausible scenario for the leap from *Titus Andronicus* to *Hamlet*.

By viewing these quartos as the playwright's own originals—allowing the authorial chips to fall where they may—we achieve, not just one, but a whole slew of simplifications—together with a much clearer sense of how our greatest literary artist grew over time—and how he brought his audiences, and all later writers of English plays and novels, along with him. How can any aspect of Shakespeare Studies be more interesting than this?

Also, by viewing these early quartos as first or early versions of a play that would be revised by the author himself over a period of years—in some cases several times—it becomes apparent that the weaker the staging, the less fully realized the characters, the looser the versification, the more archaic the language, the more reckless with historical fact—the earlier the quarto—while the better the staging, the more modern the language, etc., the closer in time it must be to 1609, when—for some reason yet to be determined—all publication of his plays in quarto came to a halt.

It's simply not possible to lump these plays in quarto together into some sort of general category with characteristics shared by all—or even by most. All are different—not just because they occurred at different moments in historic time and their author's life—but because each has a history of its own unlike any other. The only thing the quartos share is that each represents a different stage in a particular play's development (where we have it) to what it had become by 1623. Nor, as Feuillerat shows, is the Folio version necessarily the purer version, the one most truly *Shakespearean*. Just as each play has its own history, its own original purpose—each has its own history of publication, closely allied with that purpose—whether social, political, or personal to the author, and/or the acting company that used it to achieve such astonishing success in the fields of literary art, commercial enterprise, and public education.

All of these are issues that stand waiting in the wings until those who should be taking seriously the task of explaining how these immensely influential works of dramatic literature came to be written, leave off counting feminine endings and begin dealing with their *provable connections* to the *social and political history of the periods* when they were created. Until *this story* is told—the world will continue to believe that Shakespeare's identity doesn't matter.

~~ Dismembering the curricula ~~

Back in the mid-nineteenth century, when John Churton Collins was finding it so difficult to persuade Oxford University to create a Chair in English Lit—the University's resistance was largely due to the notion that because people read for pleasure—there was no point in creating a department to *study* them—how and why they were written—as that would simply lead to a lot of meaningless "chatter about Shelley" (Maguire 36).[173]

Now it would seem that Collins was wrong and his critics were right. Although "the chatter" is no longer about Shelley—it's never been about much of anything. The flight from reality—that is, the effort to replace the reading and discussion of works of literature with the reading and discussion of abstract theories—began with efforts by scholars like Pollard and Greg to view literature from the perspective of science rather than as poetry and/or entertainment.

The newbie English departments—dissatisfied with merely reading and then discussing with undergraduates what it is about the great works of literature that has set them apart—plunged ever more deeply into the abstract, adopting ideas and terms from one science after another—while ignoring those studies that *might* have offered real perspective, like history, mythology, biography and psychology.

There would have been nothing wrong with this flight into

---

[173] This comment, by Churton Collins's arch enemy at Oxford, history professor Edward Freeman—is not so offhand as it may seem. Shelley's hatred for his *alma mater* was almost as notorious with his Victorian readers as was his poetry, his leftist politics, and his shocking lifestyle.

IV Shakespeare in Our Time

theory had they kept these ideas within their graduate think tanks—but when they began teaching them to undergraduates—replacing discussions of meaning, style, purpose and pleasure with arcane spinoffs from the language sciences—students began dropping out. A people's literature is meant for *people*, young *people*, not proto-philologists. As an article in the *New York Times* of June 22, 2013 informs us, in 1991—

> 165 students graduated from Yale with a B.A. in English literature. By 2012, that number was 62. In 1991, the top two majors at Yale were history and English. In 2013, they were economics and political science. At Pomona this year, they were economics and mathematics. . . . At Pomona College . . . this spring, 16 students graduated with an English major out of a student body of 1560.

It's true that the Humanities have suffered over the past half century due to dwindling job opportunities and skyrocketing college tuitions, leaving many students with no option but to focus on a degree that they, and their parents, hope will guarantee enough of a living after college that they will be able to repay their student loans.

But it's clear that a large part of the reason why students who would have been eager to major in English in the past are avoiding it today is because they were turned off by AP English classes in high school, where theory so infected the study of literature that high school teachers were teaching semiotics because that's what they themselves were taught as high school students. Worse—it may be that kids who who've been turned off literature by these AP classes will not only *not* study English Lit in college if they can avoid it—all pleasure having been drained from it by Theory—they will, from then on, avoid like the plague anything that the world labels *Literature*.

As Gerald Graff, professor of English and Education at the University of Illinois at Chicago, wrote in *Professing Literature: An Institutional History* (1987)—"By the turn of the century it was a commonplace among educators that English courses were boring or baffling students rather than acculturating or indoctrinating them" (100). True enough, yet his choice of terms—*acculturating* and *indoctrinating*—sounds an awful lot like *brainwashing*.

Was the purpose behind the institution of English departments an attempt to open the delights of literature to a broader public—or was it to indoctrinate it with an elitist white male protestant Oxbridge/Ivy League world view? Was it because there was something important to their future lives to be discovered with semiotics? Or was it because—as the new kid on the post-doc block where established programs in fields like economics and science could boast ground breakers like Marx and Darwin (Byron and Shelley being somewhat questionable as father figures)—English departments had to come up with some means of establishing themselves at the postgrad level—where research and theory reign supreme—in hopes that their theories will get published and their jobs made more secure.

It's certainly a great paradox that as the English language has risen over the past half century to become the *lingua franca* of the world—English departments in the English-speaking universities have become trapped in a process that appears to be causing the Humanities—the noble tradition bequeathed them by the Greeks, Romans, Erasmus and Shakespeare—to fade away to little more than a handful of terms. As William Chace, President and Professor of English Emeritus at Emory University and Honorary Professor of English Emeritus at Stanford, asks in his article from the Autumn 2009 issue of *The American Scholar*—"The Decline of the English Department"—

> What are the causes for this decline? There are several, but at the root is the failure of departments of English across the country to champion, with passion, the books they teach and to make a strong case to undergraduates that the knowledge of those books and the tradition in which they exist is a human good in and of itself. What departments have done instead is *dismember the curriculum*, drift away from the notion that historical chronology is important, and substitute for the books themselves a scattered array of secondary considerations (identity studies, abstruse theory, sexuality, film and popular culture). In so doing, they have distanced themselves from the young people interested in good books.

Here, as with Graff, we find expressed the very attitude that has

IV Shakespeare in Our Time

caused the collapse. It isn't *chronology* that matters—it's the great issues of the day and the mood of the public. It's epic, satire, romance, memoire—*not* what trope some writer got from some earlier writer. Most of all, it's the *story!* And not just those they tell—but their own as well. Knowing Shelley, who he was, why he was expelled from Oxford, what sent him into exile and drove him to suicide, what made him write, and—beyond all else, why it is that we can still get shivers when we read his poetry?"

Lines like "if winter comes, can Spring be far behind?"—milked for centuries by his admirers for their relevance to the winter of life and the spring we all hope will follow in "that bourne from which no traveller returns"—are what take Shelley and his life, and ours—beyond mere chatter. It's the *people* who wrote these works and those who have kept them alive over the centuries by reading and publishing and repeating them as they shave or drive to work—that are what made Literature central to the Humanities. It's what once gave so many intellectually hungry young people the impetus to finish high school and continue on to college.

Where's the history?

"Dismembering the curriculum" is bound to occur where the natural bond between Literature and History has been severed. Without the works that it spawned, history loses its greatest means of expression, while literature—cut off from those events that show its relevance—loses its meaning for our daily lives. Disconnected, rootless, it floats in the bloodless atmosphere of Swift's Laputia. Only when Literature and History are studied in tandem do they become meaningful, grounded, whole, important, pulsating with life. Only when they are taken together does History become story—and Literature provide medicine for what ails the soul.

Could it be that the problem with Literature was never that it had no such post-graduate departments—but that *it did not, and does not, need them*—since all they do has been to allow Tweedledum to battle Tweedledee with nothing to show for it but a loud and unintelligible rattling of terms? Since there's no substance to these shadows—interest can only derive from the intensity of the struggle

—the meaner the combatants, the more interesting the fight, never mind the fact that no one has the slightest idea of what it's all about. In a 1947 attack on the "New Criticism" an oppositional theorist castigated Literature's "'aloof intellectual"—its 'aping' of science —its reduction of literary commentary to 'a circumscribed end in itself.'" Graff notes that—

> the sins of which [such] scholars accused the New Critics were precisely the ones for which New Humanists and other generalists had earlier attacked research scholars—scientism, preference for nit-picking analysis over direct experience of literature itself, and favoring the special interests of a professional coterie over the interests of general readers and students. (248-9)

Again and again, the same old *cri de coeur*—repeated by each new literary *ism* as it demands attention to what should be the most important issue of all when seeking to understand a particular oeuvre —*who* wrote it and *why* did he (or she) take the time, the trouble, and the expense, not only to write it, but to get it past the censors, and, in some cases, avoid being killed in a duel?

This mare's nest of meaningless terms (too many meanings equals no meaning) should tell us that these folks have nothing to say to us about Literature in general and Shakespeare in particular. If they did they would surely prefer to speak in terms that students and ordinary readers can understand without having to translate. Because they don't, won't or (perhaps by now) can't—is it surprising to discover that they have become empty vessels, that—like Alice at the conclusion of Charles Dodgson's masterpiece, we can only cry out —"*You're nothing but a pack of cards!*"[174]

According to Graff, following World War II, the institution of programs for the influx of mature students taking advantage of the GI Bill drove the universities into the hands of "generalists" who urged "readings of the work *in se*, without reference to any external context" (171)—"external context" meaning *History* (one of those words they

---

[174] And wasn't this the very point that Carroll was making when he created them —though his target wasn't literature but the current faddish approach to math.

IV Shakespeare in Our Time

will go to lengths to avoid unless they can tack an *ism* on it). A report from Harvard asked—"what principle of synthesis would bring together in one, or even two courses, the subject matter of philosophy, the fine arts, music and literature, . . . such a broad survey of the superficial aspects of fields which have relatively little in common was productive only of 'a smattering of information.'" Again, no mention of History or Biography—but what else could they mean?

> Granted a mere smattering of information is precisely what the old fashioned survey course had usually amounted to, but did that justify abandoning historical principles altogether? The committee bordered on recognizing the need for history when it warned that "if the books read do not seem to the student to have any bearing on one another, we are losing endless educational chances." But what it hoped would give the books a "bearing on one another" was not historical continuity or context, but what it called "a common body of tradition," something very different from history, as it turned out. (169)

He sees the problem, but does he see the solution?

> Arguably in such a culture the old universals can recover their interest only by being thoroughly *historicized*. In deciding that the monuments of the humanities had to be abstracted from their history in order for their power to be recovered, the theorists of general education had removed the one condition under which the great works had a chance to recover that power. (173)

Amen. Yet he fails to follow up. Graff's solution to this chaos is to teach students *the nature of these controversies!* How can that happen when he himself is unable to distinguish among them? And even if a case could be made for one over another, what good will it do either the university or the students to take valuable time to teach them the reasons for these arcane arguments while ignoring the works themselves—diminishing them to little more than the focus of an argument, a "political football"—Hitchcock's "McGuffin"?

For all but those who choose to make a career of linguistics or philology—time would be better spent reading Austen and Alcott,

Dryden and Defoe, along with something of their biographies and the historical and political climate that surrounded and influenced them. For racial issues there's Ralph Ellison, James Baldwin, Langston Hughes, Maya Angelou—for women's issues there's Mary Wollstonecraft, Edith Wharton, Alice Walker. If this isn't the goal—then what is? Salaries for left brainers? Opportunities to get their abstruse and arcane theories published in hardback at an astronomical cost to university libraries in poorly printed editions that no one but one or two competitors in their field will ever bother to read?

Seeking specifics on the connection between Literature and History, it turns out that Graff's Chapter eleven—"History versus Criticism (1940-1960)"—isn't about either—

> That the New Criticism was "ahistorical" in its theory and practice has become a commonplace, but it would be more accurate to say that the New Critics accepted and worked within the view of history held by most of the literary historians of their time. This was a view that reduced history to atomized "background" information and saw only an "extrinsic" connection between history and literature. The New Critics followed the historians in thinking of literary history as at best a body of preliminary information that, however indispensable, could be set aside once the would be explicator had done a minimal amount of homework. Instead of challenging this narrow view, the critics echoed the historians in thinking of history as a preliminary activity from which one moved on to something more literary. (183)

No one apparently saw History (or Biography, or Psychology) as the ground out of which such writing grows and great literature is born. Tweedledee defends his narrow dismissive Newism, against Tweedledum's narrow dismissive Oldism.

Graff discusses how much a reader needs to know about the author and the situation to appreciate a poem. Responses to this range widely among the various isms. But isn't this just one more thing that defies rubricization (we too can terminize), for the amount a reader needs to know about the background of a work can range just as widely. With even the briefest snapshots of the period when it was

IV Shakespeare in Our Time

written, a student can fit a poem or play into its place in history, if history is also being taught—if they don't, the loss is to History, not Literature. Every great poem is different in this way, just as it's usually different in many ways. These problems come only with the effort to generalize, to arrive at a rubric where none is needed—where, in fact, all they do is interject an impermeable layer of pointless fieldspeak *between* the student and the story. Students need to *hear* the music—not just read about it.

Graff has very little to say about history. The word he prefers is *culture*—but like so many of the terms preferred by theorists, as a collective for history, biography, religion, psychology, education, fashion and cuisine—by attempting to say everything it ends by saying nothing. That T.S. Eliot's *The Hollow Men* is a reaction to the First World War, that Auden's "September 1, 1939" is a reaction to the onset of the Second—requires more than cold dates and dry isms. Students understand war—they've seen enough of it in films and on the news, or by the return of their own family members from the front—so why not call a spade a spade?

Graff likes the word *contextualize*—not only does history "contextualize" literature, literature "contextualizes" history. While History explains Literature—gives it meaning and context, Literature brings History to life. Early divisions between the Departments of English and History have left us eating butter without bread and bread without butter. History without literature is nothing but an assortment of dates and collective terms like "manifest destiny" or "the Monroe Doctrine," painfully memorized for tests, quickly forgotten after. Literature without history becomes so diminished in value that its traditional use as a path to self understanding is lost. Readers, the few who remain with telly and Netflix—turn to serials and whodunits.

Graff follows the rise and fall of one ism after another, culminating in the 1960s with the New Critics combining forces with the "old historians" against the threat of Deconstructionism, then—

> with astonishing speed, indeterminacy, transgressive interpretation, and even the analysis of discursive power became routinized, emerging as yet another set of self protected methodologies, fully insured against error, backed by its own fieldspeak, its own journals, conferences, and old

boy network, and immune to criticism from outsiders. (241)

Immune to outside criticism—but acutely aware of which way the ever shifting critical wind is blowing in their own departments—and whether they can trim their sails enough to survive the next round of pink slips—O truth, where is thy bling!

> Like the New Critics prior knowledge that all literature is paradoxical, the deconstructionists' foreknowledge that all texts are allegories of their own unreadability (or that they necessarily foreground the problematic of representation, mask and reveal their rhetorical conditions of possibility, undo their claims of reference by their figurality, metaphoricity, and so forth) is made suspect by its monotonous universality of application. This is not to say that deconstructive readings are invariably groundless, any more than New Critical readings were or are. But there needs to be some criterion for differentiating interesting, nontrivial cases of theoretical self undoing of the process of representation from cases that merely exemplify an alleged condition of all discourse. (242)

Got that? Was Latin dropped from the curriculum so there'd be time for stuff like this? No wonder academics are so deaf to historical questions like the skewed dating of Shakespeare's works. Nothing matters to the profs who pontificate on Shakespeare, nothing *can* matter, more than understanding the rubrics of the latest *ism* and how they can use it to reprehend the theories of their competitors in such a way that someone will want to publish their theories and so make them sufficiently important to their departments and to the University that they can dare to put a down payment on a house.

Graff's solution is more left-brain organization, more discourse, more argument spread more widely—even to the hapless student whose parents are paying through the nose for what they are told is a useful education—as though that would solve the basic problem, the missing background, the missing context, the missing connection to life—the missing *story*.

Avoiding history, avoiding biography—referring instead to *tradition* or *acculturation*—the realities surrounding the production of the Shakespeare canon continue to mean almost nothing. If the

IV Shakespeare in Our Time

English Departments didn't invent the crass response—"So long as we have the plays, what does it matter who wrote them?"—but they've created the attitude that fostered it, and that keeps it alive.

Cognitive dissonance

Nineteenth century scholars, thrown off the trail of Shakespeare's erudition by Jonson, Milton, Davenant, Dryden—yet themselves increasingly steeped in the Greek and Latin curricula created by Erasmus—were stymied by what psychologists term "cognitive dissonance"—defined as the discomfort felt by an individual is forced to hold two or more contradictory beliefs, ideas and/or values at the same time. According to the Wikipedia article—"When dissonance is present, in addition to trying to reduce it, the person will *actively avoid situations and information*" which may increase it—

> Dissonance is aroused when people are confronted with information that is inconsistent with their beliefs. If the dissonance is not reduced by changing one's belief, the dissonance can result in restoring consonance through misperception, rejection or refutation of the information, seeking support from others who share the beliefs, and attempting to persuade others.

—a perfect description of how the Academy has been treating the truth about the Shakespeare canon ever since it got sucked into the "Shakespeare problem" in the early years of the twentieth century. What history would show—should they bother to consult it—is that Shakespeare's knowledge of the Law, Medicine, Science, Music theory, English and Roman history, Roman and Greek poetry and drama, and a dozen other areas of study—simply could not possibly have come to him through English alone, or even Latin alone.[175] Why is it taking them so long to get this right? The answer, as usual, is

---

[175] The mere quantity of books in print attesting to the variety of his knowledge is reflected in the specialized dictionaries that bear his name—*Shakespeare's Legal Language, A Dictionary, Military Language in Shakespear, Shakespeare's Theatre, Music and Musical Imagery in Shakespeare,* and *Literature in Shakespeare*—to name but four.

politics—politics then, *politics* later, *politics* today—university politics having replaced Crown politics as the primary cause of the mystification.

The great Winston Churchill—descended from families already high in Court circles in Shakespeare's time—when asked what he thought about the authorship question—did not say "Hogwash!" or shout "Preposterous!" What Churchill actually said was—"I don't like to have my *myths* tampered with." Churchill did not defend the Stratford story as the truth—he called it *a myth*. If we're to save the Humanities—if we're to provide the young with words to live by— then it's time we started *tampering*—and the place to begin is with the man who did more to give Renaissance Humanism to the world than has any single other individual in history—the great artist, lover and thinker whose friends got him published under the name *William Shakespeare*. Let's find out *who he was*.

—∞— Hide Fox and all after —∞—

Now that we've come full circle—from Jonson's "less Greek" to Davenant's claim that William was his father, to the 400 years of failure to find anything that connects Davenant's namesake with a writer's biography—where do we go from here? We've seen how a series of Shakespeare organizations have failed in their attempts to resolve the anomalies Chambers termed "Problems of Chronology," i.e.—*when* the plays were *actually written*—or those he termed "Problems of Authenticity," i.e.—*who* actually *wrote them*.

We see that 200 years of data has accumulated in archives and libraries and in multi volume publications—yet from this mountain of information we also see that *nothing has ever appeared* to suggest a solid connection between William of Stratford and the life of a genuine theatrical genius. We've seen how the Shakespeare societies and the English departments of the great universities have failed— and continue to fail—with their peculiar reliance on philology. Science—however valuable when properly applied—cannot replace a tin ear or a stupefying lack of common sense.

Clearly William of Stratford could not have been the true author. With so much knowledge of Court life—Shakespeare had to

IV Shakespeare in Our Time

have been someone closely involved with the Court. With an education of the sort that could only have come from one of the universities, he had to have been connected with a university, or a tutor from a university. He had to have known Italy at close hand. And to have gone from *Titus Andronicus* to *King Lear* in a single lifetime *he had to have been a genius!* What then do we mean by a *literary genius?* If there's one thing that you get from studying the history of that time—it's how limited were his options.

England is a small island, roughly the size of American states like Alabama or Oregon. In addition it was cut off from the rest of Europe by twenty miles of turbulent ocean water. Comparing it then with its population now, the entire island from Scotland to the tip of Cornwall was roughly a third of what London is today. London—the only real city then—was roughly three times the size of any other British town. During Shakespeare's time it's estimated to have grown from about 150,00 to 200,000—just barely the size of a modern city.

While higher education was increasing during the author's time, it was still in its infancy. In the mid-16th century the entire population of Cambridge University was about 1000 students and faculty. It took seven years to get a Master's degree—so by the second or third year a student would most likely have known just about everyone on campus. It would take another three centuries before English would replace Latin as the major language spoken on campus by everyone but stable boys. And since mundane service duties were handled by less affluent students known as *sizars*—who like the other students, were fluent in Latin—whatever form of English they used where they came from, was limited to family, friends and washerwomen.

As for the Court—Shakespeare's obvious knowledge of that closed community—tightly bound by family (blood) connections—suggests he was born into it—for anyone who came to it from a lesser station in life—and there were certainly writers who did (Ben Jonson for one)—consisted of about 200 persons all told. With death the only means by which a man could advance at Court, those members of the community who were involved in literary or theatrical activities can be counted on the fingers of one hand. Who among that small community might qualify as a literary genius?

Ellen Winner's *Gifted Children*

In 1996, Boston College Professor of Psychology and Harvard Senior Research Associate Ellen Winner published a book that explains what to look for. In *Gifted Children; Myths and Realities* she examines the elements required for the unusual child destined to become what she terms a "creator." She begins by describing the characteristics of gifted children—a limited group out of which only a handful will rise to the level of *creator*. Atypically, these children are—

> precocious. They begin to take the first steps in *the mastery of some domain* at an earlier than average age. They also make more progress in this domain than do ordinary children because learning in the domain comes easily to them. By domain, I refer to *an organized area of knowledge such as language, music, mathematics*—

From the start they insist on marching to their own drummer—

> Gifted children not only learn faster than average or even bright children but also learn in a qualitatively different way . . . . they need minimum help or *scaffolding* from adults in order to *master their domain*—and much of the time they teach themselves. The discoveries they make about their domain are exciting and motivating and each leads the gifted child on to the next step. *Often these children independently invent rules of the domain and devise novel, idiosyncratic ways of solving problems.*

These children have what she terms a "rage to master"—

> They are intrinsically motivated to make sense of the domain in which they show precocity. They exhibit *an intense and obsessive interest, an ability to focus sharply*. . . . They experience "states of flow" while engaged in learning—optimal states in which *they focus intently and lose sense of the outside world*. The lucky combination of obsessive interest in a domain along with an ability to learn easily leads to high achievement. (3-4)

IV Shakespeare in Our Time

Later she defines "the right personality structure for mastery"—these

> children are highly motivated to work to achieve mastery, *they derive pleasure from challenge* and, at least *by adolescence, they have an unusually strong sense of who they are and what they want to do as adults.* . . . [They are] *fiercely independent and nonconforming* . . . [and] they tend to be more introverted and lonelier than the average child, both because they have so little in common with others and because they need and want to be alone to develop their talent. These qualities of thought and feeling add up to a kind of subjective experience that is both more pleasurable and fulfilling, and *more painful, isolating, and stressful* than that of the average child. (212-3)

She addresses several common myths regarding giftedness—

> the common sense "folk" psychology . . . that giftedness is entirely inborn: you either have it or you don't. The abilities of Mozart, Picasso, Newton, or Einstein are so unfathomable to us that we explain them by saying that these individuals were just born geniuses. The environment has no interesting role to play if talents are inborn and fixed. . . . Psychologists like to attack folk psychologies in general . . . but psychologists have their own myth: that giftedness is entirely a product of the environment [and that] the right kind of training, begun at an early age, is sufficient to account for even the very highest levels of giftedness. (143)

She shows that, in fact, both factors must be present for such children to excel in any domain. They must be born with talent—in her terms, a "rage to master." At the same time *they must also have the support of caregivers who value their efforts*, who can provide them with what she terms an "enriched environment"—one in which education is valued and which includes "opportunities for reading, playing and talking." Without these—no matter how great the inborn gifts—nothing can develop. (186).

But giftedness in childhood can only go so far. Only a few go from gifted child or prodigy in a domain to becoming *a creator* in that domain—Says Winner, "Those who traverse this route must make the profound transition from being an expert in an established domain—to being someone who *disrupts the domain and remakes it—leaving it forever altered."*

Moreover, they must be born *when the zeitgeist is right*—when a domain is ready for the kind of change that the creator envisions. *A domain can change only so much and thus can accommodate only a very few creators at a particular time.* So the factors that predict them include not only personal traits but also historical and cultural factors.

In her final pages she goes into detail on characteristics of creators as determined by numerous tests and studies. To become a Creator requires not only early ability but also a *rebellious personality,* a desire to shake up the status quo." Creators are—

> *hard driving, focused, dominant, independent risk takers.* They have experienced stressful childhoods and they often suffer from forms of psychopathology. . . . Creators must be willing to sacrifice . . . [They are] workaholics. The most creative people are also the most prolific. . . . [They] must be able to persist in the face of difficulty and overcome the many obstacles in the way of creative discovery. They must persist because of what has become known among creativity researchers as the "ten year rule"– that it takes about ten years of hard work in a domain to make a breakthrough.

Winner details the research that led to this "ten-year rule"—

> Even Mozart did not produce his first masterpiece until after about ten years of composing. A willingness to toil and to tolerate frustration and persist in the face of failure is crucial. . . . *Creators are strong, dominant personalities with an unshakable belief in themselves.* They must be able to believe in themselves, for otherwise they would be felled by the inevitable attacks that come when one goes against the established point of view.

The only child syndrome

Several times in the course of the book Winner describes the need creators have to be alone. Prodigies are often "only children," raised

IV Shakespeare in Our Time

in the company of adults, allowed to go their own way to a much greater extent than ordinary children.—Such children often suffer from being so different from their peers, feeling odd or out of place among them. Even so they prefer being alone to being bored in the company of ordinary children.

> They set challenging goals for themselves and believe that they can achieve what they aspire to. Those who would be recognized must also be able to tolerate competition—some even thrive on it. . . . Creators are independent and nonconforming. . . . Caring about pleasing everyone cannot be a priority for anyone who is going to challenge an established tradition. . . . Creators must be willing to sacrifice comfort, relaxation, and personal relationships for the sake of their work. *They are often ruthless and destructive of personal ties.* . . . Creators have to be willing to risk failure, since *anything new is likely initially to be denounced.* [Those] who produce the most works are most likely to produce a masterpiece, but *they also produce the most failed works.* Perhaps the most important of all is the desire to set things straight, to alter the status quo and shake up the established tradition. Creators do not accept the prevailing view; they are *oppositional and discontented.* (292-298)

Winner examines the typical family life of great creators—

> The future creator seems to grow up in a family that is *much less child-centered and supportive*, and far more stress filled than does the gifted child not destined to become a creator. Three-fourths of the eminent creators studied by [leading researchers] experienced some kind of extreme stress in their early family life—poverty; death of a parent; divorced or estranged parents; rejecting, abusive or alcoholic parents— fathers who experienced professional failure or bankruptcy; and so on. They came from *atypical families—irritable, explosive families, often prone to depression or to large-scale mood swings.* . . . Particularly shocking is the frequency with which eminent individuals have lost a parent in childhood. . . . In [one] study of major creators, over a fifth had lost one or

> both parents in childhood . . . the only other groups with such high levels of parental loss are delinquents and depressive or suicidal psychiatric patients.

As she continues she approaches our area of inquiry—

> Family trauma is more often characterized by those who became *writers, artists, musicians and actors* in comparison to those who became scientists, physicians and political leaders. . . . [In one study] of eminent twentieth-century figures, 89 percent of the novelists and playwrights, 83 percent of the poets and 70 percent of the artists had difficult family lives, while this was true for only 56 percent of the scientists. . . . The same distinction was found in a comparison between Nobel Prize winners in science v. literature; those in literature were more likely to come from *unstable family environments.*

Winner draws a number of conclusions from these studies. Regarding family trauma—

> Trauma could make a child feel different from the start and thus lead to a willingness to be different. *The perception that one's environment is unpredictable may lead to the desire to achieve in order to gain control over one's destiny.* . . . Loss of a parent may also lead to a kind of compensation—*a desire to replace the lost object by creating one's own object, whether a work of art* or a scientific theory. A horror of the void left by death could stimulate a child to create an ideal world and to lose [him]self in its creation. The desire to replace emptiness and the lost object with an ideal created world may be so strong that [he] is not overly critical.

Such a world is a good description of the island of Ephesus where a shipwrecked family is reunited in *The Comedy of Errors*—or the magical isle of *The Tempest*, where a father and daughter are wafted to safety out of the grasp of an evil relative—or Illyria in *Twelfth Night* where brother and sister are washed ashore following another Shakespearean shipwreck.

Comparing Winner's detailed analysis with Shakespeare's erudition—what sort of biography should we be looking for?

IV Shakespeare in Our Time

Certainly we would expect to see at least some of the following—*a "rage to master"—an enriched environment with an enlightened caregiver—a stressful home life, a solitary childhood, a painful childhood trauma—a parental failure—the early death of a parent—an indomitable will—an oppositional and discontented nature.*

Except for his father's business troubles, we see none of this in anything we know about William of Stratford. It must be for this reason that—despite the genius attached to his name—among the *creators* whose biographies and careers names by Winner—Darwin, Edison, Freud, Gandhi, Goethe, Bach, Beethoven, Mozart, Hayden, and Picasso—all of whom altered their domains—she never mentions the man whose domain was the English language—she never mentions *William Shakespeare*.

How lucky we are that the true author—whose biography corresponds in every way to her prescription—has finally been found.

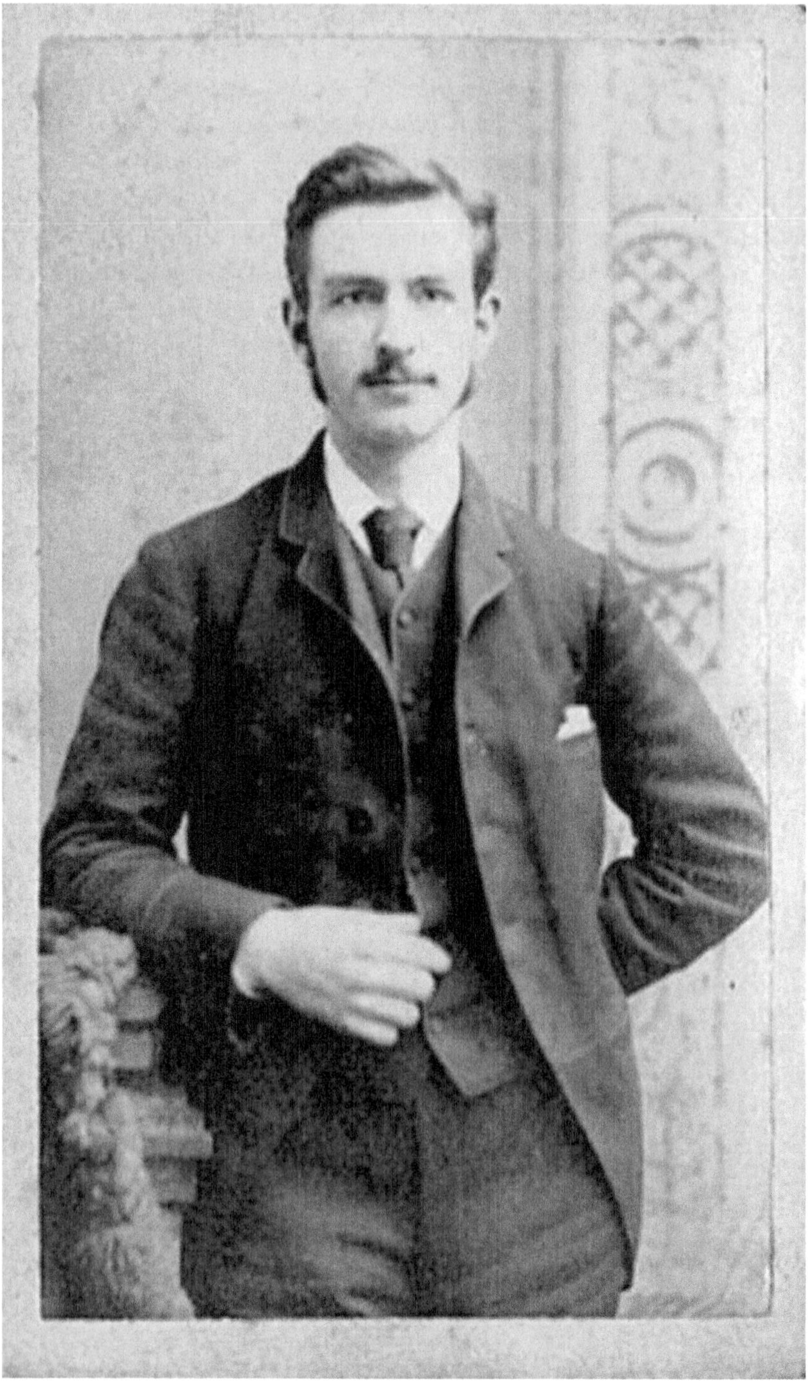

IV Shakespeare in Our Time

~ *"Shakespeare" Identified* ~

> He who will really fight for the right, if he would live even for a little while, must have a private station and not a public one.
>
> Aristophanes

In the years following World War I a progressive British school teacher in his forties went in search of a publisher who would help him provide the world with evidence for yet another Shakespeare candidate, one Edward de Vere (pron. de Vare[176]), the 17th Earl of Oxford. This was not easy, for the publishing community was weary of a subject that after almost a century of argument had ground to a halt. Stymied by how promising paper trails tended to vanish at critical points—Francis Bacon's candidacy had come to a standstill as notable Baconians slipped over the edge of genuine scholarship into attempts to communicate with the dead.

Most publishers had never heard of the Earl of Oxford—and when they sought to learn more they were hardly enthused—due to his exceedingly bad reputation with English historians. To the homophobic readers of the nineteenth century there were the hideous implications of the masculine pronoun in *the Sonnets*. Nevertheless, despite such warnings—among them the fact that his own name inspired mirth—Fate was kind to John Thomas Looney[177] and in 1920 his book—*"Shakespeare" Identified*—was published—to great

---

[176] In Shakespeare's time, the name *de Vere* (or *de Veer*) would have been pronounced *de Vare*. We know this because in a letter from Sir Thomas Stanhope to Lord Burghley, July 15, 1590—in speaking of Burghley's granddaughter Elizabeth—referred to her as "Lady Vayer" (Akrigg 32). Apparently "the great vowel shift" that altered how English vowels were pronounced had not yet occurred. As in Chaucer's time, an internal *e* was still pronounced as we pronounce long *a* today. So Oxford's family name, descended from his Norman ancestors, was pronounced *Vare*, or *Vair*—as it's spelled in France. In Latin the word *ver*, meaning *truth*—verity, verily—is also pronounced *vair*.

[177] Some have argued that it "must have been" pronounced Loaney, but Looney's biographer, James Warren—was informed by J. T.'s descendants—that the name should be pronounced like Mooney or Rooney, as they are on the Isle of Man.

Educating Shakespeare

praise from questioners and fury from The Birthplace Trust.[178]

Having taught the plays to sixth formers—struggling with their questions about the author—Looney conceived of a method that he thought might succeed where others had failed. So entirely missing was Shakespeare from recorded history—he guessed that his true identity may have been suppressed from the very beginning. Trusting his poet's ear—he began by thumbing through collections of early verse in search of something that *sounded* like Shakespeare.

Almost immediately he found what he was looking for. On page 25 of *Palgrave's Golden Treasury*—surrounded by Shakespeare poems before it and after—there was a poem attributed to an *E. Vere, Earl of Oxford,* that stopped him cold. In Shakespearean iambics, neatly punctuated with trochees and spondees—the rhyme scheme and reference to Apollo fairly leapt off the page—

> If women could be fair and yet not fond,
> Or that their love were firm not fickle, still
> I would not marvel that they make men bond,
> By service long to purchase their good will,
> But when I see how frail those creatures are,
> I muse that men forget themselves so far
>
> To mark the choice they make, and how they change,
> How oft from Phoebus do they flee to Pan.
> Unsettled still like haggards wild they range,
> These gentle birds that fly from man to man.
> Who would not scorn and shake them from the fist
> And let them fly, fair fools, which way they list?
>
> Yet for disport we fawn and flatter both,
> To pass the time when nothing else can please,
> And train them to our lure with subtle oath,
> Till, weary of their wiles, ourselves we ease.
> And then we say, when we their fancy try,
> To play with fools, Oh what a fool was I.

---

[178] It seems that Henry Clay Folger, founder of the Shakespeare Folger Library in Washington, D.C.—now and for many years militantly opposed to the authorship question—had himself begun as a questioner (Whittemore "Reason #22").

IV Shakespeare in Our Time

There it was!—with one of Shakespeare's favorite metaphors—women as "haggard hawks." But who was *E. Vere, Earl of Oxford?* Looney began digging through histories of that time for evidence. It seems this *E. Vere* wasn't hard to find—of the eighteen authorial characteristics compiled from years of reading the plays, it seems the Earl of Oxford had them all—

> 1) A matured man of recognized genius—2) apparently eccentric and mysterious—3) of intense sensibility—a man apart—4) unconventional—5) not adequately appreciated—6) of pronounced and known literary tastes—7) an enthusiast in the world of drama—8) a lyric poet of recognized talent—9) of superior education, classical, the habitual associate of educated people—10) a man with Feudal connections—11) a member of the higher aristocracy—12) connected with Lancastrian supporters—13) an enthusiast for Italy—14) a follower of sport (including falconry)—15) a lover of music—16) loose and improvident in money matters—17) doubtful and somewhat conflicting in his attitude to woman—18) of probable Catholic leanings, but touched with skepticism. (104)

Locked in combat with each other over textual minutia—the infant English Departments had no time for John Looney's "biographical fallacy." As for the History Department—horrified by the fact that Oxford's enemies had charged him with murder, pederasty and, most terrible of all—ingratitude towards the great Lord Burghley—they dropped his theory like a radioactive potato. Nevertheless—despite how the Academy has remained entrenched against anything that threatens their beloved scenario—a handful of dedicated scholars and courageous publishers have gradually moved the argument to the point where the Earl of Oxford now dominates all candidates but the sacred William.

To Looney's list of characteristics a few more must be added. First, there must be reasons, not only why the true author would hide his identity—but why it has remained hidden for so long. There must be substantial evidence that he was deeply—not just marginally—involved with the London Stage. Most important of all—there must be evidence of an unusual education, one that explains the otherwise inexplicable depth of his knowledge of English Law, Pharmacology, Medicine, Astronomy, ancient Greek, ancient Roman Literature and History—the kind of education available then to none but a very privileged few.

With half his plays based in Italy plus references to France of the sort that he could not have learned from what books there were then—there must also be evidence that he had actually spent time in those countries—particularly in Italy, where he would have been exposed to the Commedia dell'Arte—there being nothing of the sort anywhere else at that time. Do the events of his life connect with the plots of the plays? Was he the right age to have written the quartos in his youth that are presently considered his sources? And did his childhood conform to Ellen Winner's prescription?

The answer to all of these is a resounding affirmative. That as the 17th Earl of Oxford he was also England's premiere aristocrat for most of his life[179] may be something of an historical anomaly—but a close look at the history of the period reveals that he could hardly have accomplished what he did from any less privileged a position—for he was born at the very dawn of the English Reformation, when "Art" was, as Shakespeare put it, "tongue-tied by authority."

Oxford's Stage credentials

As for evidence of his involvement in the Theater—in *Shakespearean Playing Companies* (1996), Andrew Gurr, scholar and author of some of our most recent and authoritative works on the Renaissance Stage —describes Oxford as "an independent and very persistent promoter of playing groups, both of men and of boys, for . . . twenty years," and that his companies "dominated at Court 1583-84" (307, 201).

In *Wits Treasury*—the very book that in 1598 had introduced *William Shakespeare* as the author of ten currently popular plays—Oxford was noted as having been "best for comedy." Regarding Shakespeare's knowledge of Italy—Oxford spent his twenty-sixth year in Venice—location for several of Shakespeare's greatest plays.

---

[179] Following the execution of the 4th Duke of Norfolk in 1572.

IV Shakespeare in Our Time

Birth of the London Stage

In the months following Oxford's return from Italy, March 14th 1576—the first three successful commercial theaters ever built in England opened for business within weeks of each other. Four years later, a fracas at one of them revealed him as the true patron of several of the top three London acting companies over the past ten years. In 1584, a lawsuit attempting to close one of these theaters revealed him as its patron. In 1602, a company bearing his name as patron along with that of his close friend and contemporary, the Earl of Worcester, became the Queen Anne's Men—second in importance to the King's Men, formerly the Lord Chamberlain's Men, chief producer of Shakespeare's plays through the reign of Queen Elizabeth and well into that of King James. Though provided by widely divergent documentation—these dates show Oxford with close to thirty years of close involvement with the London Stage from its first beginnings.

As for connections between his life and Shakespeare's art—almost every play reveals some situation that Oxford had to deal with in his own life—in particular the seven plays that reflect—in plot or subplot—the breakup of his marriage.[180] While there were accounts then of Richard III that suggest a man more sinned against than sinning—Shakespeare's portrayal of this last of the Plantagenet kings as a cruel and tyrannical villain reflects how he was probably seen by Oxford's ancestors—the 11th and 12th earls of Oxford—executed by Richard's Yorkist brother, Edward IV. Richard's defeat at Bosworth Field—the battle that put Elizabeth's grandfather on the throne—was engineered by the 13th Earl of Oxford (Seward *Roses* 305[181]).

Born in 1550, fourteen years earlier than William of Stratford, Oxford's early life fits the timing of the earliest extant versions of Shakespeare's history plays—their style with the styles of the periods that followed. Oxford's personality and early years match—point for point—Ellen Winner's description of a *creator*—as does the life that left him—as Hamlet mourns—with the "wounded name" he bears to

---

[180] *Pericles, Cymbeline, Winter's Tale, All's Well, Much Ado, Hamlet,* and *Othello.*

[181] In his *Wars of the Roses* (1995), historian Desmond Seward focuses on five leading individuals from the period, one of them John de Vere, 13th Earl of Oxford.

this day in conventional English History. Most conclusive is the fact that eight of his most vulnerable learning years—from age four to twelve—were spent with one of England's most highly respected educators—possibly the only one alive at that time who could conceivably have taught him all that "Shakespeare knew."

"That noble Theseus of Learning"

It may be the identification of Sir Thomas Smith—educator, scholar and statesman—Oxford's tutor and surrogate father—that gives us the most conclusive evidence that the Earl of Oxford was Shakespeare—for every one of the areas of unusual expertise that we've examined so far—his phenomenal knowledge of the Law and legal terms, of medicine, pharmacology, horticulture, astronomy, Greek and Latin literature, English and Roman history—all can be traced to Smith—partly through his reputation and his writings—but most directly through his 400-volume library as recorded in 1698 by his first biographer—the historian John Strype (274-81).

Although Oxford may not have appreciated it until after Smith was gone—among the benefits that his rank bequeathed him—not least was a childhood spent with "that noble Theseus of learning"—as he was described by Strype. Praised as "the shining light" of Cambridge University—once Smith transferred to the Court of Edward VI, he became the moving force in publishing, distributing and legalizing the Book of Common Prayer—cornerstone of the Church of England. As Secretary of State—first under Edward VI (1547-49), then under Queen Elizabeth (1572-76)—Smith's long career in government service followed his earlier years as scholar and teacher of Greek literature and Roman law at Cambridge, where—shortly before entering government service—he served as the university's greatly admired Vice-chancellor. According to Strype—

> He bore a great part, both in the University, the Church and in the Commonwealth . . . the best scholar in his time, a most admirable orator, linguist and moralist . . . an ingenious poet, an excellent speaker, of exquisite skill in the Civil Law, in Astronomy, in natural philosophy, Physic and Divinity. (157)

IV Shakespeare in Our Time

Appointed University Orator in 1533 at age twenty (Dewar 13), Smith was succeeded first by his friend and colleague John Cheke, then by Roger Ascham—who would become tutor to Edward VI and Queen Elizabeth. Of Smith's achievements Strype notes—

> While at Cambridge he endeavored to polish the English tongue—and was noted to be one of the three there that were the past masters of [the same]. He invented a new alphabet of twenty nine letters and sought a better spelling.
>
> His profession was the Civil Law, and he was the first Regius Professor of it in the University, placed therein by the Royal Founder Henry VIII, whose scholar he was. . . . He was a great Platonist, which noble and useful philosophy he and Cheke brought into study in the University, accustomed before to the crabbed, barbarous, useless, schoolmen.
>
> He was renowned for his knowledge of medicine ("physick") and chemistry ("the handmaid of physick") for which he had "apartments in his house for his stills and laboratories."
>
> [He was an] excellent Linguist and a Master in the knowledge of the Latin, Greek, French and Italian tongues. [H]e excelled in Roman History, and was] very curious and exact [in the art of gardening]. (27, 211, 214, 218)

Smith's 20th-century biographer Mary Dewar adds—

> Throughout his life Smith maintained interests far outside the range of the classical and legal scholar and statesman. His interest in mathematics and passion for scientific studies never left him. . . . He studied throughout his life astronomy, architecture, natural phenomena, drugs and medicines. His own chemical experiments with his precious "stills" were an abiding interest, at times almost a ludicrous preoccupation. . . . An official dispatch to Lord Burghley on state affairs in the 1570s was accompanied by a bottle of one of his own concoctions "against my Lady of Oxford's miscarriage". . . . He read widely in the poets and had a tendency to break into lamentable verse himself. (14-15, 141)

It's fair to assume that during their eight years together, Smith taught his young charge as much as he could about those subjects most dear to him. As a Reformation pedagogue Smith shared the belief, absorbed from Erasmus, that humanity would improve only when the nobility—who still held pride of place at the Courts of Europe—were trained from childhood in the ancient Wisdom Tradition.

If the world of literary criticism has found it difficult to locate the author of the Shakespeare canon, it's at least partly because his story is so unique. Only a handful of courtiers from that period of intense training—among them Oxford's rival as the Court's leading poet, Sir Philip Sidney—Sidney's sister Mary, the Countess of Pembroke, herself a respected poet and translator—and his cousin Sir Francis Bacon, the father of modern English prose—received educations similar to the one Oxford got from Smith—and although, like him, they were courtiers by birth—their power to establish themselves as *creators* (in Winner's terms) was nowhere near his—due to the credit that could not be denied to someone of his rank.

In many ways Oxford was the product of a great experiment, one that the passionate educators of the English Renaissance were driven to attempt—though sadly for him, one that may have been seen by his tutor, and that was certainly seen by his guardians—as having gone terribly wrong. Trained in statecraft by these pillars of the English Reformation, it seems that Oxford—denied what he felt was his right to a voice in his nation's government—used his status as a peer, his literary talent and his vast and profound education—to create a forum in which he could wield the powers he was born with, gifts of language—and an imagination as profound and compelling as his incomparable intellect.

❦ APPENDICES ❦

APPENDIX A Source of the Name *Shakespeare*

Among the many important facts that the Academy fails to note about the name *Shakespeare* are two that should be obvious—first—that it is not and never was a typical English name. Second—that it's a *pun* that describes what he does—that is, by *shaking* his *spear* (his *pen*) he fills the stage with *spears*, which—in Green Room slang[182]— means *actors* who have not yet gone onstage—or stagehands with backstage duties who can "swell a scene or two" by throwing on a toga, grabbing a prop spear, marching across the stage while waving it and shouting—thus to create the illusion of an army or a mob.

If this seems farfetched it would not have seemed so to those who appreciated the wordplay that Samuel Johnson called a *quibble*, for which—like Atalanta—who lost the race because she had been distracted by the golden apples—Shakespeare would "sell his soul." It seems the philologists, whose word is law at the universities, either don't recognize a pun when they see one—or, unlike Atalanta—won't be lured from their race for top Shakespeare dog by distracting facts.

A multitude of spellings

The most obvious issue for anyone researching the name is the trouble the Stratford scribes had with spelling it. Although spelling was still a matter of personal self expression—there being as yet no confirmed orthography—how a word is spelled in a letter can tell us how it was pronounced. With an ordinary English name like Brown, where an *e*

---

[182] The Green Room in a modern theater refers to the room offstage where actors wait before and after going on. It may have been painted green, a restful color, but more likely the term originated before there were theaters—when actors needed a *room* (in a wagon or tent) on the village green in which to get costumed before performing for the public before there were indoor theaters. Thus "Green Room slang" refers to things shared privately among professional actors.

might be added at the end—or Smith, where the *i* might be replaced with a *y*—nothing comes close to the 83 different versions of William's surname as it appears in the Stratford files from 1562 through 1635 (Chambers *Facts*).

According to Chambers—based on his years of delving through the record—the name first appears in 1248 with a *William Sakspere* (hanged in Gloucestershire for robbery)—after which—though never numerous—it continues to pop up here and there, though primarily in Warwickshire. Among the various spellings—the (unhyphenated) version of the name the Lord Chamberlain's Men used on their published plays appears now and then—along with the more common *Shakspere* or *Shackspeer*—the less common *Schakespere, Saxper, Shaxespere, Schackspere, Schackespeire, Shakyspear, Shakysspere, Chacsper, Shakisspere*, etcetera. Long story short—the one preferred by the actors was not totally unique—but it did not predominate until *after* 1598 when it first appeared on the title page of the second editions of *Richard III* and *Richard II*. Even as late as 1605 a scribe connected with the Court Stage spelled it *Shaxberd*.

Focussed on how often it occurred and the many ways it was spelled—Chambers never comments on this unusual variety, possible reasons for it, or, most important, how it may have been pronounced.

1066 and all that

English names from the Elizabethan period were primarily derived from one of two languages brought to England over the preceeding centuries by continental invaders who brought their written languages with them. By the sixteenth century the Celtic language spoken by most of England had been altered by the most determined of these invader settlers, the Anglo-Saxons, who did have a written language, perhaps created as a means of communicating with the Romans. Also known as Old English—it provides most of the one-syllable root words ending in a consonant that constitute the bones of modern English. The other source was French—brought to England in 1066 by William the Conqueror and his army of aristocrats.

Saxon names tend to identify a geographic feature, a hill, field, or river—a trade like Smith, Miller, or Carter—a parent like Wilson,

Appendix A Source of the Name *Shakespeare*

Thomson, or Johnson. Since *Shakespeare* is certainly not a patronym—French would seem the more likely source. The surname of Shakespeare's great predecessor, the poet Geoffrey *Chaucer*, derived from *chausseur*—French for *shoemaker*.

How they pronounced *Shakespeare*

We know how the Stratford scribes spelled William's name—what we don't know is how they pronounced it. *Sh* in English sounds like the French *J*—*"je suis jolie,"* "joie de vivre"—just as William's name, if pronounced with a "short" a—is Shackspere—which *sounds* so much like *Jacques-Pierre*—a double name of the sort French Catholics still give their sons—two saints's names linked by a hyphen, like the French actor *Jean-Pierre* Aumont, or the French filmmaker *Jean-Luc* Goddard. If William's name was generally pronounced with a short *a*—it probably began as a French given or first name—which suggests that his ancestor first came to England with William of Normandy.

By the 1500s, most of the upper levels of the English aristocracy were descended from French noblemen who came in with William the Conqueror—as with names like *Seymour*, originally *St. Maure*—or *Devereux*, Robert (*"Robair"*) *d'Evreux*. If William's surname was originally a first name, it suggests that he was descended from a serf or bond slave who came over with his Norman seigneur in or after 1066. From time immemorial, laborers on that level had no fixed surnames.

By the 1590s the name *Jacques-Pierre* having long since been anglicized into something easier to say in English—exactly what we can't know for certain—but the spellings left by scores of scribes offer suggestions as to how the citizens of Stratford pronounced it before the Lord Chamberlain's Men established the pronunciation we use today. As Dr. Ewan Johnson, research associate at Lancaster University in Lancashire—whose area of expertise is the "Norman diaspora"—has affirmed (via email)—Stratford was located at the center of the area settled by the French in and after the Norman invasion. He also affirms that the French nobility were accompanied by "large numbers of servants."

Educating Shakespeare

According to E. K. Chambers, of the 83 different spellings of Shakespeare, those that begin with "*Shack, Schak, Shax* are nearly as common as those that begin with *Shake or Shakes.*" We distinguish between words like *back* and *bake* by how they're spelled. So if *Shakespeare* originated with the French *Jacques-Pierre*, it would make sense that in Stratford and elsewhere—those who knew the name solely from *hearing* it *spoken* would have pronounced it *Shack or Shacks.*[183] But for the actors to make it work as a pun, it had to be spelled so that it would be pronounced Shake—which has got to be the reason why they inserted a hyphen between *e* and *s*.

If the name was pronounced as a *three*-syllable word in Stratford, as is suggested by spellings like *Shak-es-peer* or *pyeer*—by *Shakespeyr, Schakespeire, Shakesspere, Shakisspere*—as listed by Chambers—such spellings suggest a situation where the scribe was copying the name from a document where it was spelled as the name was spelled in French. Unaccustomed to the French habit of glossing or ignoring final consonants—such a scribe might have seen *Jacques* as two syllables, *Jack-ess* thereby creating the *kes* or *kiss* that appear in some versions of the name. Where the final syllable includes a *y*—*pyeer, pyere*—it certainly *sounds* like *Pierre*.

That pesky hyphen

If William's name was chosen by the Lord Chamberlain's Men as a much cover for the real author because it could be understood by the literati as a *conundrum*—a *pun*—in which a shaking spear suggests an aggressive pen—then the name would have to be pronounced *Shake*, not *Shack*. But if the name was an anglicization of *Jacques-Pierre*,[184] then wherever it had taken hold around the nation, it would likely be *heard* as *Shacks*-pair, *Shacks*-pyair, or *Shak*-es-pyair.

---

[183] That the English nickname *Jack* came from *Jacques* is without dispute. Jacques (French for James) has a particular meaning for the French as slang for members of the lower class—a rebel or a rascal—but always lower—as is the Jack to the King and Queen of the face cards. The *Jacquerie* instigated the French Revolution. In English it's a tool for heavy lifting—in crime, hijacking.

[184] Sigmund Freud, who loved Shakespeare, believed that *Jacques-Pierre* as the origin of the name—as he explained in letters to colleagues (Ernest Jones 18).

Appendix A   Source of the Name *Shakespeare*

For centuries the illiterate workers like those who made up the audience of "groundlings" at the public theaters had been confusing outsiders and authorities by using what today is know as "Cockney rhyming slang"—hiding from listening ears the actual subject of their conversation with rhymes and puns. Considering how the word *bread* might have become slang for *money*—if originally "bread and honey" was Cockney slang for *money*—when the word *honey* was eventually dropped, the word *bread* remained as a slang term for *money*.

As for the hyphenated *Shake-speare*, why—when the name first appeared in print on the title page of *Richard III*—were its *two syllables* hyphenated between the *e* and the *s* if not to establish the first syllable as *Shake* rather than *Shak* (*bake* rather tha*n back*)? Because *Shak would have spoiled the pun*, and the pun was necessary if the actors were to inform those with ears to hear that it was really just a cover name like *Cuthbert Curry-knave* or *Martin Mar-prelate*.

Efforts by orthodox theorist David Kathman to prove the Stratford scenario by referencing Chambers is yet another example of the peculiar nature of the academic mind. One can only wonder how he dares to claim that "Shakespeare was by far the most common spelling of the name in both literary and nonliterary contexts" in the face of Chambers's evidence for the exceptional number and variety of spellings. When he states that "there is no evidence that the variant spellings reflected a consistent pronunciation difference, but there is considerable evidence that they were seen as . . . interchangeable"— which pronunciation does he mean—*Shake* or *Shack*?

Kathman's a financial systems analyst—he's not a poet. While the two are not totally incompatible—David Kathman is no T.S. Eliot.

APPENDIX B Shakespeare's Hand

Perhaps the simplest of all the historical caveats that argue that William of Stratford was no more than a stand-in for the true author is the evidence that not only had he no real involvement with the London Stage, what evidence there is suggests that he could not even write his own name. Hard as it is to prove a negative, that 300 years of research by dedicated scholars have failed to turn up so much as a paragraph that they can declare with *certainty* was penned by William's own hand should tell us something about his qualifications for the Crown of Bays he's been awarded over the centuries.

As for facts as opposed to conjectures—all that is known for certain that was penned by William himself are the six scribbles that, towards the end of his life, he scrawled on four legal documents in which it seems he was not certain about what came after *Shak*.

a) The 1612 Mountjoy suit deposition: *Willm Shackper*
b) The 1612 Blackfriars Gatehouse deed: (William) *Shakspear*
c) The 1612 Blackfriars mortgage: *Wm Shakspea*
d) The 1615 will, page 1: *William Shacksper*
e) The will, page 2: *Wllm. Shakspere*
f) The will, page 3: (by me William) *Shakspear*

On a) and c) he didn't complete the word, as though he couldn't recall how it ended. Note that on b) the clerk wrote the "William"—and that in the final signature on page 3 of his will, the first three words, "By me William" were also written by the clerk.[185] Also note that despite spelling his own name six different ways, not once is it spelled as it was printed on the titles of *Richard III* and *Richard II*.

---

[185] The final three of these come from the three pages of William's will, written shortly before his death in 1616. That the will itself was subjected to alterations after it was first committed to paper by a scribe has been discussed by a number of authorship scholars, most recently and thoroughly by Bonner Miller Cutting in chapters 6 and 7 of *Necessary Mischief* (2005).

Appendix B Shakespeare's Hand

The Wikipedia article titled "Shakespeare's handwriting" is yet another example of the academic attempt to pull the wool by mixing a pennyworth of fact with a pound of maybe. After stating that William's handwriting is known from the six surviving legal signatures, it plunges immediately into conjecture—"*It is believed* by many scholars that the three pages of the handwritten manuscript of the play *Sir Thomas More* are also in William Shakespeare's handwriting." While it's true that "many" have so stated—what isn't true is that this "proves" that of the four different "hands"—A, B, C, and D—scribbled on this rare surviving playscript—that "hand D" was Shakespeare's has *not* been proven—nor can it be—since there is nothing with which to compare it.

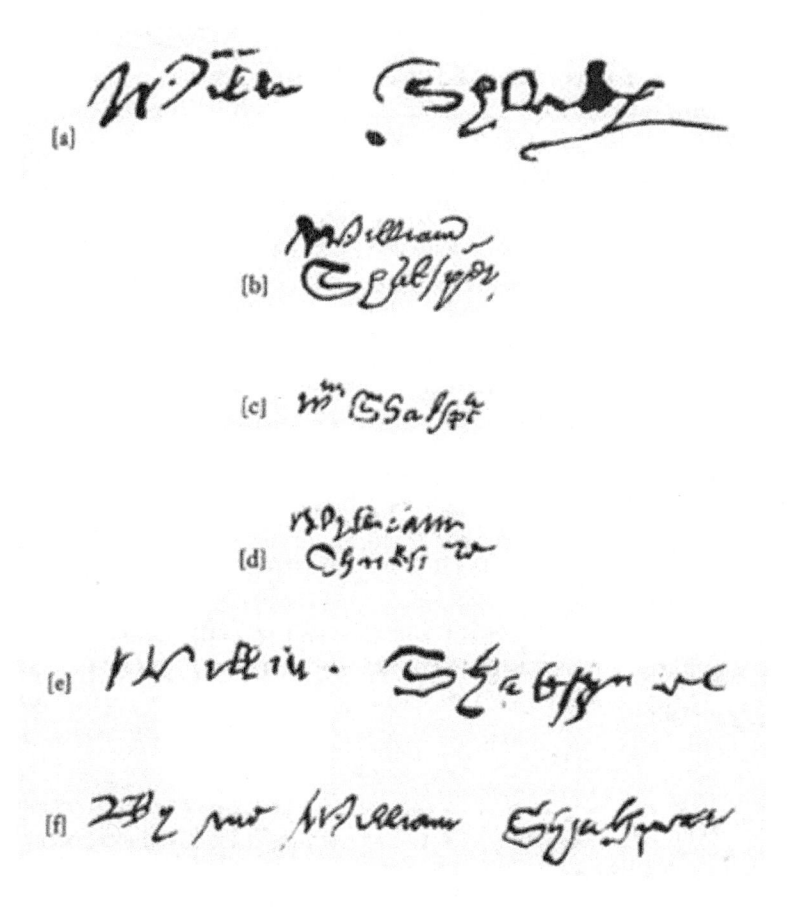

319

Educating Shakespeare

The letter C

Desperate for something to support this colossal leap of faith—all that the authors of the Wikipedia article can offer are comments by those members of the Lord Chamberlain's Men—Hemmings, Condell, and Jonson—whose primary purpose, of course, was to support and promote the wellbeing of the Company on which their livelihoods depended—which meant hiding the identity of their playwright.

As an example of the tortured tergiversations of three centuries of misattribution—the Wikipedia article offers the following—

> By the late nineteenth century, paleographers began to make detailed study of the evidence in the hope of identifying Shakespeare's handwriting in other surviving documents. In those cases when the actual handwriting is not extant, the study of the published texts has yielded indirect evidence of his handwriting quirks through readings and apparent misreadings by compositors. To give one example of this, in the early published versions of Shakespeare's plays there is a recurrence of an upper case letter "C" when the lower case is called for. This might indicate that Shakespeare was fond of such a usage in his handwriting, and that the compositors (working from the handwriting) followed the usage.

Or it "might indicate" a desperate grasping at straws.

"The Play of Sir Thomas More"

Among the handful of original documents relevant to the Stage that remain from Shakespeare's time is an undated handwritten copy of *The Play of Sir Thomas More*, as it seems to have been submitted in the form of "foul papers" to Sir Edmund Tilney—recently appointed the Crown's first theatrical censor by his cousin, the Earl of Sussex, Elizabeth's first appointed Lord Chamberlain. This working draft was apparently submitted to Tilney in response to Sussex's determination in 1572 that plays produced at Court be critiqued by a censor before they could be performed.

It's clear from the sections marked through by horizontal pen lines—doubtless made by Tilney in his role as censor—that he

Appendix B Shakespeare's Hand

wanted these cut. The play's subject—Sir Thomas More, Lord Chancellor under Henry VIII—best known today for his stand against the King's break with the Pope as portrayed in *A Man For All Seasons*—here portrayed as a kind and witty humanist—should be difficult to assign to anyone other than Shakespeare—which has, of course, not prevented the clueless Academy from trying—as it's obviously far too early for William of Stratford.

While six separate hands are identified as having scribbled corrections or additions at one time or another on the manuscript or attached bits of paper—Hand D, has been focussed on by academics as Shakespeare's, functioning here as merely one of six correctors. Since Hand D is an example of what is known as the *Secretary Hand*, this has given the Academy cause to claim that William was capable of writing something other than his six attempts at a legal signature that are all that can be be attributed to him with certainty.

Hopefully someday—when the rest of the facts involved have found their proper place in the Shakespeare story—this exceptional survivor of the centuries will be given the treatment it deserves by scholars actually pursuing the truth.

APPENDIX C Shakespeare's Coat of Arms

The notion that William of Stratford was known in his time as a gentleman derives from the "Gent." that occasionally appears in the record after his name. That he could call himself "Gent." was due to the Coat of Arms that he'd acquired for his father shortly after their name appeared on the Queen's Warrant in 1595 (along with the names of two leading actors from the Lord Chamberlain's Men) —seemingly for having participated in some way in the Christmas Revels of 1595 at Court. It is our contention that this entry in the Queen's Exchequer was made by a clerk who copied it from a request for payment submitted by actor John Hemmings—who (we contend) was responsible for inserting William's name into what records he could as a means of protecting the Lord Chamberlain's Men and their playwright from threats to the London Stage by the recently appointed Secretary of State, Robert Cecil. If Cecil knew the value of the record —and how to manipulate it—so did Hemmings.

Source of the Coat of Arms

In the Library at the College of Arms—still located in the same place in London as it was in 1596—there remain two tattered paper drafts containing sketches for a proposed Coat of Arms drawn up by the then Garter King of Arms (or more likely his clerk) granting William the Coat of Arms he had requested for his father, John Shakspere. A note at the foot of one describes "This John" as having presented a "pattern" (design) on paper twenty years earlier. There is no sign of the earlier design, but an ink sketch in the upper left corner of the extant draft is of a bird—referred to in the text as "a falcon"—holding an upright object, apparently meant to represent a *spear*—doubtless a pun on the applicant's surname. This, we must assume, had been copied, along with the text, from the earlier application.

From this we surmise that sometime before 1576—which was when John Shakspere's finances began to go awry—"this John"— then at the peak of his lifelong effort to better himself—had taken the

Appendix C Shakespeare's Coat of Arms

three-day trip to London to obtain the document that would allow him to call himself a "gentleman"—something that carried more weight than mere social status—as it cast him as a man of established credit, making it easier to get loans from money-lenders (there were as yet no banks in England). Hoping that marriage to a distant member of a local gentry family would be sufficient to qualify him for the coveted document—also possibly aware that such certificates were becoming easier to obtain than they would have been in feudal times—it seems clear that John Shakspere had been willing and able to pay the Herald's fees at that time, or he would not have made the three-day trip to London.

Right away we see how William's modern biographers have framed these facts to suit their narrative. As Schoenbaum puts it—

> William's father had made a preliminary approach to the Heralds' office at some time after he became bailiff of Stratford in 1568, but then, as troubles closed in on him, let the matter drop. The heralds demanded heavy fees when the Shakespeares, beset by creditors, could ill afford them. (*A Life* 167)

Upper left corner of the rejection of John Shakspere's Coat of Arms.

323

By attributing John Shakspere's failure to get the Coat of Arms to financial woes that according to the record had not yet occurred—Schoenbaum attempts to sidestep what should be the obvious fact that Shakspere Sr. had been rejected by the Heralds for the same reason that such applications were *always* rejected—*weak credentials*. *Yeoman* he was from birth and *yeoman* he would remain—that is, until his son came into the bounty he acquired in 1595 for the use of his name on the plays.

The Coat of Arms grant provides more than just a footnote on the authorship controversy. The timing of William's application—only months from when his name would be recorded in the royal Warrant as a member of the Lord Chamberlain's Men—must have been meant to confirm his status as actor, as there was no other way that that could have been done at that time. As the company's manager, Hemmings was one whose job it was to submit such a request for payment to the Queen's Exchequer following the Court entertainments of the 1594-95 winter season.

"Not without Right"

In the upper left hand corner of the earlier paper, above the drawing of the bird and pen, is the legend in upper and lower case: "Non, sanz Droict," Law French for "No, without Right." Just below this is written the same legend, but without the comma—a line was then drawn through it as if to mark it out. Next to these two, in much larger capital letters, is written: "NON SANZ DROICT" – also *sanz* comma.

It hardly takes an expert to grasp that without the comma, the meaning of the line has been changed from "No, without right," to—well, to what? According to the Stratford line of defense it meant "Not without right" in Law French—but if that was the intended meaning it would have been written "Pas sans Droict." But it would still make no sense. Without right to what? The mythographers however, were not about to let it go—that "Gent" is just too crucial to their vision of William as someone capable of writing plays—someone who could possibly have been friends with an Earl like Southampton.

Appendix C Shakespeare's Coat of Arms

The motto

That there is nothing extant that might illuminate this further is no surprise. The fact that these two papers have survived is interesting. How many of such applications have survived the centuries?

As for the meaning of "Non, sans droit"—Schoenbaum shifts into academic superhyperbole—"Could the phrase conceivably signify heraldic endorsement?"—"Probably not," he answers himself—"more likely it represents a motto" which was brought to the herald by "the bearer"—namely William of Stratford (167). The notion of a motto was not new with Schoenbaum—it had occurred to scholars as long ago as Malone.

The obvious interpretation of the original line was to repeat the rejection from twenty years earlier on grounds that—according to the chief Herald then—John Shakspere's credentials were not sufficient for a Coat of Arms. What else could "No, without right" mean?—Apparently almost anything but the unavoidable, undeniable, obvious *truth*—that unpleasant thing that keeps getting in the way.

A "classic simplicity"

That Shakspere's application was rejected for lack of credentials is also implicit in its barren design. Schoenbaum refers to the kind of designs accepted by the Heralds as inclined to "fussiness and over-elaboration" as compared with what he fatuously terms the "classic simplicity" of John Shakspere's design (167). This is sheer and utter nonsense—an obvious refusal to acknowledge the facts..

The images on Coats of Arms had no more to do with Art than shapes of numbers have to do with the amounts they represent. Traditional heraldic symbols—the traditional elements of a Coat of Arms represent the applicant's credentials—his family connections —his personal accomplishments—if any. In John Shakspere's case, that the only images on either the upper level or the shield are puns on his name emphasizes the fact that he simply had nothing else to offer—which was, of course, the reason why his application was rejected. It was accepted in 1596 purely because—unlike John Shakspere—Hemmings had clout.

Efforts to connect the Coat of Arms with John's son's supposed career as a writer by claiming that the spear was meant to be a pen is untenable—partly because he applied for it long before said son was old enough to do any writing—but also because *it doesn't look like a pen*—or even what we would normally think of as *a spear*. If it looks like anything that would be a *lance*—which were used only by young male courtiers dressed in heavy armour for performing at the royal Tilts. Weighted at the holding end for balance, it neither looked like —nor functioned anything like—a *spear*.

If all this seems absurd for a humble dealer in sheep products, it's because these Coats of Arms—with their claims of ancestral achievements dating back to the Crusades—were already losing what real world value they once carried. For Shakspere Sr. its value lay in the credit it bestowed, making it easier for him to get loans with which to buy land—land being the best investment for men of his class.

With the fame that came to the name Shakespeare in the 1590s, the original Coat of Arms design took on a life of its own—acquiring first a *helm*, suggestive of either military service or jousting—*mantling*, flags blowing in the wind, a mere decoration—and the jousting lance—none of it having any connection whatsoever to an ancient ancestor or his life as Mayor of a Midlands market town.

In reporting the questionable nature of the evidence that John Shakspere deserved a Coat of Arms—while calling it "sufficiently vague"—Schoenbaum addressed the violent character of the Herald who had signed off on it, William Dethick—and the "heraldic tempest in a teacup" in which it became involved in 1602 when the then York Herald Peter Brooke accused Dethick of "elevating base persons." Of the 23 men who, according to Brooke, did not merit the Coat of Arms awarded by Dethick—*John Shakspere* was fourth on his list.

Malone's notion that "Not without right" was "a family motto" ranks high as one of the most absurd the world has been asked to swallow with regard to William of Stratford. No one—however ignorant or muddle-headed—would ever adopt as a motto a meaningless double negative like "Not without Right." In fact, no academic has ever attempted to deconstruct this particular anomaly —probably because as a motto it is so utterly meaningless. Both 20th-century literary historians Schoenbaum and Chambers had to admit

Appendix C Shakespeare's Coat of Arms

that the family appears never to have used it either then or later. Of course not. They may have been illiterate, but they weren't stupid.

Conjured up during a period when there were no newspapers and few people could read—when none but antiquarians would have known or cared about Dethick's battle with York Herald Brooke—Shakespeare's connection to the popular plays that were making London the entertainment capital of the nation would not be made public for another two years. When in 1598 a version of his name appeared for the first time on two of London's currently popular plays—hyphenated in such a way as to insure that it be seen, and heard, and pronounced *Shake*-spear (not *Shack*-spear, as it was most likely pronounced in Stratford)—it carried with it—for "those who had ears to hear"—a rather obvious pun, which sent the signal that the Lord Chamberlain's Men intended to keep the matter of their playwright's real identity to themselves.

"Not without Mustard"

The following year—shortly after getting in trouble for a play he helped write for Pembroke's Men (*The Isle of Dogs*)—young Ben Jonson was hired as a playwright by the Lord Chamberlain's Men. By the following year he had one ready—the first of the "citizen comedies" intended to appeal to a public with little interest in plays about England's past or stories from the Greek Romance tradition. *Every Man in His Humour* got Jonson started on his career as a successful London playwright. The following year, his second opus, *Every Man Out of his Humour*, unlike the mildly satirical "humor" of his first, was fiercely spiced with theatrical satire—the character Sogliardo, probably meant to be played by the popular comedian Will Kempe, was undeniably a caricature of William of Stratford.

In Act II, Scene 1, The knight Puntarvolo enters in company with Carlo Buffone and Sogliardo, described in the play as—"an essential clown . . . so enamoured of the name of a gentleman, that he will have it, though he buys it." Sogliardo complains of his treatment by the College of Heralds. Keeping in mind that the Earl of Oxford's heraldic symbol was a boar—and that the word *rampant* in heraldry refers to the upreared posture of the animals that support either side of

Educating Shakespeare

the shield on a Coat of Arms—note that Sogliardo is most impressed by how many colors are involved (colors have nothing to do with the symbology of heraldry—as in the following exchange between Sogliardo, and the players Carlito and Puntarvolo—

SOG. ... By this parchment, gentlemen, I have been so toiled among the harrots [heralds] yonder, you will not believe! they do speak in the strangest language, and give a man the hardest terms for his money, that ever you knew.

CAR. But have you arms, have you [the Coat of] arms?

SOG. I'faith, I thank them; I can write myself gentleman now; here's my patent, it cost me thirty pound, by this breath.

PUNT. A very fair coat, well charged, and full of armory.

SOG. Nay, it has as much variety of colours in it, as you have seen a coat have. How like you the crest, sir?

PUNT. I understand it not well, what is't?

SOG. Marry, sir, it is your boar without a head, rampant. A boar without a head, that's very rare!

CAR. Ay, and rampant too! Troth, I commend the herald's wit, he has deciphered him well: a swine without a head, without brain, wit, anything indeed, ramping to gentility. You can blazon the rest, signior, can you not?

SOG. O, ay, I have it in writing here of purpose; it cost me two shilling the tricking. ...

PUN. It is the most vile, foolish, absurd, palpable, and ridiculous escutcheon that ever this eye survised.

CAR. 'Slud, it's a hog's cheek and puddings in a pewter field [cold cuts on a platter]. ...

PUN. Let the word [the motto] be—"Not without mustard!"

Appendix C Shakespeare's Coat of Arms

Generations of orthodox scholars have been at a loss to explain this exchange—so a little insight might be in order. At some point in 1595 William begins making trips to London to see what more he can do for himself. Jonson describes Sogliardo as coming up "every term to learn to take tobacco, and see new motions [plays or puppet shows]." Someone in the company, most likely Hemmings, finds him a place to stay in St. Helen's parish. When the tax collectors get too nosy, Hemmings arranges for him to stay with costumers who live near himself and Henry Condell.

William, of course, was aware that he must not refer in any way to anyone, including the actors, about his arrangement with the Company. To do so would be to kill the goose that lays the golden eggs with which he's just acquired New Place in Stratford, and is arranging to have a bust made of his adored father who just recently has passed on. The actors understand that they must show him a good time and keep him separated from questioners.

In writing *Every Man Out* for the Lord Chamberlain's Men in 1599—Jonson couldn't resist using the story behind William's Coat of Arms to amuse the actors and their audience. Images of the heads of beasts were a commonplace on crests, so a body without a head was obviously a joke. It was also a metaphor for what was being done to Shakespeare's identity. The body without a head represents the body of Shakespeare's work minus its head. That William was feasting off the boar's head—the works that came from the head of the man whose totem was a Blue Boar—seems pretty straightforward. If we try hard, maybe we can still hear the laughter echoing down the corridors of Time—when "Not without right" became "not without mustard."

APPENDIX D *The Stratford* Bust

Issues surrounding the Bust on the wall of Trinity Church in Stratford are foremost in pressing the issue of Shakespeare's identity. If we are to know who he was, we want to know what he looked like. One thing is clear from the start, he certainly did not look like the absurdity still staring down from the memorial on the wall of the Stratford church. How best to begin if not by quoting the great American satirist Mark Twain in his essay *Is Shakespeare Dead?*

> *I haven't any idea that Shakespeare will have to vacate his pedestal this side of the year 2209;* . . . it is a very slow process. It took several thousand years to convince our fine race—including every splendid intellect in it—that there is no such thing as a witch—it has taken several thousand years to convince the same fine race—including every splendid intellect in it—that there is no such person as Satan—it has taken several centuries to remove perdition from the Protestant Church's program of post-mortem entertainments—it has taken a weary long time to persuade American Presbyterians to give up infant damnation and try to bear it the best they can— and it looks as if their Scotch brethren will still be burning babies in the everlasting fires when Shakespeare comes down from his perch.
>
> *We are The Reasoning Race.* . . . [W]hen we find a vague file of chipmunk-tracks stringing through the dust of Stratford village, we know by our reasoning powers that Hercules has been along there. I feel that our fetish is safe for three centuries yet. The bust, too—there in the Stratford Church. The precious bust, the priceless bust, the calm bust, the serene bust, the emotionless bust, with the dandy mustache, and the putty face, unseamed of care—that face which has looked passionlessly down upon the awed pilgrim for a hundred and fifty years and will still look down upon the awed pilgrim three hundred more, with the deep, deep, deep, subtle, subtle, subtle expression—of *a bladder.*

Appendix D The Stratford Bust

Present version of the Stratford Bust.

Stratford busted

Was there ever anything more ridiculous than the Stratford Bust—the face that launched a thousand quips? Roughly a hundred years after Mark Twain the issue was addressed with passionless sobriety by authorship scholar Richard Whalen in his article in *The Oxfordian*—"The Stratford Bust: A Monumental Fraud" (2005). That it took 27 pages to follow the development of the present effigy suggests the quagmire faced by Whalen when he set about to explain it.

Two different busts for two different men

As Whalen tells it, the story involves two very different busts for two very different individuals. The first dates to 1634 when a William Dugdale, a gentleman from Warwickshire—while collecting material for a book he was writing on local artefacts—sketched the bust as it then appeared on the wall of the Stratford Church. His sketch—buried for centuries among his family papers—finally coming to the notice of Shakespeare scholar Charlotte Stopes in 1909—depicts a thin bald man with a drooping mustache standing with his hands resting on an extremely large bag, knotted in each of its four corners. Dismissed by early biographers like Halliwell-Phillipps as "inaccurate" or "badly done"—since it tended to throw Shakespeare Studies into chaos—it's been ignored or dismissed ever since by almost every scholar who bothers to mention it. While Sam Schoenbaum thought it "authentic enough"—to Chambers, the gaping gulf between Dugdale-Hollar's "bagged commodities"—as Charlton Ogburn later described it—and today's tasselled pillow—was "a mare's nest."

Enter *The Woolpack Man*

In 2005—shortly before Whalen's article was published—novelist-playwright Richard Kennedy of Newport Oregon had two insights. The first had to do with exactly what was in that knotted bag—the second identified the original bag holder. After checking with his local reference library and the London College of Heralds—Kennedy put up a website he titled *The Woolpack Man* on which he informed the Authorship community that the bag must have been what was known in the sixteenth century as a *woolsack*—one of the thousands of

Appendix D The Stratford Bust

cheaply made hempen bags in which sheepmen packed raw wool during sheep-shearing season—their knotted corners providing hand holds that made them easy to carry and toss from man to man into carts piled high with other bags of wool.

Carters would then distribute the bags to homes where women with spinning wheels would spin the raw wool into yarn—those with looms then weaving the yarn into rolled sheets of woolen fabric which factors would sell to merchants who would ship the rolls of fabric overseas, creating what in time became the nation's most profitable trade commodity.

The Stratford Bust as sketched by *William Dugdale in 1634*

England and the wool trade

The quality of English wool was due to the kinds of sheep bred over the centuries whose thick wool protected them from the damp and chilly climate. At 50 degrees north latitude—surrounded by the cold and windy Atlantic ocean, these sheep produced the kind of warm protective covering that made English wool a cut above that from anywhere else. As wool became increasingly valuable—raising sheep became increasingly popular with landowners, eventually leading to bitter and sometimes violent disputes over land use, loss of fam land, and overgrazing. But there was no changing the fact that while land once dedicated to to producing vegetables and hay, products which required the work of farm hands and teams of horses or oxen, when converted to raising sheep, required nothing more than a single shepherd and his dog.

The Woolsack

Over time, as an island surrounded by water—as England's native ship-building became the means for developing new sources of trade —as they grew in mercantile power, they had to establish colonies where their ships could find ports. Expanding into what they're still fond of calling the British Empire—seeking symbols with which to represent the nation's triumphant rise in world culture—the English came to acknowledge the role wool had played in this greatest of all success stories. Even the humble bags in which it had once been stored became symbolic of the status accorded their contents. This led to the creation of *The Woolsack*—a large red blocklike object that Speakers in the House of Lords still sit on or stand near while speaking. Today all pronouncements of governmental authority are said to be made "from the Woolsack"—not, as in earlier centuries—from the throne.

Birth of the Birthplace

Until the First Folio—in which a dedicatory poem mentioned "thy Stratford moniment"—the town of Stratford-on-Avon was never remarkable for anything more than a place where those in the market for sheep and sheep products could gather once a week to buy and sell

Appendix D The Stratford Bust

the living animals as well as their hides and meat.

Despite efforts by Caroline Spurgeon and others to portray it as the sort of quiet country village suggested by Shakespeare's imagery––16th-century Stratford was a noisy, smelly, crowded market town.

The Bust as "improved" by Wenceslaus Hollar in 1656.

Once a week it would be filled to the brim with shouting herdsmen, bawling sheep, and the cries of vendors selling snacks to the factors who were there to buy the living animals and their products. The brewery that provided the ale for market day and the tannery that created leather from the animal hides, both located a few blocks from each other in the center of town, both produced the foulest of smells.

The Forest of Arden that supposedly lay just outside of town was long gone by the Shakspere's time—replaced by strips of market garden along the outer limits of the town—since there was no room between the closely packed village dwellings for more than a few herbs and a little lettuce. Clearly Spurgeon's image of the quiet life where Shakespeare got his images was a product of her imagination.

By 1634—Stratford having been identified by the First Folio some fifteen years earlier as Shakespeare's hometown—word having gotten around that there was a bust, presumably of the Bard himself, in the church there—a local antiquarian William Dugdale thought he'd have have a look at it, possibly even get a drawing of it for the book he was writing on local antiquities. Thus did the bust of John Shakespeare begin its long, strange series of "improvements" until it eventually arrived as the present "bladder" of Mark Twain's disdain.

Shakespeare's face

The search for a worthy image of Shakespeare has been a necessary accompaniment to the search for his identity. To fill the void, portraits of various otherwise unidentified persons from his time have been used over the years to illustrate books and articles about the author for whom they had no certain image. As a result, almost any relatively intelligent looking chap from that time was apt to end up on a book cover. According to Wikipedia, "more than 60 portraits purporting to be of Shakespeare were offered for sale to the National Portrait Gallery within four decades of its foundation in 1856." There are at least six of these portraits still in contention—the Chandos, the Cobbe, the Janssen, the Grafton, the Sanders, and the Soest. (The Droeshout—the bizarre frontispiece to the First Folio—seems to be losing its claim to authority).

Appendix D The Stratford Bust

With Looney's discovery the search has shifted to locating dependable images of the 17th Earl of Oxford. So far there's the Welbeck, a copy of a portrait painted while he was in France in 1575 —the Ashbourne, painted in his early forties—a Hilliard miniature, probably from his thirties—and most important, the portraits by George Vertue, the great artist-engraver of the eighteenth century, whose version of Shakespeare has so many points of similarity to portraits known to be of the Earl of Oxford that we feel justified in adopting one in particular as Shakespeare's image.

One version of the Bust made by Vertue for Pope's edition of Shakespeare that reflects the face he portrayed as Shakespeare in his portfolio of engravings of famous men.

Vertue's Shakespeare

George Vertue (1784-1856) is known by art historians as the premiere artist-engraver of the first half of the 19th century. Developments in the print industry had made it possible by then to create complex, realistic images by means of copper or steel engravings of a sort that far surpassed the woodcuts of earlier times. Considerable artistic skill was required for Vertue to copy by sight, by means of a sharp pointed metal tool, the face in a painting onto one of these metal plates, which he used to create copies on heavy paper.

Accustomed to Court life from childhood (his parents had been servants in the household of the exiled James II)—George was the close friend of Sir Edward Harley—2nd Earl of Oxford (by the second creation). In their time, the Harleys—first the father, then the son and and his wife—were leaders of Court society and patrons of poets, artists and antiquarians. Edward's father, Robert Harley, first Earl of Oxford (by the 2nd creation) was Queen Anne's Secretary of State, then Chancellor of the Exchequer—finally Lord Treasurer.

A poet himself, Harley Sr. was the Maecenas of what has been termed the Silver Age in English literature (following the Golden Age of Shakespeare, Spenser, Sidney, Bacon and Milton). Lifelong friend and confidante of peers inclined to the arts and antiquities, patron of Daniel Defoe (*Robinson Crusoe*), Jonathon Swift (*Gulliver's Travels*), Alexander Pope (*Rape of the Lock*), and John Gay (*Beggars Opera*)—he was also a founding member of—and contributor to— the famous Scribblers Club—whose members are known to have plotted over interminable cups of coffee the literary tricks they played on their political enemies and a complacent bourgeoisie.

When Harley died in 1724, his entire estate, library and antiquities—including numerous portraits of former lords and ladies —passed to his son—who then doubled the already huge collection by marrying Henrietta Cavendish Holles—direct descendant of Oxford's cousin Horatio Vere. Their daughters then doubled it yet again by marrying the Duke of Portland, which made her—Margaret Holles, Duchess of Portland—the richest woman in England—and owner of the entire collection gathered over time at Welbeck Abbey. There are moments in history when the forces that have been holding things together for centuries give way—many things changing all at

Appendix D The Stratford Bust

once. With the death in 1714 of the last of the Stuarts—the Whigs were in and the Tories were out. No longer able to manipulate the market to their advantage—wealthy Tories were forced to let go of some of their immense holdings of goods as well as estates.

By the 1750s—with husband and father both gone—the expense of maintaining these collections convinced the Duchess and her mother to contribute them to the nation as the founding collection for the British Museum which then became the founding collection of the British Library. For help with this overwhelming task they

Vertue's Shakespeare *from his* Portfolio of Illustrious Poets.

turned to George Vertue to examine, evaluate and catalogue these would certainly have seen the resemblance between the portrait of Oxford we know as the Welbeck and possibly others whose existence remain unknown.

Vertue and Shakespeare

George Vertue began working with and for Edward Harley at about the same time that he was commissioned by Alexander Pope to provide the frontispiece for Pope's six-volume edition of the plays.
Although Vertue would have been familiar with the images used to introduce earlier editions—such as the ridiculous Droeshout from the First Folio, and those used later—Vertue chose to use something totally different, one he must have found in the Harley collection. Surrounded by an elaborate oval frame is the face he would repeat elsewhere, possibly copied from a painting he'd found at Welbeck Abbey. That such a practiced eye chose it to represent it as Shakespeare in his *Portfolio of Famous Poets*, strengthens our belief that it's the same face we see in known portraits of Oxford.

Vertue's virtue

As much antiquarian as artist, George Vertue has been described by a contemporary as deeply concerned that his engravings be as truthful as possible a true reflection of his subjects looks. Alexander Chalmers—in his *Biographical Dictionary* of 1812—attributes Vertue's failure to complete a portrait series of the faces of famous men from before his time—Birch's *Heads of Illustrious Persons of Great Britain*—a series originally planned by Vertue himself—to his "rigid regard for veracity, which made him justly scrupulous of authenticating the likenesses of deceased characters without the clearest proofs" (30.321). One wonders which "deceased character" Vertue was finding it so difficult to "authenticate" in his series of England's greatest poets, that he left it for his rival to finish.

Appendix D The Stratford Bust

Oxford in his twenties, forties, and fifties. Note the pursed upper lip, the curve of the eyebrows, and the similar shape of the nose, a strong identification at a time when noses came in many different shapes.

Vertue's "other Shakespeare"

It seems that Alexander Pope had his edition of Shakespeare ready to publish several years before it finally saw print in 1725 (it had taken time to get enough subscribers). The date inscribed by Vertue on the frontispiece he created for Pope's Shakespeare was 1721, but two years earlier, in 1719, he had engraved another very different face as Shakespeare's in his own series "Twelve Heads of Poets"—published at some point between 1726 and 1729.

It's this image that in 2004 caught our attention from the end of the long central hall of the Folger Library—lined on either side with glass cases filled with Shakespeare related items—propped upright in the center of a glass case. The intelligent face, the penetrating glance, the tightened upper lip—all so different from any of the other images of Shakespeare. Labelled by the so-called experts as yet another copy of the Chandos—as can easily be seen by anyone with relatively reliable vision and an ounce of common sense—his "Shakespeare with collar" *DOES NOT resemble the Chandos* (p. 15) *in any way.*

The face in this engraving—and in Vertue's illustration of the Bust (p. 349)—both so similar to the Welbeck and the Ashbourne from different stages in Oxford's life, all reflect intelligence of the sort not found in any other image of Shakespeare. It just isn't possible that Vertue could have come up with such a face out of his imagination. Because there are mentions throughout the literature of

other portraits of Oxford that haven't yet been located or identified—
—we propose that the portrait of *Shakespeare with a collar* on which Vertue based his engravings must have been painted when Oxford was in his fifties, when his curly hair was beginning to recede from his temples. Putting them together, we have the *Welbeck* from his twenties, the *Hilliard* from his thirties, the *Ashbourne* from his forties, and the *Vertue* from his fifties—all but the Hilliard reflecting the same nose, and most uniquely on the later paintings, the tight or pursed upper lip.

APPENDIX E Henslowe's Spelling

In a history rampant with ambiguous original texts and unanswered questions, resolution of a major issue may sometimes rely on the interpretation of a single phrase or letter of the alphabet. Such is the case with the enigmatic "ne" with which theater entrepreneur Philip Henslowe kept his running account of box office receipts from plays produced at his theater in Southwark during the six years covered by his journal (1591-1597). His account is immensely important as it's the best—in some ways the *only*—record we have of how a public theater functioned back then.

Henslowe kept track of each day's receipts on a line divided into three columns—first came the date—then the title of the play—and finally the amount it brought in that day. With few exceptions, this was the format he followed throughout—as in an early entry—"Rd at harey of cornwall the 25 of febrearye 1591. . . xxxij s" meaning —"Received from 'Harry of Cornwall' on February 25, 1591, 32 shillings." Six days later the line reads, "ne—Rd at harey the vj the 3 of marche 1591 . . . iij*li* xvj*s* 8 *d*'—which told him that *Harry the Sixth*, performed on the 3rd of March—brought him 3 pounds 16 shillings and 8 pence. Why the "ne" for this play and not for the other? Scattered throughout the journal—"ne" appear fairly infrequently—its most obvious significance that on days where it appears the take is apt to be somewhat higher than usual.

Since 1923—when E. K. Chambers published his four-volume account of *The Elizabethan Stage*, the more or less tacit agreement has settled on the idea that Henslowe's "ne" meant *new*, as suggested in his section on the Admiral's Men (2.145-6). Its importance rests primarily on the fact that it set the earliest possible date—the *terminus a quo*—for several of Shakespeare's most important plays. Although almost every respected researcher, including Chambers himself, has admitted that "ne" *cannot* mean "*new*"—because some of the plays so noted were obviously not, in fact, new (nor were they new to Henslowe)—yet *new* has continued to be the automatic explanation, such as this from the 1966 *Shakespeare Encyclopaedia*—

> Philip Henslowe . records a performance of a *Hamlet* on July 11, 1594 at the theater at Newington Butts, when it was jointly occupied by the Admiral's Men and the Chamberlain's Men. Henslowe failed to mark it "ne" (new), so it was probably old stuff. (285)

—which shows how a single minor point can influence how an entire bit of theatrical history can be misinterpreted by a single letter. It was actually not Chambers who first suggested that "ne" meant *new*—but our frisky friend John Payne Collier, as Chambers's precursor W.W. Greg attests in Chapter III of his 1908 book on the Diary. Nor was it Chambers who added these caveats, since it's clear he was simply following Greg's conclusion that—although it was "impossible to suppose that Henslowe would have written 'ne' for 'new,' yet what else the letters can stand for it seems impossible to guess'" (2.149). However, said Greg—

> Happily their exact significance is a matter of no practical importance. We can treat them as we should a conventional sign, and infer their significance from their observed use: (i) that the play was new to the stage and had never before been acted; (ii) that it was new to the company, but had been previously represented by some other body; (iii) *that it was new in its particular form, having received alterations since it was last acted.* From this it is a legitimate inference that where a title occurs for the first time in the Diary, and is not marked with the letters "ne," the play was an *old stock piece* which had been previously acted by the same company' (*Diary* 148).

First it should be noted that The Rose had been in operation for four years before Henslowe began his daily account—so whether a title appearing for the first time in his account was an "old stock piece" could hardly be determined by the presence or absence of "ne." Second, neither Greg, nor Chambers, could foresee that—far from "a matter of no importance"—"ne" would become a permanent stumbling block—for so deeply has the idea that it meant *new* sunk into the shared psyche of the Academy—that like a rock in the middle of a free-flowing stream it continues to create confusion around a matter of the utmost importance—namely, *dating the plays!*

Appendix E Henslowe's Spelling

Without knowing for certain what Henslowe was tracking with "ne"—how can we know whether "(i) the play was new to the stage and had never before been acted," if in fact that was not his purpose? —How can it tell us that "(ii) it was new to the company," since there's no way of knowing whether it had been performed during the four years before Henslowe began keeping track, or (iii) whether it had previously been performed by another company?

Other alternatives have been suggested—that "ne" stood for Newington Butts, the alternate theater used by Henslowe's actors on occasion (Frazer 35)—that it indicated a play for which Henslowe had to pay a licensing fee, which required that he raise the ticket price (Foakes xxxiv)—that it indicated that the play brought in twice the usual fee, and so forth. Yet none of these have stuck, chiefly because none seemed important enough to add a fourth column to an account containing only three other facts—name, date, and the day's receipts. What makes the most sense is the third possibility suggested by Greg and Chambers—namely that "ne" meant that the play "had undergone a substantial process of revision before revival"—for surely, in reviewing the response to a particular play, Henslowe would want to know the reason for that day's increased box office.

Henslowe's *e*

Yet this theory too has failed, either because it has not offered a word or phrase for which "ne" could be either an acronym or an abbreviation—or possibly because Greg, and all who have followed him, disliked the idea of revision, for which the Stratford bio allows no time. As Roslyn L. Knutson states in her article "Henslowe's Diary and the Economics of Play Revision for Revival" (1985)—even Greg had to fudge on revisions—"defending the sign 'ne' as the mark of new plays, he offered as an exception a play 'new in the sense that it was *a revival with alterations*'"—purest flimflam, since a "revival with alterations" cannot be considered a *new* play. More sensibly she continues—

> In the Cambridge editions of Shakespeare's plays, J. Dover Wilson systematically identified textual variants and cruxes in

the early plays as evidence of revisions.... Over the years, editions of and monographs on plays with more than one textual version have reinforced the association of major alterations with a play's return to the stage after some period of retirement. For such an apparently widespread playhouse practice, G.E. Bentley developed a "rule of thumb": "almost any play... kept in active repertory by the company which owned it is most likely to contain *later revisions*." (1)

Chambers fudged as well in *Facts and Problems* when he states—

Plays which had been laid aside were often revived. A stock favourite was called a 'get-penny'.... Conceivably three or four plays marked 'ne' in Henslowe's accounts for 1594 may have been revived and are not strictly new; the significance of 'ne' is not quite clear." (215)

What *is* clear is that Chambers—like Knutson and virtually all academics—refused to admit a conclusion that threatens the Stratford scenario. What is also clear is that—contrary to Greg's sidestepping —"their exact significance" is a matter of the utmost "practical importance"—both to Henslowe, for whom it was important to his business—and to all Shakespeare scholars because it directly affects the entire history of the canon.

Revision! Revision! Revision!

As Albert Feuillerat—who almost alone among his colleagues was strongly in favor of a Shakespeare who revised—explains in *The Composition of Shakespeare's Plays* (1953)—

Henslowe's Diary is filled with illuminating information on the art of making old plays look like new ones.... To distinguish the different types of revision Henslowe makes use of three terms with a remarkable regularity: "mending," "additions," and "altering." (7-8)

Feuillerat spends all twenty pages of his introduction identifying and describing the practice of turning old plays into new in dozens of

Appendix E Henslowe's Spelling

instances throughout the period—for if the audience could be convinced that they were seeing something new, or that something familiar had been improved—the box office would increase. The appetite for new plays during the early years of the public stage is reflected in Henslowe's practice of hiring as many as four or five writers to get him fresh new fodder as fast as possible.

Today—bound by copyright laws and respect for authorial rights—no producer would think of "mending" a play without the author's permission—but such was not the case back in the sixteenth century. Many of the plays produced during this first early period in the development of the commercial Stage grew largely out of the long-standing folk tradition whereby popular plays, particularly comedies, were routinely updated for each new holiday with fresh new routines, satires, and characters.

To those who study Early Modern publishing, it should be clear that revision was a frequent if not always a truthful title page claim. All sorts of works announced—as did the 1590 edition of *The Spanish Tragedy*—that they were: "Newly corrected, amended, and enlarged with new additions." In his *Shakespeare: Facts and Problems*, Chambers notes that the title page of the third (1602) edition of *Richard III*, advertises itself as "Newly augmented"—although "there are no augmentations" (1.300).

As Neil Carson reports—

> In the years from 1596 to 1603 about a dozen works were "altered" or "mended" by the companies in Henslowe's theaters. . . . *Tasso's Melancholy* performed as an "ne" play by the Admiral's Men in 1595, was restaged at the Fortune in 1602, at which time Dekker was paid for two sets of alterations . . . [with] clear evidence of progressive revision. (77)

Those pesky vowels

What makes sense is that Henslowe's "ne" stood for "*n*ewly *e*mended." To quibble that if this was what Henslowe meant he would have spelled it "na" for "*n*ewly *a*mended"—is to ignore the nature of his spelling, which was so wildly phonetic that he rarely spelled a word the same way twice. That a 16th-century speller—particularly one as idiosyncratic as this self-taught businessman—would spell "amend" *emend* is hardly surprising, since both spellings meant the same thing then. Thomas Digges, Roger Ascham and Edmund Spenser, for instance, all spelled *among* "emong" (OED). As for Henslowe's handwriting, hard to decipher as it may be in places, it's not an issue with his "ne"—two versions of which can be seen in Plate II in Foakes's 2002 book on the Diary (lvi-i)—in which he explains in detail that there can be no doubt that it's spelled *ne*—NOT *na*.

Also, that Henslowe was inclined to use *e* where others used *a* is evident from the fact that he spelled words like *Alexandria* "elexandrea" and *Alexander* "elexander" (Diary 34, 56). In any case, the difference between the two—*amend* meaning to make a thing better—as with Jack Cade's nickname—"John Amend-all"—and *emend* meaning to correct a mistake—would have been far too subtle for Henslowe, whose diary was meant for no one to read but himself.

Thus "newly emended" resolves most of the problems with Henslowe's "ne." It avoids the major problem with "new." In fact, it tells us the opposite, namely that any play so labelled was definitely *not* new—and if not so old that it could be considered "an old stock piece"—it had already been seen by an audience. It makes sense of the fact that the totals for "ne" performances were generally higher than the totals for repeat performances of plays that were not so labelled—since it was undoubtedly billed as such. It also makes sense that—as an impresario—Henslowe would want evidence of the box office results of a revision. And it fits with the statement on many title pages of plays published in quarto that the text was "newly augmented"—or something that meant the same thing.

WORKS CITED

Abbreviations
BL   British Library
DNB   Dictionary of National Biography (since 2005)
OED   Oxford English Dictionary
PRO   Public Record Office
STC   Short Title Catalog

Dictionaries & Lexicons
Bartlett's Quotations: A collection of passages, phrases and proverbs traced to their sources in ancient and modern literature. Ed. John Bartlett. (1882). 15th Edition. Boston: Little Brown, 1980.
Encyclopedia of Concert Music. Ed. David Ewen. New York: Hill & Wang, 1959.
Riverside Shakespeare. Ed. G. Blakemore Evans. Boston: Houghton Mifflin, 1974.
Shakespeare Lexicon and Quotation Dictionary. Ed. Alexander Schmidt. (1902). 2 vols. 3rd ed. New York: Dover, 1971.

Books, Articles and Emails
Akrigg, G.P.V. *Shakespeare and the Earl of Southampton.* Cambridge: Harvard UP, 1968.
Alexander, Mark Andre. "Shakespeare's Knowledge of Law: A Journey through the History of the Argument." *The Oxfordian.* Vol 4 (2001): 51-120 (online).
Altrocchi, Paul. "Bermoothes: An Intriguing Enigma." *Shakespeare Matters.* 5.3 Spring (2006): 10-15 (online).
Andreski, Stanislav. *Syphilis, Puritanism and Witch Hunts.* New York: St. Martin's, 1989.
Andrews, Mark Edwin. *Law versus Equity in "The Merchant of Venice."* Boulder CO: UC Press, 1965.
Aubrey, John. *Brief Lives.* Ed. Richard Barber. (1898). Bury St. Edmunds: Boydell, 1982.
Aune, Mark. "The Uses of *Richard III*: from Robert Cecil to Richard Nixon." *Shakespeare Bulletin* 24.3 (2006): 23-47.
Baldwin, T.W. *William Shakspere's Small Latine & Lesse Greeke.* 2 vols. Urbana: U Illinois Press, 1944.

Bayley, Melanie. "Alice's Adventures in Algebra, Wonderland Solved." *New Scientist: Physics and Math.* #2739, Dec. 16, 2009.

Bentley, Gerald E. The Profession of Player in Shakespeare's Time, 1590-1642. Princeton: PUP, 1984.

Bettelheim, Bruno. The Uses of Enchantment: The meaning and importance of Fairy Tales. New York: Knopf, 1976.

Bloom, Allan and Harry V. Jaffa. *Shakespeare's Politics.* (1930). Chicago: UCP, 1964.

Bloom, Harold. *Shakespeare: The Invention of the Human.* New York: Putnam/ Riverhead, 1998.

Bly, Robert. *Iron John.* New York: Vintage, 1990.

Boas, Frederick. *Shakespeare & the Universities and other studies in Elizabethan Drama.* (1923). Folcroft, PA: Folcroft Library, 1973.

Booth, Wayne C. *The Company We Keep; An Ethics of Fiction.* Berkeley: U Cal Press, 1988.

Brooke, Tucker. *The Shakespeare Apocrypha.* Oxford: Clarendon, 1956.

Bucknill, John Charles. *The Medical Knowledge of Shakespeare.* London: Longmans, 1860.

Bullough, Geoffrey. *Narrative and Dramatic Sources of Shakespeare.* 8 vols. New York: Columbia UP, 1960.

Campbell, John. *Shakespeare's Legal Acquirements.* New York: Appleton, 1859. books.google.com.

Campbell, Lily B. *Shakespeare's Histories: Mirrors of Elizabethan Policy.* (1947). London: Methuen, 1968.

Carson, Neil. *A Companion to Henslowe's Diary.* (1988). Cambridge: CUP, 2005.

Cecil, David. *The Cecils of Hatfield House: An English Ruling Family.* Boston: Houghton Mifflin, 1973.

Chace, William M. "The Decline of the English Department; How it happened and what could be done to reverse it." *The American Scholar.* Autumn 2009. (online)

Chamberlin, Frederick. *The Private Character of Queen Elizabeth.* London: Lane, 1921. books.google.com

Chambers, E. K. *The Elizabethan Stage.* 4 vols. Oxford: Clarendon, 1923.

_____. *William Shakespeare,: A Study of Facts and Problems.* 2 vols. (1930). Oxford: Clarendon, 1966.

Collier, John Payne, ed. *Extracts from the Registers of the Stationers Company.* Vol I. The Shakespeare Society: London, 1848.

Collingwood, R.G. *The Idea of History.* 1946.

Collins, John Churton. *Studies in Shakespeare.* Westminster: Constable, 1904.

Works Cited

Croft, Pauline. "The Reputation of Robert Cecil: Libels, political opinion and popular awareness in the early seventeenth century." *Transactions of the Royal Historical Society*. Sixth Series, Vol. 1 (1991): 43-69.

Crompton, Louis. *Byron and Queer Love: Homophobia in Nineteenth-Century England.* London: Faber, 1985.

Cutting, Bonner Miller. *Necessary Mischief: Exploring the Shakespeare Authorship Question.* Jennings LA: Minos, 2018.

Davis, Frank. "Shakespeare's Medical Knowledge: How did he acquire it?" *The Oxfordian*. Vol 3 (2000): 45-58. (online)

Debus, Allen G. *The English Paracelsians.* London: Oldbourne: History of Science Library, 1965.

Dewar, Mary. *Sir Thomas Smith: A Tudor Intellectual in Office.* London: Athlone, 1964.

Duncan-Jones, Katherine. *Ungentle Shakespeare: Scenes from his Life.* London: Thomson Learning, 2001.

Edmond, Mary. *Rare Sir William Davenant.* New York: St. Martin's, 1987.

Egan, Michael, ed. *The Tragedy of Richard II Part One.* Lewiston, NY: Edwin Mellon, 2006.

Elton, Geoffrey. *England under the Tudors.* London: Methuen, 1955.

Erne, Lukas. *Shakespeare as Literary Dramatist.* Cambridge: CUP, 2003.

Everitt, E.B. and R.L. Armstrong. *Six Early Plays Related to the Shakespeare Canon. Anglistica* XIV. Copenhagen: Rosenhilde & Bagger, 1965.

Febvre, Lucien and Henri-Jean Martin. *The Coming of the Book: The Impact of Printing, 1450-1800.* Trans. David Gerard. London: NLB, 1976.

Feuillerat, Albert. *The Composition of Shakespeare's Plays: Authorship; Chronology.* (1953). Newport, NY: Books for Libraries Press, 1970.

Foakes, R.A., ed. *Coleridge's Criticism of Shakespeare: A Selection.* London: Athlone, 1989.

Foxe, John. *Book of Martyrs.* (1554). Eds. Miles J. Stanford, William Bryon Forbush. Grand Rapids MI: Zondervan, 1967.

Furness, H.H. ed. *King John.* New Variorum Edition 1919.

Gasquet, Francis & Edmund Bishop. *Edward VI and the Book of Common Prayer.* 2nd ed. London: Hodges, 1891. *books.google.com*

Golding, Arthur, trans. *Psalms of David . . . with Calvin's Commentaries* (STC 4395). London: Thomas East for George Bishop, 1571.

Graff, Gerald. *Professing Literature: An Institutional History* (1987). Chicago: UC Press, 1989.

Graves, Robert. *The White Goddess: a historical grammar of poetic myth.* (1947). New York: Farrar Straus, 1997.

Green, Martin. *Wriothesley's Roses in Shakespeare's Sonnets, Poems and Plays.* Baltimore: Clevedon, 1993.

Green, Nina. *The Oxford Authorship Site.* www.oxford-shakespeare.com.

Greenwood, Sir George. *The Shakespeare Problem Restated.* London: Bodley Head, 1908. *books.google.com*

Greg, W.W. *Henslowe's Diary.* Part II. London: Bullen, 1908.

Grillo, Ernesto. *Shakespeare and Italy.* (1949). New York: Haskell, 1973.

Gurr, Andrew. *The Shakespeare Company, 1594-1642.* Cambridge: CUP, 2004.

Handover, P.M. *The Second Cecil: Rise to Power: 1563-1604.* London: Eyre & Spottiswoode, 1959.

Hankins, John Erskine. *Shakespeare's Derived Imagery.* (1953). New York: Octagon, 1967.

Hart, Alfred. *Shakespeare and the Homilies.* (1934). New York: Octagon, 1977.

Highet, Gilbert. *The Classical Tradition: Greek and Roman influences on Western Literature.* (1949). Oxford: OUP, 1970.

Holland, Norman. "Freud on Shakespeare." *PMLA.* Vol. 75, No. 3, (June 1960): 164.

Honigmann, E.A.J. "Shakespeare's Will and Testamentary Traditions." Shakespeare and Cultural Traditions: the Selected Proceedings of the International Shakespeare Association World Congress. Eds. Tetuso Kishi, Roger Pringle and Stanley Wells. Tokyo, 1991. pp. 127-137.

Hotine, Margaret. "Richard III and Macbeth: Studies in Tudor Tyranny?" *Notes and Queries* (December 1991): 480-86.

Hume, Martin. *The Great Lord Burghley; A Study in Elizabethan Statecraft.* (1898). New York: Haskell House, 1968.

Hutton, Ronald. *The Witch: A History of Fear from Ancient Times to the Present.* New Haven: Yale U Press, 2017.

Ingram, William. *The Business of Playing: The Beginnings of the Adult Professional Theater in Elizabethan London.* Ithaca, NY: Cornell UP, 1992.

Jaffa, Harry V. "The Limits of Politics: King Lear, Act I Scene 1." *Shakespeare's Politics.* Ed. Alan Bloom (1930). Chicago: UC Press, (1964): 113-45.

Works Cited

Jayne, Sears Reynolds. *Plato in Renaissance England*. Norwell, MA: Kluwer, 1995.

Jiménez, Ramon. *Shakespeare's Apprenticeship: Identifying the Real Playwright's Earliest Works*. Jefferson N.C.: McFarland, 2018.

———. "Shakespeare in Stratford and London: Ten Eyewitnesses who saw nothing." *The Shakespeare Oxford Society's 50th Anniversary Anthology*. Fall, 2002/2005.

Jones, Ernest. *The Life and Work of Sigmund Freud*. 2 vols. New York: Basic Books: 1953-57.

Jones, Terry et al. *Who Murdered Chaucer?* New York: St. Martin's, 2003.

Joseph, Sister Miriam. *Shakespeare's Use of the Arts of Language*. (1947). Philadelphia: Paul Dry, 2005.

Jowett, Benjamin, trans. *Plato's Dialogues*, 1871. (online)

Joyce, Michael. *Plato's Symposium in English*. London: Dent, 1935.

Kathman, David. *ShakespeaeAuthorship.com*.

Kennedy, Richard. *The Woolpack Man*. http:webpages.charter.net/stairway/woolpackman.htm

Kornstein, Daniel. *Kill All the Lawyers?* Princeton: PUP, 1994.

Knutson, Roslyn L. "Henslowe's Diary and the Economics of Play Revision for Revival." *Theatre Research International* 10:1 (1985): 1-18.

Laoutaris, Chris. *Shakespeare and the Countess*. London: Penguin, 2015.

Lathrop, Henry Burrowes. *Translations from the Classics into English from Caxton to Chapman: 1477-1620*. (1932). New York: Octagon, 1967.

Levin, Bernard. *Enthusiasms*. London: Jonathan Cape, 1983.

Looney, J.T. *Shakespeare Identified as Edward de Vere, Seventeenth Earl of Oxford*. (1920). Ed. James Warren. Somerville, MA: Forever Press, 2019.

Maguire, Laurie E. *Shakespearean Suspect Texts: The "Bad" Quartos and Their Contents*. Cambridge: CUP, 1996.

Malim, Richard. *The Earl of Oxford and the Making of Shakespeare*. Jefferson NC: McFarland, 2012.

Masson, David. ed. *The Poetical Works of John Milton*. London: Macmillan, 1893.

McFarlane, K.B. *The Nobility of Later Medieval England. The Ford Lectures for 1953*. Oxford: Clarendon, 1973.

McMillin, Scott and Sally-Beth MacLean. *The Queen's Men and Their Plays*. Cambridge: CUP, 1998.

Milne, Kirsty. "The Forgotten Greek Books of Elizabethan England." *Literature Compass*. May (2007): 4.3 677–87.

Murray, Gilbert. *The Alcestis of Euripides*. New York: OUP, 1915. books.google.com

Naylor, Edward W. *Shakespeare and Music*. London: Dent, 1896. books.google.com

Noble, Richmond. *Shakespeare's Biblical Knowledge and Use of the Book of Common Prayer*. New York: Macmillan, 1935.

Ogburn, Charlton. *The Mysterious William Shakespeare: The Myth and the Reality*. New York: Dodd Mead, 1984.

Pettie, George. *A Petite Palace of Pettie His Pleasure*. (1908). Ed. Israel Gollancz. Whitefish, MT: Kessinger, 2007.

Pitcher, Seymour. *The Case for Shakespeare's Authorship of "The Famous Victories."* Binghamton NY: SUNY, 1961.

Pollard, Albert F. *The History of England: 1547-1603*. London: Longmans, 1919.

———. *England Under Protector Somerset: An Essay*. (London, 1900). Miami: Hardpress, ND.

Pollard, Alfred W. *Shakespeare's Folios and Quartos: A Study in the Bibliography of Shakespeare's Plays*. London: Methuen, 1909.

Prior, Roger. "Was *The Raigne of King Edward III* a Compliment to Lord Hunsdon?" *Connotations: A Journal for Critical Debate*. Vol 3.3 (1993/4): 243-64.

Read, Conyers. *Mr. Secretary Cecil and Queen Elizabeth*. (1955). New York: Knopf, 1961.

Reiter, Paul. "From Shakespeare to Defoe: Malaria in England in the Little Ice Age." *Emerging Infectious Diseases*. Vol 6. Feb. (2000): 16. (online)

Roe, Richard Paul. *The Shakespeare Guide to Italy: Retracing the Bard's unknown travels*. New York: Harper, 2011.

Root, Robert Kilburn. *Classical Mythology in Shakespeare*. New York: Henry Holt, 1903. books.google.com

Rowse, A.L. *Shakespeare the Man*. New York: St. Martin's, 1988.

Sams, Eric. *Shakespeare's Edmund Ironside: The Lost Play*. Aldershot, Hants: Wildwood, 1986.

Schoenbaum, Samuel. *William Shakespeare: A Documentary Life*. New York: OUP, 1975.

Scoufos, Alice-Lyle. *Shakespeare's Typological Satire*. Athens, OH: Ohio UP, 1979.

Seward, Desmond. *The Wars of the Roses: Through the Lives of Five Men and Women of the Fifteenth Century*. (1995). New York: Penguin, 1996.

Works Cited

Shaheen, Naseeb. *Biblical References in Shakespeare's Plays*. (1931). Cranbury, NJ: Assoc. UP, 1999.

Showerman, Earl. "Look Down and See What Death is Doing: Gods and Greeks in *The Winter's Tale*." *The Oxfordian*. Vol 10 (2007): 55-74

_____. "Shakespeare's Many *Much Ado's*: Alcestis, Hercules, and Love's Labour's Wonne." *Brief Chronicles*. Vol I (2009): 109.

_____. "Shakespeare's Medical Knowledge: Reflections from the ER." *Shakespeare Matters*. 11/13, (2012): .

Simpson, Richard. "The Politics of Shakspere's Historical Plays." *The New Shakspere Society's Transactions*. Vol 2. London: Trubner, 1874. *books.google.com*

Smith, Irwin. *Shakespeare's Blackfriar's Playhouse: Its History and Design*. New York: NYU Press, 1964.

Spurgeon, Caroline. *Shakespeare's Imagery and What it Tells Us*. (1935). Boston: Beacon, 1958.

Stone, Lawrence. *The Family, Sex and Marriage in England: 1500-1800*. New York: Harper & Row, 1977.

Stritmatter, Roger. *The Marginalia of Edward de Vere's Geneva Bible*. (1993): Northampton, MA: Oxenford Press, 2001.

_____ and Lynne Kositsky. *On the Date, Sources and Design of Shakespeare's The Tempest*. Jefferson, NC: MacFarland, 2013.

Strype, John. *The Life of the Learned Sir Thomas Smith Kt.* (1698). New York: Burt Franklin, 1974.

Tait, Adam. "Aconite and mandrake: crypto-pharmalogical botanicals in Shakespeare." *The UBC English Students' Association*. May 3, 2019.

Tilley, Morris Palmer. *Elizabethan Proverb Lore in Lyly's Euphues and in Pettie's Petite Pallace; with Parallels from Shakespeare*. University of Michigan Publications: *Language and Literature*: Vol II. New York: Macmillan, 1926.

Usher, Peter. "Advances in the Hamlet Allegory." *The Oxfordian*. Vol 4 (2001): 25-50.

Velz, John W. *Shakespeare and the Classical Tradition*. Minneapolis: U Minnesota Press, 1968.

Vyvyan, John. *Shakespeare and Platonic Beauty*. (1961). London: Walwyn, 2013.

Wallace, Charles W. *The Evolution of the English Drama up to Shakespeare*. (Berlin 1912). Port Washington, NY: Kennikat, 1968.

Waugaman, Richard. "What Are the Implications of the Spelling "Shake-Speare" in Ben Jonson's 1616 Folio?" *Shakespeare Oxford Newsletter*. vol 52.3: (2016): 36.

Werth, Andrew. "Shakespeare's "Lesse Greek." *The Oxfordian.* Vol 5 (2002): 11-29. (online)

Whalen, Richard. "The Stratford Bust: a monumental fraud." *The Oxfordian.* Vol 8 (2005): 7-24.

Whittemore, Hank. *100 Reasons Shake-speare was the Earl of Oxford.* Somerville, MA: Forever, 2016.

Wilder, Alec. *American Popular Song: The Great Innovators, 1900 to 1950.* New York: Oxford, 1972.

Williams, Meg. "Preface to *Poesie et Psychoanalyse: two papers on Keats and Coleridge"* by Arthur Hyatt Williams. Trans. David Alcorn. London: Karnac, 2005. (online)

Winner, Ellen. *Gifted Children: Myths and Realities.* New York: Basic Books, 1996

Dugdale's sketch of himself observing the Bust in 1638.

INDEX

Akrigg, G.P.V., 11, 305
Alexander the Great, 7, 61, 86, 143, 144
Alexander, Mark, 47
Altrocchi, Paul W., 56
Andreski, Stanislav, 205-206
Andrews, Mark Edwin, 48-50
Aristotle, 61, 67, 70, 99-101, 181, 189, 191, 195
Aubrey, John, 16, 22, 29, 34, 35, 36, 38
Aune, Mark, 250
Bacon, Delia, i, 8, 30, 40, 45, 79, 151, 153, 260
Bacon, Sir Francis, 45, 47, 49-50, 60, 76, 80, 82, 113, 115, 208, 242, 251-253, 257, 305, 312, 338
Baldwin, T.W., 24-26, 85, 89-90, 94
Bayley, Melanie, 269
Bentley, Gerald E., 12, 279, 346
Bettelheim, Bruno, 6
Bible, 1, 4-5, 75, 84, 97, 144, 155-156, 158, 160-169
Bloom, Allan, 220
Bloom, Harold, 7, 118, 210
Bly, Robert, 6
Boas, Frederick, 39
Booth, Wayne C., 259
Brooke, Tucker, 114, 151
Bucknill, John C., 51
Bullough, Geoffrey, 50, 73, 77, 148-153, 222, 280
Burbage, Richard and Cuthbert, 11, 13, 16-17, 36, 235, 239, 241, 248-249, 277

Burghley, Lord (William Cecil), 18, 20, 69, 159, 173, 184, 187, 196-197, 200-201, 211-213, 218, 224, 242-243, 247, 252, 305, 307, 311
Calvin, John (and Calvinism, Calvinist), 87, 108, 111, 155, 157, 169-170, 177, 194, 199, 203-205, 222
Campbell, Lily B., 6, 146, 195-196, 219, 221, 223, 278
Campbell, Lord Chancellor John, i, 45, 47
Carson, Neil, 347
Cecil, Robert, 215, 216, 241-246, 248-252, 322
Chace, William M., 288
Chalmers, Alexander, 340
Chambers, E.K., v, 22, 29, 31, 41-43, 151, 194, 238, 261-262, 275, 279, 296, 314, 316-317, 326, 332, 343-347
Churchyard, Thomas, 5
Coleridge, Samuel Taylor, 39, 79, 115-118, 262, 277
Collier, John Payne, 47, 116, 259-260, 274, 344
Collingwood, R.G., vi
Collins, John C., 42, 79-83, 90-92, 97, 272, 286
Courtier, The, 5, 176
Croft, Pauline, 250
Crompton, Louis, 203
Cutting, Bonner Miller, 10, 318
Davenant, William, 30, 32-39, 274, 295, 296
Davis, Frank, 51-52

de Vere, Edward, 17th Earl of Oxford, 173, 222, 238, 305-310, 327, 337-338, 353
Dewar, Mary, 311
Dickens, Charles, ii, 4, 40
Dodgson, Charles, 269, 290
Drayton, Michael, 18, 262
Dryden, John, 27-28, 33, 35, 37-38, 73, 89, 117, 292, 295
Edmond, Mary, 33, 35-36
Edmund Ironside, 281
Egan, Michael, 148, 280
Elizabeth Tudor, Queen of England, 15, 18, 48, 49, 122, 124, 136, 159, 171-174, 184, 191, 200-201, 212-216, 221-228, 230-234, 239-242, 244, 246-247, 252, 305, 309-311, 320
Elizabethan, Elizabethans, 8, 41-43, 76, 91, 98, 111, 117, 121-122, 157, 167, 193-194, 198, 219, 222, 271, 275, 282, 314, 343
Elyot, Sir Thomas, 66, 74, 99, 192, 199
Erne, Lukas, 255, 283
Everitt, F.B., 281-282
Falstaff, 6, 52, 102, 138, 161, 165, 178-181, 228, 242-246
Febvre, Lucien, 182-183
Feuillerat, Albert, 106, 108-110, 152, 276-280, 285, 346
Field, Richard, 20-21, 190
Fleay, Reverend Frederick, 151, 260-266, 269
Foakes, R.A., 117, 345, 348
Foxe, John, 74, 147, 155, 243
Fuller, Thomas, 37
Furness, H.H., 219
Furnival, Frederick, 260-266
Gascoigne, George, 16, 108, 115
Golding, Arthur, 74, 81, 115
Gorboduc, 5, 221-222
Graff, Gerald, 287-294

Greene, Robert, 76, 115, 145, 152, 188, 261, 272
Greenwood, Sir George G., 47
Greg, W.W., 31, 43, 265-267, 269, 271-278, 282, 286, 344-346
Grillo, Ernesto, 121-122, 124, 130
Gurr, Andrew, 234, 238, 308
Hall, Dr. John, 18, 75, 148
Halliwell-Phillipps, James O., 30, 260, 266, 272, 332
Handover, P.M., 249-250
Hart, Alfred, 207-208, 210, 213-214, 218
Hazlitt, William, 117-118
Hemmings and Condell, 13-15, 21-22, 33, 36-38, 245, 267, 320, 322, 324-325, 329
Henrietta, Queen, 33, 338
Henslowe, Philip, iii, 13, 275, 277-279, 343-348
Highet, Gilbert, 83-87, 201
Holinshed, Raphael, 74, 115, 146-150, 190
Honigmann, E.A.J., 13
Hotine, Margaret, 250
Hume, Martin, 244
Ingram, William, 262
Jaffa, Harry V., 220-221
James VI of Scotland, James I of England, 31, 38, 47, 49, 86, 143, 209, 215, 225, 249, 251, 253, 305, 309, 316
Jayne, Sears R., 181, 185, 190-193
Jiménez, Ramon, 16-17, 281
Johnson, Samuel, 4, 28, 47, 116-118, 141, 179, 262, 269, 313
Jones, Ernest, 33, 316
Jonson, Ben, i, 12, 15-16, 19, 22, 26-28, 31-33, 36-43, 52, 73, 75, 78, 80, 84, 88-91, 107, 115, 118, 143, 193, 235, 255, 295-297, 320, 327, 329
Joseph, Sister Mariam, 97-99, 101, 103-104, 107
Jowett, Benjamin, 180

Index

Kathman, David, 20, 317
Keats, John, 39, 40, 116,-118
Kempe, Will, 11, 52, 228, 327
Kennedy, Richard, 332
King's Men (See also Lord Chamberlain's Men), 15-18, 32, 309
Knutson, Roslyn L., 278, 345-346
Kornstein, Daniel, 51
Kyd, Thomas, 152, 261-262
Laoutaris, Chris, 242
Lathrop, Henry B., 93, 152, 185-188, 200
Levin, Bernard, iii
Lewis, C.S., 2, 5, 98, 187
Lodge, Thomas, 115, 196, 198-199, 262
Looney, J. Thomas, 305-307, 337
Lord Chamberlain's Men, v, 11, 14-15, 18-19, 21-22, 31, 37, 150, 212, 226, 229, 232, 235, 239, 242-251, 280, 283, 309, 314-316, 320, 322, 324, 327, 329, 344
Lyly, John, 76, 115, 139, 208, 238
Maguire, Laurie E., 79-80, 262, 265-268, 270-276, 279, 282, 286
Malone, Edmond, 1, 30, 35, 42-43, 47, 241, 266, 269, 272, 275, 325-326
Mark Antony, 6, 101, 207, 209
Marlowe, Christopher, 13, 23, 41, 84, 108, 113, 115, 151-153, 200-201, 223, 233-235, 247, 255, 261, 263
McFarlane, K. B., 171
McMillin, Scott, 216, 222, 227, 280
Milne, Kirsty, 192-193
Milton, John, 4, 27, 28, 37, 94, 295, 338
More, Sir Thomas, 148, 158, 182, 207-208, 250, 319, 320-321
Munday, Anthony, 50, 77, 257

Nashe, Thomas, 19, 145, 151-152, 196, 198, 200, 208, 212, 255, 261, 266
Naylor, Edward W., 138-141
Noble, Richmond, 160-163, 165-168, 213
Ogburn, Charlton, 332
Ophelia, 6, 52, 174, 197
Padua, 123-124, 128, 137, 182, 190
Peele, George, 151-152, 208, 261-262
Pettie, George, 76, 115
Pitcher, Seymour, 280
Plato, 60-61, 67, 87, 119, 142, 169, 177-185, 189-196, 220
Pollard, Alfred W., 151, 264-267, 274-277, 286
Pope, Alexander, 4, 13, 28, 30, 35, 116, 118, 158, 262, 269, 337, 338, 340-341
Prince Hal, 6, 149
Prior, Roger, 229, 230-232
Read, Conyers, 197, 244
Reiter, Paul, 53
Riche, Barnabe, 74, 115
Robertson, J.M., 47, 269, 277
Roe, Richard P., 125-133
Root, Robert K., 90-97
Rowe, Nicholas, 28-29, 37-39, 117
Sams, Eric, 281
Schoenbaum, Samuel, 9, 10, 14-15, 31, 323-326, 332
Scott, Sir Walter, 4, 227
Seward, Desmond, 309
Shaheen, Naseeb, 160, 162
Shakespeare, William
  All's Well that Ends Well, 51, 74, 123-124, 131, 176, 179, 309
  Antony and Cleopatra, 6, 74-78, 103-104, 118, 170
  As You Like It, 52, 65, 74, 100, 167

Comedy of Errors, 74-75, 80, 105, 137, 165, 170, 262, 302
Coriolanus, 6, 52, 74, 87, 104, 163, 207, 220
Cymbeline, 58, 77, 81, 142, 162, 175, 309
Hamlet, 1, 5-7, 52, 56, 62, 66, 70-78, 83, 87, 91, 94, 101, 103-105, 127, 130, 138, 139, 153, 161, 164, 166, 174, 179, 197, 199, 210-213, 218, 249, 255, 262, 274, 276, 285, 309, 344
Henry IV, 95, 100, 142, 165, 168, 178, 209, 227-228, 242, 244, 255, 281
Henry V, 6, 44, 46, 75, 77, 81, 96, 100, 103, 181, 207, 214, 216, 262, 266, 281, 283
Henry VI, 81, 91, 145, 151-153, 162, 165, 244, 255, 261-266
Henry VIII, 142, 153, 165, 262
Julius Caesar, 63, 74, 75, 101, 138, 144, 184, 207, 220, 271
King John, 81, 145, 153, 208, 216, 219, 222-227, 255, 280-281
King Lear, 5, 40, 45, 55, 64, 75, 163, 220-221, 227, 273, 283, 297
Love's Labour's Lost, 52, 77, 100-102, 106, 111, 117, 170, 174-176, 179, 242, 262, 278
Lucrece, 15, 51, 74-75, 114, 130, 141, 179
Macbeth, 1, 6, 56, 75, 81, 91, 94, 101, 138, 179, 220, 250, 262
Measure for Measure, 46, 53, 74-75, 78, 104, 122-123, 162, 175
Merchant of Venice, 36, 45-50, 58, 62, 75, 77, 94, 122-124, 129, 143, 176, 178, 220, 242

Merry Wives of Windsor, 52, 74, 77, 81, 105, 179, 246
Midsummer Night's Dream, 6, 53
Much Ado, 54, 77, 81, 91, 98, 100, 105, 134, 136-137, 162, 214, 228, 255, 283, 309
Othello, 6, 32, 54, 74-75, 78, 118, 121-123, 137, 142, 168, 175, 220, 271, 309
Pericles, 5, 54, 74, 77, 142, 208, 309
Richard II, 6, 58, 106, 141, 148, 150, 163, 208, 217, 228, 242, 255, 257, 262, 280, 284, 314, 318
Richard III, 6, 52, 81, 110, 114, 148, 152-153, 162, 165, 208, 227, 242, 248-255, 257, 261-262, 280-281, 284, 314, 317-318, 347
Romeo and Juliet, 1, 6, 54, 74, 103, 106, 114, 125-126, 137, 141, 170, 174-175, 262, 274, 276, 283
Sonnets, 39, 56-57, 91, 165, 171, 305
Taming of the Shrew, 74, 81, 104-105, 123, 128-129, 137, 141, 153, 262
Tempest, 56, 58, 63, 74, 81, 103, 132, 138, 141-142, 302
Timon of Athens, 53, 74, 87, 262
Titus Andronicus, 5, 74, 81, 90, 94, 153, 261, 271, 285, 297
Troilus and Cressida, 29, 52-53, 62, 66, 74-78, 85, 87, 89, 94, 100, 142, 207, 262
Twelfth Night, 52, 74, 77, 123-124, 137, 141, 178, 283, 302
Two Gentlemen of Verona, 74, 126, 142, 153, 262

Index

Venus and Adonis, 10-11, 15, 17, 19-21, 43, 54, 56, 62, 65, 74, 80, 96, 120, 190, 256
Winter's Tale, 42, 45, 54, 74-75, 91, 94, 100, 123, 130, 137, 141, 175-176, 208, 262, 309
Shakspere, John, 8, 14, 20, 322-326
Shakspere, William, 9, 16, 21, 24, 27, 29, 31, 263, 318
Shelley, Percy Bysshe, 4, 116, 118, 286, 288-289
Showerman, Earl, 53, 87, 90-94
Sidney, Sir Philip, 115, 166, 171, 195-200, 312, 338
Simpson, Richard, 223-225
Smith, Sir Thomas, 147, 159, 191, 241, 249, 310-312
Southampton, Henry Wriothesley, Third Earl of, 11, 15, 42-43, 97, 324
Spurgeon, Caroline, 58, 66, 83, 89, 103, 112-115, 335-336
Steevens, George, 30, 47, 266, 272
Stone, Lawrence, 25, 156, 263
Stritmatter, Roger, 160, 162

Strype, John, 310-311
Swift, Jonathan, 116, 276, 289, 338
Tait, Adam, 54
Taylor, Gary, 275
Tennyson, Alfred Lord, 4, 262
Thomas of Woodstock, 148, 208, 280-281
Tilley, Morris P., 76
Troublesome Reign of King John, 281
Usher, Peter, 68-72
Velz, John W., 28, 39, 85-89
Vertue, George, 337-341
Vyvyan, John, 75, 87, 169-170, 173-180, 278
Wallace, Charles W., 236
Watson, Thomas, 188, 261, 272
Werth, Andrew, 90-91
Whalen, Richard F., 332
Whetstone, George, 5
Whittemore, Hank, 306
Williams, Meg, 117-118
Winner, Ellen, 298-302, 308-312
Wolsey, Cardinal, 158, 182, 191, 236

Educating Shakespeare

Acknowledgements

With heartfelt thanks to those who have helped me on this long journey —Jim Warren, Toni Fallon, Dave and Maxine Clark, Tom Goff, Susan and Bruce Campbell, Donna Cosco Hermle, Malcolm Blackmoor, Mark Rylance, Charles Beauclerk, Mike and Sally Llewellyn, Val and John Nicholson, Elizabet Imlay, Alex MacNeil, Bill Boyle, Earl Showerman, Bonner Cutting, Chris Paul, and Donna Drybread. Thanks also to the participants in the Concordia Authorship Conferences whose generous contributions to the Fellowship created by Professor Daniel L. Wright gave me six weeks of study in England in 2004—Paul Altrocchi, Lynn Andrews, Alan Ashby, W.P. Blair, Judith Branz, James Brooks, Marjorie Burren, Donald Coxe, Barbara Crowley, Frank Davis, Richard Desper, Samuel Gold, William & Marilyn Gray, Marguerite Gyatt, John Hamill, Robert & Norma Howe, Mark Jackson, Ramon Jimenez, Richard Joyrich, David Leech, Anne & Karl Lemp, Lynn & Roy Morris, Barbara Murray, Sally & James Newell, Robert O'Brien, Robert Prechter, Virginia Renner, Sam Saunders, Phylis Scofield, John Shahan, Kathryn Sharpe, Wenonah Sharpe, Karyn Sherwood, Earl Showerman, Eveline Smith, Jean Stearns, Ted Story, Paul Streitz, Susan Sybersma, Peter Usher, John Varady, Donald Wexler, Richard Whalen, and John Wood.

About the author

Independent scholar, artist, poet with credits from Bennington College, Boston University, Northeastern University, and Concordia University, in 1986 Stephanie Hopkins Hughes was provoked into researching the Authorship Question by Charlton Ogburn's *The Mysterious William Shakespeare*. In 1994 she was appointed creator and editor of *The Oxfordian*—the first annual journal of the Shakespeare Oxford Society —by its then president Charles Beauclerk. She has spoken at conferences in the US and UK during years of research at Hatfield House, the British Library, the Fitzwilliam Museum in Cambridge and the Bodleian in Oxford, Oxfordian sites from Ankerwycke in Berkshire, Castle Hedingham and Hill Hall in Essex, Wivenhoe on the coast, and Wiltshire House. From 2005 her blog *politicworm.com* continues to get upwards of 100 hits a day from individuals and nations all over the world. She can be reached at *Stephanie@politicworm.com*.

Printed in Great Britain
by Amazon